Advanced
3ds max 5
Modeling & Animating

Boris Kulagin

A-LIST, LLC
295 East Swedesford Rd.
PMB #285
Wayne, PA 19087
702-977-5377 (FAX)
mail@alistpublishing.com
http://www.alistpublishing.com

This book is printed on acid-free paper.

All brand names and product names mentioned in this book are trademarks or service marks of their respective companies. Any omission or misuse (of any kind) of service marks or trademarks should not be regarded as intent to infringe on the property of others. The publisher recognizes and respects all marks used by companies, manufacturers, and developers as a means to distinguish their products.

Advanced 3ds max 5 Modeling & Animating

By Boris Kulagin

ISBN: 1-931769-16-8

Printed in the United States of America

03 04 7 6 5 4 3 2 1

A-LIST, LLC titles are available for site license or bulk purchase by institutions, user groups, corporations, etc.

Book Editors: Eric Bruns, Julie Laing

Contents

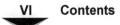

Acknowledgments

This book would have been impossible without the help of the management and my colleagues at A-LIST Publishing, so I sincerely thank them.

I am also thankful to:

Pavel Osharin, my colleague and friend, for invaluable notes and help in the writing of this book

The management of Realtime School — Director Eugeny Landyshev, head of studies Sergey Tsyptsyn, and teacher Mikhail Shagin — for high praise of my unpretentious work

Pavel Kuznetsov, Cuneyt Ozdas, Peter Watje, Fred Moreau, Laszlo Sebo, Steve Johnson, Ivan Kolev, and ChaoticDimension for permission to use their plug-ins and scripts

Special thanks to:

Dmitry Morozov, the chief artist of Moscow studio Ariorh and a teacher at Realtime School, for permission to use his work as the cover illustration and for comments on it

Lorenza Cappello, press secretary of ItalDesign Giugiaro, for 11 pounds of the company's development materials; they were invaluable during the preparation of Lesson 15

Arild Wiro Anfinnsen for permission to use his experience with modeling in Lesson 16

All of my students at Realtime School and Moscow Electronic Machinery Institute; much in the book was tested on them

My family for moral support, patience, and understanding

And thank *you* for purchasing this book. I hope it will be useful.

Yours sincerely,
Boris Kulagin

Introduction

About This Book

This book focuses on practical work with the 3ds max modeling and animation package from Discreet and is a follow-up to the book "3ds max 4: From Objects to Animation." We describe the process of creating several projects from start to finish, covering modeling, lighting, material creation, the assignment of materials to objects, and final rendering.

Target Readers

Like our previous publication, this book mainly addresses those who already have taken their first steps in 3D graphics with the help of 3ds max (i.e., people who can create boxes, circles, spheres, and more complex objects, then animate them using the key animation method). In addition, we assume that our readers are advanced users of the Microsoft Windows OS. 3ds max is a full-value package integrated with Windows, and its interface and file system follow the rules of Microsoft's operating system. Therefore, we decided not to focus on opening the system, starting the applications, or opening files; for 3ds max, these actions are as standard as those for any application within Windows. We wanted to raise the plank higher and focus on projects without being distracted by keys, buttons, and other elements of the interface.

While writing the first book, we decided that it would be unfair to cut off novices in 3D. This decision turned out to be appropriate, and we have continued the tradition. So, this book also provides several levels of material.

First, actions are described. These are highlighted by bullets, for example:

❏   Open the Scene.max file

To simplify searches for a required command, we provide the levels in a different font, for example:

Main menu → File → Open

It should be mentioned that we have considerably reduced the bulk of the material on such levels by excluding the obvious. At the same time, the *Additional Lessons* section provides several lessons for the beginners. Start with these lessons if you encounter difficulties.

Finally, there are many notes, explanations, and tips highlighted in the text as follows:

▸ *Note*

You can decide whether or not to read the text thus highlighted. As a rule, it does not affect the results of the lesson. However, if you are a beginner, we recommend that you pay attention to the information stated in these sections.

While planning this book, we discussed the contents both with colleagues and readers, and they unanimously agreed that we should not repeat material from our previous publication. We tried to satisfy this request by reducing the number of "overlaps" with material of the previous book and by making references to it where necessary.

Doing the Lessons

The lessons are combined into two large projects. You can do them successively to create your own variant of each project. If this is not interesting to you, the necessary information for each lesson is provided on the CD-ROM (projects, textures, etc.). The finished variant for each lesson also is on the CD-ROM, and you can always compare your results with ours.

Apart from these lessons, we thought it appropriate to offer several additional exercises, combined in the *Additional Lessons* section mentioned above. Their levels are different, but we think that both beginners and advanced users of 3ds max will find them interesting.

The lessons in this book do *not* follow the "from simple to difficult" principle. They are *equivalent* and rather complicated, so you can do them in any order. However, if you are a beginner, we recommend that you complete them sequentially. Some details are explained thoroughly in the first lessons that you will need to know for subsequent lessons. From one lesson to another, your attention will be less focused on *how* to do something than on *what* will have to be done.

Finally, we completed all the lessons ourselves in the course of writing this book. Therefore, in some cases, the solution to a problem may not seem optimal. Moreover, errors and inaccuracies are possible. If you think you can do better, you are welcome to try. Don't be afraid of experimenting, for no book can teach you anything unless you persistently delve into various aspects of the package.

System Requirements

Conceptually, unlike other top packages for 3D graphics, 3ds max can run on computers considered "weak." To avoid any ordeals and to enjoy the work, your computer should be Intel Pentium III-based with a clock rate of no less than 300 MHz, RAM of 256 MB, a video display board, hardware supporting Direct3D or OpenGL, and video memory of no less than 32 MB. Microsoft Windows 2000 or XP is desirable, although 3ds max also can run on Windows 98SE or NT4 SP 6. A monitor with a 17-inch screen is preferable.

We recommend that you update your copy of 3ds max to version 5.1. Updates eliminate some problems, and often the bugs of previous versions have been fixed. See the detailed information at **http://www.discreet.com**. Version 5.1 is the base one in this book.

A three-button mouse or, better, one with a wheel is recommended. The central button and the wheel of the mouse are actively used in 3ds max for navigating in the viewports. The three-button mouse is referred to in this book.

What occurs on the screen as you work with 3ds max depends on the configuration of your computer and especially on the settings of its video system. Therefore, if you see something different from what is shown in the pictures of this book (especially related to the viewports), don't be upset; it is possible that this is because of differences in configuration.

Terminology

For more information on terms used in 3ds max, see *Appendix A* at the end of this book.

The elements of the interface are worth special mention. Fig. I.1 shows the active window of 3ds max. The indicated elements have names corresponding to those occurring in the text.

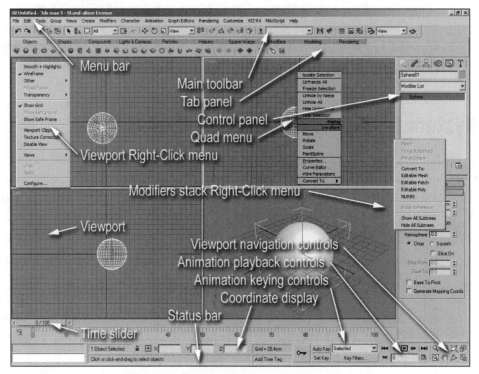

Fig. I.1. Interface elements of 3ds max

As it follows from its name — Quad menu — the context menu may consist of four sub-menus (Fig. I.2, *a*). In the first lesson of the book "3ds max 4: From Objects to Animation," we found it necessary to indicate the name of the quadrant, for example:

Context menu/Tools 1 → Sub-objects → Face

There is no such notation in this book because we hope that you already are familiar with these menus.

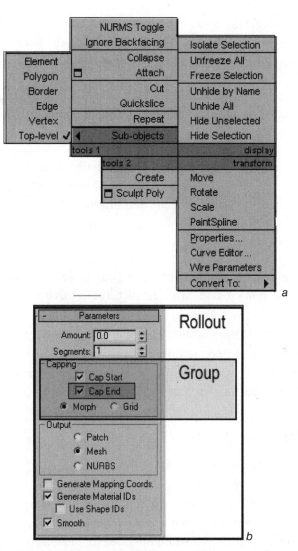

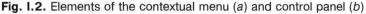

Fig. I.2. Elements of the contextual menu (*a*) and control panel (*b*)

In addition, many operations in 3ds max 5 can be performed using additional context menus (Additional Quad Menus) called by shortcuts (<Ctrl>, <Alt>, and <Shift>) and the right mouse button. For this, we decided to use the following form:

<Ctrl>+Context menu → Rectangle

To determine the position of any element on the control panel, we decided to use the terms "rollout" and "group" (Fig. I.2, *b*). Thus, the full path will look like this:

Control panel → Parameters rollout → Capping group → Cap End flag

In cases with few parameters (as in the following example), we decided to use an abbreviated record to avoid overloading of the text:

Control panel →... → Cap End flag

A few words about shortcuts. Traditionally, these key combinations are shown as follows: <Ctrl>+<A>. The brackets "<>" contain the keys. The "+" symbol indicates that these keys should be pressed simultaneously.

Presets

You can adjust 3ds max according to your preferences, but if you want the image on your screen to coincide with the pictures in this book, do the following:

❑ If possible, set the resolution of your monitor to 1152 × 864 pixels or more.

❑ Open the 3ds max settings (Main menu → Customize → Preferences → General) and deactivate the **Use Large Toolbar Buttons** flag. Then close 3ds max (<Alt>+<F4>) and restart it.

Exclusions

As explained above, this book skips items described in "3ds max 4: From Objects to Animation." When repetition was unavoidable, the material was presented in a more concise form with references to the previous book.

The main target of this material is to create reels to be demonstrated on the monitor. We don't dwell on animation intended for video, large images for printing trades, or modeling for games or the Internet. In each case, the requirements are different and can vary greatly, so it is impossible to take into account all peculiarities.

A description of the MAXScript language — an excellent tool for enhancing the features of 3ds max — is also omitted. We decided not to touch on this topic for two reasons. First, not being connoisseurs of MAXScript, we prefer to use the customized tools of the 3ds max package. Second, programming on MAXScript may well be the subject of a separate book.

Where possible, we tried to use the customized tools of 3ds max, so you will find descriptions only of the few plug-ins we used and those too good not to mention.

In addition, we only described features of 3ds max that are used in the lessons. When preparing the lessons, we tried to use as many of them as possible, but some remain untouched.

Other Sources

The "User's Manual" supplied with 3ds max must become your handbook.

Much can be picked up from the online help and interactive lessons supplied with the 3ds max package.

Finally, we recommend our book "3ds max 4: From Objects to Animation." Between these two books, we cover almost all features of the package.

What Is on the CD-ROM

The CD-ROM supplied with this book contains everything necessary for the lessons. You will find finished and intermediate files of the scenes, visualized images, and reels in the Video for Windows (AVI) format using the standard Microsoft MPEG-4 endec (see *Appendix D*).

A Little Advice

When starting a 3D project, almost every beginner fears (and we mean fears!) that he will never be able to do it. This keeps many people from starting the work. Don't be afraid of anything! Perseverance wins, they say. Everything is possible if much labor is spent, accompanied by an ounce of talent and the sense of proportion inherent in any of us. Trust us on this; we used to be dummies, too.

You may be discouraged if, when all the lessons are done, you realized that many, many experiences are ahead before you become a 3D master. This is true, though, and you should be prepared to continue your 3D education. This book is just a first step in your professional career; the rest depends on you.

Many beginners, inspired by some knowledge and experience, are eager to make everything "real" and get upset when they fail. Don't be upset! We are fond of the motto: "If you can't make it life-like, make it better!" We are not suggesting that you simply make boxes and balls and then snarl: "None of you fools know fine art when you see it." Try to make the viewer *believe* in the truthfulness of what's going on, even if this means going too far with the effects or stressing points you would hardly pay attention to in reality. Remember that it is not life that you model, but the perception of life interpreted through the virtual camera objective.

There are many packages besides 3ds max, so study them. First, focus on 2D graphics packages that will help you to finish your work. Then study packages of video editing and video effects that will allow you to compile your pieces and add sound and special effects. And the main thing: Find and study good books on fine arts, photography, and cinematography. These can be helpful.

A Small Digression

The cover illustration is made in 3ds max. We asked Dmitry Morozov, the author of the picture and the chief artist of Moscow studio Ariorh, to tell us about its creation.

"This work was done quite long ago, in late 2000. The scene was prepared for a demo reel of the studio. We used 3D Studio MAX 3, the plug-ins Character Studio 2, Digimation Shag:Hair, SimCloth, mental ray, and, of course, Adobe Photoshop for drawing the textures.

"The sketches were made by Timur Mustaev.

"The model of the character — hunter — is made using a combined technology. The rough model was based on the splines, with further 'upholstering' using the **Surface** modifier, and then finished up on the editable mesh level (**Edit Mesh**).

"All textures were made manually, merged on four channels: **Diffuse**, **Specular Level**, **Glossiness**, and **Bump**, and a separate set of textures was prepared for each channel.

"Hair is created using the Shag:Hair plug-in, clothes — SimCloth.

"For the posture and animation of the character, the Character Studio plug-in was used — at that time the only possible solution." (In version 3 there was an option for using "bones" and "skin," but these tools left much to be desired, especially the inverse kinematics system. — Boris Kulagin)

"The mechanical 'war-elephant' was initially created using **NURBS**, for their mapping was simpler, then finished up on the polygon level. All textures are drawn.

"The landscape was made using the standard **Displacement** based on the vertices' map.

"Rendering was made using mental ray.

"The whole work from the modeling stage to final rendering took 12 days."

Other works of the studio can be found on its website at **http://www.ariorhstudio.com**.

Project I

A Lunar Expedition

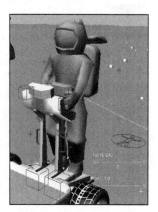

We began working on this book on the eve of the 40th anniversary of the first manned flight into outer space. On April 12, 1961, Yuri Gagarin, a citizen of the former U.S.S.R., became the first man in history to defy gravity and complete an orbit around the Earth in the Vostok 1 spacecraft. It is therefore perfectly natural that the first series of lessons in this book are dedicated to cosmic flight. When you successfully complete these lessons, you should end up with something akin to the Project-1.avi file on the accompanying CD-ROM.

Here's what you'll need to do:

- ❏ **Lesson 1: The Script.** In this first lesson, we'll make a quick draft of the script, estimate the work time, and decide which events to include and their order.
- ❏ **Lesson 2: Spaceship Modeling.** In this lesson, we'll create the model of an interplanetary spaceship from scratch, mostly using primitives that will need to be touched up later. Although advanced users of 3ds max might shun this method, simple modeling with "blocks" and "balls" is very effective.
- ❏ **Lesson 3: Modeling the Lunar Module and Rover.** Here, you will learn more interesting methods of modeling and texturing. In addition, you will learn how to create and configure inter-object hierarchical links, and connect animation parameters using the **Wire** system.
- ❏ **Lesson 4: Modeling and Animating an Astronaut.** In this lesson, we will model an astronaut in a spacesuit, create a skeleton, and prepare it for further animation. We will also teach him how to walk.

❏ **Lesson 5: Modeling Space and Animating the Flight of the Spaceship.** In this lesson, you will create the Earth, the Moon, the Sun and the stars, as well as animate the flight of the interplanetary spaceship. At first glance, you might think there is nothing too complicated in this type of animation. However, it will help us understand how to solve a number of interesting problems, such as combining objects with significantly different sizes (actually, by several orders of magnitude).

❏ **Lesson 6: Animating and Modeling the Landing on the Moon.** This lesson consists of two parts. The first part shows the approach to the surface of the Moon, as seen from a "TV monitor" camera on the lunar module. The second part shows the actual landing of the module, as seen from a camera on the Moon. It will show you interesting methods for animating objects, and elements and properties of materials used with Wires.

❏ **Lesson 7: Animating the Astronaut and Lunar Rover.** In this lesson, our astronaut will take his first steps on the Moon, climb in to take the controls of the Moon research vehicle, and start on his way.

❏ **Lesson 8: Rendering the Scene and Assembling the Movie.** In this last lesson, we will use Batch methods to render the scene in 3ds max. We will then compile the clip using the Video Post module.

All the work in this project is aimed at one goal — creating the illusion that what happens appears real, even if it lacks pizzazz. You should also note that this project was created for teaching purposes, so we tried to put as much of 3ds max's capabilities in it as we could. That is why our model is relatively simple, and why the modeling, texturing, and animating methods we used might, in contrast to the model, seem more complex than necessary.

Lesson 1

The Script

We decided to devote a relatively large amount of time to this lesson, since we think that a well-planned script is one of the basic conditions for the success of any project. Many beginning animators don't give this step enough attention, which is too bad. This stage is absolutely necessary to clarify exactly how and what you need to do. As a minimum, you must be able to estimate the duration of the clip, determine the composition of the models, and be able to render the animation. This process allows you to predict how much effort will be required and how long the project will take. It is also helpful to divide the project into stages.

The importance of this preliminary work is especially evident when working as a team, even one composed of just two people. You won't be able to work without coordinating your actions: You'll constantly run into conflicts and waste your time by repeating work, eventually leading to missed deadlines.

▶ Note

There are some people who are of the opinion that deadlines are made to be missed. To a certain extent that's true: In the work process, problems always arise. Usually, the problem is that the workload is heavier than was expected (sometimes to a much greater extent than was originally planned), and constant battles with the software, the operating system, or the hardware don't make things any easier. This doesn't only apply to the work of "creative artists." There was one case where IBM missed the deadline for its System 360 operating system by more than a year! However, all of this doesn't mean that you shouldn't set any deadlines at all.

Finally, if you have a well-planned script ready, you have a subject for discussion with the client. There's no worse situation than one in which the artist tries to convey an idea for a project to a client by waving his or her hands and using telepathy; nothing good comes of this. It's much more effective to show the client a stack of papers with models that have already been sketched and captioned, stages already designed, etc.

So, let's get down to writing the script and making some sketches. As a rule, when working "for yourself," it's usually enough to have some very simple drawings. We decided not to show you our sketches, and asked our colleague, Pavel Osharin, to do them for us; he does a much better job. You can see that the result of Pavel's work is a bit different from what we came up with (Fig. 1.1). This is yet another point proving the necessity of planning the project in detail before starting: If the concepts and actions of two people who have been working together for around five years don't agree right off the bat, we think you can see how the no-planning method will work for people who just recently met!

Episode 1. Spaceship flying toward the Moon. This episode consists of two sequential fragments. In the first fragment, a camera pans smoothly, capturing first the Earth and then the Sun. In the second scene, we see the station flare its engines and change trajectory (Fig. 1.1, *a*). The duration of each of these fragments is about 8–10 seconds, and as a whole comes to somewhere around 16–20 seconds. We'll need a model of the Earth for this episode, as well as one for the Moon, space, and the flying interplanetary station. We'll also need some effects — glow and flare, in particular. It would also make sense to employ a two-second fade-in at the beginning of the clip.

Episode 2. First phase of landing. A camera on the lunar module displays an approaching and shifting lunar surface (Fig. 1.1, *b*). This episode lasts 10 seconds. The display might be stylized in such a way as to look like the image displayed on a monitor. Models include the lunar surface and a highly detailed fragment of the lunar module. A blinking light that illuminates a fragment of the hull would add a nice touch.

Episode 3. Second phase of landing. Actual landing on the lunar surface (Fig. 1.1, *c*). The camera follows the module from the lunar surface. The duration of this episode is about 10–15 seconds. The required models consist of the lunar surface and lunar module. Additional effects — flowing dust baring the solid rock of the lunar surface.

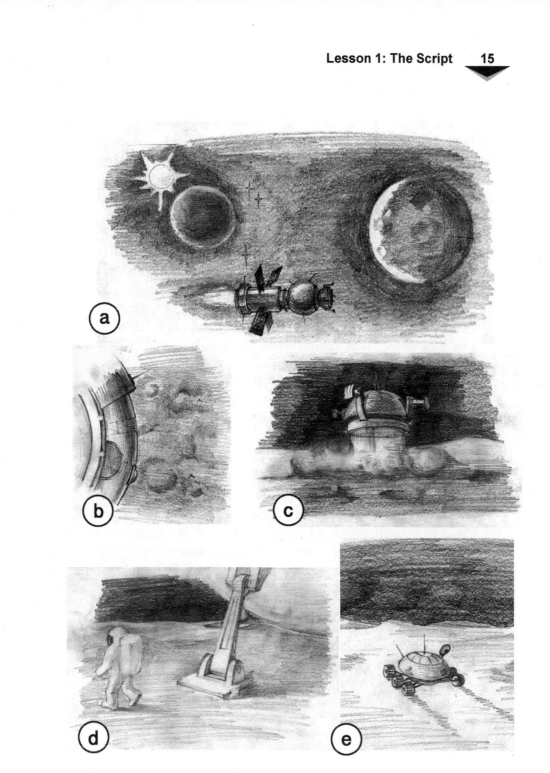

Fig. 1.1. Sketches for the script

Episode 4. First steps on the Moon. An astronaut moves along the lunar surface towards the lunar vehicle (Fig. 1.1, *d*). The camera follows his movements, while moving in an arc. This episode lasts approximately 10–12 seconds. The models used include those in the previous episode, plus the astronaut in a spacesuit and the lunar vehicle. As for effects, it would be interesting to show the exposure of light reflected off the spacesuit. This effect is clearly visible in lunar photos. And, of course, we shouldn't forget the footprints made by the astronaut's boots.

Episode 5. Beginning the investigation of the Moon. The moon research vehicle, operated by the astronaut, moves away from the lunar module, leaving tracks on the lunar surface (Fig. 1.1, *e*). The camera rises gradually, following the research vehicle, and showing the panorama of the Moon and Earth rising above the horizon. This episode lasts approximately 15–20 seconds. The clip concludes with the fade-out effect.

Summary. The total duration of the clip is about one minute and is intended exclusively for demonstration on a computer monitor. Provided that the frame rate is at 30 frames per second, it will consist of about 1,800 frames (640×480 pixels without fields).

It is tempting to begin creating model sketches right now. However, since the structure of this book is designed such that the lessons are independent from one another, we decided to distribute the sketches by appropriate lessons.

You can, however, begin the work of sketching the models at this time.

Our final advice for this lesson is related to your interaction with the customer. Unless it is absolutely necessary, try to avoid demonstrating intermediate results. As a general rule, models without texture, covered by default 3ds max colors, will surprise those who have no idea about the process. It's much better to postpone the final demonstration by a couple of days than to have to say something to the customer like: "Don't look at this too closely, it will look different." It will only confuse and disappoint him or her, and in no way will it help you produce a favorable impression or improve your reputation.

Lesson 2

Spaceship Modeling

To design our spaceship, we looked at the U.S. Apollo space program and Russian manned space projects (Fig. 2.1). But, before we start modeling, the main task should be determined. From this, we can see that there is no need to create an incredibly detailed model. Most of the time, the spaceship will be relative far from the camera. During the small period of time that the spaceship is near the camera, at a distance where its details could be discernable, it will move at a fairly high speed relative to the observer, and its motion will blur those details.

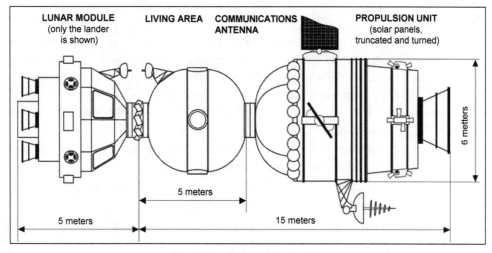

Fig. 2.1. Spaceship sketch

Spaceship Geometry Creation

The first thing to do is to determine the set of individual objects. The main structure consists of the propulsion unit, lunar module (see *Lesson 3*) and living area. Three solar panels, directed at the Sun, and a communications antenna, directed at the Earth, are attached to this complex.

We will model the parts of the spaceship using geometrical primitives. 3ds max provides an extensive selection of primitives, with material indices (**Material ID**) for various pre-assigned surfaces and texture coordinates (**UVW Coordinates**) generated automatically. The examples to be discussed demonstrate when this helps and when this hampers modeling.

Before we start the process, we recommend that you specify the measurement units. It should be mentioned that, in 3ds max, the units are somewhat arbitrary and not as important as in CAD systems, but their use adds a certain austerity to the modeling process and helps avoid problems when several projects are united in one.

❐ Make one unit of 3ds max equal to one millimeter — the unit commonly used in engineering to denote linear sizes:

Main menu → Customize → Units Setup → System Units Setup

![System Unit Scale panel: 1 Unit = 1.0 Millimeters, Respect System Units in Files checked]

➤ **Note**

The developers of 3ds max do not recommend changing this parameter without utter necessity. Frankly, we do not quite understand why: After many years of work with 3ds max, we never encountered any difficulties. We therefore recommend that you see the effects and why they occur for yourself. We will use millimeters as the measurement unit in this lesson and meters in the next one. Problems (if any) will arise when all the objects are shown in one scene.

It is usually sufficient to specify the units to be displayed. 3ds max will work internally with inches by default and convert them into the units you specify for display.

If you load a file with system units different from those in current use, the **Respect System Units in Files** flag should be checked. You will then be able to adjust the object to conform with the current system units, or adjust the system units to conform with those of the file. If the flag is not checked, 3ds max will ignore the units of the file being loaded, which may lead to unpredictable results.

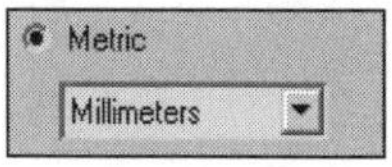

❏ Set the units for display:

Main menu → Customize → Units Setup → Millimeters

❏ Enable snaps to grid points:

Main menu → Customize → Grid and Snap Settings → Snaps (Fig. 2.2, *a*)

❏ Set the grid spacing to 100 millimeters:

Main menu → Customize → Grid and Snap Settings → Home Grid (Fig. 2.2, *b*)

The **Inhibit Perspective View Grid Resize** option requires explanation. When it is checked, the grid in the projecton preview window can only be resized to the extent specified by the **Perspective View Grid Extent** parameter. When it is unchecked, the grid is not so restrained, as in the previous versions of 3ds. You can use this option as you please.

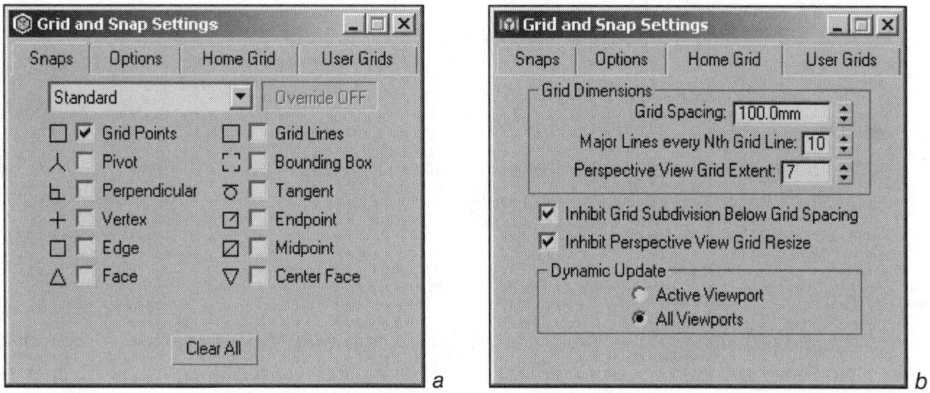

Fig. 2.2. Snaps (*a*) and **Home Grid** (*b*) settings

▶ *Tip*

Later, you will be able to access this window by simply clicking the right mouse button in the main panel.

❏ Activate snaps to the grid (<S> key).

❏ In the **Front** viewport at the coordinate origin, create a cylinder with a radius of 3000 millimeters, height of 4000 millimeters, and the parameters shown in Fig. 2.3:

Main menu → Create → Standard Primitives → Cylinder

Parameters

Radius:	3000.0mm
Height:	4000.0mm
Height Segments:	1
Cap Segments:	1
Sides:	18
☑ Smooth	
☐ Slice On	
Slice From:	0.0
Slice To:	0.0
☑ Generate Mapping Coords.	

Fig. 2.3. Cylinder parameters for modeling the propulsion unit

❗ *Explanation*

By default, 3ds max partitions cylinders by height into 5 segments. In our case, this is absolutely unnecessary. Set the **Height Segments** parameter to 1.

Check the **Generate Mapping Coords** flag.

▶ *Tip*

It is often convenient to create a primitive using the keyboard (Control panel → ... → Keyboard Entry).

▶ *Note*

To avoid repetition, in the future we will not indicate where to initiate the creation of a primitive. There are four primary methods in 3ds max: first, via the main menu (Create → Standard Primitives, Extended Primitives); second, in the control panel (Create → Geometry); third, in the context menu, accessed by holding the <Ctrl> key while pressing the mouse button, then select **Primitives** (there are only a few in this menu, but you can add more if you want); finally, via the **Objects** panel. It is a matter of preference which way you choose.

❏ Go to the **Perspective** viewport and maximize it to full screen (<Alt>+<W> key combination).

❏ Switch to **Shaded** object display in the viewport (<F3> key) and turn on the rib display (<F4> key).

❏ Select the **AutoGrid** flag in the control panel.

☐ Rotate the view as you feel comfortable and create a truncated cone (corresponding to the mid-flight engine nozzle) with the parameters shown in Fig. 2.4.

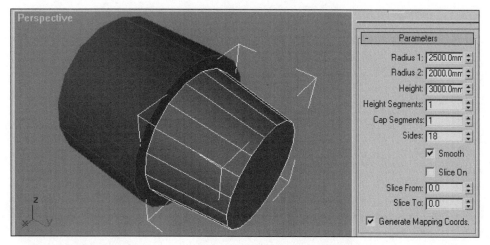

Fig. 2.4. Truncated cone, corresponding to the rear side of the propulsion unit, and its parameters

 Explanation

Set the **Sides** value to match that of the cylinder.

☐ Align the cone and cylinder. Begin as follows:

   Main panel → Align

☐ Click on the cylinder and set the parameters in Fig. 2.5.

 Note

We assume you know how to navigate viewports, and will not cover that here. See *Lesson 12* for further information.

 Note

In our book "3ds max 4: From Objects to Animation," we repeatedly recommended that you assign unique and meaningful names to your objects. Now would be a good time to do so with this example, but it is not necessary, as all parts of the spaceship will be combined into a single object.

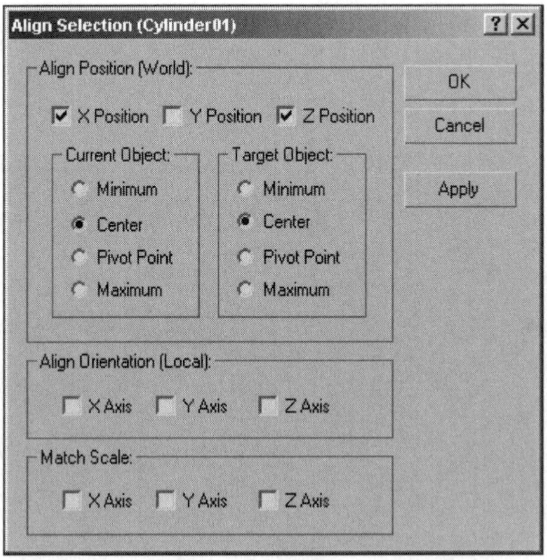

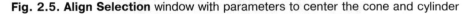

Fig. 2.5. Align Selection window with parameters to center the cone and cylinder

In our opinion, further modeling is straightforward and will not be considered in much detail. The following discussion is a brief outline of the steps to be taken.

First, ensure that the **Generate Mapping Coords** parameter is checked when creating each primitive, because 3dx max deselects it by default.

Turn the truncated cone into a mid-flight engine nozzle by applying the **Edit Mesh** modifier. Select the polygon covering the nozzle and delete it (Fig. 2.6, *a*):

Main menu→ Modifiers → Mesh Editing → Edit Mesh

Context menu → Sub-object → Polygon

Put ring tubes (**Tube**) along the nozzle. Place the tubes so that part of them extend inside (Fig. 2.6, *b*).

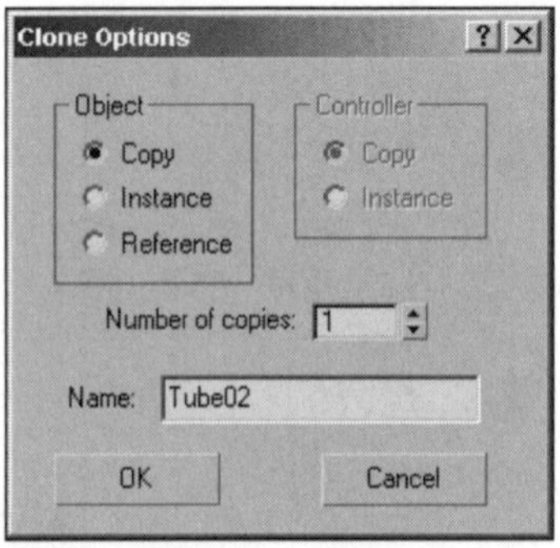

► *Tip*

After creating the first ring, you can copy it several times, adjust the parameters and move them along the longitudinal axis by holding the <Shift> key.

For the rings on the propulsion module, use **Chamfer Cylinder** primitives with a small chamfer value (Fig. 2.6, *c*). Many users neglect the chamfers, thinking they would be invisible anyway. In reality, they are visible, maybe too much! The chamfers create a feeling of authenticity that the works of beginners often lack.

You can also use the **Chamfer Cylinder** primitive for the lunar module (Fig. 2.6, *d*). Once it is created, use the **Edit Mesh** modifier to delete the unnecessary polygons.

❗ *Warning*

Don't **Collapse** the stack of modifiers, as you may still need to change the cylinder's parameters.

Use the common cylinder "decorated" with flanges to make the transfer hatch from the propulsion module to the living area.

You can easily build the living area by simply copying the lunar module, deleting the **Edit Mesh** modifier and correcting the parameters (Fig. 2.6, *e*).

Finally, make the hatch between the living area and the lunar module.

Try to render the spaceship by pressing the <F9> key in the perspective window.

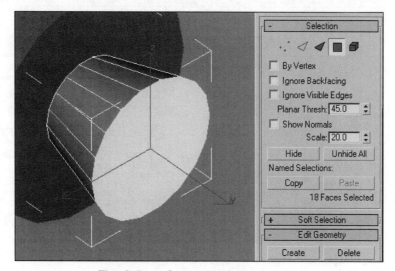

Fig. 2.6, *a.* Spaceship-body creation

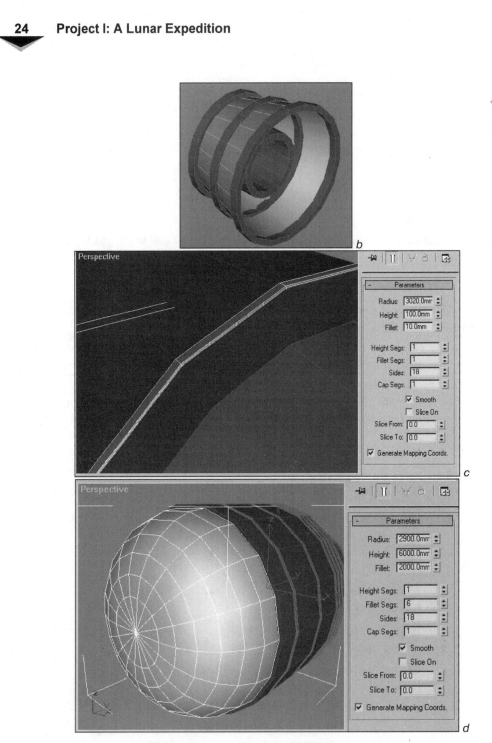

Fig. 2.6, *b—d.* Spaceship-body creation

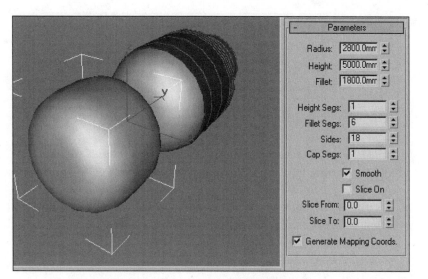

Fig. 2.6, e. Spaceship-body creation

At this point, you can see that most of the elements are disturbingly angular. This is easy to fix: Double the number of sides in the primitives' parameters. This should be done for the propulsion module (both the front and rear parts), the living area and the lunar module, as well as for the "seams" of these objects.

 Note

For the lunar module, this procedure is a little difficult. When you try to change the primitive's properties, you will be warned that there is a modifier in the stack (**Edit Mesh)** that strongly depends on these parameters (Fig. 2.7). Confirm your wish to continue and make the necessary changes. You will see that the result of the **Edit Mesh** modifier leaves much to be desired. We will not go into detail explaining this problem, but note that it can be solved by deleting the modifier from the stack and applying it again.

Tip

It is easier to select components of objects with the basic projections; in this case, on the **Left** or **Top** viewport.

 Note

The current intermediate stage of construction of the spaceship is on the companion CD-ROM in the file \Lessons\Lesson02\scenes\lesson02-01.max.

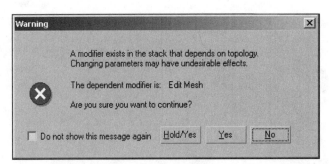

Fig 2.7. Warning that a modifier in the stack depends on the primitive's parameters

Continue editing by creating the engines used to orient the spaceship. We suggest that you make them separately from everything else. To do so, select all of the objects and hide them:

Main menu→ Edit → Select All *or* <Ctrl>+<A> keys

Context menu → Hide Selection

▶ *Tip*

The keyboard hotkey for the **Hide Selection** command is not initially defined in 3ds max. We recommend that you to assign it:

Main menu → Customize → Customize User Interface → Keyboard inlay

Select the **Hide Selection** command in the **Action** list.

Click in the **Hotkey** window and press the key that you think is most suitable for this command (we selected the <*> key on the numeric keypad).

If this key is already defined, you will be warned in the **Assigned to** window. If so, select another key or key combination.

Press the **Assign** button to save your choice.

We recommend that you to assign hotkeys for **Hide Selection**, **Hide Unselected**, and **Unhide All**. We selected the combinations <*>, <Ctrl>+<*>, and <Alt>+<*>, respectively, where the <*> key is on the numeric keypad.

For our purposes, the orientation engines function as a unit on the surface of the spaceship, with the nozzles pointed in various directions. It is not very difficult to build them:

❐ Draw a **Box** in the **Top** viewport with dimensions of $600 \times 300 \times 300$ millimeters.

❐ Convert it to an editable mesh object:

   Context menu → Convert to → Convert to Editable Mesh

❐ Select the upper polygon and reduce its size, so that you end up with a truncated pyramid (Fig. 2.8, *a*):

   Context menu → Sub–object → Polygon
   Context menu → Scale *or* <R> key

❐ Create the nozzles in the same manner as that of the mid-flight engine
(Fig. 2.8, *b*).

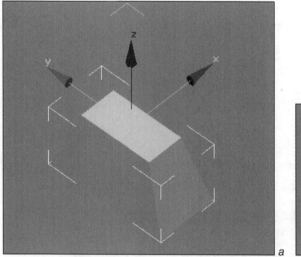

a   *b*

Fig. 2.8. Orientation engines

❐ Select the truncated pyramid and attach the nozzles to it:

   Context menu → Attach

❐ Select and delete the polygons covering the exhaust of the nozzles:

   Context menu → Sub-object → Polygon

Now you have to place the orientation engine on the surface of the propulsion
module. You can do so by simply dragging it, but there is another method you

should try: aligning the normals of the appropriate surfaces (**Normal Align** command).

☐   Unhide all objects:

> Context menu → Unhide All

☐   Select the orientation engine and position it near the rear end of the propulsion module. Use the **Normal Align** command:

> Main panel → Normal Align

☐   Select the bottom surface of the orientation engine. This surface will be marked with a blue arrow representing its normal (Fig. 2.9, *a*).

☐   If necessary, adjust the viewport in order to select the surface on the propulsion module with which the engine will be aligned. This surface will be marked with a green arrow.

☐   Enter the parameters in the dialog box so that the engine is positioned correctly (Fig. 2.9, *b*).

☐   Adjust the orientation engine if necessary.

▶ *Tip*

It is convenient to move the engine using local coordinates.

Main panel → Reference Coordinate System → Local *or* <Alt>+ Context menu → Local

Fig 2.9, *a*. Using the **Normal Align** command

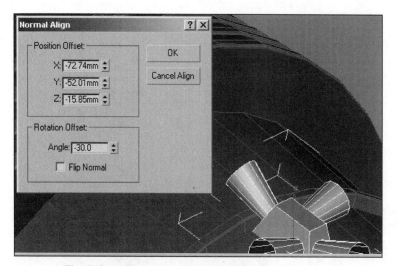

Fig 2.9, *b.* Using the **Normal Align** command

Now you have to make copies of the engine for three other sides of the propulsion module. To do so, clone the object and turn it around the module's center by following these steps:

Main panel → Reference Coordinate System → Pick

❏ Select the object which will be used as the center of rotation.

❏ Select the object's center as the **Transform Coordinate Center**.

❏ Turn the object 90 degrees around the Z-axis while holding the <Shift> key.

❏ Set the **Clone** dialog parameters as shown in Fig. 2.10, *a*. You should have the result shown in Fig. 2.10, *b*.

We will not consider the process of editing the remainder of the spaceship body in detail, except for a few cases that deserve special attention. You can find the result on the CD-ROM in the file \Lessons\Lesson02\scenes\lesson02-02.max.

We built the open aerial towers using the quadrangular truncated cone, divided into several sections by height, and by applying the **Lattice** modifier (Fig. 2.11, *a*). Then we applied the **Edit Mesh** modifier and worked on the vertices:

Control panel → ... → Modifier List → Lattice, Edit Mesh

Fig. 2.10. Clone Options window (*a*) and the result of copying
the orientation engines (*b*)

The aerial dishes were made with the use of the **Semi-sphere** primitive (Fig. 2.11, *b*), also with further modification by the **Edit Mesh** modifier.

The solar panels were built using the **Box** primitive with large partitions (Fig. 2.11, *c*). You will see later how this partitioning is used.

The docking hooks come from a **Box** adjusted with the **Edit Mesh** modifier and duplicated around the general center (Fig. 2.11, *d*).

The portholes consist of **Semi–sphere** and **Tube** primitives.

We also put handholds and ladders on the surface of the spaceship using renderable shapes. They are what visually determine the size of the ship, for the size of astronauts who use them is implied and gives a subconscious estimate of the size of the whole construction. In order to attach them to the surface of the ship, we first had to set the parameters shown in Fig. 2.11, *e*.

Note

Notice that the **Sides** and **Steps** values are small. Modeling efficiently and recognizing when great precision is not needed can save you several minutes or hours at final rendering.

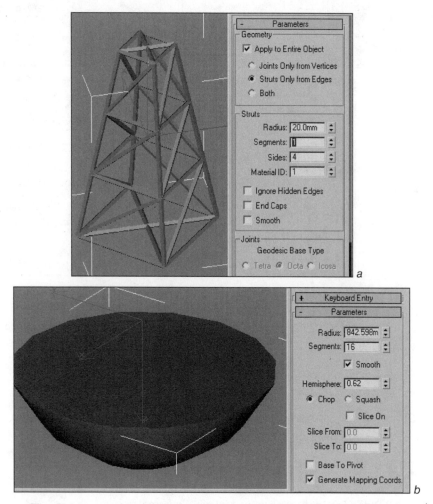

Fig. 2.11, *a* and *b*. Modeling different elements of the spaceship

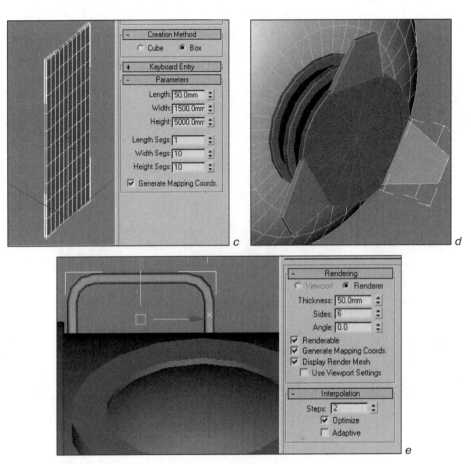

Fig. 2.11, *c–e*. Modeling different elements of the spaceship

As a final step, we selected all the objects and specified that they are made of the same material:

❑ Select all objects.

❑ Open the material editor (<M> key).

❑ Select any preview window (**Material slot**) and press the **Assign to Selection** button.

▶ *Tip*

We want to use a double-sided material, so make sure the **2-Sided** flag is checked in the material's parameters.

Fig. 2.12. Result of rendering the spaceship

The basic geometry of the spaceship is ready (Fig. 2.12). Now it is time to look at different materials.

Material Creation and Assignment

First of all, group the entire spaceship together in the following way:

❏ Select the propulsion module (we named it Cylinder01) and convert it to an **Editable Mesh** or **Editable Poly** object type — it does not matter which in our case:

   Context menu → Convert to → Convert to Editable Mesh

❏ **Attach** all the other objects to it:

> Control panel → Edit Geometry → Attach List

❏ Select all objects and press **Attach**.

❏ Rename your spaceship as SpaceShip and the only material used thus far as SpaceShip_Test.

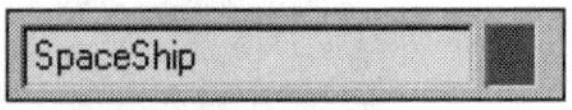

Now it is time to check the way textures will look on the surface of our model. To do so, most professionals use **Checker**.

❏ Assign the **Checker** texture to the **Diffuse** channel:

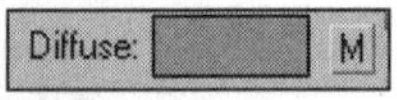

> Material editor → Blinn Basic Parameters → Diffuse
>
> Material/Map Browser → Checker

❏ In the texture parameters, set the **Tiling** recurrence value for **U** and **V** coordinates to 5 (Fig. 2.13), and see how the texture looks in the viewports.

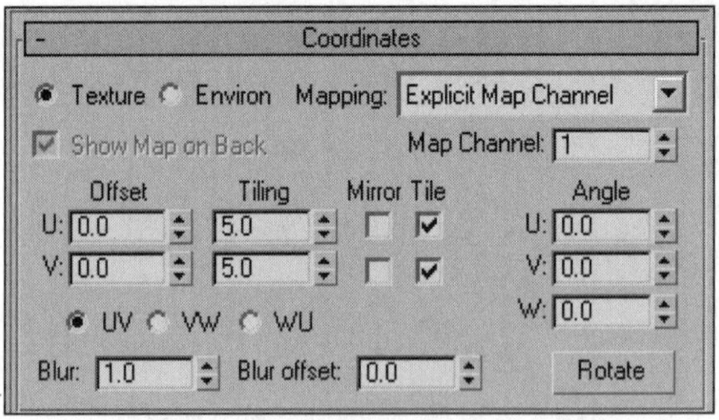

Fig. 2.13. Parameters of the **Checker** test texture

So, what do we have now? 3ds max did not apply the new texture to primitives that were modified. Also, texture coordinates were only retained for objects with modifiers supporting them (e.g., **Lattice**). The coordinates were destroyed if the **Edit Mesh** modifier was applied, and at least one sub-object was deleted — something you should keep in mind in the future.

In any case, the default coordinates are almost useless here. You can edit them using the **UVW XForm** modifier — give it a try if you like — but in this case it is easier to reassign them completely.

Now, let us look into the **Material ID** parameter. It defines which sub-material (of the aggregate set of materials defined by a **Multi/Sub-object**) each sub-object (polygon or plane) is assigned.

❏ Switch to the polygon-selection mode:

>   Context menu➔ Sub–object ➔ Polygon

❏ Select the polygons with a material index of 1:

>   Control panel ➔ Surface Properties ➔ Material ➔ Select By ID

❏ Type "1" in the window's input field and press **OK** (Fig. 2.14).

► ***Tip***

You can highlight the selected polygons (**Shade selected faces**) by pressing the <F2> key.

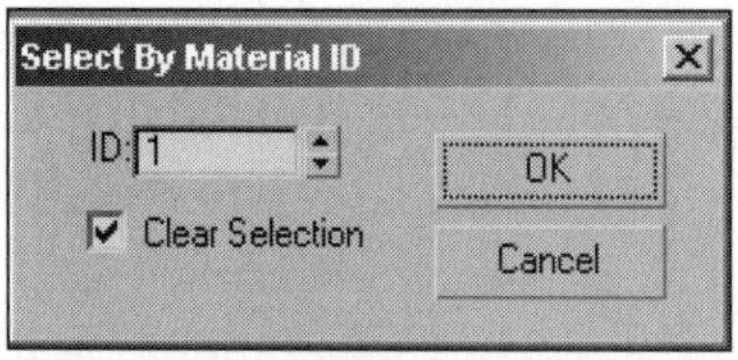

Fig. 2.14. Select By Material ID window

Try to select polygons with other indices. Their values will not be affected, but it doesn't do much for us either, because, in our case, it is difficult to identify the materials and surfaces.

Generally, automatic texture-coordinates generating and assigning the material index to various surfaces are not as useless as they may seem. On the other hand, familiarity with the manual procedure can be much more efficient when you create plain objects, especially several objects of the same geometry with different materials. However, when more complicated objects are modeled (the kinds of things found outside a spaceship), these functions are more of a hindrance than an assistance.

In our book "3ds max 4: From Objects to Animation," we described in detail how to create and assign materials in the "traditional" method used with the first version of 3ds max. Starting with version 3, however, 3ds max introduced the capability to "drag and drop" materials onto various sub-objects, with the composite set of materials created and updated automatically. The material indices are also assigned automatically, according to the sub-materials selected. We recommend that you use this method.

❏ To begin, assign a material index of 1 to all polygons:

      Context menu → Sub-objects → Polygon

      Main menu → Edit → Select All *or* <Ctrl>+<A> key combination

      Control panel → Surface Properties → Material → ID field → 1

Now define the materials. The main one will be used for the body of the spacecraft, but materials for the solar panels, portholes and the nozzle of the mid-flight engine are interesting as well. Materials for other, smaller details are not as important, except that they should adhere to the general style.

We looked at a lot of photographs of spacecraft and found that there are two main types of surfaces: bright and metallic (typical at the start of the space age), and dim white paint on metal. You can find the first type of material in the examples supplied with 3ds max (Apollo.max).

We recommend that you create a modern material, a white matte surface, with identification markings and a few other elements. Seams and rivets are out of the question, because they will never be seen. However, the skin of the spaceship is made up of metal sheets that cannot be painted absolutely evenly and, in addition to affecting color, reflect light at different angles and give a feeling of discontinuity. Let's create such a material:

❏ Open the material editor and select any free preview window. Rename the material SpaceShip_Body.

❏ Use the image in ship_body-diffuse.tga as the texture for the **Diffuse** channel, and the image in ship_body-gloss.tga for the **Specular Level** and **Glossiness** channels (Fig. 2.15, *a*).

There are two ways to do this. The "traditional" one uses the **Material/Map Browser** in the material editor, the other uses the **Asset Browser**. In the first case, simply click the button next to the corresponding parameter, select

Bitmap and load the file. In the second case, launch the browser:

Control panel → Utilites → Asset Browser

Find the file and drag it onto the corresponding button.

Now let's consider the images contained in these files.

Even though the image in ship_body-diffuse.tga has a white background, we are not going to use the coloring, because it is more convenient to control the color with 3ds max. This file also uses the transparency channel (alpha-channel). Let's make use of that fact.

❑ Switch to texture-editing mode and enter the parameters shown in Fig. 2.15, *b*.

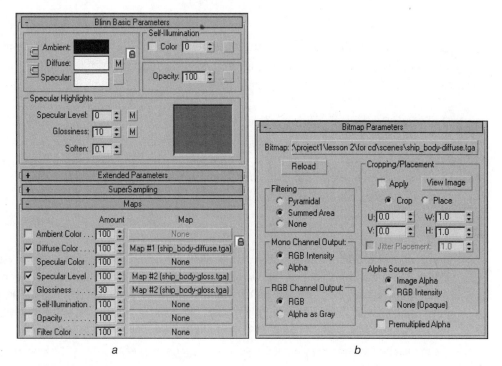

a   b

Fig. 2.15. Texture assignment (*a*) and parameters of the **Diffuse** channel (*b*)

Explanation

In the **Bitmap Parameters** menu, set the **Alpha Source** to **Image Alpha**.

Uncheck the **Premultiplied Alpha** flag, because the texture was made in Adobe Photoshop with the usual transparency channel.

Select **Summed Area** in the **Filtering** group. This algorithm is rendered slower, but its smoothing effect is of higher quality than that of **Pyramidal**. This is especially important if you use the alpha channel.

Leave the rest of the parameters unchanged. Briefly, they are used as follows. The **Mono Channel Output** parameter specifies what part of the image will be interpreted as mono-chrome, e.g., when the texture is transparent or represents a **Bump**. On the other hand, the **RGB Channel Output** parameter enables you to choose the part of the image that should be in color. The **Cropping/Placement** group allows you to trim and position the image.

The ship_body-gloss.tga file does not use the alpha channel. As you can see, it simply con-tains the "sheets of metal" of which the body of the spaceship is built. In addition, darker areas correspond to identification signs and elements applied to the **Diffuse** texture. This is done to create the illusion that the signs were made with another color on top of the main paint.

We will consider the rest of the parameters later. Right now, we must assign a material to the objects comprising the body of the spaceship and orient the tex-tures.

❏   Switch to polygon-editing mode:

     Context menu→ Sub-object → Polygon

❏   Progressively select the polygons constituting the body of the spaceship by holding the <Shift> key (Fig. 2.16).

▶ Tip

If you work with **Editable Mesh** objects, it is often convenient to check the **Ignore Visible Edges** flag in the Control panel. This will allow you to select several polygons simultaneously, if the angle between them is less than the **Planar Threshold**. Unfortunately, there is no such option when working with **Editable Poly** objects. However, in both cases, you can easily se-lect polygons in side projections with the **Crossing** method. See details in *Lesson 12*.

It can also be useful to highlight the selected polygons by pressing the <F2> key: They will be shown in red.

Fig. 2.16. Polygons that will use the SpaceShip_Body material

❏ Apply the SpaceShip_Body material from the material editor to the selected polygons, or simply press the **Assign Material to Selection** button.

Test the rendering by pressing the <F9> key. As you can see, the material has been applied to the spaceship, but it looks strange. The problem is with the texture coordinates.

❏ Use the **UVW Map** modifier without deselecting the polygons:

   Control panel → Modifier List → UVW Map

▶ *Note*

There are many ways to access commands in 3ds max. For example, **UVW Map** can also be found at Main menu → Modifiers → UV Coordinates *or* at Tab panels → Modifiers. From here on, we will not stick to a single method, but will use the most convenient one in each situation.

The **Tab Panel** and **Floating Toolbars** deserve special attention. 3ds max is constantly evolving toward greater convenience. These panels appeared in 3D Studio MAX 3, and the ability to edit their contents was, undoubtedly, a step in the right direction. 3ds max 4 has since introduced more options, such as editing the **Quad Menu** and Main menu, making the toolbars less useful. Do not hesitate to use them if you like but, in the future, we will refer to them only when necessary.

❏   Activate the **Smooth+Highlight** viewport by pressing the <F3> key.

❏   Show the material in the viewport:

     Material editor → Show Map in Viewport

▶ *Note*

When the **Diffuse** texture uses the alpha channel, sometimes the viewport displays the material incorrectly. If so, temporarily switch it off in the **Diffuse** texture's parameters, but do not forget to reselect it later.

❏   Set the **UVW Mapping** parameters shown in Fig. 2.17 in order to get the right image.

❗ *Explanation*

We deliberately made the textures inaccurate, so that you could become familiar with the **UVW Map** modifier.

❏   Select **Cylindrical** mapping for the texture.

❏   Select the **Gizmo** and rotate it along the longitudinal axis so that the exhibition's logo is visible:

     Context menu→ Sub-object → Gizmo
     Context menu→ Rotate

❏   Try different values for recurrence on the **U** axis until the logo is round.

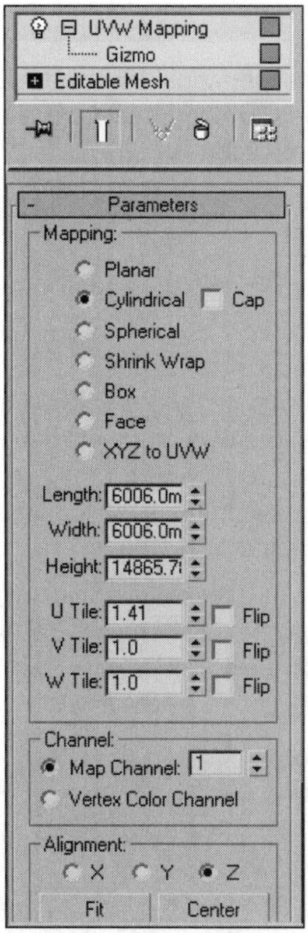

Fig. 2.17. UVW Mapping parameters for the spaceship body

We will now set the final material parameters. In order to do so, you will need to determine approximately where the camera and sources of light will be located.

First, get rid of the **Ambient** light, because we don't need it:

Main menu → Rendering → Environment → Global Lighting → Ambient → Black

There are two main sources of light in our scene. One of them simulates sunlight — very bright, giving contrast between lit and unlit areas. The second simulates light reflected by the Moon — dimmer and softer. Light from distant stars pales in comparison with that from the Sun and Moon and will not be used as a source of illumination. In our example, the Earth is almost in line with the Sun and therefore will also not be used. It is much more important to consider the light reflected off various parts of the spaceship onto other constituent elements. To that end, we suggest you use several low-power point sources.

▶ *Note*

It may seem that ambient light could be used for that purpose. Such light uniformly high-lights objects from all sides. Unfortunately, because it highlights *all* objects without exception, it cannot be used in our scene.

☐ Create the camera and sources of light as shown in Fig. 2.18, *a*:

Tab panel → Lights & Cameras

▼ *Explanation*

Since both the Sun and Moon are a great distance from the spaceship, their rays are considered parallel. Therefore, the type of source is parallel (**Direct**). You can use either a **Free Direct** or **Target Direct** source in each case; we prefer the second type. By making the center of the lit object the target, it is easy to move the source without being afraid that the object will no longer be illuminated.

Shine the beam of light so that the whole object is lit, but not more. This is easy to do using the view from the light source (<Shift>+<4> keys) and the **Light Hotspot** and **Light Falloff** tools. If there are several directional light sources in the scene, 3ds max will ask you to select one from a list.

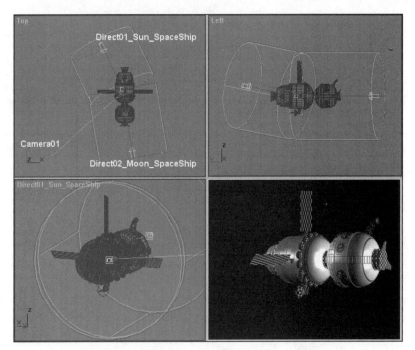

Fig. 2.18, *a*. Camera and light-source positions

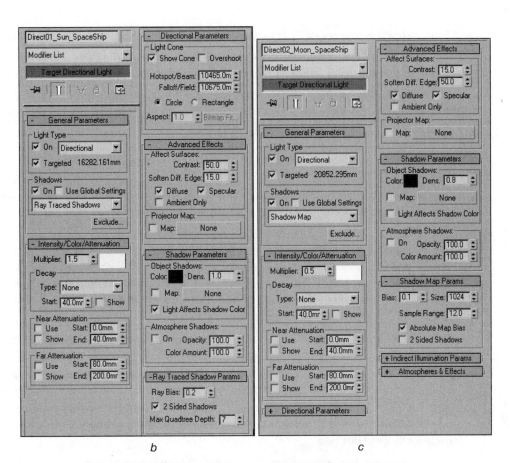

Fig. 2.18, *b* and *c*. Parameters of light imitating the Sun (*b*)
and the Moon (*c*)

Note

You will need to test the rendering many times while choosing the light and material parameters. If your computer is powerful enough, interactive rendering (Viewport context menu → Views → ActiveShade) in one of the viewports can be extremely helpful. Unfortunately, it does not react to all changes in the scene. You may want to use the **Initialize** command in the **ActiveShade** context menu on those occasions.

Tip

While adjusting an object's parameters (e.g., a source of light), you often have to select and move other objects. To avoid having to reselect the original object several times, you can **Pin** its parameters on the control panel with the **Pin Stack** button.

❏ Rename the sources of light as **Direct01_Sun_SpaceShip** and **Direct02_Moon_SpaceShip**. Such long names are needed to avoid ambiguity when selecting objects by name, as there will be at least five light sources in the spaceship flight scene: three for the Sun and two for the Moon.

❏ Parameters for **Direct01_Sun_SpaceShip** and **Direct02_Moon_SpaceShip** are shown in Fig. 2.18, *b* and c, respectively.

Explanation

You can leave the moonlight white, but the color of the sunlight should be given a yellow cast. To change the color, adjust the HSV (**Hue–Saturation–Value**) representation, wich allows you to work with understandable terms, such as "light yellow" and "bright red."

Light in space is very bright due to the absence of an atmosphere, making the border between lit and unlit areas very sharp. Furthermore, since the Sun is so far away and its angular size is so small, its shadows are similarly very sharp. These characteristics are simulated by the **Multiplier**, **Contrast**, **Soften Diff. Edge**, and **Ray Traced Shadows** parameters of the **Direct01_Sun_SpaceShip** light source.

Moonlight is not as bright and softer and, since its angular size is so large, it can not be treated as a point source of light. We suggest your shadows be of the **Shadow Map** type. Select values for **Size** and smoothing (**Sample Range**) so that they are a little bit blurred and do not have any "steps." In the process, you will need to test the rendering many times using the <F9> key. **ActiveShade** can not display such subtlety. We also selected the **Absolute Map Bias** flag to prevent the shadows from shaking during animation, which is typical for those of this type.

Try adjusting the light parameters for yourself. You will undoubtedly notice two more shadow types: **Advanced Ray Traced** and **Area Shadows**. These types appeared in 3ds max 5, and are based on the **Ray Traced** algorithm. The first type enables you to blur shadow borders, whereas the second is used to obtain so-called **Soft Shadows**. The results of these algorithms are extremely realistic, but require considerably longer to render. If that is not an issue, then experiment with them — "soft shadows" usually work quite well for the moonlight. You should be aware that shadows of this type sometimes cause strange artifacts to appear on object surfaces — blurred lines along objects' ribs. This is because the shadows are being drawn in front of the object. The solution is simple: the shadow's **Bias** should be a quarter more than the **Spread**.

❏ Place several omnidirectional (**Omni**) point sources of light around the body of the spaceship (Fig. 2.19, *a*), copying each one as an **Instance** of another. This will give you the ability to edit the parameters for all of them simultaneously.

Use a small **Multiplier** and pale-blue color. Also, turn off shadows and **Specular** surface reactions to the light (Fig. 2.19, *b*).

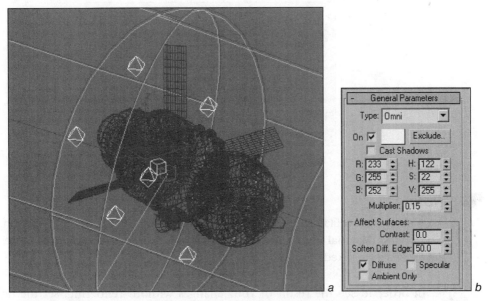

Fig. 2.19. Additional sources to simulate light reflected by various parts back onto the spaceship: positioning (*a*) and parameters (*b*)

Generally, adjusting light parameters is laborious and largely a matter of personal preference. If you do not like our result, feel free to adjust them as you see fit. Also, do not forget that we have not finished with the material parameters yet. It is time to return to them.

As mentioned before, the composite material created by the "drag and drop" method is created and automatically updated as sub-materials are added. Let's verify that this is true:

❏ Open the material editor and select any free preview window.

❏ Load the spaceship's material using the "dropper" (**Pick Material From Object**).

As you can see, it consists of two sub-materials: the one used in the beginning (**SpaceShip_Test**) and the current one (**SpaceShip_Body**) (Fig. 2.20). Rename the composite material as **SpaceShip** and edit the **SpaceShip_Body** sub-material by pressing the button.

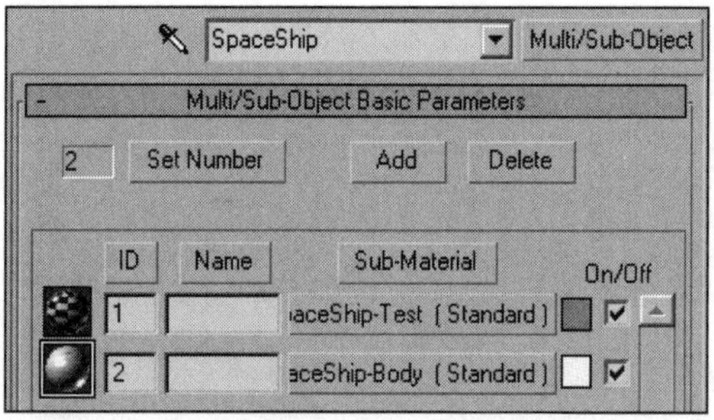

Fig. 2.20. SpaceShip composite material

> ## Note
>
> Alternatively, you could edit the **SpaceShip_Body** material through the corresponding preview window (**Material Slot**). Changes will be reflected in the composite material because the materials are linked.

In order to see the result of your changes without rendering, set the light in the preview windows to correspond to the light in the scene.

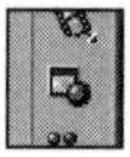

☐ Open the material-editor settings with the **Options** button.

☐ Make the color and multipliers of the light sources match the parameters of the Sun and Moon (Fig. 2.21). At the same time, activate the **BackLight**.

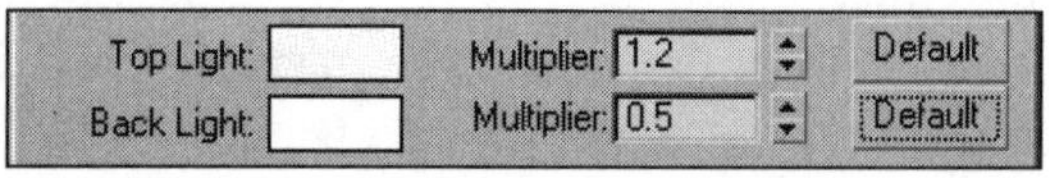

Fig. 2.21. Making the sources of light in the material editor match those in the scene

Now the working model looks similar to what will be seen after rendering.

> ## Tip
>
> If your computer is powerful enough, you can open a larger preview window with the Context menu → Magnify command, or double-click on the current preview window.

And so the magic begins! Although not complicated, our only difficulty was in the unusual nature of our lighting conditions and we spent about an hour looking at the alternatives. That is enough for this lesson, but further refinements could be made with additional textures or the use of another **Shader**. Still, we managed to obtain an acceptable result with the parameters shown in Fig. 2.22.

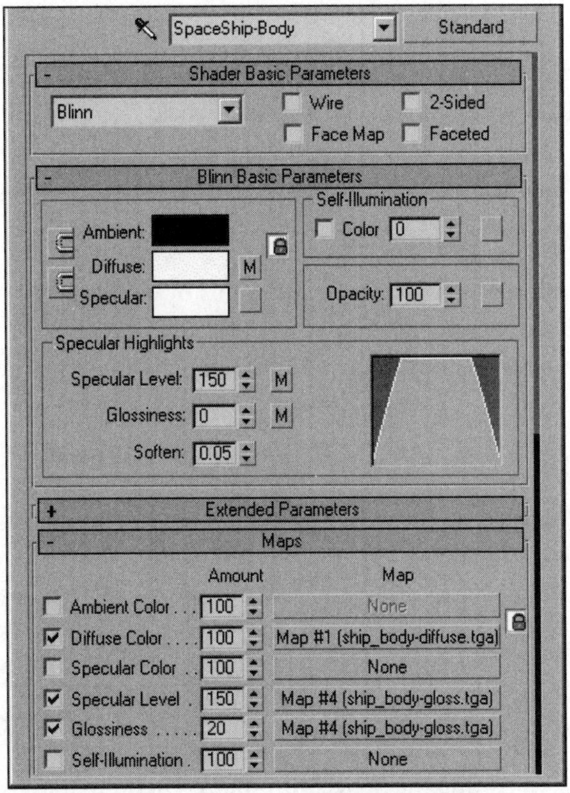

Fig. 2.22. Parameters of the **SpaceShip_Body** material

▌ *Explanation*

We never changed the **Shader** to be anything other than the **Blinn** type. You can try other ones, e.g. **Oren–Nayar–Blinn**, for finer control, but they are also more complicated.

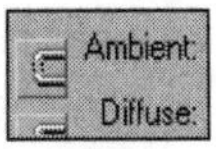

We made the **Ambient** light black even after we specified to **Unlock** it from the **Diffuse** light. That measure was more preventative than practical. We did not use the **Ambient Light**, so its parameters would not affect anything.

We made the **Diffuse** light the same color as the **Specular** light — white.

Several light parameters depend on the **Specular Level** and **Glossiness** channels of the textures. We set the **Specular Level** to 150 for demonstration purposes only. When textures are used that have a channel with the **Amount** equal to 100 or more, 3ds max ignores all the base parameters of the material. You can see this for yourself by changing the **Specular Level** — the material will appear the same.

Now let's look at other materials. First of all, make the material for the ends of the propulsion module:

❏ Copy the **SpaceShip_Body** material by moving it into any preview window.

❏ Rename it **SpaceShip_Back**.

❏ Deactivate all textures. You can do this by applying the **None** texture type from any blank texture button, or switch to texture-editing mode, press the **Bitmap** texture button and select **NONE** in the material and texture ▢ NONE browser.

❏ Change the material type from **Standard** to **Blend** by clicking on the appropriate button.   ⬤ Blend

❏ Save the current material as a sub-material.

❏ Rename the new material **SpaceShip_Back_Blend**.

❏ Use the image in Ship_body_back-mask.tga as a mask for material blending.

Replace Material   ☒

  ○ Discard old material?

  ◉ Keep old material as sub-material?

  [OK]   Cancel

❏ Go back to editing the **SpaceShip_Back_Blend** material:
  Material editor → Go to Parent

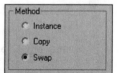

❏ Swap materials 1 and 2 so that they are in the right place. The material should be as shown in Fig. 2.23.

Method
  ○ Instance
  ○ Copy
  ◉ Swap

❏ Edit the first material, rename it **SpaceShip_Back_Metal**, and set its parameters according to Fig. 2.24.

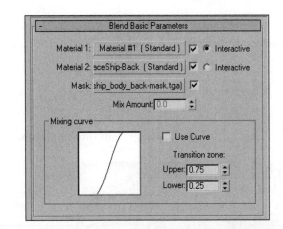

Fig. 2.23. SpaceShip_Back_Blend material structure

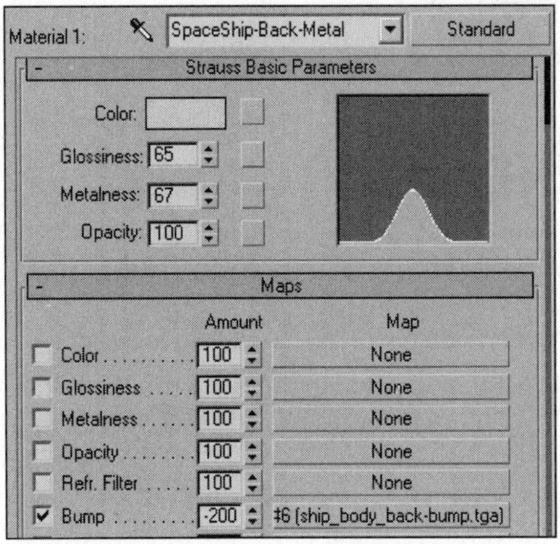

Material 1: ⟍ SpaceShip-Back-Metal ▼ Standard

Strauss Basic Parameters

Color:
Glossiness: 65
Metalness: 67
Opacity: 100

Maps

	Amount	Map
☐ Color	100	None
☐ Glossiness	100	None
☐ Metalness	100	None
☐ Opacity	100	None
☐ Refr. Filter	100	None
☑ Bump	-200	#6 (ship_body_back-bump.tga)

Fig. 2.24. SpaceShip_Back_Metal material parameters

Explanation

Select the **Strauss** shader type. This type enables you quickly to create simple materials simulating plastic and metal.

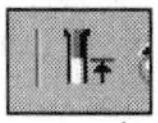

Set the parameters so as to have a metallic shine. You may want to deactivate the final resulting image temporarily in the preview window by pressing the **Show End Result** button.

Apply the ship_body_back-bump.tga file to the **Bump** channel. Since this image is in black and white, you must make the **Amount** negative in order to obtain protrusions and not indentations.

Edit the second sub-material and reduce its **Specular Level**. To navigate between sub-materials and textures, it is often convenient to use **Go Forward to
Sibling**.

❏ Use the **Edit Mesh** modifier and select the polygons corresponding to the end
surfaces as shown in Fig. 2.25, *a*.

❏ Assign the **SpaceShip_Back_Metal** material to those surfaces.

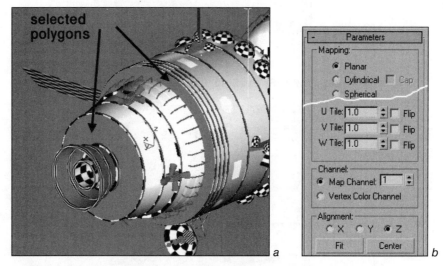

Fig. 2.25. Polygons comprising the end surface of the propulsion module (*a*)
and parameters of the **UVW Map** modifier (*b*)

❏ Maintain the same selection and apply the **UWV Map** modifier with the parameters shown in Fig. 2.25, *b*. Everything should be self-explanatory. The only
remaining option is to **Fit** the modifier's Gizmo more precisely on the surface.

The last material with a texture from a raster file is the one for the solar panels —
Lessons\Lesson02\scenes\ship-cell.tga. As you can see, the texture is very simple:
It consists of a black rectangle with white edging 1 pixel wide. 3ds max also has
a standard texture type called **Bricks** that is used to create excellent regular textures
(Fig. 2.26). We often use it and it would work well in this case. You might want try
it, but we recommend using the raster file instead. It renders faster because
the processor does not have to generate the texture and, more importantly, rendering with a raster file is more predictable.

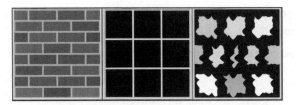

Fig. 2.26. Examples of **Brick** textures

❏ Select a free preview window and rename the material SpaceShip_Cells.

❏ Make the type of shader **Strauss**, although in this case it is not very important and any other would do.

❏ Use the raster file specified above for the **Color** channel (**Diffuse**, if another type of shader is used) and ship-cell.tga for the **Bump** channel (Fig. 2.27, *a*).

❏ Check the **Face Map** and **Faceted** flags in the material parameters. Note how the material image changes in preview window (Fig. 2.27, *b*).

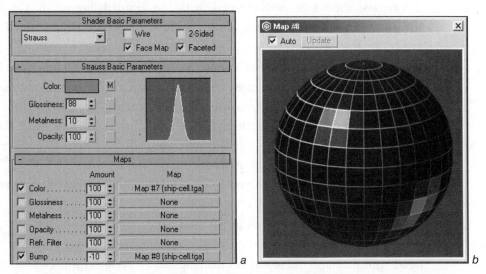

Fig. 2.27. SpaceShip_Cells material parameters (*a*) and how it appears in the zoomed preview window (*b*)

❗ *Explanation*

The **Face Map** flag applies the texture to every polygon. In our case, this is a very useful feature. For this reason, we recommended you create the solar panels from strongly segmented blocks. You can also achieve this by simply increasing the **Tiling** of the texture, but there is another reason to use this flag, which will be considered in *Lesson 5*.

The **Faceted** checkbox keeps the individual facets on surface of the object.

❏ Select the polygons corresponding to the surfaces of the solar panels and assign the **SpaceShip_Cells** material to them.

At this point, we think you can create the rest of the materials and assign them to the corresponding parts of the spaceship on your own. We will only make a few notes here:

❏ Try to name the materials reasonably. It is not necessarily that they are as long as ours, but you should be able understand them.

❏ Materials for one-sided surfaces (those that have no thickness, such as the aerials) should be double-sided, with the **2-Sided** flag set in the parameters of the material. (Don't confuse it with the **DoubleSided** composite material, which is completely different!)

❏ For some materials, it would be a good idea to assign a large texture of standard **Noise** type as the **Diffuse** texture, and blend it with the **Diffuse** color by setting the **Amount** parameter to approximately 10. By default, standard texture types are defined so that they do not need texture coordinates to be assigned. Keep in mind that you are working in millimeters and, although the units are not displayed in the material editor, standard textures use them. So it is up to you to set reasonable dimensions in comparison to the size of your spaceship.

❏ There are 24 preview windows in the material editor and it is quite possible that you will run out of them. Beginners tend to get very upset with this, and often address their dismay to various fora. The solution is simple: select any material and press the **Reset Mtl/Map to Default State** button. Then select **Affect only mtl/map in the editor slot?** in the window that appears (Fig. 2.28). There is also another way to do this: You can create a new material and substitute an existing one with it in the material editor by pressing the **Get Material** button and selecting the type of **New** material or texture.

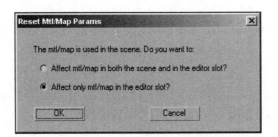

Fig. 2.28. Reset Mtl/Map Params window

☐ In order to select polygons easier, it is often convenient to hide the polygons that have already been assigned a material. Once you have finished assigning materials, don't forget to unhide them:

Control panel → Selection → Hide, Unhide All (for Editable Mesh)

Control panel → Edit Geometry → Hide Selected, Unhide All (for Editable Poly)

☐ It is also useful to hide the camera and light sources while you are working:

Control panels → Display → Hide by Category

☐ When you are done, minimize the stack of modifiers and convert all objects to an **Editable Mesh** or **Editable Poly**. It should be noted that the second type is not very stable and may present surprises, so, after everything else is done, we recommend that you convert the objects to an **Editable Mesh**:

Context menu → Convert to → Convert to Editable Mesh, Editable Poly

☐ Save your work to the lesson02-final.max file.

Lesson 3

Modeling the Lunar Module and Rover

To model the lunar module and the lunar rover, we will use the main — polygonal — method available in 3ds max. Polygons were first introduced in the third version of 3ds max, and they considerably simplified modeling by using triangular surfaces joined by invisible edges. Initially, there was only one type of object — **Mesh**. You could edit every part of it and, with the third version, that included individual constituent polygons. This greatly simplified modeling, but working with these triangular surfaces still left much to be desired.

The fourth version of 3ds max introduced a new object — **PolyMesh**. At first glance, the differences between Mesh and PolyMesh are insignificant, but PolyMesh distinguishes itself by working with "real" polygons and multi-angular surfaces.

▶ Note

The "real" polygons available with PolyMesh are still composed of individual triangles, automatically generated by 3ds max. This process occasionally makes mistakes but, unlike other packages, you can manually correct the triangulation process in 3ds max.

The toolkit for working with polygonal objects was considerably expanded in 3ds max 5, satisfying even the recognized authorities in polygonal modeling, such as Nendo and Mirai. In this lesson, we make maximal use of the new features, even when they are not the most efficient, so that you can become acquainted with them.

The toolkit for work with mesh objects, however, has not changed and is the same as in 3D Studio MAX 3. It is therefore not recommend to model with mesh objects, except to use the **Edit Mesh** modifier. There is no similar modifier for polygons, which is a shame. Hopefully, it will appear in subsequent versions.

The lunar module consists of two main parts: the living area for the crew during their orbit around the Moon and return to Earth, and the propulsion module to land and remain on the Moon (Fig. 3.1). There is no need to divide these parts into separate objects in our project, because we will not animate the return to Earth; it is quite possible, though, that you will want to animate the return by yourself.

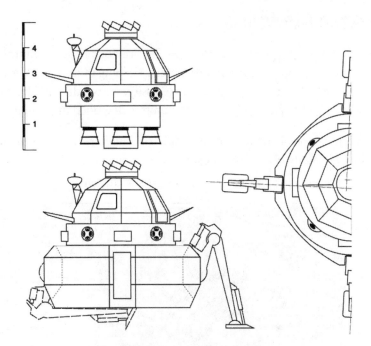

Fig. 3.1. Lunar module sketch

Very important notice. So that we do not distract you, keyboard shortcuts to commands used in this and subsequent lessons are listed below.

❏ Selection mode — <Q> key; moving mode — <W>; rotation mode — <E>; scaling and scaling type change — <R>

❏ Sub-object selection — keys <1>–<5>; toggle work with sub-objects or objects — <Ctrl>+<B> key combination

- Selection type (rectangle, circle, polygon, lasso) — <Ctrl>+<F>; selection of all sub-objects or objects — <Ctrl>+<A>; undo selection of all sub-objects or objects — <Ctrl>+<D>; invert selection — <Ctrl>+<I>; activate or deactivate **Selection Lock Toggle** of sub-objects or objects — <Space>; object selection by name window — <H>
- **Snap Toggle** — <S>; **Angle Snap Toggle** — <A>
- Viewport display mode toggle — <F3>; selected polygons highlight — <F2>; edge display on shaded viewport views — <F4>

Living Area Modeling

Before you model, specify the units. In the previous lesson, millimeters were used; in this one, we propose that you use meters. Keeping in mind the developers' warning not to change the units without utter necessity, we would still like you to see the effects when they are changed. Setting the units is described in detail in *Lesson 2*.

- Create an octahedron with a radius of 2 meters and height of 0.5 meters as the base of the living area (Fig. 3.2):

    Main menu → Create → Extended Primitives → Gengon

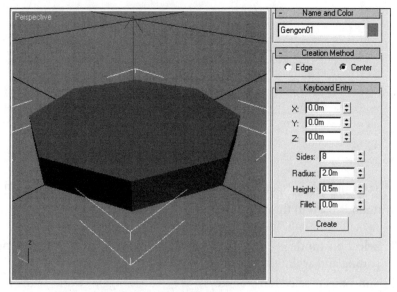

Fig. 3.2. Octahedron representing the living area

▶ *Tip*

When creating a primitive, it is convenient to enter the necessary parameters using the keyboard.

❑ Note that the grid pitch is large — 10 meters, which is very inconvenient. Correct this by setting the pitch to 0.1 meter (Fig. 3.3). To make the grid useful in the projection viewport, either uncheck the **Inhibit Perspective View Grid Resize** flag, or increase the value of the **Perspective View Grid Extent** parameter:

     Main menu → Customize → Grid and Snap Settings → Home Grid

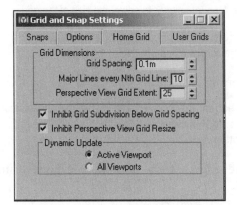

Fig. 3.3. Grid pitch setting

❑ Rename the object **Living Module** and convert it to an **Editable Poly**:

     Context menu → Convert to → Convert to Editable Poly

▶ *Note*

The editing that follows may not seem the most direct, but we are using this simple example to demonstrate as many methods as possible of editing polygonal objects. If you want to accomplish the same task in an easier way — do it!

Use the central upper vertex of the object to create another integral polygon.

❑ Switch to vertex operation mode, select the vertex, and apply the **Chamfer** command (Fig. 3.4, *a*). Note that there is a window icon to the left of the command. If you press this icon, the settings window of the command will appear. Such icons are provided for many commands:

     Context menu → Chamfer icon

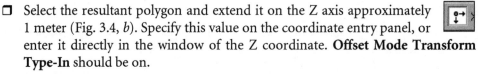

☐ Select the resultant polygon and extend it on the Z axis approximately 1 meter (Fig. 3.4, *b*). Specify this value on the coordinate entry panel, or enter it directly in the window of the Z coordinate. **Offset Mode Transform Type-In** should be on.

☐ Extrude the polygon by approximately 0.5 meter and make its size comply with that of the docking unit with a diameter of 1.6 meter (Fig. 3.4, *c*). It is convenient to do so by entering these parameters into the **Bevel** command:

Context menu → Bevel icon

Enter 0.5 for Height and press the OK button

Use Outline Amount spinner to adjust the size of the grid in Left view

☐ Rotate the view in the projection viewport as you like (or use the **Bottom** view), and select the edges of the bottom polygons.

▶ *Tip*

When selecting edges, it is convenient to use the **By Vertex** and **Ignore Backfacing** flags. In this case, we can simply click the left mouse button on the central bottom vertex.

☐ Remove the edges of the bottom polygons using the **Remove** command (Fig. 3.4, *d*):

Context menu → Remove

▶ *Note*

Only the **Remove** command should be used for this purpose! If you use the <Del> key, you will have an unnecessary "hole."

By default, the **Remove** command has no key combination. It is worthwhile to assign a shortcut, for it often will be useful in modeling polygons (Main menu → Customize User Interface → Keyboard → Remove (Poly)). It would be nice to assign a combination like <Alt>+<Del>. Unfortunately, the <Del> key is reserved in 3ds max, so choose something else (e.g., <Alt>+<End>).

☐ Select the bottom polygon (now it is the only one) and **Extrude** it by approximately 0.8 meter (Fig. 3.4, *e*):

Context menu → Extrude icon

☐ Select the polygons in the circle (marked by white contour lines in the illustration) and **Extrude** them by 0.4 meter in the direction of the **Local Normal** by setting the corresponding **Extrusion Type** (Fig. 3.4, *f*).

▶ *Tip*

This selection can easily be made as follows: Select one lateral edge, then select all lateral edges using the **Ring** command of the **Selection** drop-down menu on the control panel. Convert the selection composed of edges to a selection of polygons using the **Convert to Face** command on the context menu.

❏ Make the bottom round by selecting the edges and applying the **Chamfer** command twice (Fig. 3.4, *g*). To stay in the settings window, press the **Apply** (not **OK**) button for the first adjustment.

❏ Build the bottom part (Fig. 3.4, *h*) with the **Inset** and **Extrude** commands after selecting and removing the unnecessary edges.

▶ *Tip*

This selection can be made as follows: Select the central polygon, use the **Convert to Edge** command on the context menu, expand the selection by pressing the **Grow** button in the **Selection** drop-down menu on the control panel, and apply the **Remove** command.

It is a good idea to also assign key combinations to the **Grow** and **Shrink** commands, for example, <Ctrl>+<=> and <Ctrl>+<–>.

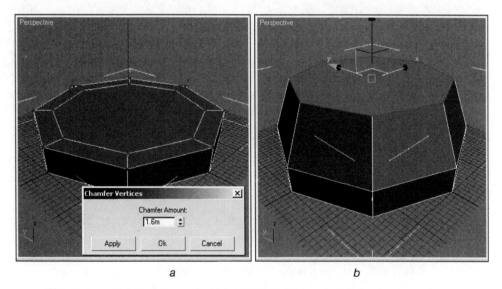

a   b

Fig. 3.4, *a* and *b*. Sequence of creating the living area's basic geometry

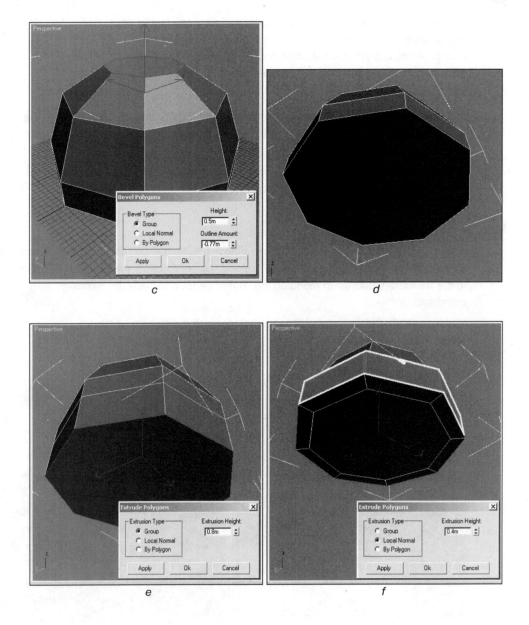

Fig. 3.4, c–f. Sequence of creating the living area's basic geometry

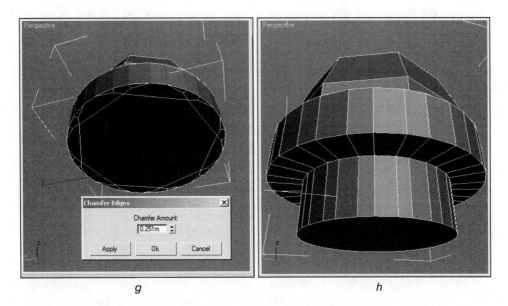

Fig. 3.4, *g* and *h*. Sequence of creating the living area's basic geometry

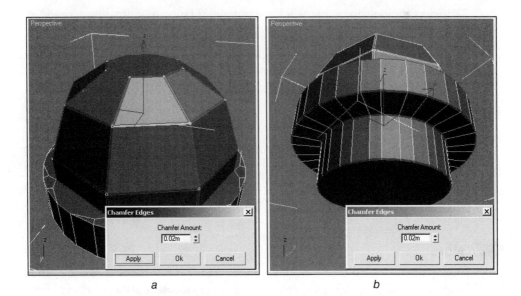

Fig. 3.5. Chamfering

We must now chamfer some edges, namely, those on the top of the module and those on the bottom circle.

❑ Select all edges on the top part and use 0.02 meter for the **Chamfer Edges** command (Fig. 3.5, *a*).

❑ Select one edge on the circle, press the **Loop** and **Ring** buttons on the control panel, and apply the **Chamfer Edges** command (Fig. 3.5, *b*).

The next step is to assign smoothing groups to the polygons. In our case, it is possible to do this automatically:

❑ Select all polygons.

❑ Apply the **Auto Smooth** command.

> Control panel → Polygon Properties → Smoothing Groups → Auto Smooth

Choose a value that gives a good result. The value is simply a specification of the maximal angle (in degrees) between two polygons to which smoothing will be applied.

Now make the portholes and hatch. They can be created separately, but we recommend that you train yourself in "batch" modeling.

❑ Select the polygons that will have portholes (shown with white arrows) and apply the **Inset** command (Fig. 3.6, *a*).

❑ Select the vertices of the polygons that will contain the portholes using the **Convert to Vertex** command. Make the chamfers (Fig. 3.6, *b*):

> Context menu → Convert to Vertex
>
> Context menu → Chamfer

❑ Leave only the required subset of vertices selected using the **Shrink** command. Use the **Chamfer** command again, ensuring that the vertices do not merge (Fig. 3.6, *c*).

❑ **Extrude** and **Bevel** the polygons (Fig. 3.6, *d*).

▶ *Note*

During your work, the geometry may start to "break." If that happens, use the **Undo** command to return to camfering the vertices and use the **Retriangulate** command on the selected porthole polygons. 3ds max has difficulties with multangular polygons, and the **Retriangulate** command helps improve the situation.

Be very careful with the **Bevel** and **Inset** commands. When a polygon is reduced in size, 3ds max does not keep track of its intersections with other polygons. (We encountered such a situation when modeling the glass of the portholes.) Even a small distortion between polygons leads to problems during rendering as a result of incorrect smoothing. The solution is to select the pair of vertices and apply the **Collapse** command.

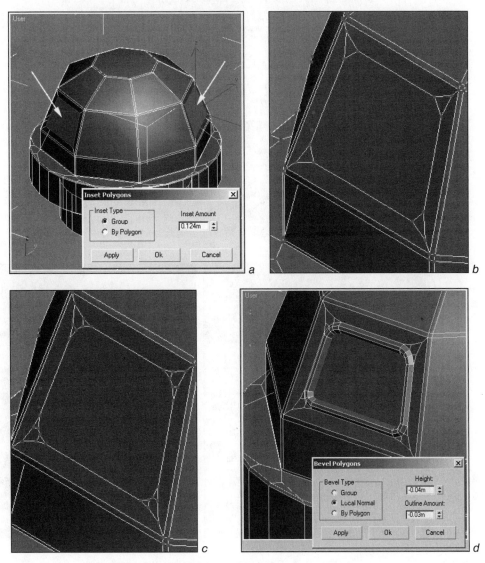

Fig. 3.6. Sequence of creating the porthole

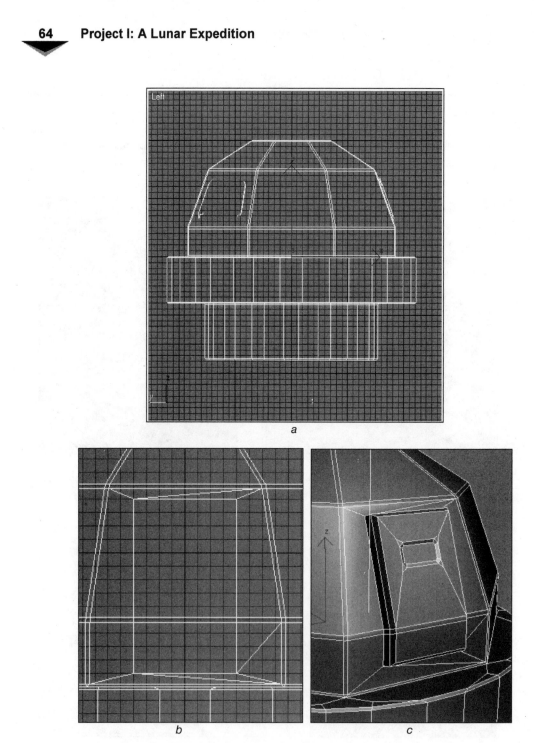

Fig. 3.7. Sequence of modeling the hatch

❑ Check the smoothing groups as described earlier.

❑ Make the hatch a little differenly.

❑ Go to a "direct" projection (e.g., **Left** view).

❑ Rotate the lunar module around the vertical axis so that you directly face one of the facets (Fig. 3.7, *a*).

► *Tip*

You can calculate the precise angle by dividing 360 by 8 and then by 2 with the integrated calculator. Press <Ctrl>+<N> in the window specifying the angle to turn the Z axis in the coordinate entry panel. You may want to use the Y axis when working with the **Rear** view, but the coordinate entry panel can interpret values as either absolute or relative. In the first case, all transformations take place in the world coordinates system; in the second case — with current coordinates. The mode is selected with the **Absolute/Offset Mode Transform Type-In Toggle** of the coordinate entry panel.

❑ Display the grid (<G> key) and activate snaps to the grid (<S> key).

❑ Check the **Ignore Backfacing** flag.

❑ **Cut** the polygons as shown in Fig. 3.7, *b.* Don't worry about the unnecessary edges, as they will not impede your work:

> Control panel → Edit Geometry → Cut

► *Tip*

Try to make the hatch yourself. You might want to use the **Insert Vertex** command instead **Cut**. (Our hatch was made in this way.) You will have to remove unnecessary edges and add others. Don't spend too much time on the process. Try to make the polygons with no more than four angles. You can find our result (Fig. 3.7, *c*) on the CD–ROM in \Lessons\Lesson 03\lesson 03-living_module.max.

Propulsion Module Modeling

The propulsion module is modeled using curves.

❑ Create a **Rectangle** in the **Top** view to match the dimensions of the living area (Fig. 3.8, *a*):

> <Ctrl>+Context menu → Rectangle

▶ *Tip*

There are no guidelines in 3ds max, but they are not necessary because the grid is usually enough. In this case, however, it is convenient to use cross hairs for the cursor (Main menu → Customize → Preferences → General → UI Display → Display Cross Hair Cursor). If you plan to use this option often, you might want to assign a key combination, for example <Alt>+<H>.

☑ Display Cross Hair Cursor

❏ Rotate the rectangle 45° around the vertical axis and convert it to an **Editable Spline**:

>   Context menu → Convert to → Convert to Editable Spline

❏ Divide each segment into two equal parts:

>   Context menu → Sub-object → Segment *or* <2> key
>   Select all segments (<Ctrl>+<A>)
>   Control panel → ... → Divide

Divide [1] ⬍

❏ Select the resulting vertices and convert them to **Bezier**:

>   Context menu → Sub-object → Vertex *or* <1> key
>   Context menu → Bezier

❏ Bend the segments into curves. To do so, simply **Scale** the vertices relative to the common center:

>   Context menu → Scale *or* <R> key
>   Main Toolbar → Use Selection Center

▶ *Note*

3ds max has one "subtlety" when working with splines, which you probably encountered while scaling the vertices. Although the segments are curves (**Curve**), they remain straight. Both the explanation and solution are simple — during curve interpolation, by default, segments are optimized to remain straight up to some very small vertex angle. You can activate and deactivate this optimization in the **Interpolation** rollout. Leave it on for now, because we just began editing and everything might be corrected later by itself. Actually, that is exactly what will happen.

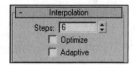

❏ Select the vertices and make chamfers of about 0.6 meters:

> Control panel → Chamfer

❏ Make **Fillets** on the resulting vertices:

> Control panel → Fillet (Fig. 3.8, *b*)

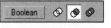

Now, make cavities for the landing props.

❏ Create a rectangle with rounded corners in the **Top** view where the cavity should be.

❏ Rotate it so that the landing props can fold easily (Fig. 3.8, *c*).

❏ Duplicate the rectangle (we called it **Rectangle01**) by turning it 90° around the center of the propulsion module while holding the <Shift> key:

> Main Toolbar → Reference Coordinate Center → Pick → select Rectangle01
>
> Main Toolbar → Use Transform Coordinate Center
>
> Rotate the rectangle while holding the <Shift> key
>
> Use the Copy cloning type with 3 copies

❏ Select **Rectangle01** and **Attach** all four rectangles to it:

> Context menu → Attach

❏ Select the main spline we created initially and make the cavities from the rectangles using subtraction (Fig. 3.8, *d*):

> Context menu → Sub-object → Spline
>
> Control panel → Boolean → Subtraction

❏ Remove "unnecessary" vertices to simplify the geometry (Fig. 3.8, *e*). It also makes sense to reduce the number of interpolation steps in the curve's parameters.

❏ Create a **Circle**, then align and attach it to **Rectangle01**.

❏ **Hide** the living module:

> Context menu → Hide Unselected

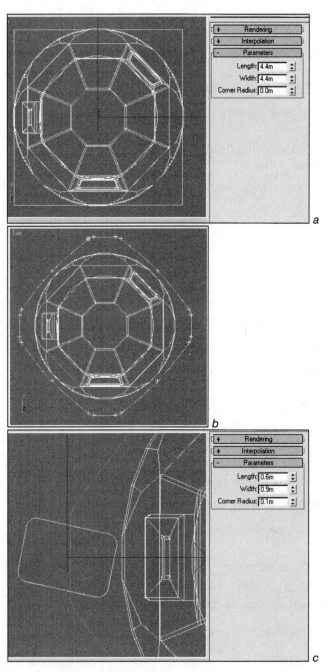

Fig. 3.8, *a–c*. Modeling the propulsion module

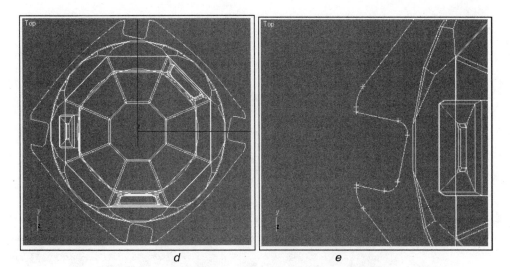

d   *e*

Fig. 3.8, *d* and *e*. Modeling the propulsion module

► *Note*

Strictly speaking, the editing procedure that follows is not the most efficient. It would be more straightforward to create a surface based on the curves we have already constructed by applying the **CrossSection** and **Surface** modifiers. Try to do this, if you understand what we mean.

☐ **Extrude** the **Rectangle01** object by 1 meter (Fig. 3.9, *a*):

   Main menu → Modifiers → Mesh Editing → Extrude

☐ Convert it to an **Editable Poly.**

At this point, it would be nice to **Bevel** the top polygon but. In this case, however, it would cause the polygons to overlap. So, we must take a more difficult route:

☐ Select the top polygon and **Extrude** it by about 0.4 meter (Fig. 3.9, *b*).
☐ Select the edges of the top of the central hole — it must be done manually, because the **Loop** command does not work for some reason.
☐ **Scale** them relative to the common center (Fig. 3.9, *c*).

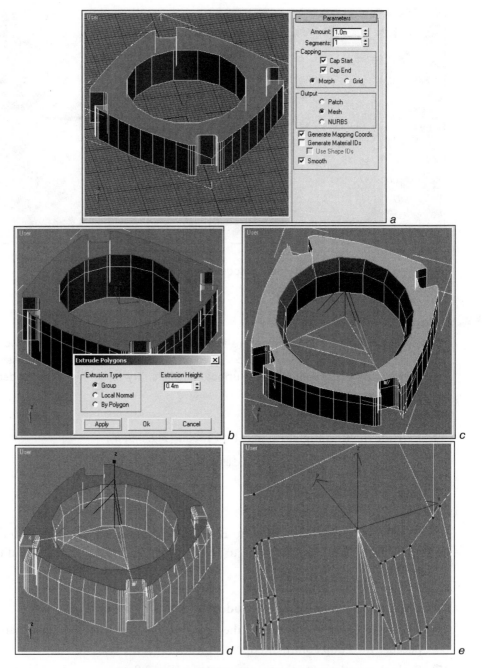

Fig. 3.9, *a–e*. Editing the propulsion module

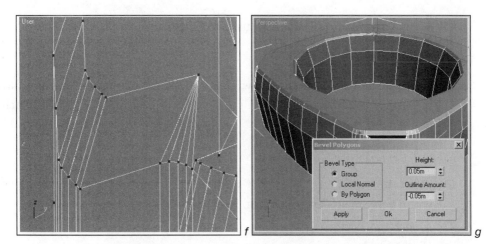

Fig. 3.9, *f* and *g*. Editing the propulsion module

❑ Return to polygon editing and reduce the size of the top polygon as required (Fig. 3.9, *d*).

❑ Select the vertices comprising the exterior curve and merge them using the **Collapse** command (Fig. 3.9 *e*). Be sure not to include redundant vertices!

❑ Merge the vertices one by one with the **Target Weld** command to obtain proper cavities (Fig. 3.9, *f*).

❑ Select the top polygon and give it a little facet using the **Bevel** command (Fig. 3.9, *g*).

You can make the bottom part in the same way, but there is also a more interesting method.

❑ Select the top polygons. To do so, select the top polygon and use the **Grow** command:

    Control panel → Selection → Grow

❑ Create a new object with the **Detach** command and copy it (Fig. 3.10, *a*).

❑ **Mirror** the resulting object and move it down (Fig. 3.10, *b*). We are using the Y axis, but you might be working in another view or with different coordinates:

    Main panel → Mirror

☐ To line up the objects precisely, use the **Align** command (Fig. 3.10, *c*):

　Main panel → Align

☐ Select **Rectangle01** again. (Now is a good time to rename it, for example, as **Service Module**.) Select and remove the bottom polygon, then attach the new object:

　Context menu → Attach

☐ Select the vertices on the border of the two elements and **Weld** them together with a very small **Threshold** (Fig. 3.10, *d*).

☐ Model the bottom part as in our sketch by selecting and moving vertices (Fig. 3.10, *e*).

☐ Put the final touches on the module by assigning smoothing groups to the polygons.

☐ Unhide the **Living Module** and position the modules next to each other (Fig. 3.10, *f*):

　Context menu → Unhide All

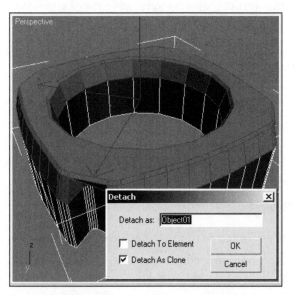

Fig. 3.10, *a*. Editing the propulsion module (continued)

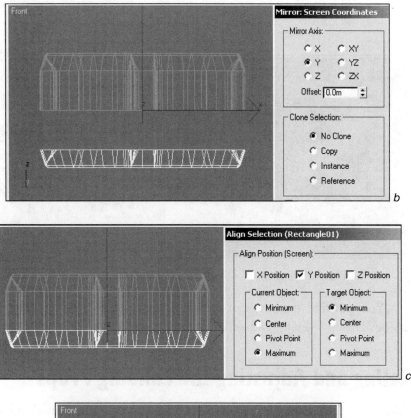

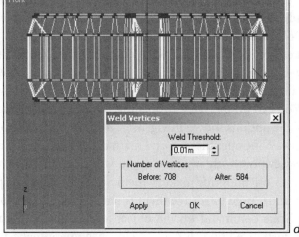

Fig. 3.10, *b–d*. Editing the propulsion module (continued)

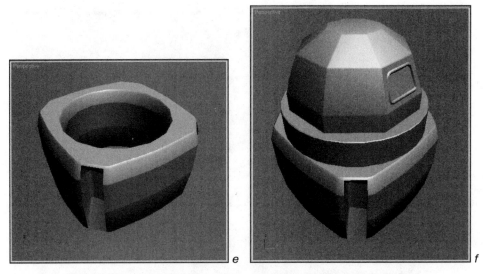

Fig. 3.10, *e* and *f*. Editing the propulsion module (continued)

You can find the result of our work on the CD-ROM in Lessons\Lesson03\ scenes\Lesson03-living-and-service-modules.max.

Modeling and Adjusting the Landing Props

Modeling the landing props is easy: Use curves as the basis and apply either the **Extrude** or **Bevel** modifier (Fig. 3.11). Finish them with a conversion to **Editable Poly** or use of the **Edit Mesh** modifier.

The sketches for this lesson were made in the vector editor Xara X. To avoid repeatedly drawing the same things, we exported the objects in AI 88 format (Adobe Illustrator) and imported the curves into 3ds max (Main menu → File → Import). You can do the same by loading Lessons\Lesson03\ai\leg.ai from the CD-ROM. Use the options shown in Fig. 3.12, *a* and *b*, when importing.

Before we continue, there is one matter that needs to be addressed. Independent of the viewport with which you are working, 3ds max will position the imported curves on the grid, making them so small that you probably will not see them. The initial urge to rescale them is natural, but doing so will cause problems. Using the **Scale** command on the object level scales the local coordinates, which may make further editing difficult. Many beginners make this mistake and later become perplexed at the strange behavior of their objects. Briefly, the reason is as follows: When a block $1 \times 1 \times 1$ meters is scaled twice by all coordinates, its size in local units remains the same. In other words, it is still the same block with 1 meter sides, but its "local meter" becomes equal to two "system meters." Rather unintuitive, isn't it? Yes, but such is the ideology of 3ds max, and it has a logical basis. It allows us, for example, to attach procedure textures with XYZ coordinates to objects but prevent them from assuming a life of their own.

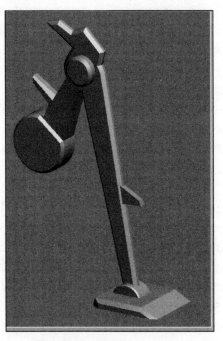

Fig. 3.11. Landing prop

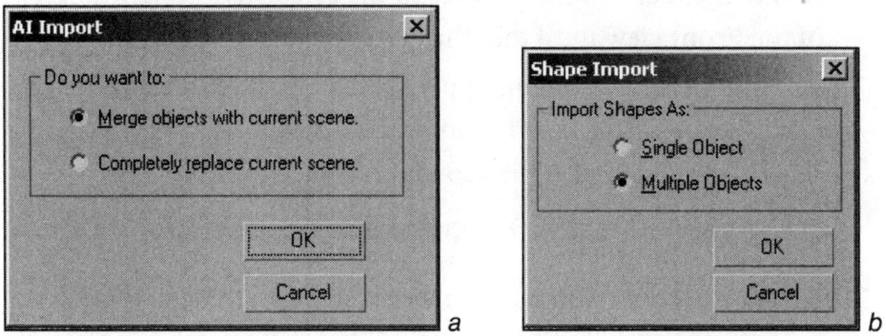

Fig. 3.12. Options when importing files in AI format

So, what should we do? There are three possibilities. The first method is to scale not on the object level, but on that of the sub-objects (e.g., vertices). In our case, that will merge all of the objects into one, with further detachment (**Detach**) into separate objects. You can get around that by applying the **Edit Spline** modifier to all selected objects and converting them to **Editable Spline**. That will give you several objects.

The second method is to apply the **XForm** modifier to all selected objects and scale its gizmo. Using this modifier in such a way does not affect the local coordinates. You will then have to convert all of the objects to **Editable Spline**.

The third method is to use the **Scale** command on all of the objects, and then **Reset XForm**. In this case, you will also have to convert them to **Editable Spline**.

So, which one should we use? Choose any one, or a combination of them. The goal is to remind you once again that 3ds max provides different ways to solve problems; the solution only depends on preference.

After a bit of playing, we found the least "painful" and most demonstrative way, which we suggest you use.

- ☐ Find the imported curves in the **Top** viewport. When scenes are imported and merged (**Merge**), 3ds max will select them unless the **Lock Selection** button is pressed. Simply use the **Zoom Extents Selected** button on the navigation panel or press the <Z> key. Otherwise, select the curves by name (they are called **Shape1**, etc.) by pressing the <H> key (Fig. 3.13, *a*).

- ☐ Select and remove the curves shown in Fig. 3.13, *b* — we will substitute them with corresponding 3ds max objects.

- ☐ Select all curves again.

- ☐ Rotate them around the center of the selected objects with respect to the X axis of the **Front** view until that they face forward in that view.

- ☐ Go to the **Front** view and apply the **Edit Spline** modifier to the selected objects (Fig. 3.13, *c*). Note that the modifier appears in italics in the stack. This means that the modifier is applied to several objects:

    Main menu → Modifiers → Patch/Spline Editing → Edit Spline

- ☐ Switch to vertex editing, then select and scale the landing prop objects relative to the common selection center, so that they match the scale of other objects in the scene (Fig. 3.13, *d*).

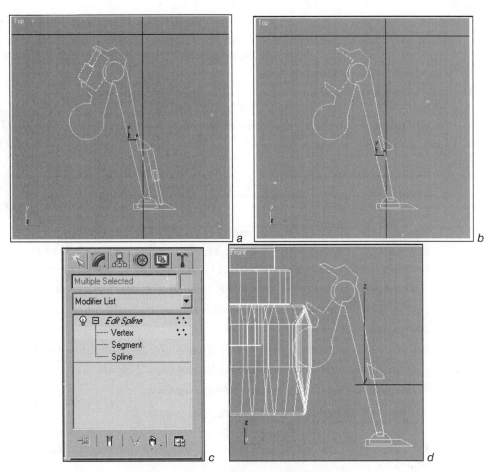

Fig. 3.13. Modeling the landing prop

❏ Convert them to **Editable Spline.** At this point, you can select **Collapse All** from the right-click context menu of the modifiers stack and edit as necessary to obtain the result shown in Fig. 3.11.

❗ *Explanation*

In our example, we mainly used the **Extrude** and **Bevel** modifiers. When necessary, the **Edit Mesh** modifier can also be used to create chamfers, move vertices, and create polygons. You also should note how frequently and practically the **Align** command was used. The \Lessons\Lesson03\scenes\Lesson03(lunar-ship).max file contains our version of the landing prop. In this file, we deliberately did not convert the objects to a base type, so that you could understand different aspects of object creation. It was quite an accomplishment! It would have been much easier to convert the objects after **Extrude** and **Bevel** were used to the **Editable Poly** type!

Adjusting the kinematic connections between objects of the landing prop is much more interesting.

☐ To begin, create a cylinder as the axis for the first segment of the prop. By anatomical analogy, this is the "hip joint." Its use will be explained later.

☐ Rename the objects. We called them **Leg0-01**, **Leg1-01b**, etc. (following the analogy from hip joint to foot). The first index corresponds to the object's position in the hierarchy, the second to the number of the prop. When copied, 3ds max will substitute the proper index — 01, 02, 03, etc. Convenient, isn't it?

☐ In the **Top** view, center the objects relative to each other with the **Align** command.

☐ Select all of the prop objects, center their pivot points relative to each object, and align them relative to world coordinates (Fig. 3.14, *a*):

Control panel → Hierarchy → Pivot → Affect Pivot Only

Press the Center to Object and Align to World buttons.

☐ In a side view, move the pivot points to the center of rotation for each object (Fig. 3.14, *b*).

☐ Turn off the **Affect Pivot Only** button.

☐ **Select and Link** the objects (Fig. 3.14, *c*):

Main panel → Select and Link

Select an object, click on it with the left mouse button, move the cursor to the next object, and repeat. Fig. 3.14, *c*, shows the linking scheme. (You don't need to move the objects.)

You can check whether you linked the objects correctly by pressing the <H> key to open the selection by name window. Check the **Display Subtree** flag. You should see the list of objects, the one at the top left being the "parent" and the one at the bottom right being the "youngest child."

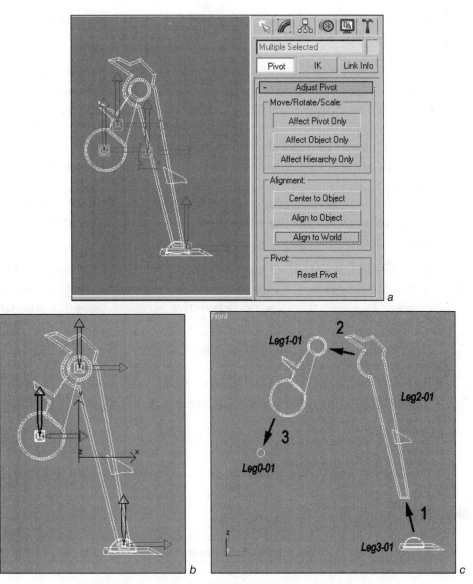

Fig. 3.14. Pivot-point settings for the landing prop (*a* and *b*)
and how the objects are welded together (*c*)

Note

It is time to check an important setting for animation. Open
the settings menu (Main menu → Customize → Preferences →

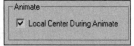

Animation) and make sure **Local Center During Animate** is selected. It will avoid confusion during further animation.

We named our file with the landing prop links as Lesson03(lunar-ship-linked-leg).max. Of course, you need not name your file in the same way.

We will now make the hydraulic pumps. This is nothing but a simulation, so the construction does not have to "work" properly. The mechanics only need to realistically interact with the other parts of the prop.

There are two objects we can use for this in the **Dynamics Objects** class: **Spring** and **Dumper**. In the book "3ds max 4: From Objects to Animation," we considered the use of **Spring** in detail. **Dumper** is used similarly, and there is no reason not to use it. Still, we would like to show you a more universal method to create such objects.

❏ Create four **Point** object-helpers. There is only one advantage in using points to a **Dummy** object — they can be absolutely invisible. It makes sense to create them in either the **User** or **Perspective** viewport using the **AutoGrid** flag (Fig. 3.15, *a*):

AutoGrid ☑

   Control panel → Create → Helpers → Point

❏ Rename the points as **P1-01, P2-01**, etc. — this will simplify editing in the future.
❏ Link them using the **Select And Link** command as follows:
   • **P1-01** with **Leg1-01**
   • **P2-01** with **Leg2-01**
   • **P3-01** with **Leg2-01**
   • **P4-01** with **Leg3-01**

▶ *Tip*

When you select objects merged together or positioned side by side, you could select the wrong one. Click the left mouse button until you get the right one.

❏ The hydraulic pumps are modeled by two cylinders and two pistons. We used the **Chamfer Cylinder** primitive. Neither their orientation nor size matters much so far, but it is important that their pivot points are on the bottom, which is typical for such primitives (Fig. 3.15, *b*):

   Main menu → Create → Extended Primitives → Chamfer Cylinder

▶ *Tip*

Once you have created one of the primitives, you can copy it three times.

☐ Rename them **Dumper1-Base-01, Dumper1-Piston-01, Dumper2-Base-01, Dumper2-Piston-01**.

☐ Use the **Select And Link** command as follows:
- **Dumper1-Base-01** with **P1-01**
- **Dumper1-Piston-01** with **P2-01**
- **Dumper2-Base-01** with **P3-01**
- **Dumper2-Piston-01** with **P4-01**

▶ *Tip*

Selecting an object by name in order to link it is very useful — press the **Select And Link** button and select the object you want to link, if it is not yet selected. Then open the selection by name window (<H> key), select the object to which you want to link, and press the **Link** button.

We will continue editing with **Dumper1-Base-01** for illustration.

☐ **Align** the **Dumper1-Base-01** object with its "ancestor" (**P1-01**) using pivot points with respect to all axes (Fig. 3.15, *c*).

▶ *Tip*

You can select the object for alignment using the method described above.

☐ Make the **Dumper1-Base-01** object "face" **P2-01**. To do so, select **Dumper1-Base-01** and use the **LookAt** controller:

> Main menu → Animation → Constraints → LookAt Constraint

☐ Drag it to face **P2-01**.

☐ Set the parameters shown in Fig. 3.15, *d*.

❗ *Explanation*

In this lesson, we will use constraints (**Constraint**) as the animation controllers. In most cases, they are a logical choice.

When constraints are assigned, 3ds max automatically toggles the control panel to the **Motion** panel, as these are the parameters you will need to edit.

Pay attention to the **Assign Controller** rollout — we deliberately opened it to make things clearer. Take a look at the animation controllers' window. You will see that the **Rotation List** controller is used for **Rotation**, and it already has two lines: **Euler XYZ** — the default controller assigned to the object, and **LookAt Constraint** — the one we needed.

The **Available** line implies that you can add more controllers.

These features appeared in the first versions of 3ds max, but they became simpler to use over time thanks to the developers.

The next rollout — **PRS Parameters** (position/rotation/scale) — is to some extent an anachronism. Only the bottom buttons are really used. Right now, the **Rotation** button is pressed, which is relevant for this stage of work.

The **Rotation List** rollout is the list of controllers being used for rotation. The **LookAt Constraint** controller is currently selected, which is also indicated by the arrow to the left. This is the controller whose parameters you will need to adjust.

What about the **Euler XYZ** controller? In our case, it does not need to be adjusted. If, however, you want the object to do more than simply face another object (e.g., follow a trajectory or surface), you can use this "redundant" controller with a proper **Weight**.

The **Set Active** button displays the settings of the selected controller. This does not interfere with the other controllers!

The **Delete**, **Cut**, and **Paste** buttons are self-descriptive and used to delete or to copy controllers between objects.

At last, we have reached the **LookAt** parameters.

The **Add LookAt Target** and **Delete LookAt Target** buttons allow an object to simultaneously trace not one but several targets. You can shift attention between them with the **Weight** parameter.

The **Keep Initial Offset** flag should be unchecked in our case. If you check it, you will understand what it means.

The **Set Orientation** button forces rotation of the object, which is not necessary in our case.

There is also a group of parameters that orient the object along various axes. Play with them to see what happens.

❏ Set the rest of the objects as needed (Fig. 3.15, *e*).

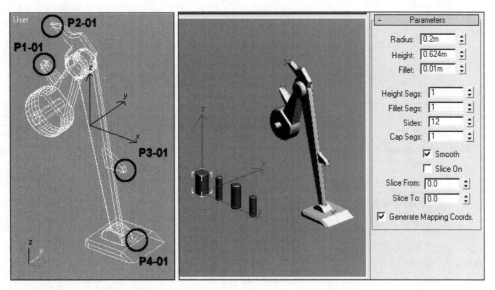

a

b

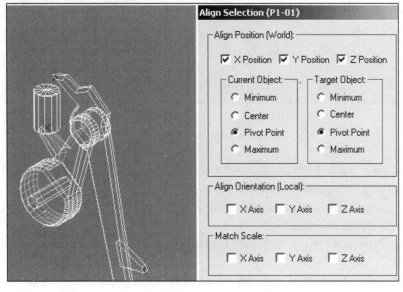

c

Fig. 3.15, *a–c.* Modeling the hydraulic pumps

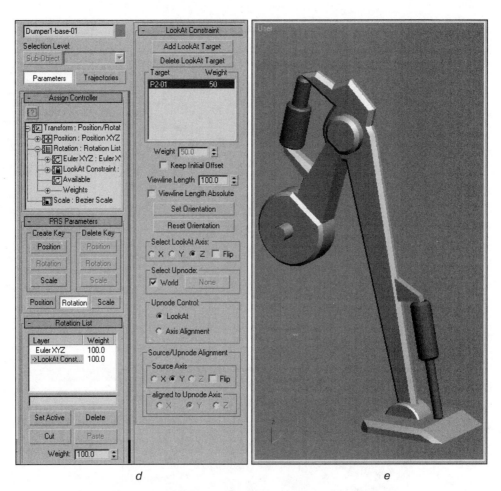

d   *e*

Fig. 3.15, *d* and *e*. Modeling the hydraulic pumps

We did not model the hydraulic objects on the lowest fundamental level, but you can do so and make them more convincing if you'd like.

Our file with the adjusted hydraulic pumps is Lesson03(lunar-ship-linked-leg-with-dumpers).max.

Now it is time to duplicate the landing props and position them appropriately.

❏   Select **Leg0-01** in the **Top** view and rotate it about 5° clockwise around the vertical axis using the **Pivot Point** as the center of rotation (Fig. 3.16, *a*). Notice that all linked objects are also rotated.

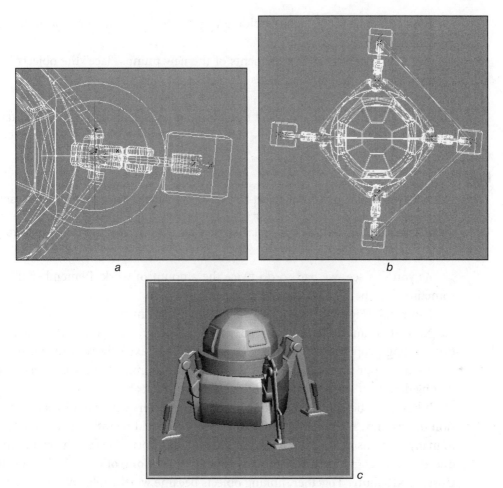

Fig. 3.16. Copying and adjusting the landing props

☐ Select all objects forming the prop. To do so, double-click the left mouse button on **Leg0-01**, which is the "parent" for the rest of the objects.

☐ Rotate the selected objects 90° around the living area while holding the <Shift> key. To create three copies (Fig. 3.16, *b*): Switch to rotation mode, use **Pick** coordinates, and click on the **Living Module**.

Use the **Transform Coordinate Center** as the center of rotation. It will shift to the pivot point of the **Living Module**.

Rotate the objects 90° while holding the <Shift> key, and enter "3" in the window that appears.

What do you notice? The elements of the new pumps "face" the objects in the original. You will have to adjust this for each of them.

❐ Go to the **Motion** panel, select one object at a time, add a new **LookAt** target, and delete the previous one.

▶ *Tip*

It is not necessary to use **Point** object-helpers as the targets; you can use the corresponding elements of the pump instead. But there is one limitation — objects cannot "face" each other. This complies with 3ds max logic that does not support bidirectional object hierarchy.

As you can see, we had to do twice the amount of work. Remember this, for sometimes it is better to skip a step and do it later.

Our result (Fig. 3.16, *c*) is in Lesson03(lunar-ship).max.

Now, it is time to look at animation — or, rather, its settings. If we had only one landing prop, we would not concern ourselves extensively with the process. But we have four props, and it takes some work to animate them all. (Imagine animating dozens of such props — it is better not to think about it!)

It has never been possible to link objects' parameters with equations in any version of 3ds max. Although intuitive, that process would be rather painstaking and, in many cases, its complexity would not justify the effort. The fourth version introduced a less complicated method with the **Wire Controller** and the so-called **Custom Attribute**. Together, linking objects became worthwhile. We will use these features here:

❐ Create a **Dummy** object, rename it **LUNAR SHIP**, and place it somewhere near the lunar module (Fig. 3.17, *a*). As you may have already guessed by its name, this is the "main object" with which the others are to be linked:

    Control panel → Create → Helpers → Dummy

❐ Create an additional parameter (**Custom Attribute**) for the **LUNAR SHIP** and adjust it as shown in Fig. 3.17, *b*:

    Main menu → Animation → Add Custom Attribute

Explanation

It is very important to set the **Custom Attribute** parameters right away. This can be a bit difficult to specify in 3ds max (a weakness that will probably be corrected in future versions):

Parameter Type — Float

UI Type — Slider (The **Name** parameter indicates the significance of the extreme values.)

Float UI Options — Range From 0.0 **To** 1.0, and **Default** set to 1.0, which corresponds to the "landing" position. This will be adjusted later in the process of binding with coefficients.

Test this new parameter in the **Testing Attribute** section.

When everything is ready, press the **Add** button.

Excellent! The parameter has been added, but so far it is nothing but a slider on the control panel. Now, we have to link it to the prop and its rotation around an axis. In the third version of 3ds max, the previous, inconvenient **TCB Rotation** controller from 3D Studio for DOS was superceded by two animation controllers for rotation — the **Euler XYZ Rotation** and **Local Euler XYZ Rotation** controllers. The latter provided rotation animation in local coordinates, which was very effective and made many users extremely happy with 3ds max, including the authors of this book. In 3ds max 4, this controller was removed from the main interface without explanation, although it still existed behind the scenes in MaxScript for the sake of compatibility with projects implemented in earlier versions. In the end, there is only one controller left for independent rotation around three axes — **Euler XYZ**. This controller uses coordinates of the **Parent** (i.e., local coordinates of the first "ancestor") for reference. For objects without a hierarchical chain, the "ancestor" is the **World**. Foreshadowing events to come, all of the landing props will be connected to the propulsion module and, to correctly animate the **Leg1-##** objects, the **Leg0-##** objects will be used. The purpose of such objects is to determine intermediate coordinates. Objects of any type can be used, including **Dummy**, for it is only their orientation that matters.

Link the slider named **Off__Landing__On** with rotation of one of the objects of the landing prop (we will use **Leg1-01**) around the Y axis:

Tip

To determine the axis around which to rotate the object, switch to **Parent** coordinates and select the object. It is quite possible that this is a different axis in your case.

☐ Select the LUNAR SHIP, click the right mouse button, select **Wire Parameters** and then choose the **Off__Landing__On** parameter (Fig. 3.17, *c*).

☐ Drag to the **Leg1-01** object, click the left mouse button, and select Transform → Rotation → Y Rotation (Fig. 3.17, *d*).

☐ Select the "right arrow" in the window that appears: It means that the parameter on the left side is the **Master** relative to the one on the right. Press the **Connect** button (Fig. 3.17, *e*).

Leg1-01 and all of its "descendent" objects will have changed position. Now try to move the **Off__Landing__On** slider. The position of **Leg1-01** will change. We seem to be off a bit, but this is not a problem, because the **Wire** system allows you to enter correcting coefficients into the leg's expression to make it work the way you want. Find a value you like and don't forget to **Update** when you make changes!

-(Off___Landing___On - 1)*2.5

▶ *Note*

Keep in mind that the rotation parameter uses radians instead of degrees.

▶ *Note*

At this point, we slightly adjusted the geometry of the propulsion module because it seemed too tall. We simply moved the vertices with respect to the folding props.

☐ Link the **Off__Landing__On** slider with all the other props. You can copy the expression you decided upon for the first leg into the clipboard and paste it into the others. All of this can be done without leaving the window by pressing the **Show All Tracks** button, finding the necessary parameters, and pasting the expression from the clipboard (Fig. 3.17, *f*).

Frankly speaking, this process is rather boring but, if you master it now, it will be easier later. If you are having difficulties, we saved our work as Lesson03(lunarship-wired-step1).max.

The next step is to prevent the **Leg2-##** objects from protruding into the propulsion module when they fold. The solution is to link the **Off__Landing__On** slider with the rotation of the **Leg2-##** objects around the Y axis, as shown in Fig. 3.17, *g*.

Note

The imperfections at this point are obvious. The props intersect each other when they fold, and the hydraulic pumps do not work at all. The latter fact is not important and nobody will notice it, but intersecting objects are far too obvious for keen viewers. You should therefore make the props fold in slightly different ways. It should be mentioned that editing links in 3ds max is not easy but, for this purpose, a mediocre link editor is used (Main menu → Animation → Wire Parameters → Parameter Wire Dialog). Still, we managed to adjust the props so that they do not fold into one plane. To do this, we selected the **Off__ Landing__On** slider on the left part of the window, pressed the **Find Next Parameter Wired** button on the right, and changed the linked objects' parameters. We failed to avoid having the objects cross during folding, but at least they look decent when completely folded. Additional rotation of **Leg0-##** by 2 degrees helped obtain the desired result (Fig. 3.17, *h*).

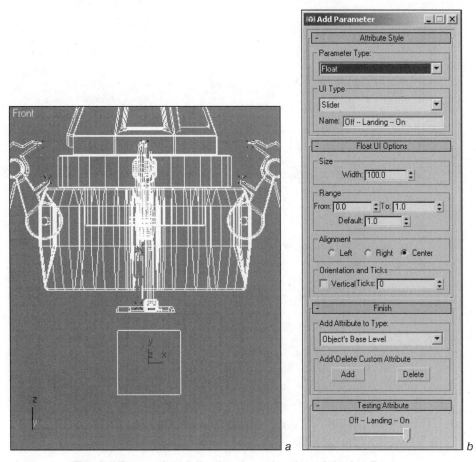

Fig. 3.17, *a* and *b*. Adjusting the animation of the landing props

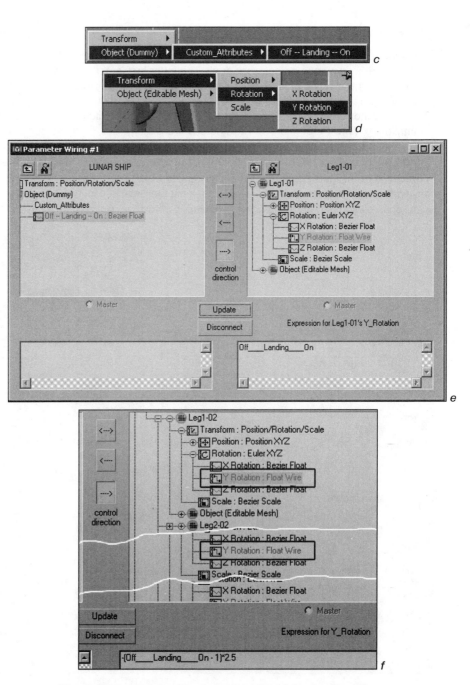

Fig. 3.17, *c–f*. Adjusting the animation of the landing props

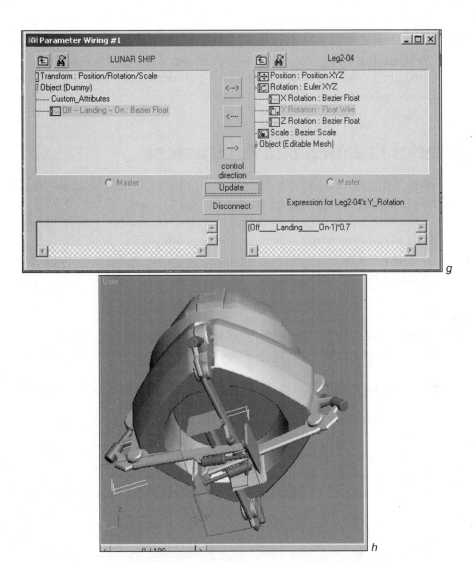

Fig. 3.17, *g* and *h*. Adjusting the animation of the landing props

❐ Use the **Select and Link** command to link the landing props (**Leg0-01, Leg0-02,** etc.) to the propulsion module (**Service Module**), and the **Living Module** and **Service Module** to the LUNAR SHIP.

Save your work. Our file on the companion CD-ROM is called Lesson03(lunar-ship-wired-step1).max.

▶ *Tip*

Try to adjust the animation of the **Leg3-##** objects yourself, so that the props behave correctly when unfolding. It is quite possible that another parameter for the **LUNAR SHIP** should be introduced to rotate these objects.

Material Creation and Assignment

We will use the materials from the previous lesson for the lunar module. Once you have materials that give good results, there is no need to create them from scratch. That is even more important in this case, because the body of the lunar module is made of the same material as that of the spaceship.

There is a large selection of materials in 3ds max libraries that will be of great assistance.

▶ *Note*

Don't rely solely on the materials in the libraries. As a rule, the ones provided would need serious tuning and adjusting for our project. They are most handy for secondary objects.

There are several ways to load a material from a library, including the following:

❑ Open the material editor and **Material/Map Browser**:

Main menu → Rendering → material editor, Material/Map Browser

❑ Set the **Browse From** toggle in the Material/Map browser to **Mtl Library**. By default, the contents of the 3dsmax.mat library will be displayed, but you can open other libraries with the **File**, then **Open** commands.

❑ You can transfer materials and textures from the library to any preview window of the material editor. You can also transfer textures to the buttons of the texture channels.

You can create your own material libraries, but it is more direct to use a previous project file as the library.

❑ In the library selection window, expand the **Files of type** drop-down menu and select **3ds max**.

❑ Load the file with the spaceship as the material library. We named it lesson02(final).max on the CD-ROM in the Lessons\Lesson02\scenes folder. You may use the file you created instead.

❑ Transfer the **SpaceShip-Body** material (we have it as a sub-material of the composite **SpaceShip** material) into any preview window of the material editor.

❑ Rename it **LivingModule-Body**. This is necessary to avoid problems when merging objects with duplicate material names. Don't assign the material to any objects just yet.

► *Tip*

Uncheck the **Root Only** flag in the **Show** group.

It is quite possible that you will not see the textures. That's all right, because we still have to make new textures.

We will need to be more detailed with the operations that follow. In the previous lesson, we applied textures to objects by sequentially selecting the object's polygons and assigning texture coordinates (**UVW Coordinates**) to them using the **UVW Map** modifier. Naturally, you can do the same here, but it will not be efficient.

We propose you use another method. The idea is as follows: Use the texture coordinates' editor (**Unwrap UVW** modifier) on the model to create a pattern for editing in a 2D graphics package.

❑ Select the **Living Module** object and hide all the other objects in the scene:

  Context menu → Hide Unselected

❑ Apply the **Unwrap UVW** modifier to it:

  Main menu → Modifiers → UV Coordinates → Unwrap UVW

❑ Enter the texture coordinates' editor:

  Control panel → Parameters → Edit

Most likely, you will see an image like the one shown in Fig. 3.18, *a.*

So, what now? Spread all of the polygons on the surface so that it's easy to draw. We can do this in one shot with a new tool in 3ds max 5:

❏ Apply the **Flatten Mapping** tool with the default settings:

    Texture coordinates' editor menu → Mapping → Flatten Mapping

You should have something similar to that in Fig. 3.18, *b*. If you use an editor that allows you to draw directly on objects (e.g., Deep Paint 3D), then this last step is not necessary. It is only required for 2D graphics packages. The burden is eased because our object contains many identical elements. Start editing. We will only consider editing part of an object's coordinates here, as the rest is absolutely the same.

❏ Undo the **Flatten Mapping** command (<Ctrl>+<Z> keys).

❏ In the texture coordinates' editor window, press the **Filter Selected Faces** button. The image will most likely disappear from the editor. If not, it is not a problem.

❏ In the parameters of the **Unwrap UVW** modifier, go to **Select Face**.

❏ Select the faces in the viewport as shown in Fig. 3.18, *c* (highlighted deep-gray). Do not select the edges of the chamfers! **Ignore Backfacing** and a small **Planar Angle** will be of great help. Note that as faces are selected, an image corresponding to the selected faces appears in the texture coordinates' editor window.

❏ After all the necessary faces are selected, use the **Flatten Mapping** command without the **Rotate Clusters** flag but with a **Face Angle Threshold** of 20°. You should get something like Fig. 3.18, *d*.

❏ Select, move, and rotate faces to obtain the image shown in Fig. 3.18, *e*. The following tools and settings will help you to do this:

    ● Switch to **Face Sub-Object Mode** and check the **Select Element** flag. This will simplify selection of the faces.

    ● Check the **Sync to Viewport** flag. This will simplify identification of the faces.

- Use the **Freeform Mode**. A frame-container will appear around the selected faces. By using the left mouse button inside the container, you can move the selected faces, scale them by dragging the corners, and rotate them by dragging the sides. You can also move the center of rotation and scaling. Hold the <Ctrl> key for uniform scaling by all axes, <Shift> for scaling and movement with respect to one axis, and <Alt> to scale relative to the center of the selection.

- You can also use the **Snap** to grid option for precise positioning, but it is not mandatory: Some inaccuracies may add a pleasant chaotic character to the scene. Nonetheless, we still recommend that you activate **Angle Snap** with the <A> key.

▶ *Note*

Some elements are not included in this group. For them, you need to apply additional signs (e.g., a logo or an inscription).

❏ After the polygons have been assigned texture coordinates, select all of them in the coordinate editor and move them to the square outlined with a bold blue line.

❏ Sometimes, as in the case of the top polygon, you do not need to use the **Flatten Mapping** command. But, to move it, you need to break the links with its adjacent faces via the **Detach Edge Vertices** command:

    Context menu of the texture coordinates' editor → Detach Edge Verts

❏ Sometimes, you need to cut the links not only with adjacent faces, but also within a polygon using the **Break** command:

    Context menu of the texture coordinates' editor → Break

❏ Just as when we created the portholes and hatch, it is often convenient to select objects here with the **Grow Selection** command. Using planar coordinates of the textures based on **Averaged Normals** may also be helpful.

Further editing consists of selecting polygons in the viewport and repeating the operations above.

Chamfers, however, are rather difficult to select in the viewport. Instead, select them in the texture coordinates' editor. First, deactivate **Filter Selected Faces** so that all polygons are shown. But how can you edit their texture coordinates? We propose that you do not to edit them. Just reduce their size and move them to an open area.

Move and scale the polygons so that they all fit inside the square outlined by bold blue lines, doing your best to preserve their relative sizes (Fig. 3.18, *f*).

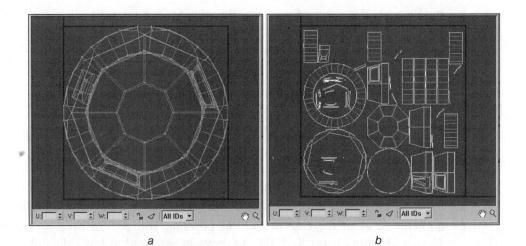

a   *b*

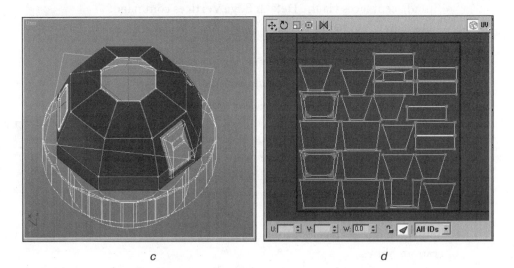

c   *d*

Fig. 3.18, *a–d*. Editing texture coordinates

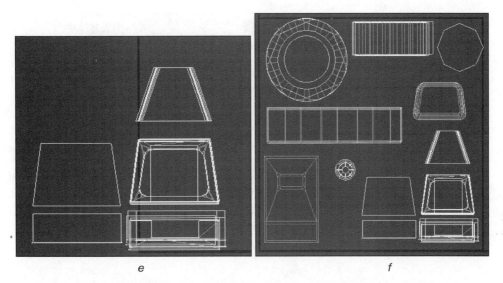

e   *f*

Fig. 3.18, *e* and *f*. Editing texture coordinates

Unfortunately, 3ds max does not save in raster format. You can achieve the same thing by copying the image on the screen to the clipboard with the <Print Screen> key and pasting it into your 2D graphic package. Be careful to cut along the borders. Then, create a new layer and start to draw!

▶ **Note**

In reality, the fifth version of 3ds max has the capability of **Rendering to Texture**, but a description of that procedure is beyond the scope of this book.

Well, what should we draw? Go back to editing the **LivingModule-Body** material as shown in Fig. 3.19. Don't pay attention to the names of the files used as textures, for they will be different.

In our case, we need two textures: one for the **Diffuse Color** channel (for inscriptions and signs) and another for both the **Specular Level** and **Glossiness** channels (for determining how the surface reacts to incident light).

What do we need to consider? The glass of the portholes and hatch window will be assigned its own sub-material, so we do not need to draw a texture. The polygons representing the sides of the module are rather severely distorted, so their inscriptions and symbols should be positioned close to the center.

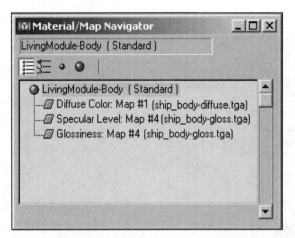

Fig. 3.19. LivingModule-Body material

We made two textures and put them in one PSD (Adobe Photoshop) file. 3ds max 5 can load files of this format either as a whole or by layers. The transparency layer is interpreted as the alpha–channel.

❏ Enter the material editor, select the **LivingModule-Body,** and open the texture **Maps**.

❏ Load the Lessons\Lesson03\scenes\living-module.psd file from the CD-ROM as the **Diffuse Color** texture:

    Material editor → Bitmap Parameters

▶ *Note*

Generally speaking, for greater austerity it would be a good idea to separate scene and texture files. Such groupings also eliminate many problems when projects are transferred from one computer to another.

❏ In the window that opens (Fig. 3.20), you can select an individual layer or the whole image for use as a texture. We named the layers correspondingly, so select the **Diffuse** layer for the **Diffuse Color** channel.

❏ Uncheck the **Premultiplied Alpha** flag in the texture parameters, because Photoshop "cannot" create textures with this kind of alpha-channel.

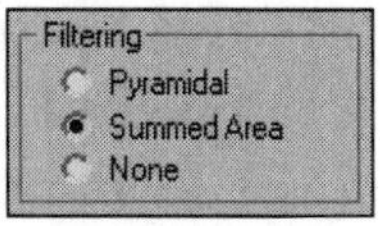

- [ ] Select the **Summed Area** filter type. It provides higher quality rendering but consumes more time.

- [ ] Load the same file for the **Glossiness** channel, selecting **Glossiness and Spec. Level**.

Tip

It is often convenient to navigate textures and materials with the **Go Forward to Sibling** button. This advances to the next element on the same hierarchical level that uses the material.

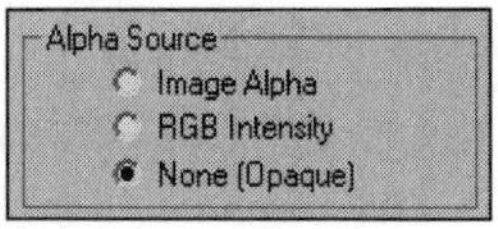

- [ ] Deactivate the alpha-channel in the parameters.
- [ ] Assign the same layer to the **Specular Level** channel.

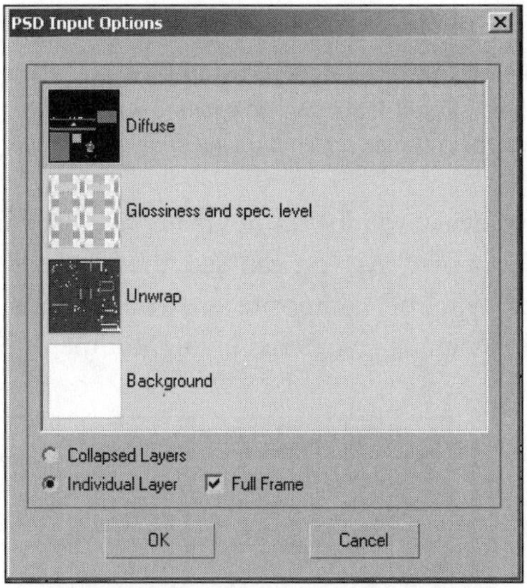

Fig. 3.20. Texture loading window for PSD files

Note

Generally speaking, working with PSD files is fairly rudimentary, lacking features such as merging multiple layers. Hopefully, this will be available in subsequent versions.

As we already mentioned, another material will be used for the glass of the hatch and portholes. In the Lesson02-final.max file, the **SpaceShip Illuminators** sub-material of the **SpaceShip** composite material can be used. Transfer it from the material and texture manager into any preview window and rename it **LivingModule Illuminatiors**.

❑ Select the **Living Module** object and move down the stack of modifiers to **Editable Poly**. You will be warned that there are modifiers on the stack that depend on the original topology (**Unwrap UVW**). Ignore the warning and press the **Yes** button.

❑ Switch to editing on the **Editable Poly** level, then select the polygons comprising the glass of the portholes and hatch window.

❑ Assign the **LivingModule Illuminators** material to these polygons.

❑ Exit editing the polygons.

▶ *Note*

Pay attention! As with most modifiers, **Unwrap UVW** can affect selected sub-objects in addition to the whole object. If you leave the polygons selected, their texture coordinates will change unpredictably. You also should not change the original geometry, remove or add polygons, etc.

❑ Select any preview window in the material editor and load the material with the "dropper." As you can see, the object is assigned the **Multi/ Sub-object** type of composite material, consisting of two sub-materials (Fig. 3.21). Rename the material **LivingModule**.

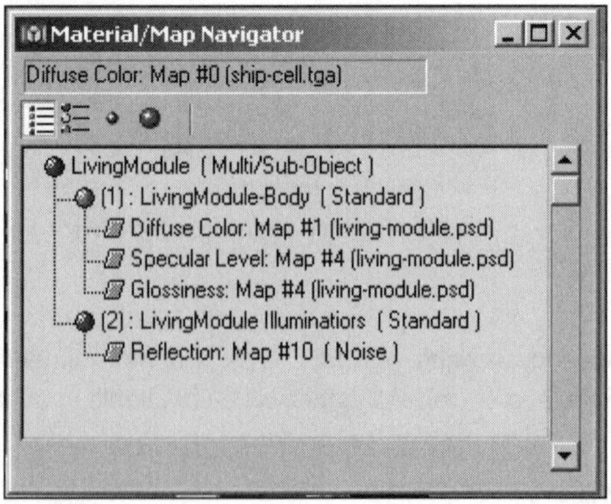

Fig. 3.21. Structure of the **LivingModule** material

Note

One thing is missing in the **LivingModule-Body** material: There is no **Reflection** texture. We did not forget about it, but there is nothing to reflect while there is no environment. We will assign it in due time.

The propulsion module can be textured in the same way as the living area, with the landing props using the **UVW Map** modifier and **Planar** type. We simply took a screenshot of the prop and applied it as the background when the textures were drawn. Other channels were also used, including the roughness channel (**Bump**). But these should have been done before duplicating the props! We spent a lot of time texturing the props by transferring the **UVW Map** modifier from one object to another.

After the main geometry is ready and the materials are assigned, there is nothing to prevent you from "decorating" the lunar module with other elements: antennas, orientation engines, etc. For this purpose, you can use objects of the spaceship: load it with the **Merge** command and then **Detach** the elements you want. Remove the extraneous parts and attach the ones you need to the living area and propulsion module with the **Attach** command. (To do so, either convert the objects to **Editable Poly**, or apply the **Edit Mesh** modifier.) Keep in mind that the objects being attached already have materials assigned to them. So, if you don't know what to do with the materials of the attached objects, select **Match Material IDs to Material**. That will add the materials of the attached objects as sub-materials and reset their indices. Try this for yourself. Our result is in the file Lesson03-LunarShip-final.max (Fig. 3.22). Isn't that easy?

Fig. 3.22. Final appearance of the lunar module

Lunar Rover Modeling

After modeling the spaceship and lunar module, modeling the lunar rover should not present any difficulties (Fig. 3.23). It looks less like a Russian "Lunokhod" than an American "Rover" in terms of size and functionality, and we will therefore use that designation.

The rover-not-assembled.max file on the CD-ROM in the Lessons\Lesson 03\ scenes folder contains our model. All objects are independent, and the modifier stacks are left as they are. After studying this file, you will have an exhaustive idea of the modeling process. We made about 70 objects, most of them primitives and rotation objects (**Lathe**) constructed by curves.

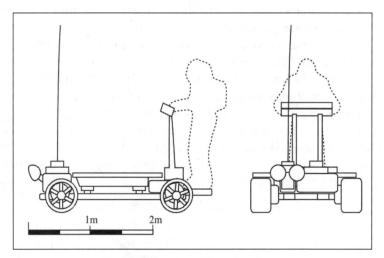

Fig. 3.23. Lunar rover sketch

The rover-assembled.max file contains the same model, but with 9 objects — only those necessary for animation. These are: base frame (**ROVER Base**), body (**ROVER bodywork**), four wheels (**ROVER xx Wheel**), two auxiliary objects to turn the rear wheels (**ROVER xx Turner**), and antenna (**ROVER Antenna**).

The rover-linked.max file contains the model linking the objects as shown in Fig. 3.24. As you can see, we used a **Dummy** object, which we named **ROVER**. As you may guess, this object serves the same role as the **LUNAR SHIP**: It is the "ancestor" for all the other objects. The pivot points were set in the same way as those of the landing props. In addition, some objects were mirrored (**Mirror**) when copying: the right wheels and the **Rover RR Turner** object. To avoid difficulties during animation, the **Reset XForm** operation was applied to them:

Control panel → Utilites → Reset XForm

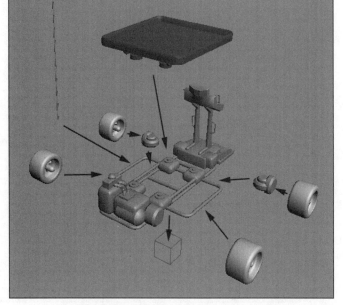

Fig. 3.24. Merging the lunar rover objects

If, as a result of this procedure, an object's normal becomes inverted, you can correct it with the **Normal** modifier using the **Flip Normals** flag:

Main menu → Modifiers → Mesh Editing → Normal Modifier

When you are done, **Collapse** the stack of modifiers for all objects:

Context menu → Collapse All

Explanation

Using the **Mirror** command in 3ds max is one of many puzzles. The idea is that it does nothing but scale the object by –100% and, as a rule, is only done with respect to one axis (i.e., **Non-Uniform Scale**). 3ds max programmers discourage such scaling, preferring the **XForm** modifier and scaling the container of the modifiers.

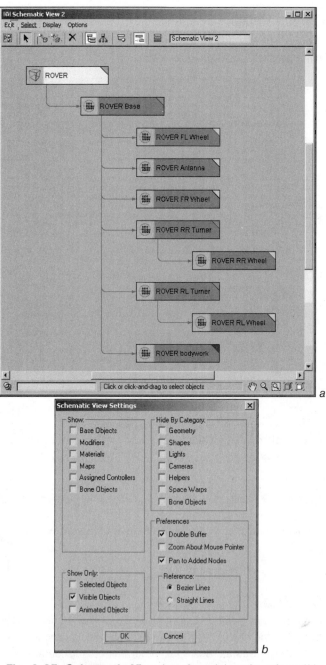

Fig. 3.25. Schematic View interface (*a*) and settings (*b*)

► *Tip*

The **Schematic View** is useful to link a lot of objects by representing the scene as a tree (Fig. 3.25, *a*). You can open it as a separate window (Main menu → Graph Editors → New Schematic View) or in one of the viewports (Viewport context menu → Views → Schematic). We do not think it is very useful in general (it is possible to do everything without it), but it is convenient to link objects by pressing the **Filters** button to set the parameters as shown in Fig. 3.25, *b*.

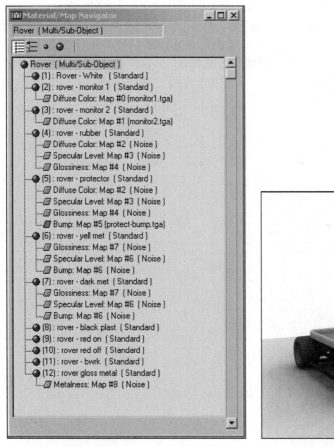

Fig. 3.26. Material structure of the lunar rover

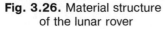

Fig. 3.27. Final appearance of the lunar rover

The rover's materials are also straightforward. There are a few raster textures for the treads and monitors, and the rest are procedural. We simply made one

Multi/Sub-object material (based on the sub-objects), assigned it to all the objects, and changed the **Material ID** for the polygons. The structure of this material is shown in Fig. 3.26. Frankly speaking, it is a bit untinished, and we will need to edit this material further and discuss to what extent it is prudent later.

You can find our version of the lunar rover in Lesson03(rover-final).max (Fig. 3.27).

Finally, we want to make a statement with which we think you will agree. It turned out that working with meters as the unit of measurement was not very convenient. As a rule of thumb, the system units should be a couple of orders of magnitude less than the average dimensions of the object — we should have operated with centimeters or inches. It is a good idea to keep this in mind in the future.

Lesson 4

Modeling and Animating an Astronaut

In this lesson you will create the main and only character of our reel — the astronaut — using the bones system (**Bones**) and direct and inverse kinematics to teach him to walk and jump. Using a new tool — character assembly — you will learn how record and load the animation reels within a short period of time, creating real animation sequences.

To create the character, we propose using polygon modeling with further smoothing. Paradoxical as it may seem, this is the main method for modeling organic objects — not only for games and interactive 3D presentations, where each "triangle" is worth its weight in gold, but also for projects within the film industry. The tedious modeling labor is repaid with interest by the ability to control each vertex and polygon of a model, especially when compared, for example, with modeling using NURBS.

The cover character is an example of polygon modeling. It was made by Dmitry Morozov, the chief artist of the Ariorh studio in Moscow. This model is absolutely polygonal.

We will create a simpler character but employ the same principles of modeling, texturing, and animation.

Astronaut Modeling

In the two previous lessons, we started modeling by setting the units. In this lesson, we suggest that you to skip this step. In the course of your work, it will be easy to change the size of the model to the required one.

A human being will wear the spacesuit, so proportions are important. It is most convenient to assign a human figure image on a background and be guided by this image during the modeling (Fig. 4.1). You will need it only in the beginning of the modeling, so we propose that you assign it only on the front view. Background drawings are described in detail in *Lesson 15*.

Fig. 4.1. Background image of a human figure

You may wonder why the figure has this initial posture. It is a compromise between two extremes. The posture "arms apart, legs far broader than shoulders" is convenient when the skeleton's affect on the model will be adjusted. But in the "operation environment" (e.g., when walking will be animated), undesirable creases and distortions appear that are difficult to remove. The "stand at attention" posture also impedes the skeleton's impact adjustment. Therefore, we chose an interim result, which we suggest you use.

❑ Set the viewport so that the background drawing is displayed in the front view (Fig. 4.2, *a*):

Main menu → Views → Viewport Background

▶ *Tip*

Load the image from the sketch.bmp file on the CD-ROM in the Lessons\Lesson04\images folder. We rendered the image, which will help you avoid difficulties during the modeling.

Synchronize the sizes of the background drawings with those in the viewport using the **Aspect Ratio Match Bitmap** toggle and the **Lock Zoom/Pan** flag.

In the viewport, you will have the image shown in Fig. 4.2, *b*.

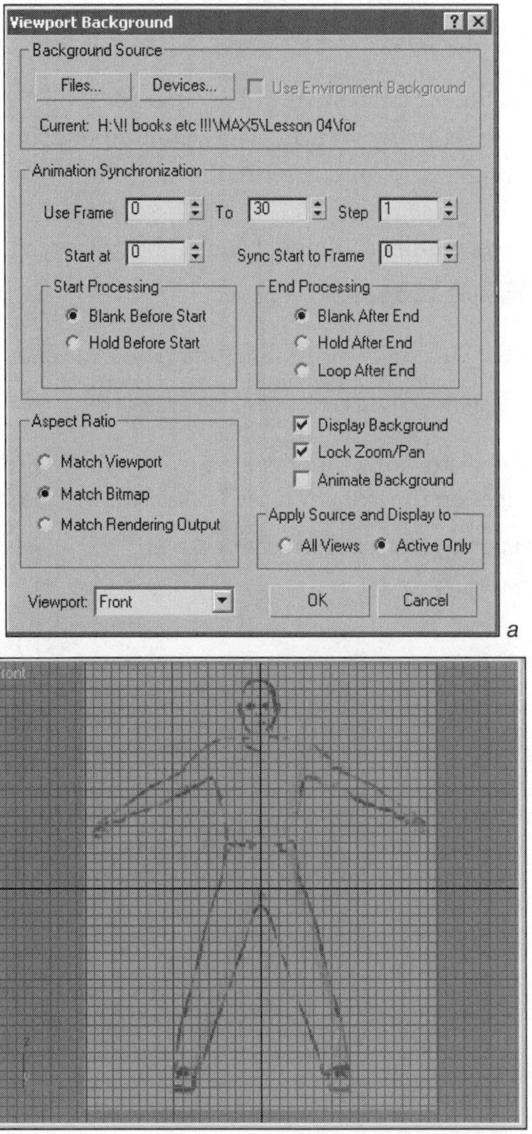

Fig. 4.2. Background image adjustment (*a*) and the viewport image (*b*)

Generally, polygonal modeling starts from a cube, but we propose simplifying the task by making a curve-based blank.

☐ Outline half of the image with a curve or a broken line, taking into account the thickness of the spacesuit (Fig. 4.3, *a*):

Main menu → Create → Shapes → Line

The gloves, boots, and helmet will be modeled later.

Note that we set many vertices. This is bound to simplify further modeling and allow you to compensate for creases in the final animation.

☐ Use the **Bevel** modifier to model half of the spacesuit (Fig. 4.3, *b*):

Control panel → Modifiers' list → Bevel

☐ Convert the object to the **Editable Poly** type and rename it **SpaceSuit**:

Context menu → Convert to → Convert to Editable Poly

☐ Remove the distortions that resulted from applying the **Bevel** modifier. Create missing edges on the front and the back of the spacesuit (Fig. 4.3, *c*):

Context menu → Sub-object → Edge or <2> key

Context menu → Create

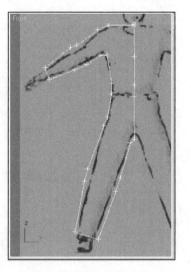

Fig. 4.3, *a*. Spacesuit blank creation

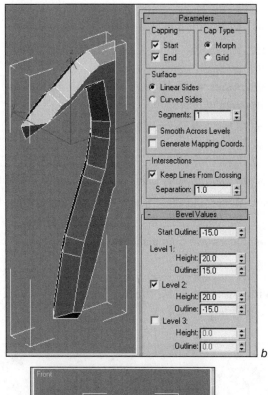

b

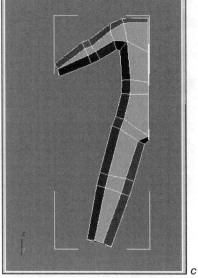

c

Fig. 4.3, *b* **and** *c***.** Spacesuit blank creation

Make further edits using the **Symmetry** modifier:

☐ Select and delete the polygons on the symmetry line of the spacesuit (Fig. 4.4, *a*).

☐ Apply the **Symmetry** modifier to the object and adjust it until you have a symmetrical model (Fig. 4.4, *b*):

Main menu → Modifiers → Mesh Editing → Symmetry

▶ *Tip*

Match the axes and the symmetry plane position (**Mirror**) to create the symmetric model.

The **Slice Along Mirror** and **Weld Seam** flags will prevent you from losing the integrity of the model.

Specify a **Threshold** value bigger than the default one.

☐ Go down the modifiers' stack and move the result of the modifiers' action to the top of the stack (**Show end result on/off toggle**). Then, edit only one side.

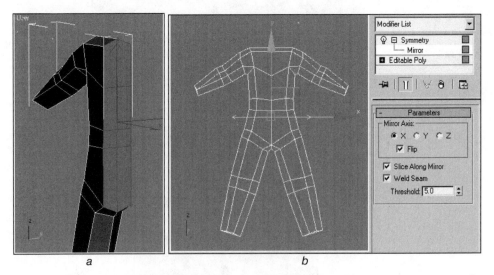

a   b

Fig. 4.4. Symmetry modifier adjustment

We are not going to describe the modeling process in detail; you should be able to solve this task if you learned the two previous lessons. The modeling then comes to moving and scaling the selected vertices and edges relative to the common center. If necessary, add vertices and edges. You can easily do this by selecting the paired edges and applying the **Connect** command.

Fig. 4.5 shows the spacesuit that has been created.

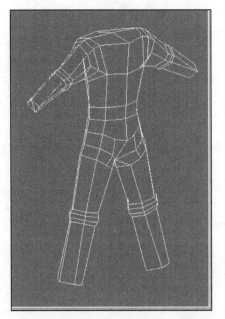

Fig. 4.5. Results of editing the spacesuit

We would like you to notice one detail: The mesh in the knee- and elbow-joints should be denser. You will be animating a low-polygon model that later will be complicated by the **MeshSmooth** modifier. The simple example will help you understand the necessity of increasing the mesh density. Fig. 4.6, *a*, shows the object, with the simple mesh in the flexion area, bent using the bones. To the left is the object before smoothing (**MeshSmooth**); to the right is the result of applying the **MeshSmooth** modifier with two iterations. As you see, this looks more like a bent sausage than the human extremity.

Fig. 4.6, *b*, shows the object with denser mesh in the flexion area. You can see that the result improved. Despite the sharp creases where the polygons penetrated each other on the unsmoothed model, everything looks better after the **MeshSmooth** modifier was applied.

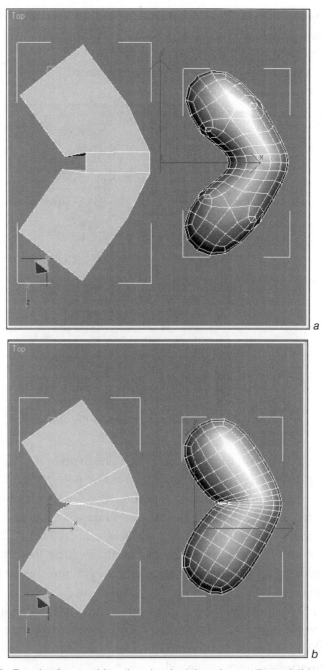

Fig. 4.6. Result of smoothing the simple (*a*) and complicated (*b*) model

❐ Model the "lunar boots" by extruding (**Extrude**) and scaling the polygons and by moving the vertices (Fig. 4.7, *a*). It is convenient to apply the **Constraints** to the edges and the polygons:

Constraints: Edge

> Control panel → Edit Geometry

We propose that you model the gloves as a separate object.

❐ As the background, create an object of the **Box** type, segmented as shown in Fig. 4.7, *b*.

❐ Try to make the object resemble a fingerless glove by converting it to the **Editable Poly** type. Add and weld by using the **Target Weld** and **Collapse** commands and moving the vertices (Fig. 4.7, *c*).

► *Tip*

As a sample, use any "pudgy" glove at hand (e.g., a ski glove). A bare hand also would work, but the modeling will be easier if you cover it with a thick glove.

❐ Extrude the fingers using the **Extrude** and **Bevel** commands and by scaling the polygons. The fingers should be able to flex (Fig. 4.7, *d*). You can extrude the polygons one by one or by selecting and extruding them together and then moving the vertices.

► *Tip*

When editing on the level of vertices and polygons, it helps to use **Soft Selection**.

Soft Selection
☑ Use Soft Selection
☑ Edge Distance: 3
☑ Affect Backfacing

❐ Move the glove to the sleeve of the spacesuit, scale it, and turn it around (Fig. 4.7, *e*).

❐ **Attach** the glove to the sleeve, then select and remove the end polygons from the sleeve and the glove.

❐ Adjust the glove precisely to the sleeve, working on the elements' level (**Elements**).

❐ "Sew together" the vertices of the glove and the sleeve using the **Target Weld** command (Fig. 4.7, *f*).

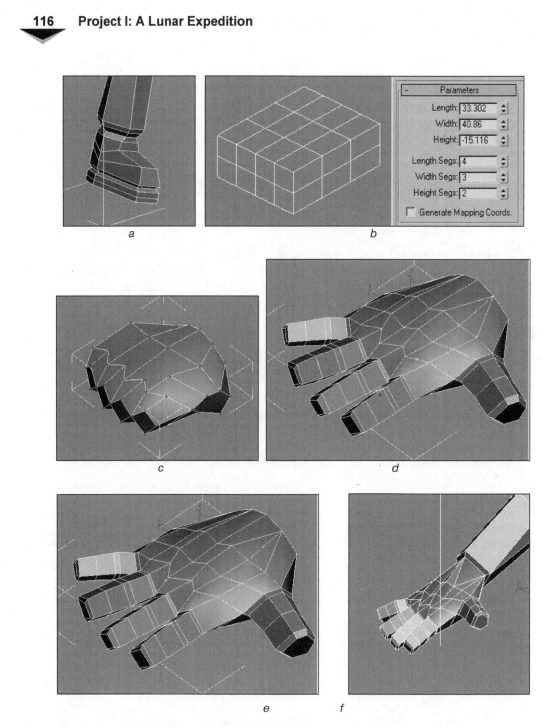

Fig. 4.7. Results of modeling the boots and gloves

- Use a sphere with few segments as the blank for the helmet. It is more convenient to create it on the top view (Fig. 4.8, *a*).
- Convert it to the **Editable Poly** type and attach the helmet to the spacesuit.
- Select and remove the redundant polygons, then merge the vertices of the helmet and the spacesuit. It is possible that you (like us) will need to create additional polygons (Fig. 4.8, *b*):

    Context menu → Create

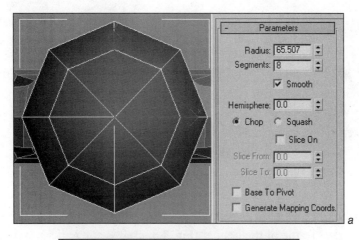

a

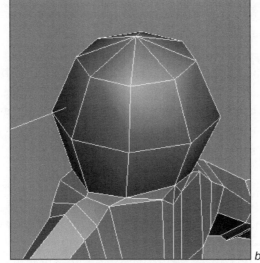

b

Fig. 4.8, *a* and *b*. Results of modeling the helmet

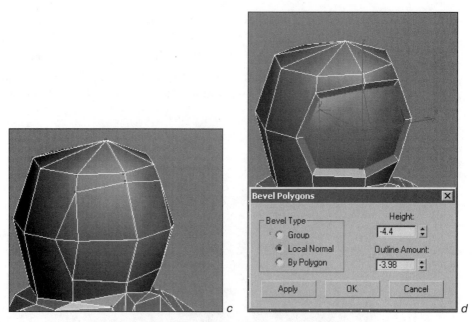

Fig. 4.8, c and d. Results of modeling the helmet

❏ Elaborate the helmet's geometry — for example, by creating the edges rimming the glass frame of the helmet (Fig. 4.8, c). It is convenient to do this by selecting the edges roundabout and applying the **Connect** command. Then move the vertices using the constraint by the edges.

At some point, the **Symmetry** modifier ceases to be helpful and becomes a burden. In our case, this occurs when you want to model the helmet's glass. If all of the main operations requiring symmetric editing are completed, you can **Collapse** the modifiers' stack:

Modifiers' stack context menu → Collapse All

❏ Use the **Bevel** command for polygons to model the glass (Fig. 4.8, d).

So, the model of the spacesuit is ready! The haversack and communication device on the chest should be made as separate objects. You can make them now if you wish, but don't attach them to the spacesuit: These objects will be linked (**Link**) with the appropriate bones of the skeleton.

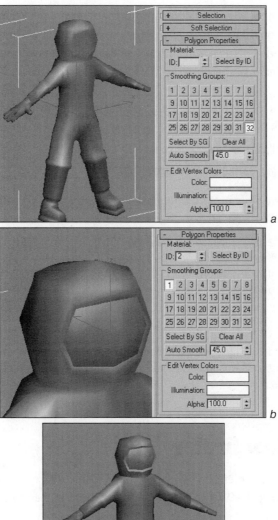

a

b

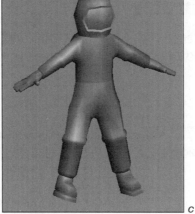

c

Fig. 4.9. Assignment of smoothing groups

At this step, it is particularly important to assign various **Smoothing Groups** to the polygons. This will give you the correct model when the **MeshSmooth** modifier is applied. This also will simplify selection of the necessary polygons during texturing by means of the **Unwrap UVW** modifier.

☐ Select all polygons and assign the same smoothing group to them (e.g., 32) (Fig. 4.9, *a*):

   Control panel → Polygon Properties → Clear All

   Press the "32" button in the Smoothing Groups.

☐ Select the polygons of the glass and assign the "1" smoothing group to them (Fig. 4.9, *b*):

   Release the "32" button and press the "1" button.

☐ Assign various smoothing groups on the glass frame, helmet, gloves, belt, boots, and the boots' soles (Fig. 4.9, *c*).

► **Note**

You can find our files with the sequence of the spacesuit modeling on the CD-ROM in the Lessons\Lesson04\Scenes folder. They are named Lesson04-01.max ... Lesson04-05.max.

Mapping Coordinates

It is most convenient to edit, or "map", the texture coordinates using the tools of the **Unwrap UVW** modifier. We used these in *Lesson 3* to map the lunar module.

► **Note**

Finish the geometry of the spacesuit before you map coordinates! After the texture coordinates are assigned and edited, it is extremely undesirable to go back down the stack.

☐ Apply the **Unwrap UVW** modifier to the **SpaceSuit** object:

   Main menu → Modifiers → UV Coordinates → Unwrap UVW

▶ *Note*

It is important that the object being edited is in the state of object editing (Context menu →
Sub-object → Top Level). Like most modifiers, the **Unwrap UVW** modifier can be applied
to sub-objects.

☐ Go to the face selection level (**Select Face**).

☐ Select the polygons of the main part of the spacesuit.
If smoothing groups were assigned, you can do this by us-
ing the **Select SG** button and entering a value in the field.
(Our value is 32.)

☐ Open the map coordinates' editor using the **Edit** button. You will have
an image similar to that shown in Fig. 4.10, *a*.

☐ Unhide only the selected polygons in the map coordinates' editor window using the **Filter Selected Faces** button.

☐ Unwrap these polygons. To do this, use the **Normal Mapping** operation
(Fig. 4.10, *b*):

   Map coordinates' editor menu → Mapping → Normal Mapping

We obtained the sweep we wanted (Fig. 4.10, *c*)!

▶ *Note*

Frankly speaking, we never found out why this refers to **Top/Bottom** rather than
Front/Back. Just take it for granted.

☐ Move the resultant sweep outside the area bordered by thick blue lines.

☐ There should be no problems with the glass and the frame. It is only important
to break the link with the other elements:

   Map coordinates' editor context menu → Detach Edge Verts.

☐ The map coordinates of the helmet (without the glass and the frame) are edited
in the same way as the spacesuit.

You can do the same operation with the polygons of the belt, but it is best to
extrude in one-line stitching (**Stitch**) the appropriate vertices. This will make it
more convenient to draw the texture. After the **Normal Mapping** operation, turn
one of the resultant elements 180° and transfer it to the second element of the belt.

Then select the vertices of the face neighboring the vertices being stitched. (The appropriate edges will be colored violet.) Finally, stitch the vertices (Fig. 4.10, *d*):

     Map coordinates' editor context menu → Stitch Selected

► ***Tip***

To turn the element, use the buttons for a 90° turn.

> Rotate +90
> Rotate -90

Everything should have been easy so far; the new tools of 3ds max considerably simplify mapping! However, the gloves and the boots will require more effort.

❐ Select the polygons of the soles in the viewport and press the **Planar Map** button on the control panel. In the map coordinates' editor, you will have the image shown in Fig. 4.10, *e*.

> Planar Map

❐ Do the same operation with the "fingertips". You will have to do this four times: for the thumb of the left glove, for the thumb of the right glove, for the rest of the fingers of the left glove, and for the fingers of the right glove.

The palm part of the gloves presents some complications. **Normal Mapping** can be used, but this will lead to undesirable distortions. It is better to use the following method:

❐ Select the upper part of one of the gloves in the viewport (Fig. 4.10, *f*). The additional selection features of the **Unwrap UVW** modifier will be helpful.

❐ Press the **Planar Map** button on the control panel to obtain the sweep of the glove in the editor's window.

❐ Do similar operations with the other parts of the gloves (Fig. 4.10, *g*).

❐ It will be even more complicated with the boots. As with the gloves, you can obtain the sweep of the boot shown in Fig 4.10, *h*, by selecting the side, back, and front surfaces and by moving, turning, and scaling the elements using the **Planar Map** button.

► ***Tip***

It may be helpful to check the **Select Element** flag in the map coordinates' editor parameters.

> ☑ Select Element

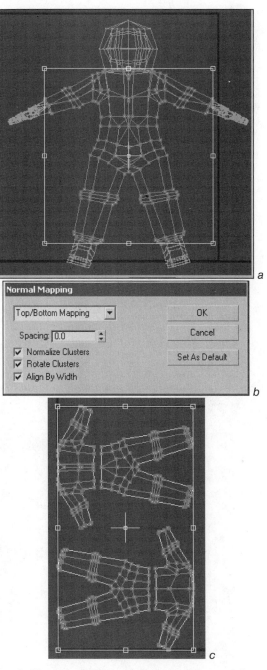

Fig. 4.10, *a–c.* Editing the texture map coordinates

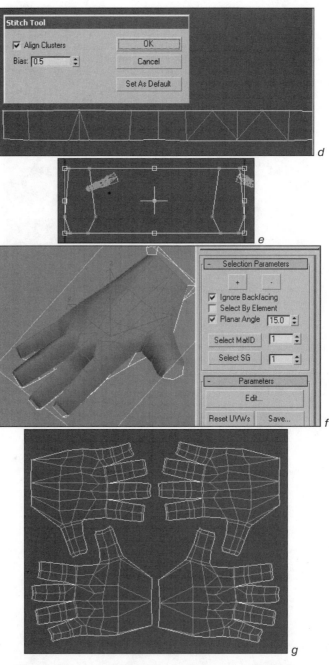

Fig. 4.10, *d–g.* Editing the texture map coordinates

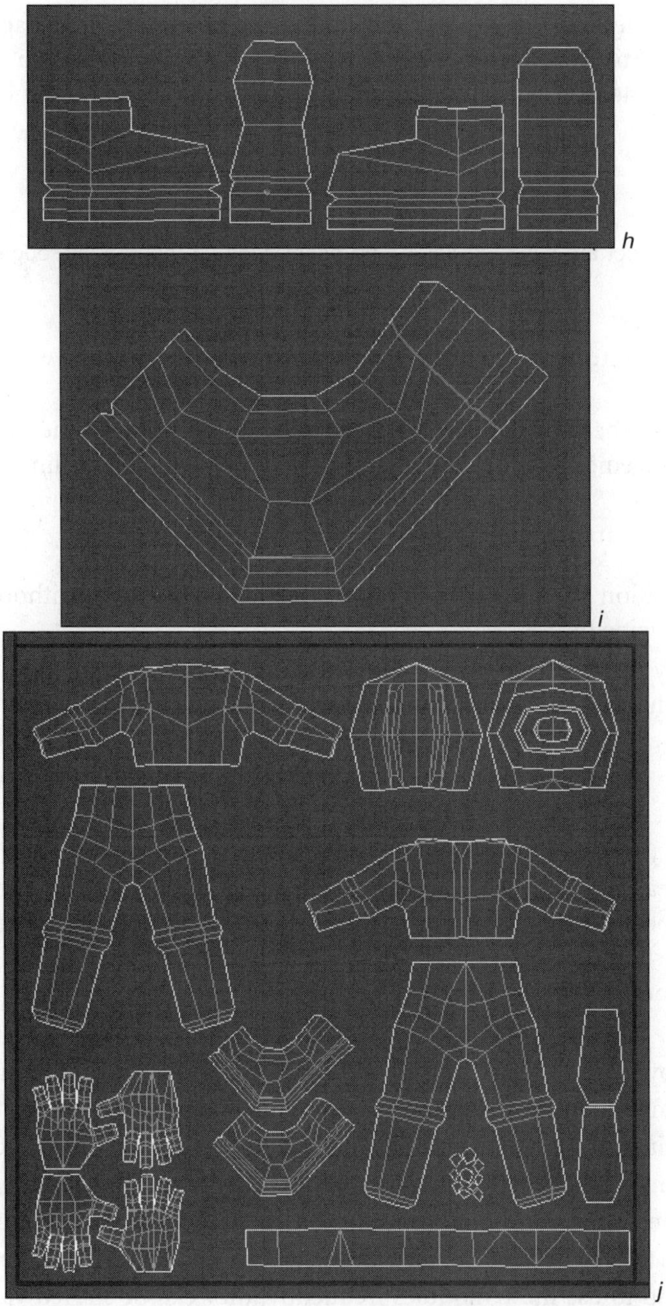

Fig. 4.10, *h–j*. Editing the texture map coordinates

❏ By selecting the edges (deactivating the **Select Element** flag) and using the **Stitch Selected** command, you can make the sweep of the boot (Fig. 4.10, *i*). You must simultaneously stitch several edges located on the same face.

▶ *Note*

Don't select the edges in pairs! The editor finds the appropriate edges; these are colored violet.

The texture maps of the second boot are set in the same way.

❏ After the texture maps are assigned to all polygons of the model, position all of the elements within the area bordered by the thick blue line (Fig. 4.10, *j*).

Below are a few tips on the elements' positioning.

❏ Position the elements as close together as possible without prejudice to the drawing process.
❏ Try to observe proportions. The minor elements (e.g., the fingertips) may be reduced, but the belt should be wider because it will have buckles.
❏ Leave small gaps between the elements. As an example, note how we handled the frame and the glass of the helmet: These elements rest one within another, but there is a small gap.
❏ In the previous lesson we proposed that you merge equal elements. Strictly speaking, this is not always necessary. You can use this method to prepare a model for the reel, but if the model will be employed in a video game that supports modern means of interactive rendering (e.g., **LightMap**), such merging should be avoided.

Now you must save the sweep as a bit-map file. As in the previous lesson, you can simply transfer the image from the map coordinates' editor to the bit-map image editor using the clipboard with the <Print Screen> key. However, we cannot recommend this method because it lacks precision. Therefore, we suggest that you use one of the additional modules on the CD-ROM in the Plugins folder, either Texporter, created by Kuneit Ozdas or Unwrap, created by Peter Vatier. If you do not plan to use these modules frequently, they can be started via the plug-in manager directly from the CD-ROM.

❏ Open the plug-in manager:

   Main menu → Customize → Plug-In Manager

❏ Call the plug-in manager's context menu, then select **Load New Plug-in.**
❏ Find the Texporter module on the CD-ROM (\Plugins\Texporter 3.4\plugins\ Texporter3.dlu) and load it.

The extension of the file (dlu) implies that this is the utility. So search for it in the **Utilities** panel:

   Control panel → Utilities → More... → start Texporter by pressing OK

❏ Specify the parameters as shown in Fig. 4.11, then select the object by pressing the **Pick Object** button. Save the sweep as a file.

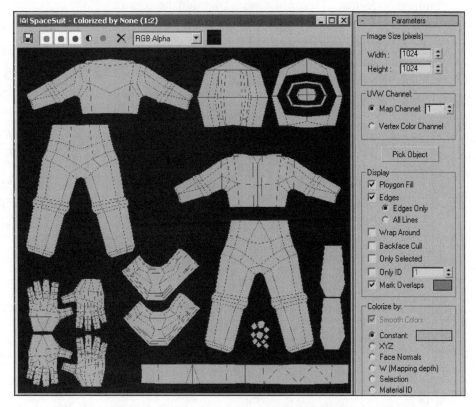

Fig. 4.11. Parameters and result of the Texporter utility performance

Note

Make the size of the image large. Through habit we use powers of "2," which are desirable for maps' creation in games. You may ignore this rule; it is only important that the image is square.

The Texporter module lets you record a large variety of information, but we propose that you limit yourself to the necessities. The online help of the module contains information for all of its features.

Save the image as the file of any format without compression (e.g., TGA). You don't need to use the alpha-channel.

You can find our file with the sweep (unwrap.tga) on the CD-ROM in the Lessons\Lesson04\images folder. The textures themselves, drawn using this file, are in the Lessons\Lesson04\Scenes folder. In this lesson, we abandoned the Adobe Photoshop format in favor of a more traditional solution.

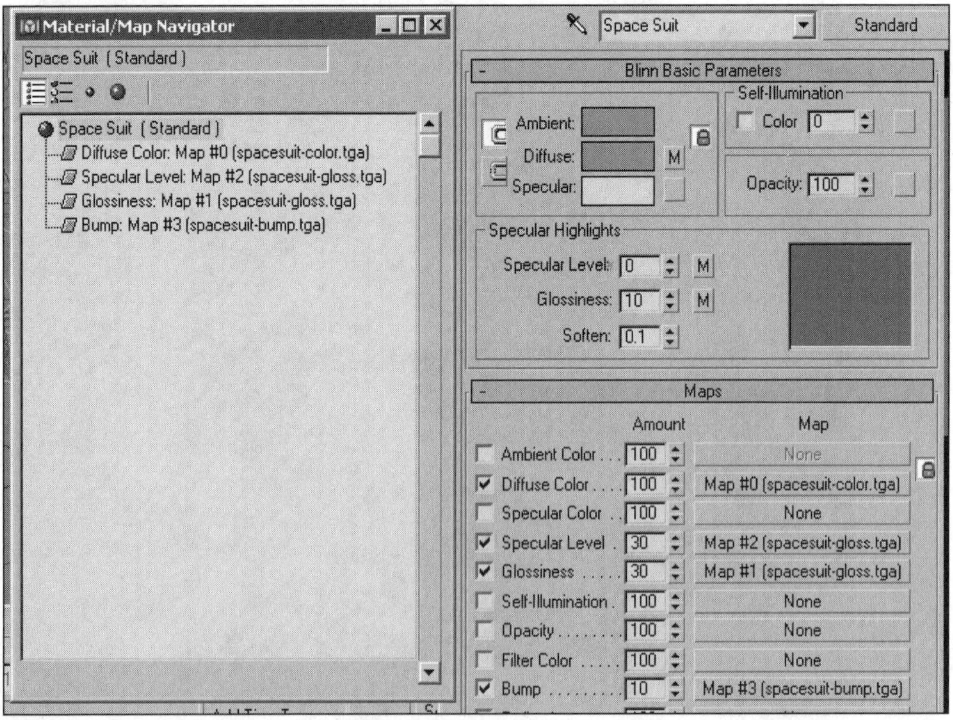

Fig. 4.12. Structure and main parameters of the **SpaceSuit** material

This folder also contains the Lesson04-08.max file with the result of the map coordinates' editing.

❑ Create a material, name it **SpaceSuit,** and assign it to the **SpaceSuit** object. The structure of the material and its main parameters are shown in Fig. 4.12. As you can see, the parameters are simple: Three textures are assigned on the appropriate channels with different **Amount** values.

❗
Do it yourself

You can make the material more complex by mixing the textures. For example, mix the spacesuit-gloss.tga and spacesuit-bump.tga files using the complex texture of the **Mix** type assigned on the **Glossiness** channel. Using the **Mix** type, you can add the texture of the **Noise** type to the **Bump** channel.

Now, everything is ready to create and adjust the skeleton of our astronaut.

Skeleton Creation and Adjustment

You will animate your character using bones (**Bones**). These have been available from the first version of 3ds max, but they really became useful with the introduction of the **Skin** modifier in version 3. Further efforts of the developers in this area considerably improved the skeleton bones and the model-merging idea. An excellent inversion kinematics system appeared as well as many other novelties, of which the developers of version 5 deservedly may be proud. There is, however, a flip side: Although the upgrades up to version 5.1 are well debugged, some functions are still unstable. Save your project as often as possible.

Our book "3ds max 4: From Objects to Animation" dealt perfunctorily with the creation, adjustment, and animation of skeletons. Some things are repeated in this lesson, but we decided to consider the process here in earnest, mainly from the point of view of animation convenience.

Before we proceed to the skeleton, make the **SpaceSuit** object transparent by selecting it and pressing the <Alt>+<X> shortcut.

❑ Set the transparency mode display in the parameters of the viewport:

Viewport context menu → Transparency → Best

❐ **Freeze** the **SpaceSuit** object to keep it from interfering with the skeleton creation:

Context menu → Freeze Selection

Start the skeleton creation with the leg bones.

❐ Create the leg bones (**Bones**) using the left view (Fig. 4.13, *a*). Note that for illustration, the bones are shown without the object in this figure:

Main menu → Character → Bone Tools

Press the Create Bones button and create a chain of bones top-down. Complete the creation with a right click. Don't remove the small bone appearing at the end of the chain!

❐ Rename the bones as follows (top-down): **Bone-Thigh-R**, **Bone-Shin-R**, and **Bone-Ankle-R**. Such names are necessary for further references. However, you can rename the objects as you wish.

❐ On the front view, move the bones until they corresponded to the right leg. To do this, press the **Bone Edit Mode** button in the **Bone Pivot Position** dialog and move the bones (Fig. 4.13, *b*).

▶ *Note*

The **Bone Edit Mode** button toggles 3ds max to the same mode as the **Don't Affect Children** button in the **Hierarchy** panel. This again confirms the slight difference between bones and simply linked objects in 3ds max. In the book "3ds max 4: From Objects to Animation," we suggested that bones and objects linked hierarchically will become "closer." So far, the development trends of 3ds max confirm these suggestions.

❐ Change the sizes of the bones so that they approximately coincided with the size of the leg using the **Fin Adjustment Tools** menu (Fig. 4.13, *c*). This will simplify further linking of the "skin" (**Skin**) to the bones.

▶ *Note*

Unlike those in other packages, the bones in 3ds max are real geometric objects with sizes; they can be visualized, and materials can be assigned to them.

To create the leg bones, we decided to ignore tradition. Usually, a complex chain is created that enables the foot to bow during movement. We assume that lunar boots bear stiff soles like those of downhill-ski boots, so we propose using a simple geometric object, such as **Box**, as the foot bone.

❏ Create an object of the **Box** type of the boot's size, then move and turn it according to the boot's position. Rename it **Bone-Foot-R**. This object will also be the bone (Fig. 4.13, *d*).

❏ Link (**Link**) the **Bone-Foot-R** object to the **Bone-Ankle-R** object using the **Select and Link** command.

❏ Make the bones for the left leg. To do this, mirror (**Mirror**) the objects-bones of the right leg with copying on the front view.

❏ Select all the bones of the right leg. (It is sufficient to double-click on the **Bone-Thigh-R** object.)

❏ Apply the mirror operation (**Mirror**) with copying and move the resultant object to the required position (Fig. 4.13, *e*).

❏ Rename the objects using the "L" index (**Bone-Thigh-L**, etc.).

Prior to version 4, there was only one type of inverse kinematics in 3ds max. For the sake of compatibility, it was retained in the new version and called **History Dependent IK Solver**. It's a good tool but has a complicated setting. We propose using the modern system of inverse kinematics, which has a similar name (**History Independent IK Solver**) but different settings.

❏ Create an inverse-kinematics link between the **Bone-Thigh-R** and **Bone-Ankle-R** objects. Rename the new object as **Leg-IK-R**:

   Select the Bone-Thigh-R object.

   Main menu → Animation → IK Solvers → HI Solver

   Drag the "line" to the Bone-Ankle-R object and click with the left mouse button.

Try to move this object (blue cross). The bones should perform motions.

▶ *Note*

After any moves, return the object to its previous placement using the **Undo** command (<Ctrl>+<Z>)!

Everything works well, but selecting this object is not convenient. In addition, you need to control the turns of the knee. Therefore, two more objects are necessary: one responsible for moving the **Leg-IK-R** object, and another for the knee turns.

☐ On the top view, create two helper objects (**Helper**) opposite the right leg. The first one, of the **Dummy** type, will control the movement of the **Leg-IK-R** object. It is this object that you will animate. Rename it as **Foot-R** and move it to the foot level. The second object, point (**Point**), is used to control the turns of the leg. Move it to the knee level and rename it **Knee-R** (Fig. 4.13, *f*):

  Control panel → Create → Helpers → Standard → Dummy, Point

☐ Link the **Leg-IK-R** object to the **Foot-R** object using the **Select and Link** command and see what happens.

The **Knee-R** object is linked in a different manner.

☐ Select the **Leg-IK-R** object and switch the control panel to the **Motion** mode.

☐ Press the **Pick Target** button in the **IK Solver Properties** menu and click with the left mouse button on the **Knee-R** object.

Try to move the **Knee-R** object. The knee of the right leg "traces" the **Knee-R** object.

To turn the foot, you must specify another parameter.

Try to move the **Bone-Foot-R** object around the pivot point (**Pivot Point**). It is around this point that the objects' rotation is performed during animation. Our object turns around the current pivot point, but not the way we want it to. Move the object's pivot point until the rotation corresponds to the desired one.

☐ Select the **Bone-Foot-R** object and switch the control panel to the **Hierarchy** mode. Open the **Pivot** panel in the **Adjust Pivot** menu and press the **Affect Pivot Only** button.

☐ Move the pivot point to the position corresponding to that of an ankle (Fig. 4.13, *g*).

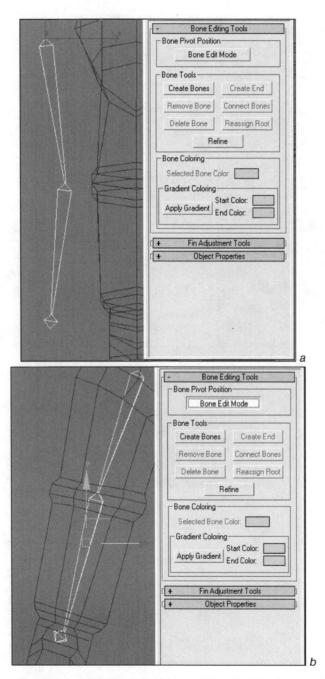

Fig. 4.13, *a* and *b*. Adjustment of the right leg bones

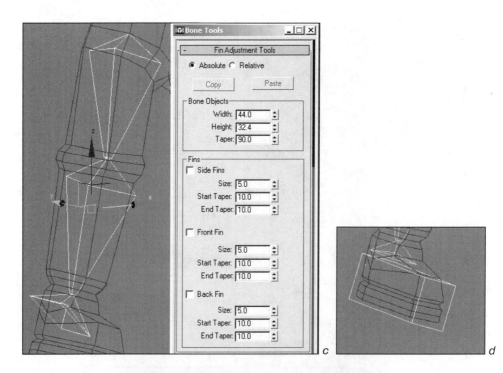

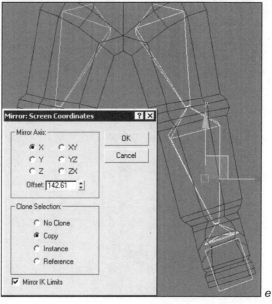

Fig. 4.13, *c–e*. Adjustment of the right leg bones

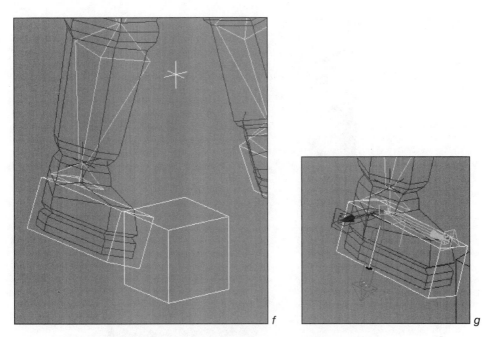

Fig. 4.13, *f* and *g*. Adjustment of the right leg bones

You don't need to create a controlling object for this bone; it will be easy to access. However, note that such a control object is created in the same way as that for the arm bone. This process will be described below.

Adjust the bones of the left leg.

▶ *Tip*

To avoid certain incidents later, select all bones of the left leg and apply the **Reset Pivot** operation in the **Hierarchy** panel.

❑ Create an inverse-kinematics link between the **Bone-Thigh-L** and **Bone-Ankle-L** objects.

❑ Copy the **Foot-R** and **Knee-R** objects and rename them **Foot-L** and **Knee-L**. Move them to the required position and link the appropriate objects with them.

❑ Adjust the pivot point of the **Bone-Foot-L** object in the same way as for the **Bone-Foot-R** object.

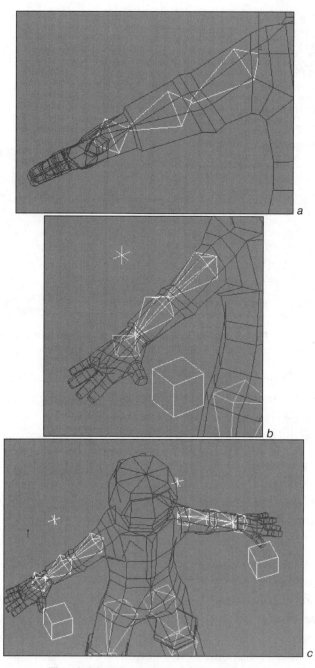

Fig. 4.14. Adjustment of the arm bones

It is convenient to make the right arm's bones on the front view.

☐ Make a chain of bones beginning from the shoulder joint.

☐ Rename them (from the shoulder) **Bone-Shoulder-R**, **Bone-Forearm-R**, and **Bone-Hand-R**.

☐ Move and adjust them so that they are within the right arm of the astronaut, their sizes being proportionate to the arm (Fig. 4.14, *a*).

☐ Display with duplication the bones of the right arm and move them into accordance with the left arm. Rename them as **Bone-Shoulder-L**, etc.

☐ Create an inverse-kinematics link between **Bone-Shoulder-R** and **Bone-Hand-R**. Rename the object as **Arm-IK-R**.

☐ Create auxiliary objects similar to those you created for the legs. Rename them **Arm-R** and **Elbow-R**. Link them with the **Arm-IK-R** object through the steps used to link the **Leg-IK-R** object (Fig. 4.14, *b*).

The process is the same for the left arm (Fig. 4.14, *c*). Select all bones of the left arm and apply the **Reset Pivot** operation.

▶ *Note*

The scheme for the arms is a little simple: It provides no option for twisting the forearm. A more complex scheme can be used for this purpose by creating two or more bones to control the forearm. Then the inverse-kinematics link can be created up to the first bone after the elbow joint; the rest of the bones obey direct kinematics laws. You can do this if you want, but it doesn't make sense in our model. To employ this feature in full, a more complex mesh for the forearm is required.

The hand should be able to twist freely around all its axes. All of these features are inherent to the **Bone-Hand-R** and **Bone-Hand-L** objects. However, the process of their animation is extremely inconvenient. Let's use a resourceful method to animate these bones.

☐ Create a helper-object of the **Point** type close to the right hand. To make it different from the other points, display the additional elements (Fig. 4.15, *a*). Rename this object **Hand-Twister-R**.

☐ Select the **Bone-Hand-R** object and assign the animation controller of the **Orientation Constraint** type to it.

> Main menu → Animation → Constraints → Orientation Constraint
>
> Drag the "line" to the Hand-Twister-R object and click with the left mouse button.

❏ Set the parameters in the control panel as shown in Fig. 4.15, *b*.

▶ *Tip*

Change only one parameter: Check the **Keep Initial Offset** flag.

The parameters of the controllers-constraints are considered in detail in *Lesson 3* in the example of the **LookAt** controller.

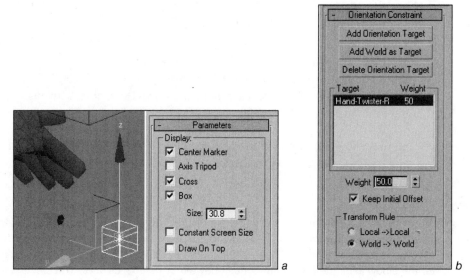

Fig. 4.15. Hand-twisting adjustment

❏ Link (**Link**) the **Hand-Twister-R** object to the **Bone-Forearm-R** object.

Try to rotate the **Hand-Twister-R** object in the **Parent** coordinates:

    <Alt>+Context menu → Parent

The **Bone-Hand-R** object repeats the rotation. Now try to move the controlling object, **Arm-R**. The **Hand-Twister-R** object performs the rotation of the **Bone-Forearm-R** bone. Isn't it nice?

Do the same for the left hand.

Now you will not encounter problems while creating the finger bones.

❏ Create a separate chain of bones for each finger. Make them on the top view and fit them to the glove's form (Fig. 4.16, *a*). When the bones are created, re-move the end bones by pressing the right mouse button.

▶ *Note*

Note that the bone chains of the fingers start from the bone in the palm. This is a matter of principle that will enable you to animate the finger flexion without problems.

❑ Rename the finger bones as **Bone-Finger-X-Y-R**, where **X** is the number of the finger beginning from the thumb (from 1 to 5), and **Y** is the number of the bone beginning from the palm (from 0 to 3).

▶ *Tip*

To quickly rename objects, you can use the **Rename Objects** tool (Main menu → Tools → Rename Objects).

❑ Use the **Select and Link** command to link the **Bone-Finger-X-0-R** bones to the **Bone-Hand-R** object (Fig. 4.16, *b*).

For the fingers, we propose only the fist option. You can adjust each finger separately because the same principle is used.

To simplify animation, in *Lesson 3* we used the option of creating additional parameters (**Custom Attributes**) of the object with further linking using the **Wire** system. In this lesson, it is more convenient to use screen manipulators.

❑ Create a screen manipulator in the right bottom corner of the viewport of any view. Rename it **Fist-Slider-R** (Fig. 4.16, *c*):

    Control panel → Create → Helpers → Manipulators → Slider

Leave the default values of the manipulator's parameters; they will be corrected later.

To enforce the manipulator, activate the **Manipulate** mode. Now you can change the value by moving the slider of the manipulator:

    Main panel → Select and Manipulate

Use the **Wire** system to link the value of the manipulator and the rotation of the **Bone-Finger-X-1-R — Bone-Finger-X-3-R** bones around the Y axis (**Y Rotation**).

In *Lesson 3* we mentioned that the **Euler XYZ** controller used for rotation employs the coordinates of the parent object. For the **Finger-X-1-R** objects, such objects are **Finger-X-0-R**. The rotation will be correct.

❏ Select the **Fist-Slider-R** object and link the **value** parameter with the rotation of the **Bone-Finger-5-R** object around the Y axis:

Context menu → Wire Parameters → Object (Slider)→ Value

Drag the "line" to the Bone-Finger-5-R object and click with the left mouse button.

Select in the menu Transform → Rotation → Y Rotation

Press the "→" button in the dialog that appears to indicate that the parameter in the left window is the control, relative to the parameter in the right window. Press the **Connect** button (Fig. 4. 16, *d*).

Try to move the slider of the manipulator. You'll notice that the finger is twisting too actively. Reduce the **Maximum** value in the parameters of the controller-manipulator. (Set the value to 1.)

Repeat the operation for the bones of all fingers. You can simplify the task by finding the required parameters in the right window and linking the **value** parameter with them. Note that the objects are linked hierarchically, so the parameters are represented as a tree. Open separate "branches" using the "+" symbol.

➤ *Note*

Unfortunately, the basic 3ds max application does not provide a tool that enables you to complete this task in one motion. You can search for the appropriate plug-in or script on the Internet (e.g., **http://www.scriptspot.com**).

Do the same operations for the fingers of the left hand (Fig. 4.16, *e*).

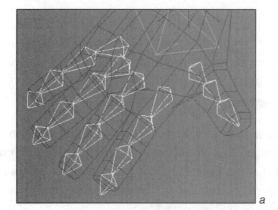
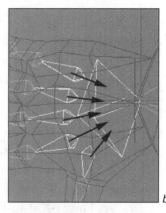

Fig. 4.16, *a* and *b*. Creation and adjustment of the finger bones

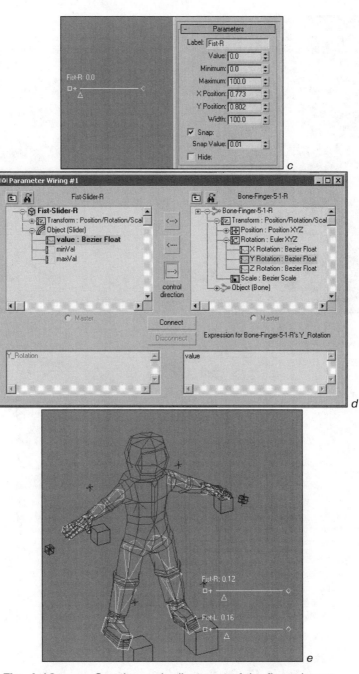

Fig. 4.16, *c−e.* Creation and adjustment of the finger bones

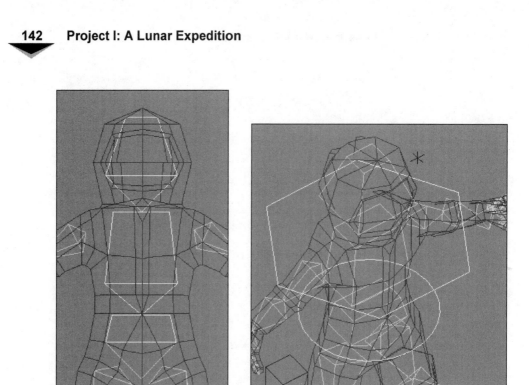

a
b

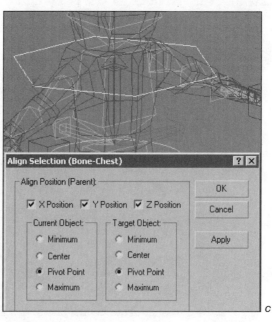

c

Fig. 4.17. Creation and adjustment of the body bones

You have three more object-bones to create: those for the abdomen, chest, and helmet. Let them be the objects of the **Bone** type; unlike the boxes, they do not require additional pivot points.

❑ Create a chain of bones on the front view starting from the abdomen. The small bone at the end of the chain results from the completion of the bone creation. Remove this small bone; it will not be used.

❑ Match the sizes of the bones with those of the model (Fig. 4.17, *a*).

❑ Rename the objects (bottom-up) **Bone-Abdomen**, **Bone-Chest**, and **Bone-Helmet**.

❑ To simplify the body's tilt animation as well as the chest's flexion and twisting, create the additional **_BODY** and **Chest** objects. Let them be shapes (**Shapes**) — a circle and a hexagon (Fig. 4.17, *b*):

> Main menu → Create → Shapes → Circle, NGon

❑ Use the **Select and Link** command to link the **Bone-Abdomen** object to the **_BODY** object. Link the **Bone-Chest** and **Chest** objects using the **Orientation Constraint** controller in the same manner used for the hands. Note that an object can have only one "parent", so an attempt to link the **Bone-Chest** object directly to the **Chest** object would lead to an undesired breakage of the previous link.

❑ Match the pivot point of the **Chest** object with that of **Bone-Chest**:

> Control panel → Hierarchy → Affect Pivot Only
>
> Main panel → Align → click Bone-Chest object
>
> In the dialog, select the option that matches the pivot points by all coordinates (Fig. 4.17, *c*).

❗ *Do it yourself*

If you wish, you can adjust the rotation of the helmet, which is rigidly attached to the spacesuit.

❑ Link the objects in the following way using the **Select and Link** command:
1. **Bone-Thigh-R, Bone-Thigh-L** — to the **Bone-Abdomen** object
2. **Bone-Shoulder-R, Bone-Shoulder-L** — to the **Bone-Chest** object
3. **Foot-R, Foot-L, Knee-L, Knee-R** — to the **_BODY** object
4. **Arm-R, Arm-L, Elbow-R, Elbow-L** — to the **Chest** object (Fig. 4.18)

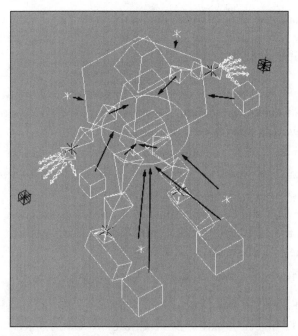

Fig. 4.18. Final linking of the bones and control objects of the skeleton

Try to move the main object (**_BODY**). All bones and the control objects should move together. If this is not the case, then there is an error.

▶ *Note*

In reality, not all links are necessary, and some are even harmful. Thus, many of them will have to be broken during the animation.

Now, the skeleton is ready and adjusted for further animation!

You can find our Lesson04-10.max ... Lesson04-14.max files with the sequence of the skeleton's creation on the CD-ROM in the Lessons\Lesson04\Scenes folder.

Linking the Skeleton with the Model

The model of the astronaut has been created, and the skeleton is also ready. Now we will link the skeleton to the model and adjust the effect of the bones using the **Skin** modifier.

► *Note*

Some modifiers, including **Skin**, **Unwrap UVW**, and **Flex**, are difficult to call simply "modifiers." These are already "systems" or "packages within a package" that include multiple features and settings. So far, the developers of 3ds max have tried, when defining modifiers, to adhere to the principles laid in the first version. However, we feel that the boundaries of these principles tend to narrow as new versions are released.

Before you apply the **Skin** modifier, ensure that all bones are in their correct positions relative to the model; move them, if necessary. This is especially applicable to the finger bones. When we created our model and the bone system, we deliberately made several errors. We thought about correcting these errors but decided to leave them. We will use them to show solutions to problems that may result from inaccurate adjustment of the bones to the model's geometry.

❐ Make the **SpaceSuit** object available for editing (**Unfreeze**):

  Contextual menu → Unfreeze All

❐ Apply the **Skin** modifier to the **SpaceSuit** object:

  Main menu → Modifiers → Animation → Skin

On opening the contextual menu of the modifier, we were surprised to find that this menu contained almost all the necessary commands (Fig. 4.19). Praise the 3ds max developers for this! Old habits die hard, however, so we will refer to the commands in the control panel when describing further operations. Nevertheless, we recommend active use of the contextual menu.

3ds max allows any geometrical object, right up to curves (**Shapes**), to be used as bones. We used objects of the **Box** type as bones for the boots.

❐ Add all of the bones to the list in the **Skin** modifier:

  Control panel → Parameters → Add button above the list of bones

  In the selection-by-name dialog, choose all objects whose names begin with "Bone" and press the **Select** button.

► *Tip*

In the selection-by-name dialog, you can easily select objects by typing in the first letters of their names.

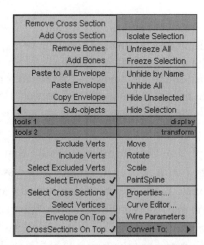

Remove Cross Section	
Add Cross Section	Isolate Selection
Remove Bones	Unfreeze All
Add Bones	Freeze Selection
Paste to All Envelope	Unhide by Name
Paste Envelope	Unhide All
Copy Envelope	Hide Unselected
◄ Sub-objects	Hide Selection
tools 1	display
tools 2	transform
Exclude Verts	Move
Include Verts	Rotate
Select Excluded Verts	Scale
Select Envelopes ✓	PaintSpline
Select Cross Sections ✓	Properties...
Select Vertices	Curve Editor...
Envelope On Top ✓	Wire Parameters
CrossSections On Top ✓	Convert To: ►

Fig. 4.19. Contextual menu of the **Skin** modifier

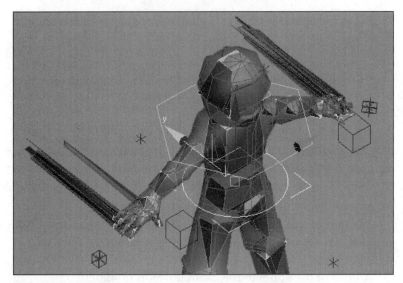

Fig. 4.20. Insufficient effect of the skeleton's bones on the model

Select the **_BODY** object — the oldest in the hierarchy — and move it. We left some vertices of the fingers and hands in place (Fig. 4.20). This shows that the effect of the bones is insufficient on these vertices.

If everything is OK, don't be too happy; a redundant effect of the bones is as unwanted as an insufficient effect. Now, try to edit the bones' effect on the vertices of the model.

During editing, you repeatedly will have to move the control objects to follow the bones' effect on the model. To do this, you will have to toggle between the **SpaceSuit** object and the control objects by selecting them in turn. To avoid extra manipulations, we propose that you animate the control objects, properly bending the bones in an intermediate frame.

❑ Go to an intermediate frame (e.g., 50) by moving the   ‹ 50 / 100 ›
   Time Slider.

❑ Press the **Auto Key** button (Animation recording).   Auto Key

▶ *Note*

The full name of this button is **Toggle Auto Key Mode** (Toggle on/off animation recording).

❑ Move the control objects of the legs and arms by changing the posture of the astronaut (Fig. 4.21).

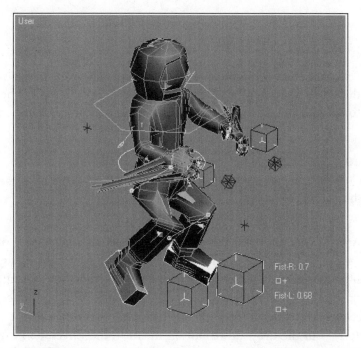

Fig. 4.21. Changing the astronaut's posture to control the bones' effect

❏ Release the **Auto Key** button.

Now you can change the posture of the object by moving the slider.

❏ Go back to the zero frame.
❏ Select the **SpaceSuit** object. **Hide** the rest of the objects to avoid confusion:

Contextual menu → Hide Unselected

The **Skin** modifier allows you to edit the bones' effect on the model's vertices in two ways. The first method, editing each bone's area using the effect area (**Envelope**), is the simplest but least accurate one. When the skeleton was created, we insisted that you accurately match the bones' sizes to those of the model. The **Skin** modifier adjusts the effect area based on the sizes of the bones, but not always in the best way. The second method is to directly assign each bone's effect, or "weight" (**Weight**), to each vertex of the model. This method is more laborious, but more accurate, too. Which is to be applied? Both. The truth is usually somewhere in between; it depends on the task. Let's test this premise.

❏ Go to the working mode with the **Envelopes**:

Control panel → Edit Envelopes

❏ Select the **Bone-Abdomen** envelope. This can be done in two ways: by selecting the **Bone-Abdomen** bone from the list, or by clicking with the left mouse button on the gray line corresponding to the center of this bone's envelope.

▶ *Note*

The line corresponds to the center of the envelope, not to the bone itself! The envelopes can be moved independent of the bone's position.

As you see, the envelope consists of two sub-envelopes, or borders (Fig. 4.22, *a*). The inner envelope defines the area where the bone has 100% effect on the vertices. The outer envelope restricts the bone's effect: The bone does not affect the vertices without it. Between these sub-envelopes, the bone affects the vertices with intermediate values. The bones' effect falloff law (**Falloff**) is in the drop-down button menu in the **Envelope Properties** group of the **Parameters** menu.

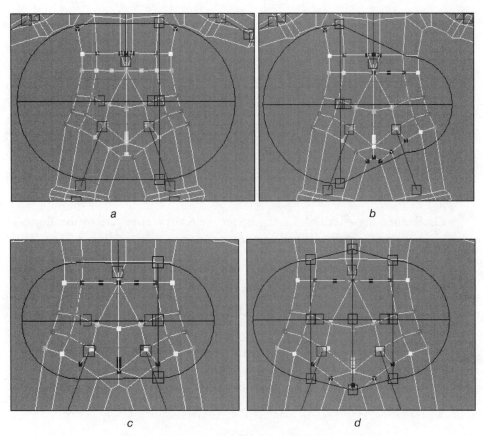

Fig. 4.22. Editing the bone-abdomen effect

In the display mode in the **Wire frame** viewport, the bone's effect on the vertices is in color: red corresponds to 100%, blue — 0%. In the **Shaded** display mode, polygons are colored correspondingly. The **Display** menu shows what is to be displayed, and how.

The envelope for the abdomen bone is too large. Reduce the size of the outer sub-envelope using the control **CrossSection**, displayed as "squares".

☐ Select one of the "squares" on the outer sub-envelope and move it, thus reducing the bone's effect (Fig. 4.22, b).

☐ Achieve symmetry by selecting and moving the square of another cross section (Fig. 4.22, c).

❏ Add one more cross section. Move the control vertices of the new cross section to allow this bone to affect the vertices between the legs of the astronaut (Fig. 4.22, *d*):

Control panel → CrossSection → Add

Click with the left mouse button approximately in the middle of the envelope.

Note that some vertices within the inner sub-envelope are colored in intermediate colors. This shows that other bones, namely, those of the chest and legs, affect these vertices. They also must be edited. At the same time, you should leave overlaps in the envelopes; the spacesuit is thick, so stretches are appropriate.

❏ Reduce the effect of the leg bones. Select the envelope of the **Bone-Thigh-R** bone and edit the control vertices of the cross sections (Fig. 4.23, *a*).

On the front view everything is all right, but the left view clearly shows that this bone ceased to affect the rear vertices of the thigh and knee (Fig. 4.23, *b*).

❏ Correct it by moving the control vertex on the symmetry line of the envelopes (Fig. 4.23, *c*).
❏ Copy the parameters of this bone's envelope into the clipboard using the **Copy** button on the control panel.
❏ Select the envelope of the **Bone-Thigh-L** bone, paste the copied parameters from the clipboard (**Paste**), and edit the position of the envelope.

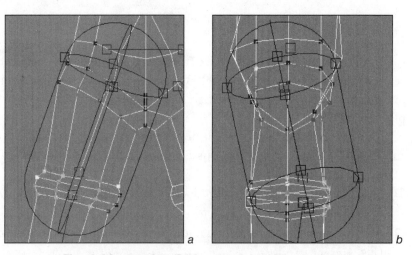

Fig. 4.23, *a* and *b*. Editing the right thigh envelope

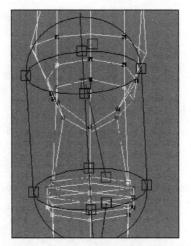

Fig. 4.23, c. Editing the right thigh envelope

The effect of the other bones of the legs, chest, and arms is edited in the same way.

To edit the bones of the helmet and boots, another method is to be used. These objects are rigid, and the effects of other bones on their vertices can lead to distortions of the geometry.

☐ Select the **Bone-Helmet** envelope.

☐ Edit its effect area (Fig. 4.24, *a*).

☐ In the control panel, activate the option for selecting vertices.

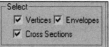

☐ Select the vertices of the helmet, assign them a weight of 1, and check the **Rigid** flag (Fig. 4.24, *b*). Thus, you will point out that only the **Bone-Helmet** bone will affect these vertices.

The effects of the **Bone-Foot-R** and **Bone-Foot-L** for the boots are adjusted in the same way.

Adjust the fingers' effect by combining these two methods.

 Do it yourself

There is another option for editing the weight of the effect — direct drawing (**Paint Weights**). We propose that you master this feature on your own. We successfully used it to adjust the fingers' effect. For illustration, this can be done in the intermediate frame.

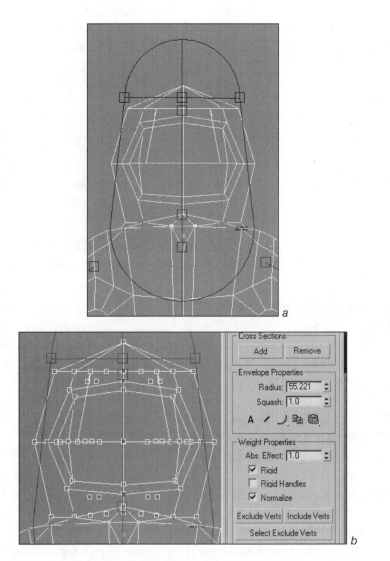

Fig. 4.24. Editing the bone-helmet effect

We encountered another problem: excessive mashing of the model in the oints. It is unlikely that you "survived" the ordeal. Further smoothing can reduce this effect, but you should not fully rely on it.

There are tools within the **Skin** modifiers that allow you to solve this problem. Use one of them on the left thigh.

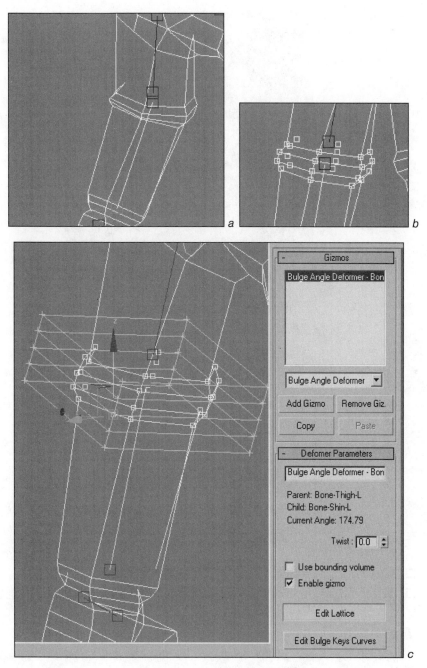

Fig. 4.25, *a–c.* Editing the **Bulge Angle Deformer** gizmo

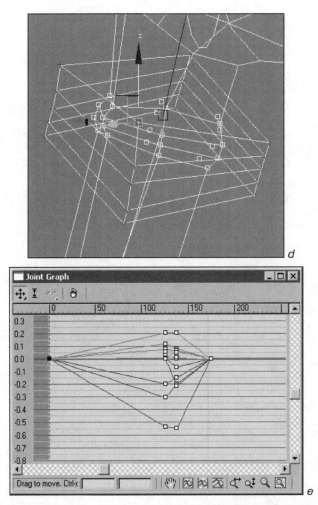

Fig. 4.25, *d* and *e*. Editing the **Bulge Angle Deformer** gizmo

Fig. 4.25, *a*, shows the "mash" we would like to remove. To do this:

☐ Go to the zero frame.
☐ Select the envelope corresponding to the **Bone-Shin-L** bone.

► *Tip*

Toggle off the display of the envelopes by checking the **Show No Envelopes** flag in the **Display** menu.

☑ Show No Envelopes

❏ Select the vertices of the left knee using the lasso (Fig. 4.25, *b*).

❏ Assign the bulge angle deformer on the selected vertices (**Bulge Angle Deformer**). It is the simplest of the three available. According to the name, its main purpose is to imitate muscles, but in our case it is also suitable:

   Control panel → Gizmos → Bulge Angle Deformer → Add Gizmo

The gizmo is formed around the selected vertices (Fig. 4.25, *c*).

❏ Go to the intermediate frame, press the **Edit Lattice** button, and obtain the desired form by moving the vertices of the gizmo (Fig. 4.25, *d*).

You can use the curve editor to adjust the gizmo's vertices according to the angle between the bones (Fig. 4.25, *e*).

To tell you the truth, this task is minute. Fortunately, after the gizmo of one thigh is adjusted, you can copy the parameters for the other one.

❏ Copy the gizmo's parameters into the clipboard by pressing the **Copy** button.

❏ Select the envelope corresponding to the **Bone-Shin-R** bone.

❏ Select the vertices of the right knee and assign the angle deformer on the selected vertices.

❏ Use the **Paste** button to paste the parameters from the clipboard.

❏ The same must be done for the elbow joints and for the hip joint (for correct performance of the buttocks).

❏ Create the backpack and the communication device (**Backpack** and **Com-Dev** objects) and link them to the **Bone-Chest** bone (Fig. 4.26). Before you do this, unhide all objects in your scene:

   Context menu → Unhide All

If you followed our advice and made the animation, get rid of it now.

❏ Select all objects.

❏ Remove the animation keys. First, select and remove the keys from the intermediate frame (ours is 50th), then remove the keys from the zero frame.

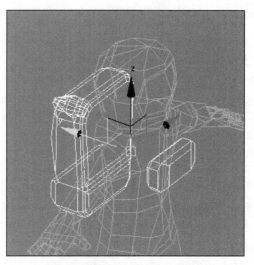

Fig. 4.26. Additional objects

Our fully adjusted model is in the Lesson04-18.max file in the Lessons\
Lesson04\Scenes folder on the CD-ROM.

Character Animation

Animating the character (**Character Animation**) is usually both the most complicated and the most interesting task. There are several packages for the Win-
dows/Intel platform created for this purpose: for example, Life Forms Studio from
Credo Interactive (**http://www.lifeforms.com**) or Life Studio from LifeMode
Interactive (**http://www.lifemi.com**). As a rule, there are no modeling tools in these
packages; you must import the model from a multi-purpose package, animate it, then
export the model to the format of the appropriate package. In most cases, you can use
source files obtained via motion capture. Some packages, such as Kaydara MOCAP
from Kaydara (**http://www.kaydara.com**), offer complex solutions.

Traditionally, the best multi-purpose package in this niche is the Maya package
from Alias|Wavefront, but gradually the other packages have intruded into this area
of the 3D graphics. 3ds max is not an exception here, with the character animation
tools becoming more advanced from one version to another.

Discussing character animation in 3ds max, it would be unfair not to mention
the Character Studio package, the 3ds max plug-in intended exclusively for character

animation. While this book was being written, the fourth version of the above package was released. It offers many new features for character adjustment and animation. Discreet has priced this package at $995. If you are serious about character animation, it must be at your disposal.

So, what is offered by 3ds max to raise the efficiency of character animation? First, notice the character assembly features (**Character Assembly**). These allow you to work with the character's objects as a whole, save animation as files, and load them when necessary.

Another novelty is animation based on the "pose-to-pose" principle (**Pose-To-Pose**). The method considerably speeds up the animation of many objects.

Let's go back to our character, the astronaut.

When linking the objects, we tried too hard and linked the control objects of the legs (**Foot-R**, **Foot-L**, **Knee-R**, **Knee-L**) and arms (**Arm-R**, **Arm-L**, **Elbow-R**, **Elbow-L**) to the base objects (**_BODY** and **Chest**). These links must be broken before the character is assembled.

❒ Select the above objects and break the links by pressing the **Unlink Selection** button on the main toolbar.

Create the **Character Assembly**.

❒ Select all objects in your scene (and the screen handlers), then create the character:

Main menu → Character → Create Character

An object will be created symbolizing the character (Fig. 4.27). Actually, this is a fake object, an "icon" to which the rest of the assembly's objects are linked. Try to move, rotate, and scale it. As you can see, all objects correctly perform these manipulations, allowing you to forget the scale of your character.

On the control panel, there are several buttons for this object that also allow you to manipulate the assembly objects and the whole character. We will use only some of these features.

Note

The developers of 3ds max strongly recommend adjusting the links of the objects' parameters using the **Wire** system after the character is assembled (i.e., "within" the character). In our case, these adjustments were made beforehand. We experimented a little and encountered no special problems or, rather, failed to notice the difference. This peculiarity already may have been corrected in version 5.1. Still, we suggest that you to follow the developers' recommendation.

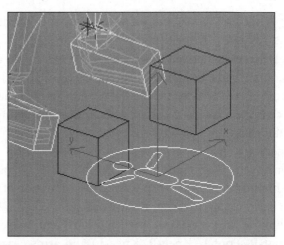

Fig. 4.27. Object of the **Character Assembly** type

To explain further operations, below is a brief description of traditional animation recording algorithms and those of the **Pose-To-Pose** animation method.

To start traditional animation recording, press the **Auto Key** button. (In previous versions of 3ds max, the appropriate button was named **Animate**.) The **Time Slider** is moved to the required frame. Any movements and other changes of the object in this frame will lead to the key creation only for the changed parameter. For further animation, go to the required frame and change the required parameter.

In **Pose-To-Pose** animation, the sequence and result are somewhat different. Press the **Set Key** button (or, rather, **Toggle Set Key Mode**), and the object will be edited (moved, rotated, etc.) in the required frame of the animation. No animation recording takes place because you specified the animation keys by pressing the **Set Key** button. The keys will be specified for all parameters highlighted in the **Key Filters** dialog, no matter if they were changed or not. The changes to parameters that are not highlighted will be ignored.

It is convenient to use the named selection sets (**Selection Set**) in **Pose-To-Pose** animation. These sets simultaneously create keys for all objects of the selection, considerably accelerating the animation process of many objects.

Let's use this method to animate our astronaut.

Character assembly could be used for this animation. You could use it by opening the drop-down list in the animation control panel (**Animation keying controls**). The **Character01** line is in this list.

The use of this method, however, will set you back a bit. Why? You will animate only the control objects, but the keys will be set on the parameters of *all* objects of the assembly. Therefore, it is better to create and use a new selection (**Named Selection Set**) consisting only of the control objects.

❑ Select the control objects and create the new selection by entering its name in the main panel line (e.g., **Control Objects**). Press <Enter>.

❑ You can add or delete objects from this selection in the **Named Selection Sets** dialog (Fig. 4.28).

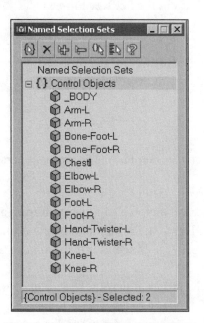

Fig. 4.28. Named Selection Sets control window

Fig. 4.29. Display Floater window

▶ *Note*

Don't include the screen manipulators in the selection! It is appropriate to animate the fingers at the end, and there is no need to create the same amount of keys for them as for the other objects.

Hide some of the objects to simplify the animation. You can do this by hiding the bones — the objects of the **Bone** type — or the character itself. In either case, it is convenient to use the floating window of the objects' display (**Display Floater**) (Fig. 4.29):

Main menu → Tools → Display Floater

We propose that you use the option for hiding objects by their type (**Hide By Category**). This will allow you to see immediately any faults in your model's adjustment. To show this, we will hide the character itself in the further illustrations.

❑ Select **Control Objects** in the drop-down list of the animation keying-controls panel.
❑ Check the **Position** and **Rotation** lines in the **Set Key Filters** dialog.
❑ Press the **Set Key** button.
❑ Put the character into its original posture in the initial frame of the animation by moving and rotating the control objects (Fig. 4.30). Press the **Set Key** button.

▶ *Note*

The control objects are set so that some of them only have to be moved, others — only rotated. Be very attentive!

Further animation is done in the same way. Go to the next frames and record the intermediate phases of movement. Fig. 4.31 shows the movement phases of the character. For clarity, the control objects are hidden, and the phases are shifted relative to each other.

The astronaut's gait turned out to be rather ludicrous, but it's up to you to correct it!

So, what advice can we give about creating animation? First, have patience; manual animation of characters is a painstaking process in any package.

Remember that the gravitation on the Moon is six times less than that of the Earth, so the spacesuit can hardly be used as a jogging outfit.

Go from general to particular during the animation: First, roughly animate the legs and the arms, then the position and bend of the torso, and later the twists of the boots, hands, etc.

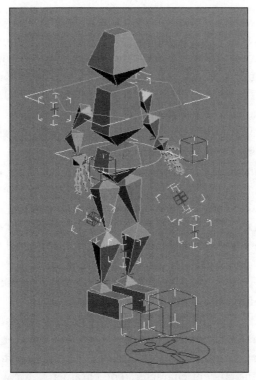

Fig. 4.30. Original posture of the character

Fig. 4.31. Phases of the character's movement

To create looped animation, your astronaut should come to a halt in the same posture as he started his motion. To do this, select all **Control Objects**. Then copy the keys from the initial frame to the last one by moving them on the time scale (**TimeLine**) and holding down the <Shift> key. The astronaut will return to his initial position. Transfer all **Control Objects** to the required place and specify the new keys in this frame.

Finally, purchase a good book on anatomy and human motions or find the appropriate information in the Internet.

Our astronaut has made his first and, frankly, rather unsteady step. The animation process took us about 30 minutes, while the duration of the animation itself is only 1.5 seconds. The ratio leaves much to be desired!

To see what is offered in 3ds max to enhance efficiency:

Select the **Character01** object. On the control panel in the **Animation** group, three buttons can be used to control the animation.

Hopefully, there is no need to explain why the **Reset All Animation** button should be left alone.

Save your animation as a file using the **Save Animation** button (e.g., as Step1.anm file).

The **Insert Animation** button allows you to load the animation parameters from file for the current character. The parameters for when our astronaut makes two identical, running steps are shown in Fig. 4.32.

Explanation

In the **Source Time Range** group, you can adjust the animation loading. To make the astronaut take the second step, the animation should be added from the last frame of the current animation. Our astronaut comes to a halt on the 50th frame, so the animation should be added approximately from the 55th frame.

The **Start Time** and **End Time** borders determine the part to be loaded.

The **Relative/Absolute** toggle, if set in the **Relative** position, allows the character to continue forward motion.

The **Apply To** group is used to specify the parameters that will be affected by loading the animation.

The large **Object Mapping** rollout allows you to reassign the objects' current correspondence and that of the file being loaded. When animation is loaded, an automatic adjustment of correspondence takes place based on the objects' names (**Auto Name Mapping**).

If something disappoints you, reassign the links among the objects (e.g., to make the astronaut step with the other leg).

In our case, there should be no hindrances, so don't hesitate to press the **Merge Animation** button. Our astronaut makes the second step fully identical to the first one.

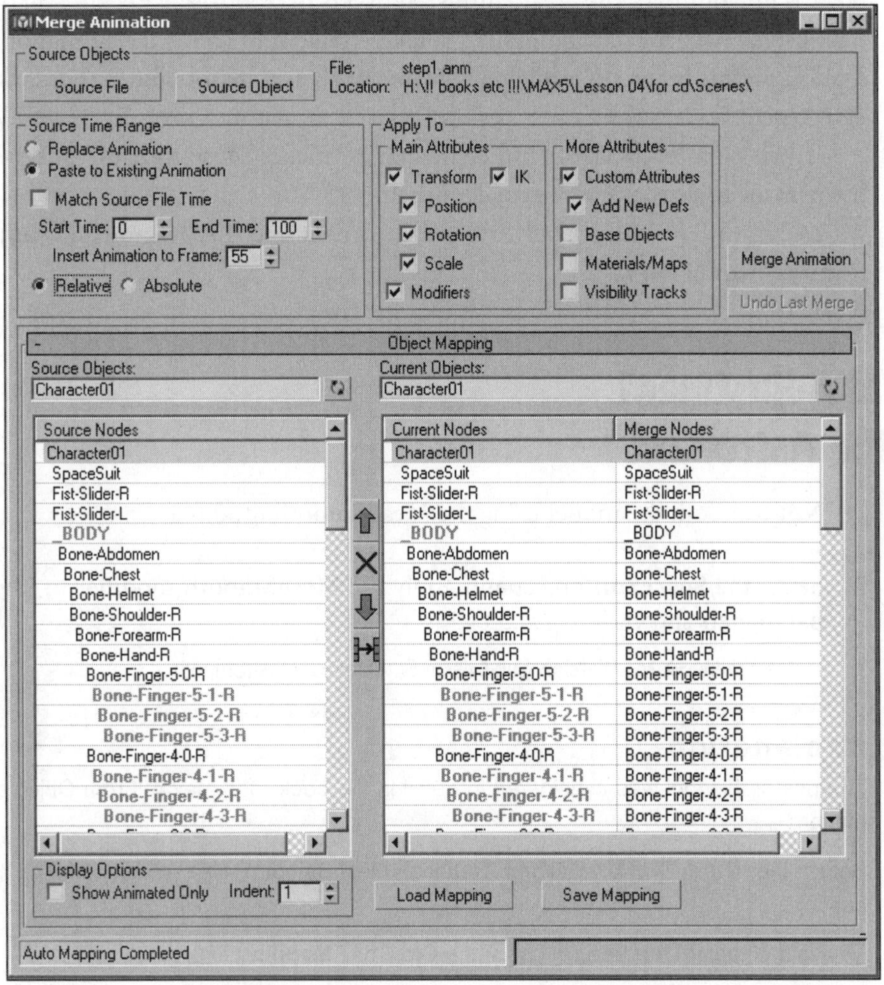

Fig. 4.32. Animation loading from the file dialog

How do we recommended that you use the Animation tool? It makes sense to create a library of separate movements. For example, three files are desirable for simple walking: start of the motion (ending with a half-step), full step, and end of the motion. You can create a single file for this and load it by parts later, but remember which frame contains each motion. Unfortunately, all of this will have to be recorded somewhere "on paper;" there are no additional options for the creation and control of the motion databases in 3ds max. It is possible that by the time this book is on your desk the great enthusiast of 3ds max, Borislav Petrov, will offer 3ds max users script for solving many problems related to character animation. Information on this project is available at **http://www.scriptspot.com/bobo/darkmoon/ eNLArge/**.

If you plan to create several characters, it makes sense to apply one system of the control objects and bones to all of them.

In *Lesson 7* we will actively use our astronaut and discuss in detail some other features of animation.

Final Adjustment of the Astronaut

Now, smooth the model using the **MeshSmooth** modifier.

❑ Select the **SpaceSuit** object and apply the **MeshSmooth** modifier to it with the parameters shown in Fig. 4.33:

Main menu → Modifiers → Subdivision Surfaces → MeshSmooth

Explanation

The use of this tool was considered in detail in the book "3ds max 4: From Objects to Animation."

Select the **NURMS** (Non-Uniform Rational MeshSmooth) type of smoothing; it is the best one.

To avoid "sagging" the texture, check the **Old Style Mapping** flag.

Smoothing once will be enough for now.

To take into account the character's sharp angles, check the **Separate by Smoothing Group** flag. When our astronaut was modeled, we focused on these groups.

To retain the shape, it is also useful to check the **Keep Faces Convex** flag.

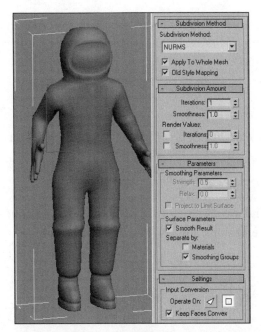

Fig. 4.33. Parameters of the **MeshSmooth** modifier used for
the character's smoothing

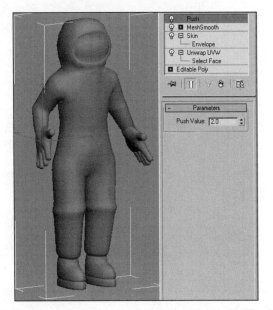

Fig. 4.34. Restoring the character's volume using the **Push** modifier

Application of the **MeshSmooth** modifier noticeably makes objects "look slender." To help the character retained his initial size and volume, apply the **Push** modifier (Fig. 4.34):

Main menu → Modifiers → Parametric Deformers → Push

❏ Save your scene.

❏ Select the **Character01** object and save your character. The astronaut, not the whole scene, will be used further on:

Main menu → Character → Save Character

You can find our Lesson04(Final).max and Lesson04(Char).chr files on the CD-ROM in the Lessons/Lesson04/Scenes folder.

Lesson 5

Modeling Space and Animating the Flight of the Spaceship

In this lesson, we will create a portion of near-Earth space and animate the flight of the spaceship.

Having completed the previous lessons on modeling, material creation and assignment, and animation, these tasks should not be difficult for you. Therefore, from this lesson on, we will dwell less on basic operations.

Before we proceed, we need to get some figures from an encyclopedia. The diameter of the Earth is about 13,000 kilometers, one of the Moon about 3,500 kilometers, and of the Sun about 1.4 million kilometers. The distance from the Earth to the Moon is about 384,000 kilometers, and from the Earth to the Sun about 150 million kilometers. We quote these figures to demonstrate the grandeur of our task and the impossibility of creating these objects and distances life-size. The spaceship itself does not exceed 30 meters. 3ds max does not work with scales differing by more than 10 orders of magnitude, which, in any case, is not needed.

Much of this lesson (and of subsequent lessons) may seem strange and illogical from the point of view of what you learned at college or university. But everything falls into place when you realize that all of this is nothing but a simulation, and all means are justified for the sake of the result.

Finally, in many respects, the sequence of operations corresponds to that of professionals when they work alone. We wrote this book primarily for those who want to work freelance, for jacks-of-all-trades. In a corporate structure, however, your work may proceed in a different order.

Modeling Space

In the previous lessons, we specifically addressed setting the system units. There is no such need in this lesson.

Fig. 5.1 shows the cosmos. This scene is on the CD-ROM in Lessons\Lesson05\ Scenes\lesson05-01.max. Let's see what it's all about.

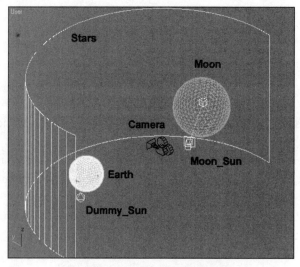

Fig. 5.1. Model of the cosmos

Explanations

Despite the figures quoted above, we made the Earth smaller than the Moon, illustrating that most of the trip has been left behind and our voyage is nearing its goal.

We used the **GeoSphere** primitive for the Earth and Moon. Unlike common spheres, these spheres consist of triangle faces, proving more round with less polygons. Both objects are at approximately the same distance from the coordinate origin.

Foreshadowing events to come, we will remark that when the global lighting system uses **Radiosity**, geospheres are also more preferable due to their regular structure.

The Moon's parameters are shown in Fig. 5.2, *a*. They are the same for the Earth, with the exception of the radius.

As with most geometrical primitives in 3ds max, the geosphere allows us to use the default texture coordinates (**Generate Mapping Coordinates** flag). But practice shows that their performance is not always as anticipated. Using the **UVW Map** modifier with spherical texture merging is not out of place (Fig. 5.2, *b*).

Main menu → Modifiers → UV Coordinates → UVW Map

▶ *Tip*

Keep in mind the wonderful option to drag-and-drop modifiers from one object to another. Combined with the <Ctrl> and <Shift> keys, you can copy, move, and create links between modifiers of various objects (**Instance**).

The **Stars** object was created using the **Arc** type of a **Shape**, with the parameters shown in Fig. 5.2, *c*, and subsequent use of the **Extrude** modifier (Fig. 5.2, *d*). The arc was made using the Center-End-End method. The center of the arc is precisely at the coordinate origin — this is very important! When creating the arc, activate the **Snap to Grid** option. It is also important that the camera is at the coordinate origin, otherwise undesirable distortions are inevitable when the camera is turned.

❗ *Explanations*

This method is rather obsolete, isn't it? 3ds max has other, more progressive methods. The first one is to assign a texture in a spherical environment (**Spherical** type of **Environment Map**). This method is excellent, for it requires no effort to synchronize the camera view, and everything is done automatically. The drawback is the necessity to use a very large image. To render a final product of 640 × 480 pixels, this image needs to be at least 4000 × 2000 pixels to avoid blurring, and the advantages turn out to be quite expensive.

The second method is to use procedure effects like StarField, integrated in 3ds max, or MilkyWay from Pavel Kuznetsov. This is more applicable in our case, but it does not paint a real picture of a starry sky in space. Is it worthwhile? You will know when you have finished this lesson. We will just add that a starry sky is a special case, and the method we propose is universal.

So, let's begin.

There are two sources of light in the scene: Moon_Sun and Dummy_Sun. The first one lights the Moon, whereas the second lights nothing, being a sort of "dummy" to create certain effects.

Based on these requirements, the sources of light need to be configured appropriately.

Neither type nor parameters matter for the Dummy_Sun. One thing is important, though: Exclude it from lighting objects. It is very easy to do:

❏ In the parameters of the Dummy_Sun, open the **Exclude/Include** window:

Control panel → ... → General Parameters → Exclude   Exclude...

❏ Set the toggle to **Include** and leave the list area below blank (Fig. 5.2, *e*). This will prevent the source from lighting any object in the scene.

The procedure for the Moon_Sun is no more difficult. This source uses Direct Light that should cover the whole Moon. To do this, edit the Hotspot/Beam size (the area of light without attenuation) on the view from the light source (<Shift>+<4> keys) with the **Light Hotspot** button on the navigation panel. In addition, only the Moon should be lit (Fig. 5.2, *f*):

Control panel → ... → Exclude → Include

Select the Moon in the left window and include it to be lit by this source by pressing the ">>" button.

Another source of this light will be considered later, when a material is assigned to the Moon.

What about the Earth? Unless we do something, it will remain in shadow. We will describe the method for the Earth below.

You have probably already asked yourself: Why so complicated? Wouldn't it be easier to create one source of light that illuminated the environment and all objects in it? We will try to explain below.

Since the Moon does not have an atmosphere, and the Sun's radiation in a vacuum is enormous, the border between lit and unlit areas is extremely sharp. The Earth, on the other hand, has an atmosphere, so the border between its lit and unlit areas is blurred. In addition, where the surface is already dark, often clouds are still lit by reflected light. The spaceship has its materials set in accordance with its light sources, and there is no reason to abandon that approach. The stars don't need sources of light at all. You can assign materials for all these objects in accordance with a source of light if you want, but practice shows that it is easier and more effective to fit light to the materials than vice versa.

Finally, there is the camera. It is positioned at the coordinate origin, at the "center of the world," and its parameters are shown in Fig. 5.2, *g*. Its focal length is 50 millimeters. When this lesson was prepared, we consulted with a professional photographer who strongly recommended using at least an 85 mm lens to avoid distortions.

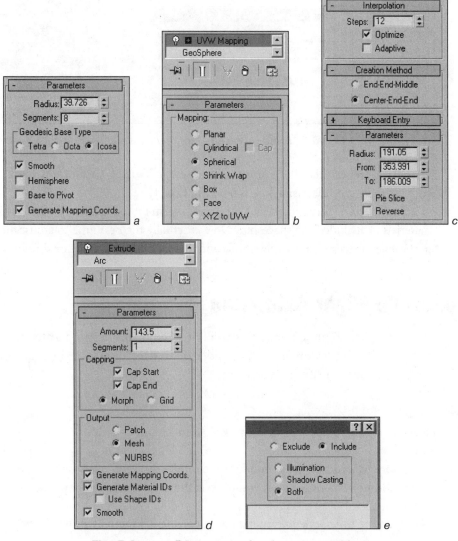

Fig. 5.2, *a–e*. Parameters of various space objects

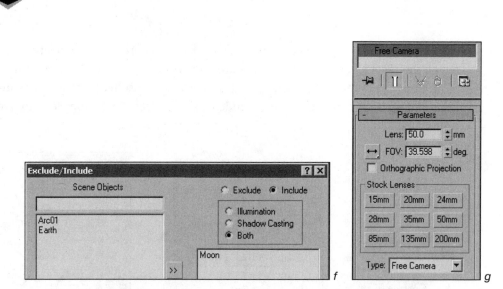

Fig. 5.2, *f* and *g*. Parameters of various space objects

When we created the camera, we used a **Target Camera** for the sake of convenience, but it is easier to animate the **Free** type.

Now, it's time for animation. Your may ask, isn't it too early, as we haven't assigned materials or included the spaceship? Now is actually the best time to adjust the animation, while the scene is relatively simple and there is no need to hide or simplify objects.

Spaceship Flight Animation

To learn more about animation, we will proceed by more complicated means than necessary. In this lesson, we will consider the **Path Constraint** in detail and teach you its wonderful features in 3ds max.

▶ *Note*

If you want to accomplish the same task in an easier way — do it.

Before we proceed, it is a good idea to set the time scale. It is our rule to do it right away, although 3ds max allows you to reset these parameters at any time.

❏   Open the time scale parameters window and set them as shown in Fig. 5.3:

     Time control panel → Time Configuration

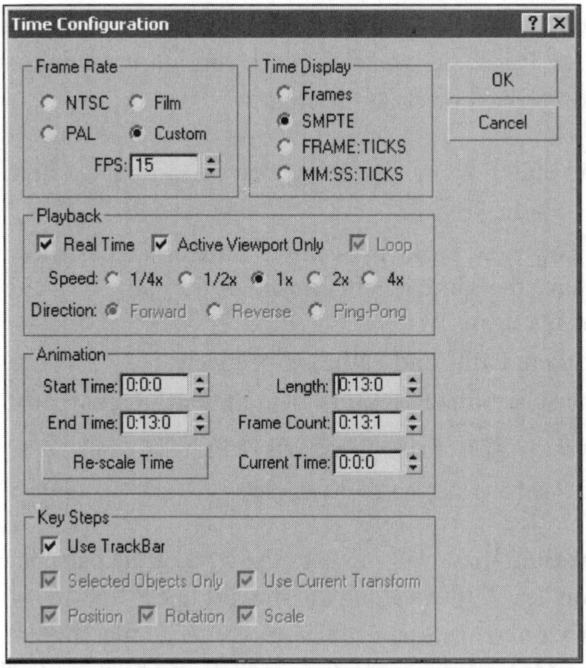

Fig. 5.3. Time Configuration window

Explanation

Use 15 frames per second for the **Frame Rate**. We plan to show the clip on a computer screen, so that should do.

The **Time Display** group determines the format in which time will be displayed on the scale. It is convenient to use the SMPTE format, where time is displayed as "minutes:seconds:frames."

The **Playback** group determines the rate and direction of animation in the viewport. Do not change these parameters.

Use the **Animation** group to set the length of animation. We will need approximately 5 seconds for the space panorama and 7 seconds for the flight. If this is not enough, you can change these parameters at any time.

3ds max has a cunning way to change the duration without opening this window. Move the cursor to the time scale and press the <Ctrl> and <Alt> keys. The start or end time is changed according to which mouse button is pressed. Move the mouse along the horizontal axis: the left button will affect the first frame of the active segment, the right button — the final frame. Pressing the middle button will change the active segment. It may be intriguing, but this option is not particularly convenient; we discovered it by accident.

Now, you can load the spaceship and lunar module, but we discourage you from doing so. It is easier and quicker to configure the animation for a simple object and load the real objects at the end.

❏ Create an object of any type at any place — we used a **Box**.
❏ Rename it SpaceShip-Base.
❏ On the **Top** view, make two simple **Line** objects as shown in Fig. 5.4, *a*. They should have the same length and lie in the same direction — from the left to the right, in our case.
❏ Rename them Path1 and Path2, respectively.
❏ Select the SpaceShip-Base and assign the **Path Constraint** controller to it.

> Main menu → Animation → Constraints → Path Constraint
>
> Drag to Path1 and click the left mouse button.

The SpaceShip–Base will move to the start of the path. Start playback of the animation. It will move along the straight line!

When a **Constraints** controller is assigned, the control panel automatically toggles to the **Motion** view with the parameters of the controller. Set them according to Fig. 5.4, *b*.

Explanation

In the third lesson, we considered the similar LookAt Constraint in detail, so we will only discuss the features specific to Path Constraint here.

The **Add Path** and **Delete Path** buttons indicate that objects can move simultaneously along several paths. The **Weight** parameter controls the path the object will take at any specific moment. There is only one path in the list so far, and the **Weight** window is inactive.

The **%Along Path** parameter controls the object's position along the path. You can see that the spinner of this parameter is highlighted by red corners. This denotes that it is animated. Look at the time scale and notice two red rectangles — keys. By moving their position on the scale, you change when the motion starts and ends.

The **Follow** flag is used to turn an object corresponding to the direction of motion. The **Bank** flag is used to tilt like an airplane. The object's orientation during motion is determined by the the **Axis** group.

The **Allow Upside Down** flag allows the object to do just that.

The **Constant Velocity** flag makes the object move at a constant speed along the entire path. Otherwise, the distance between vertices dictates the speed: the shorter the distance, the slower the movement. It is not important in our case, because there are only two vertices.

The **Loop** flag allows an object to loop around a path only if the path is closed.

The **Relative** flag enables the object to retain its original position.

Add the second path by pressing the **Add Path** button and clicking with the left mouse button on the Path2 object. Things are a bit different now. The object will move at the same distance from both paths.

Let's make the object go from one path to the other:

❏ Go to the first frame of animation by pressing the <Home> key.

❏ Leave the weight of the first path equal to 50 and enter 0 for the second path (Fig. 5.4, *c*). Notice that the object moves to the start of the first path.

❏ Go to the last frame (<End> key), activate the recording of the animation by pressing the **Auto Key** button, and invert the path weights (Fig. 5.4, *d*).

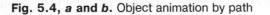

Fig. 5.4, *a* and *b*. Object animation by path

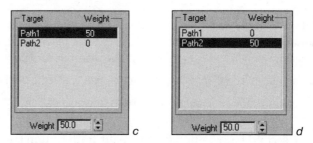

Fig. 5.4, c and d. Object animation by path

Note

Don't forget to deactivate the **Auto Key** button after the keys are set!

Play the animation, or simply move the slider. As you can see, the object smoothly goes from one path to the other.

You can change the object's trajectory by moving the paths and their vertices. By opening the curve editor and adjusting the Weight0 and Weight1 curves, you can get a steeper turn (Fig. 5.5). It is important that the object flies in front of the camera (i.e., the camera does not have to turn around its axis to see the action).

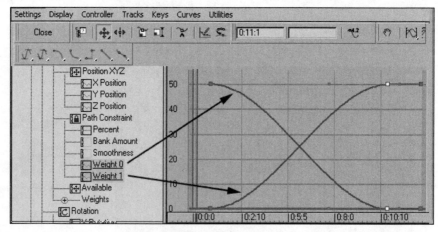

Fig. 5.5. Curve editor

The result of our work is on the CD–ROM in lesson05-02.max.

Camera Tracking

From the third lesson, you might realize that camera tracking of the spaceship can be performed using the **LookAt** controller. The task becomes a little bit complicated because the camera should initially show a panorama of space. This can be achieved by initially directing the camera at an invisible object and then using animation weights to turn and track the spaceship.

❏ Create a **Dummy** object on the grid plane (e.g., in the **Top** view) and rename it Camera–Target1 (Fig. 5.6, *a*).

❏ Select the camera and assign the **LookAt Constraint** to it:

> Main menu → Animation → Constraints → LookAt Constraint
>
> Drag to the Camera–Target1 and click the left mouse button.

❏ Set the controller so that the camera really faces the Camera–Target1 (Fig. 5.6, *b*). We will not try to explain all of these parameters, as it is the result that really matters.

❏ Add the StarShip-Base as another target by pressing the **Add LookAt Target** button and clicking the left mouse button on the object.

Play the animation. As you can see, the camera tracks a point somewhere in between the objects.

Further editing is similar to animating an object along a path. Using the weights and curve editor, make the camera track only the StarShip-Base starting with the fifth second (Fig. 5.6, *c*). To do this, you will have to **Add Keys** and adjust the curves. The **Tangents** are basically the same as **Handles** at the vertices of Bezier splines.

❏ **Close** the curve editor.

Now, animate the motion of the StarShip-Base starting from the fifth second.

❏ Select the StarShip-Base.

❏ Open the time scale context menu by clicking with the right mouse button. Show the **Selection Range:**

> Time scale context menu → Configure → Show Selection Range

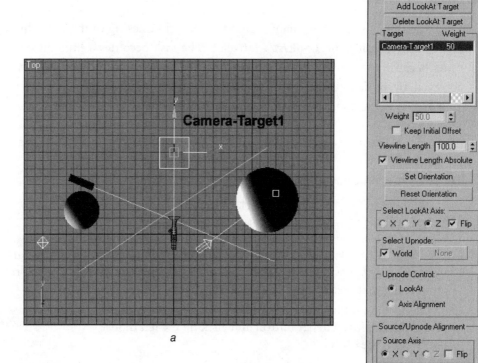

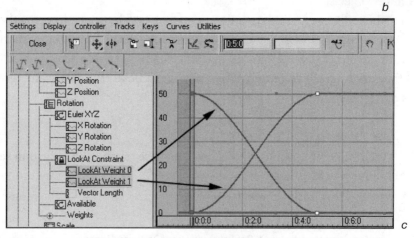

Fig. 5.6. Animation settings for camera tracking

❏ Select all the keys in the window, and drag the left square to the 0:5:0 frame (5 seconds) (Fig. 5.7). Notice that the spaces between the keys are scaled uniformly, which is exactly what we need.

Fig. 5.7. Editing the start of an object's motion

There is one more trick to perform. To accentuate the speed of the spaceship and the vastness of space, we should alter its size so that it is very small both at the start and at the end, then increase it to actual size as it approaches the camera. This is easy to do. Scale the object down to 1 percent by all coordinates (**Uniform Scale**) at the start of the motion. Use the **Auto Key** button to switch on the animation and go to the frame containing the closest approach. Scale the spaceship back to its original size and then reduce it again in the last frame. Finally, move the key that was automatically set to frame zero to the frame containing the start of the motion.

You can find our result in lesson05-03.max.

Creating and Assigning Materials and Effects

Let's begin with the stars. In this lesson, we decided not to use the automatic generation of a starry sky in order to demonstrate the most universal method to create the **Environment**, be it starry sky, city panorama, or marine view.

There are two spherical starry sky textures included in 3ds max — Stars10.jpg and Stars8.tif. The format of the first one (JPEG) compresses and degrades image quality and is therefore unacceptable in our case. The second file is better, because TIFF files do not degrade image quality.

▶ *Tip*

You can find similar files on the Internet (e.g., NASA websites). Be sure to look at the licensing agreement closely, for such files are not always free for commercial use.

This file should be touched up in a raster graphics editor. You will notice that the stars are dim and multicolored. If you saw the Stanley Kubrick film "2001: A Space Odyssey" — the most realistic science fiction movie on space exploration — you might have noticed that the stars are bright dots filling the entirety of space. Color is not important; only size and intensity matter. It is easy to achieve by adjusting contrast and color saturation in any 2D graphics editor.

We only need part of this file, because we will "pull" the texture over the area created by extrusion (**Extrude**) of the **Arc**. The vertical size will be determined by the **Amount** parameter of the **Extrude** modifier, but we need to know the width-to-height ratio of the arc to determine the horizontal size. How can we measure it?

We can use a special utility in 3ds max called **Measure**.

- Select the Stars object.
- Deactivate all modifiers, including **Extrude**, in the modifiers stack on the control panel by "turning off" the lamp to the left.
- Go to **Utilities** on the control panel while maintaining the selection.
- Press **Measure** to calculate the length of the **Shapes** group. (We have about 640 units.)

Activate the modifiers for the Stars object and calculate the **Amount** parameter of the **Extrude** modifier. (We have about 200 units.)

► *Tip*

Since we have already configured the animation, we can minimize the dimensions of the Stars object by moving it as required and changing the **Amount** parameter of the **Extrude** modifier, so that it perfectly fits within the camera view.

Now, we know the width-to-height ratio we need for the image. Based on that, cut out an area somewhere near the center. Since our sector slightly exceeds 180°, we used a piece measuring 1500 × 480 pixels.

You can make your own file, or use ours: Lessons\Lesson05\Scenes\stars.tif on the CD-ROM.

- Open the material editor, select any preview window, and rename the material Stars.

❏ Assign the Stars.tif file to the **Diffuse** texture channel.

❏ Set **Self-Illumination** to 100%.

❏ Make the material two-sided.

❏ Drag-and-drop the material on the Stars object and display the material in the viewports using the **Show Map in Viewport** button.

❏ To be on the safe side, deactivate shade casting and receipt from other light sources in the parameters of the Stars object:

    Context menu → Properties → General → Rendering Control → Receive Shadows and Cast Shadows

Now, it is time to discuss Motion Blur, which occurs when filming moving objects — "smear," as cinematographers call it. Using blur makes the image more realistic, but necessarily leads to a loss in sharpness. There are several methods for using blur in 3ds max. They can be divided into two groups: blur applied to objects and blur applied to the whole scene. Let's discuss them and choose the most suitable one for our scene.

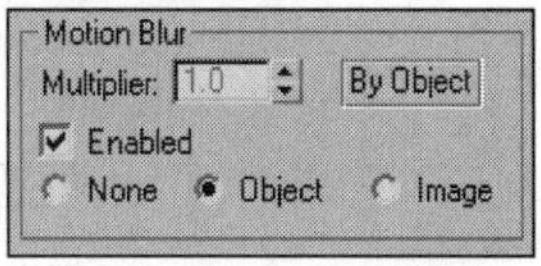

Object Motion Blur is the oldest, rooted in 3D Studio for DOS. When rendering, several copies of the object's image are shifted relative to each other (as a rule, the amount it would move during the course of a frame) and merged together. The drawbacks of this method are that the rendering time is considerably increased, and that the blur is applied to the object, not to its shadows or reflections. The advantage is that the object clearly intended will be blurred. To apply this method, adjust the parameters of the target object and check the appropriate flags in the rendering parameters (Fig. 5.8):

    Main menu → Rendering → Render → MAX Default Scanline A-Buffer → Object Motion Blur

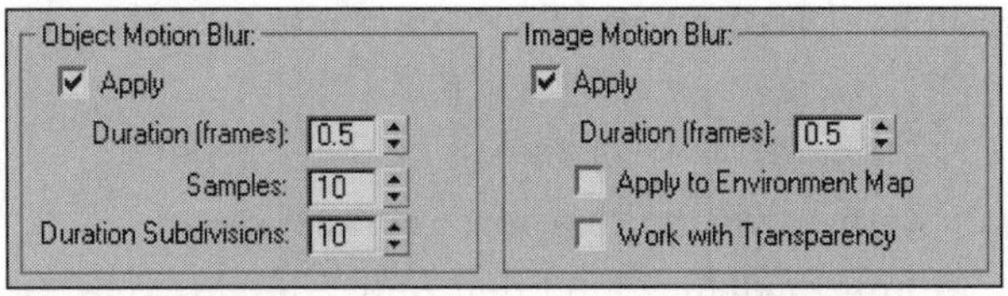

Fig. 5.8. Object Motion Blur and **Image Motion Blur** settings

Rendering **Image Motion Blur** takes much less time and gives higher quality results, when the motion of an object is more or less smooth. If the object makes sharp turns or simultaneously rotates, then you get nothing but an obscure mess. Moreover, when objects with this type of blur are overlapped, other unpleasant effects take place. In other respects, this method suffers the same drawbacks as **Object Motion Blur**. It is activated and employed in a similar way in the effects menu, mainly for quick adjustment.

When should we use these methods? They are primarily employed for objects that move quickly relative to a static or slowly moving camera.

▶ *Note*

We recently gave up explicitly using blur in 3ds max. The reason is that Rich Pixel Format (RPF) files can now record speed and direction data into a special Velocity channel for use in Discreet Combustion and better results in a shorter period of time. In addition, blurring the whole scene, either in Combustion or After Effects, makes the capability rather superfluous in any 3D package. Consideration of this and other techniques combining 3ds max and Combustion is beyond the scope of this book. However, if you really want to animate 3D graphics professionally, pay attention to it, especially since the price of the latest version (Combustion 2.1) is much lower than those of for previous versions and other professional video editing packages.

Our case is somewhat different. The camera actively rotates while tracking the spaceship, so we should not blur the whole scene.

3ds max has two types of "global" blur.

The first one uses the Video Post module during rendering. It is obsolete and therefore inappropriate for us to use. The module itself is not bad for some things, such as simple video editing, but we will not consider it further.

The second method appeared in the fourth version of 3ds max and is called **Multi-Pass Motion Blur**. It is the most resource-consuming method, but also the most "correct." We recommend that you use it.

❑ Switch to the camera view by pressing the <C> key.

❑ Select the camera via the viewport's context menu.

❑ Go to an intermediate frame that only contains stars (e.g., the 0:1:0 frame — 1 second).

❑ Make a **Quick Render** of the scene:

     Main panel → Quick Render (Production)

You should get a starry sky, a portion of which is shown in Fig. 5.9, *a*.

❒ In the camera parameters, **Enable** the **Multi-Pass Effect**, select **Motion Blur** in the drop-down menu, and make another quick rendering.

To tell you the truth, the result leaves something to be desired (Fig. 5.9, *b*).

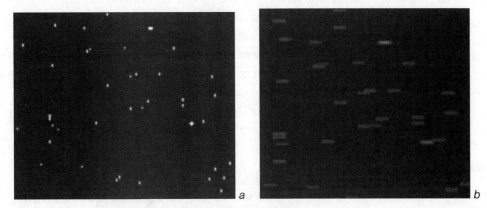

a   *b*

Fig. 5.9. Starry sky unblurred (a) and blurred (b)

3ds max is not to blame. It did what it's supposed to: blur the image by averaging the saturation values. This would work if, for example, we were looking at a mountain landscape. As for a starry sky in outer space, however, such a procedure is not appropriate. We could have done the same thing with bright and extruded lines.

This is a topic deserving more serious discussion. Computer images with "8 bits per channel" are composed of pixels with a brightness from 0 (corresponding to black) to 255 (corresponding to white). In reality, this range is much wider, reaching into the millions. In most cases, neither film nor videotape can handle such a range, but they can still show "flashes" from bright objects, such as stars — you likely have seen it many times. There are several methods to avoid this limitation, including High Dynamic Range Imaging (HDRI), but 3ds max does not support them without additional modules from third parties.

We attempted to solve this problem with the standard tools in 3ds max, but we gave up.

First, we tried using Lens Effects. Their name suggests effects performed on light entering the lens, but they are used for many purposes — we once managed to produce a very convincing fire with them. In this case, we decided to use the **Glow** effect on the Stars object. Turning off brightness, we tried to adjust them so that only parts of the object were glowing. Everything went OK! Our excitement quiclky ended, though. We tried rendering the last frames, when the Moon occupies most of the picture, and got a stray glow at the edge of the Moon. We initially decided to let it stand, because we can use depth cutoff (**Z-Buffer**) in the effect settings. Unfortunately, we still failed to obtain the desired result. Looking at the channels employed in 3ds max to create the effects, we discovered an unpleasant fact: When the channels are created, **Camera Motion Blur** is not taken into account. The **Render Effects Per Pass** flag in the multipass effects parameters was similarly useless, rendering the effects in the same way.

We wanted to give up blurring the stars completely, but something stopped us and, after greater consideration, we managed to find a solution!

Let's take a closer look:

❑ First of all, we decided to abandon blurring the whole scene in favor of blurring in-dividual objects. To do so, deactivate the **Enable** flag in the **Multi-Pass Effect**.

❑ Select the Earth, Moon, and StarShip-Base objects.

▶ *Tip*

You can do this quickly with the selection-by-name command: Press the <H> key, choose the objects while holding the <Ctrl> key, and press **Select**.

❑ Open the properties window for the objects:

Context menu → Properties

❑ Enable **Motion Blur** and use the **Object** type.

❑ Select the Stars object and go to its property window.

❑ Enable **Motion Blur** and use the **Image** type.

❑ Set the **Object Channel** parameter to 1 in the **G-Buffer** group.

❑ Ensure blur will be rendered in the parameters window:

Main menu → Rendering → Render → MAX Default Scanline A-Buffer → Object Motion Blur and Image Motion Blur → Apply

❏ Open the effects settings window:

   Main menu → Rendering → Effects

❏ Press the **Add** button and select **Lens Effects**. Rename the added effect **Lens Effects – Stars**. We will use at least one more lens effect to simulate the Sun later.

❏ Select **Glow** in the **Lens Effects Parameters** drop-down menu and transfer it from the left to the right window using the > button.

❏ Select the effect and specify the parameters shown in Fig. 5.10.

Fig. 5.10. Parameters for the effect

Explanation

- To apply changes to the settings, use the **Update Effect** button in the **Preview** group of the **Effects** menu. If your computer is powerful enough, you might want to check the **Interactive** flag, which will keep you from constantly pressing this button.

Move the time control slider to the frame where only stars are rendered (e.g., 0:1:0).

We should change the parameters in the order below.

On the **Glow Element** rollout, **Options** tab:

- Only check the **Image** type in the **Apply Element To** group.

- Check the **Object ID** flag for the **Image Source** and select the channel of the object. For the Stars object, we used channel 1, so the effect should only be applied to this object.

- Check the **Bright** flag in **Image Filters** and set the brightness to be used.

On the **Parameters** tab of the same rollout:

- Set a small value for the effect.

- The **Intensity** parameter must also be reduced from the default value.

- Make both colors white in the **Radial Color** group.

- Rename the effect Glow-Stars on the **Name** line.

On the **Lens Effects Globals** rollout, **Parameters** tab:

- Set a very small value for the **Size** of the effect. With such a value, the **Intensity** parameters have almost no effect.

The rest of the parameters are not used and can be left unchanged.

Since we started to create effects, we might as well create them for the Sun, too:

❑ Go to the frame starting the motion of the StarShip-Base. (Our frame is 0:5:0.) Position and resize the Sun (Dummy_Sun light source) and Earth objects so that both are fully visible in the camera view. If necessary, scale the Earth by all coordinates (Uniform Scale).

▶ Tip

Sometimes, it is worthwhile to display the so-called "safe frame" (Viewport context menu → Show Safe Frame). It will show the objects that will be included in final rendering.

❑ Create a new group of lens effects in the **Effects** window. We named it Lens Effects-Sun.

The parameters for these effects are slightly different and contain more elements. Before we proceed, let us briefly consider all of the different lens effects (Fig. 5.11):

❏ **Glow** is a halo around a bright object. You can see it everyday. (There is one around street lights in foggy weather.)

❏ **Ring** is also a halo, formed under the same conditions, but it is an atmosphere more than a lens effect.

❏ **Ray**, on the other hand, is related to optics and its imperfections. Sometimes, photographers use special filters to obtain this effect.

❏ **Auto Secondary** and **Manual Secondary** reflections are parasitic effects that form when light goes through the lenses of the camera. Sometimes, they appear as a polygon, depending on the aperture.

❏ **Star** extends streaks of light from bright spots. It is very effective on the surface of water, on snow, or to imitate fireworks.

❏ **Streak** is self-descriptive, often seen as a flash in photographs and movies.

Fig. 5.11. Lens effects

Which ones should we use?

We can use a halo for the Sun. Another halo can be used for the corona. To be completely honest, it is difficult to see the corona at such a distance in outer space without a filter, but we will create one for appearance. If we use blur, that implies using the camera with Rays and secondary reflections.

Setting the lens effects is a precise and interesting task, and describing all of its aspects could fill dozens of pages. If you know what you want to do, try making your own effects by combining several elements.

You can use our effect on the CD-ROM in Lessons\Lesson05\Plugcfg\ Lens Effect - Sun.lzv.

❏ Add another lens effect:

   Effects → Add → Lens Effect

❏ Load Lens Effect - Sun.lzv:

   Lens Effects Globals → Parameters → Load

❏ In the same menu, pick the light source for the effect (Dummy_Sun):

   Lens Effects Globals → Parameters → Pick Light

❏ By selecting an element of the effect on the list to the right, you can then edit its parameters.

► *Tip*

If you decided to make your own effect, create each element separately and add them gradually.

The first element in the list (we named it Sun Inner Glow) should give a bright, sharp disk (Fig. 5.12, *a*). We did so by setting a high **Intensity** of up to 200 and making the **Falloff Curve** steeper (Fig. 5.12, *b*):

   Glow Element → Parameters → Radial Color → Falloff Curve

We only assigned our elements to lights (not the image):

   Glow Element→ Options → Apply Element to

The next element — Sun Glow Crown — is set as previous elements except for a lower intensity, a slightly different falloff curve, and use of the **Noise** texture on the **Radial Color** channel, giving a blurred contour to the effect (Fig. 5.12, *c*). To do this, we transferred the texture from the "Map #1" button into a preview window of the material editor by inheritance (**Instance**), and set its parameters (Fig. 5.12, *d*).

The rest of the elements are just as easy to set. We finished with the effect shown in Fig. 5.12, *e.*

When effects (including lens effects) are used, it is important to recognize that they are applied from top to bottom, summing the individual intensity values along the way. Try to switch places of the Lens Effects-Stars and Lens Effects-Sun, and you'll get a hideous result.

❏ Save your version of the effect for use in the future.

a

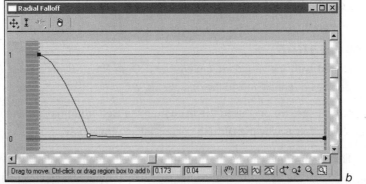

b

c

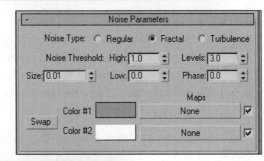

d

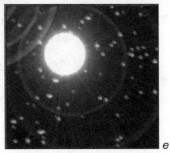

e

Fig. 5.12. Setting the lens effects simulating the Sun

We have now reached the materials for the Earth and the Moon.

The space.mat library of 3ds max contains materials for these celestial bodies. We used the Space_Moon material for the Moon. The only thing to do is to enhance the contrast of the Moon_Sun and make its light yellowish:

Control panel → ... → Advanced Effects → Contrast → 80   Contrast: [80.0]

We created our own material for the Earth, which does not require a light source.

The structure of that material is shown in Fig. 5.13, *a*.

Explanation

We started with the standard material and Oren-Nayar-Blinn shader (Fig. 5.13, *b*). This shader gives a "softer" feel to the object.

As you can see, we only used the texture on the **Self-Illumination** channel, where we also used color. This is why the **Diffuse** color is left neutrally gray.

The first texture level is of the **Falloff** type, with parameters that give a thin blue halo (Fig. 5.13, *c*). We used **Fresnel** as the attenuation type. This type is primarily used to simulate glass, but it also works in our case.

The Side channel was assigned a blue color, because it is responsible for the halo. The Front channel uses the same type of texture, but with different settings (Fig. 5.13, *d*). Towards/Away is used as the attenuating type, and Object defines the direction of attenuation (surfaces facing toward and away). Sun_Dummy is selected as the controlling object, and the mix curve was given non-linear attenuation.

Mix textures were assigned as sub-textures (Sub-Map) for the day and night sides of the Earth.

The day side (Fig. 5.13, *e*) consists of two sub-textures from raster images — EarthMap-Day.tga and CloudMap.tga — mixed with the CloudMap-Transp.tga texture.

The night side (Fig. 5.13, *f*) also consists of two sub-textures — EarthMap-Night.tga (where we tried to show the lights of big cities) and CloudMap.tga. Mixing is simply based on the **Mix Amount** parameter. Furthermore, the CloudMap.tga texture is darkened by reducing the **Output Amount** parameter (Fig. 5.13, *g*).

You can find our result in the lesson05-04.max file.

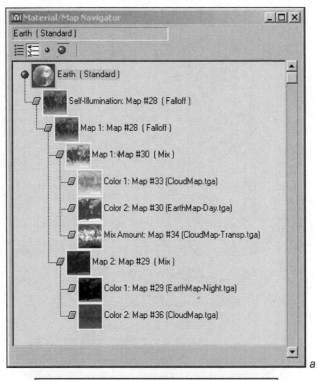

Fig. 5.13, *a* and *b*. Structure of the Earth material (*a*)
and parameters of its elements (*b*)

Fig. 5.13, *c* and **d.** Parameters of the Earth material elements

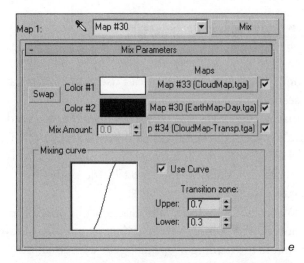

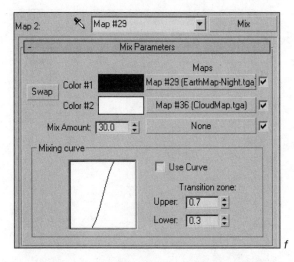

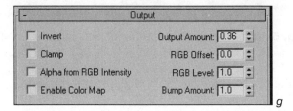

Fig. 5.13, *e–g*. Parameters of the Earth material elements

Final Assembly of the Scene

Now, all we have to do is **Merge** the spaceship we already created in the scene. Our file is lesson05(spaceship).max. You can use your own models and assemble them into your scene.

In preparing the lesson05(spaceship).max file, we loaded the spaceship and lunar module objects, docked them, and introduced another **Dummy** object called _SPACE SHIP. Names beginning with an underscore are very easy to select, coming first the list. We put this object in the center and linked (**Link**) all other objects to it.

We also included (**Include**) all objects of the spaceship in the list to be lit by the light sources (Fig. 5.14). In **Properties**, we activated **Object Motion Blur**. Do not forget to fold the landing props using the additional LUNAR SHIP parameter.

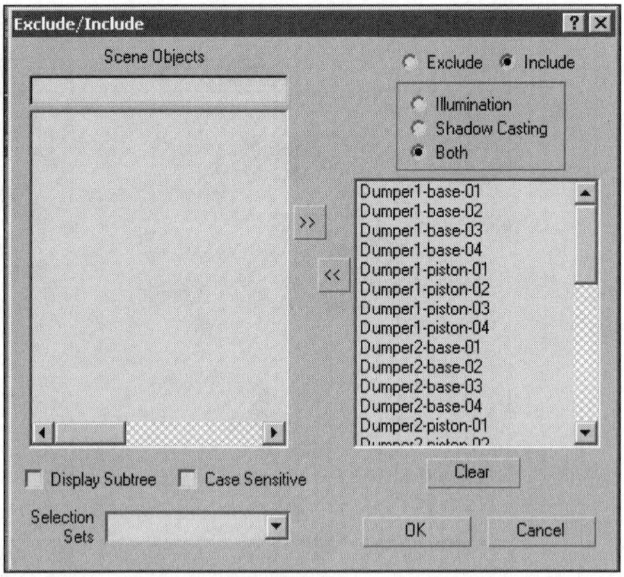

Fig. 5.14. Including all spaceship objects in the list of those to be lit by the light sources

Now, the scene is ready to be loaded into another one.

❏   **Merge** the lesson05(spaceship).max objects into your scene:

Main menu → File → Merge

❑ Select the _SPACE SHIP object, adjust its size (adjusting the size of all linked objects in the process), and position it in accordance with the StarShip-Base object.

▶ *Tip*

Do this in the **Top** view at the frame corresponding to the closest approach to the camera.

❑ Adjust the **Hotspot/Beam** and **Falloff/Field** parameters of the Direct01_Sun_SpaceShip and Direct02_Moon_SpaceShip light sources so that only the spaceship is lit. Move these sources to a position approximately corresponding to light from the Sun and the Moon.
❑ Link the _SPACE SHIP object to the SpaceShip-Base object, and **Hide** the SpaceShip–Base.

❗ *Do it yourself*

Move the solar panels and antenna so that they face the Sun and the Earth, respectively. To do this, you will have to **Detach** these objects, adjust their pivot points, and make them **LookAt** the right direction. Don't forget to link them back to the station!

Now, everything is ready for rendering! You can make test renderings of separate frames by pressing the **Quick Render (Production)** button.

The "great mystery" of 3D graphics will thus begin. The idea is to obtain the desired result (the reel) in a reasonable amount of time. This does not always happen. We encountered some problems; the main one is described below.

Using **Object Motion Blur** and **Ray Traced Shadows** at the same time leads to unreasonably long rendering. There are two solutions. One is to give up **Object Motion Blur** in favor of **Image Motion Blur**. This would considerably reduce image quality. The Stars object already uses **Image Motion Blur**, and when two objects with this type of blur are merged, undesirable side effects occur. The other option is to sacrifice **Ray Traced Shadows** in favor of a large **Shadows Map** and slight blur. We chose the second way, justifiably assuming that few people will notice fuzzy shadows in general blur.

There are a few more aspects you should discover for yourself. Lesson05-final.max should help.

Lesson 6

Modeling and Animating the Landing on the Moon

Landing on the Moon consists of two fragments. The first one is the approach of the lunar module to the surface of the Moon, viewed by a camera on the lunar module. The second is the actual landing.

Approach of the Lunar Module to the Moon

The scene shown in Fig. 6.1 should be constructed for this fragment.

It took us about half an hour to make this scene, animate it, and set up the effects. You can load the lesson06(part1).max file from the CD-ROM in the Lessons\Lesson06\Scenes\ folder and check out our version. Below is a description that will help if you wish to repeat the creation process.

▶ **Note**

You may encounter difficulties when loading the file. You probably will be warned that some modules are missing. This is because we used several effects-scripts included in 3ds max for final rendering. To use these effects constantly, you must add their paths into the list of 3ds max paths to additional modules (**Plug-Ins**). You can do this by editing the Plugins.ini file or by adding the paths directly into 3ds max. We used scripts from the \3dsmax5\scripts\PluginScripts\ folder (Fig. 6.2):

Main menu → Customize → Configure Paths → Plug-Ins → Add

Then you must restart 3ds max.

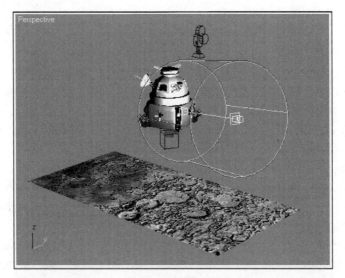

Fig. 6.1. Scene for the approach of the lunar module

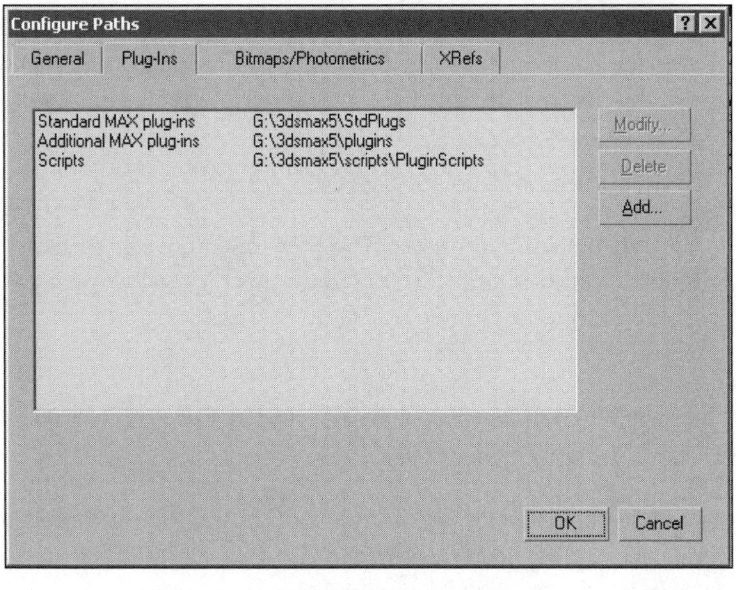

Fig. 6.2. Configure Paths window

First, specify the time parameters. This is done in the same way as in the previous lesson. Set the picture frequency to 15 frames per second (i.e., 120 frames). In general, the SMPTE format is a matter of preference.

There is no modeling in this part because you will be creating an environment.

☐ Create a **Plane** object on the **Top** or **Perspective** view. Use dimensions corresponding to those of the image in the moon-surface.tga file (600 × 1200 pixels) on the CD-ROM in the \Lessons\Lesson06\Scenes folder (Fig. 6.3, *a*).

☐ Rename the object **Moon Surface**.

☐ Open the material editor, select any preview window (**Material Slot**), and rename the material **Moon Surface**.

☐ Set the texture from the Moon-Surface.tga file on the **Diffuse** channel. There is no alpha-channel in the texture, and the default settings are satisfactory.

☐ In the parameters of the material, specify **Self-Illumination** equal to 100% (Fig. 6.3, *b*). The type of **Shader** does not matter; this object will not be lit.

☐ Activate the texture and material display in the viewport (**Show Map in Viewport**). Assign the material on the **Moon Surface** using the drag-and-drop technique.

The surface of the Moon is ready!

☐ **Merge** the lunar module with the scene. You can use our lesson06(lunar-ship).max file in the \Lessons\Lesson06\Scenes folder or create your own:

Main menu → File → Merge

Select all objects in the list and press OK.

☐ Create a **Free** camera on the **Top** view and move it so that part of the lunar module is within sight. It is easy to do this on the **Perspective** view by controlling the position on the camera view.

▶ *Tip*

For the camera view, it is useful to activate the safe frame display (Viewport context menu → Show Safe Frame).

☐ Turn and move the lunar module so that the logo is within the camera view. Make the landing props visible, too.

☐ **Link** the camera with the **LUNAR SHIP** object.

☐ Select the **LUNAR SHIP** object. Raise it and all the objects linked with it above the surface of the Moon until the **Moon Surface** appears, with a little space, within the camera view. Don't forget to fold the props using the additional **Custom Attributes** of the **LUNAR SHIP**.

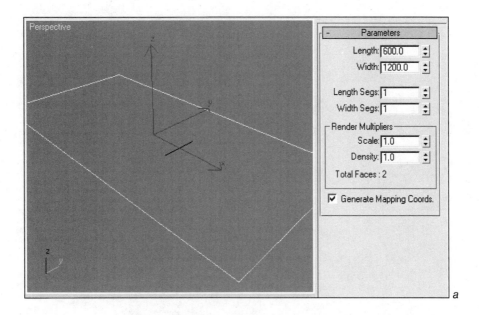

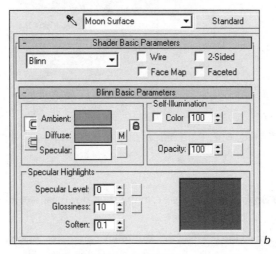

Fig. 6.3. Modeling the Moon's surface

❏ Create a **Directional** light source and rename it **Sun**. Configure and position it so only the objects of the lunar module are in the lit area. The parameters of this source are shown in Fig. 6.4.

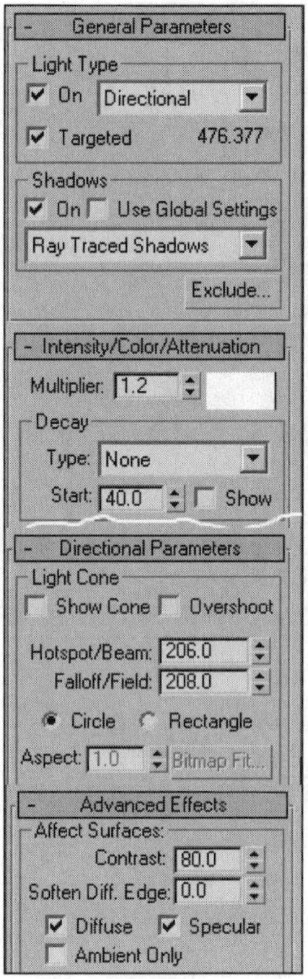

Fig. 6.4. Parameters of the light source for the lunar module

▶ *Tip*

Check the **Shadows On** flag. From the drop-down list, select **Ray Traced Shadows**; their use is relevant in this case.

Slightly increase the value of the **Multiplier** parameter. Also increase the **Contrast**.

Position only the lunar module within the lit area using the **Hotspot/Beam**.

Exclude the **Moon-Surface** object from lit objects using the **Exclude** button.

The animation is also easy to do. There is no need to animate the lunar module; it is easier and more correct to animate the Moon surface relative to the lunar module.

☐ Move the **Moon-Surface** in the zero frame so that only one side is within the camera view.

☐ Go to the last frame, press the animation-recording button (**Auto Key**), and move the **Moon-Surface** relative to the camera.

Play your animation in the camera viewport. As you see, the motion for the surface of the Moon smoothly starts and stops. But we also want the motion to be linear. To create this, we have to change the type of the keys.

☐ Open the **Mini Curve Editor**. By default, all three animated tracks of the selected object are chosen. In our case, these three tracks are for positioning (**Position**) by three coordinates.

☐ Select the keys of all three curves and press the **Set Tangents to Linear** button in the control panel (Fig. 6.5).

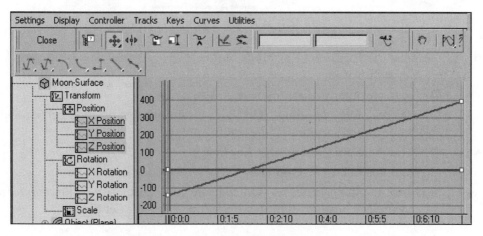

Fig. 6.5. Editing the animation curves

▶ *Note*

If a required button is not in the control panel of the **Mini Curve Editor**, display the **Key Tangents: Track View** panel:

Mini Curve Editor → right chick in the main menu → Show Toolbars → Key Tangents: Track View

☐ Close the **Mini Curve Editor** and deactivate the **Auto Key** button.

Animate the unfolding of the landing props — it really makes an impression! To do this, an additional **Off__Landing__On** parameter should be animated (**Custom Attributes**).

☐ Select the **LUNAR SHIP** object.
☐ Press the **Key Filters** button in the animation control panel to open the **Set Key Filters** window. Check the flag for **Custom Attributes** only (Fig. 6.6).

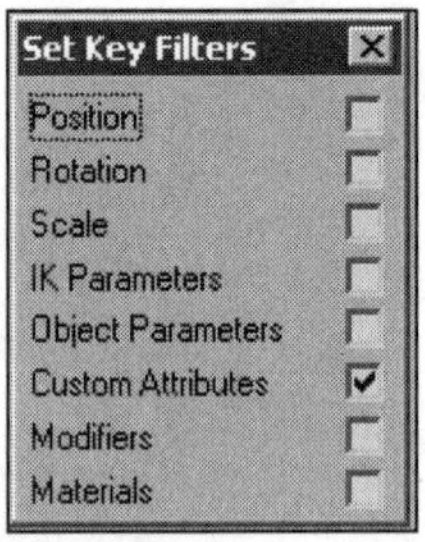

Set Key Filters	☒
Position	☐
Rotation	☐
Scale	☐
IK Parameters	☐
Object Parameters	☐
Custom Attributes	☑
Modifiers	☐
Materials	☐

Fig. 6.6. Set Key Filters window

☐ Press the **Toggle Set Key Mode** button. (This is its full name; only **Set Key** is displayed.) 
☐ Go to any intermediate frame (e.g., 4 seconds).
☐ Move the **Off__Landing__On** slider to the leftmost position corresponding to the "retracted" position of the landing props.
☐ Press the button with the **Set Key** image.

☐ Go to the frame corresponding to the sixth second of animation.
☐ Move the **Off__Landing__On** slider to the rightmost position corresponding to extended position of the landing props. Press the **Set Key** button.

Play the animation in the camera viewport. The landing props should unfold.

This could be the end of this fragment, but we propose that you to another feature of 3ds max — freehand drawing of animation curves. So far, this feature is unavailable in any other 3D package or video editors. Frankly speaking, when we first discovered this feature, we were unsure of its purpose and where it could be used. Gradually, we found many areas for its application. Here we want to describe one of them to you.

The landing of the lunar module entails inevitable errors corrected by the orientation engines. It is possible to simulate these adjustments by applying an animation controller of the **Noise** type to the rotation of the object. We will do so in the next lesson to simulate the jolting of the lunar rover moving on an uneven surface. In this lesson, though, we propose that you to use the freehand drawing of the animation curves.

☐ Select the **LUNAR SHIP** object and open the curve editor. You can open it in a separate window:

    Context menu → Curve editor

☐ Select the **X Rotation** track of the rotation controller. While there is no curve yet, the value of this parameter is shown as a hatched line in the editor.

☐ Draw a curve using the **Draw Curves** tool. Its amplitude must not exceed 2-3 degrees (i.e., points on the vertical axis) (Fig. 6.7, *a*).

☐ There will be too many keys. You can "thin" them out using the **Reduce Keys** command (Fig. 6.7, *b*).

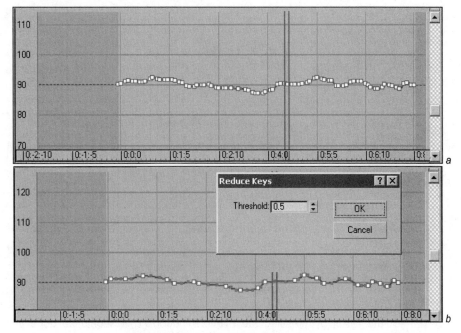

Fig. 6.7. Drawing animation curves

❏ Draw the curves for rotation around the Y axis (**Y Rotation**).

Play the animation. You'll see a slight image tremor on the camera view — this is what we need.

If the amplitude turned out to be too large, you can reduce it by selecting all keys and using the **Scale Values** tool.

The animation is ready!

To enhance realism, we propose that you apply several effects to it.

First, use the **Depth of Field** (DOF) effect. There are three methods of implementing this effect in 3ds max.

▶ Note

As with blur, the use of the DOF effect in a 3D package is justified only when there is no video editor at hand. The same principle applies to effects.

One of these effects can be adjusted and applied in the **Effects** window, whereas the other one is used in the Video Post module. Frankly speaking, the results of both effects aren't worth discussing. Their only advantage is quick rendering, but we still want to dissuade you from using them.

We propose that you use the slowest but most correct method: the **Camera Multi-Pass Effect**.

❏ Select the camera and set the **Depth of Field** parameters as shown in Fig. 6.8.

❗ Explanation

Activate the **Depth of Field** effect.

Deactivate the **Render Effects Per Pass** flag. This will considerably increase the speed of final rendering.

Increase the camera **Target Distance** near the Moon surface.

Using the **Total Passes** and **Sample Radius** parameters to obtain a slight blur of the lunar module. We found that six passes will suffice for the desired effect. Check the result by pressing the **Preview** button. This should be done in the camera viewport.

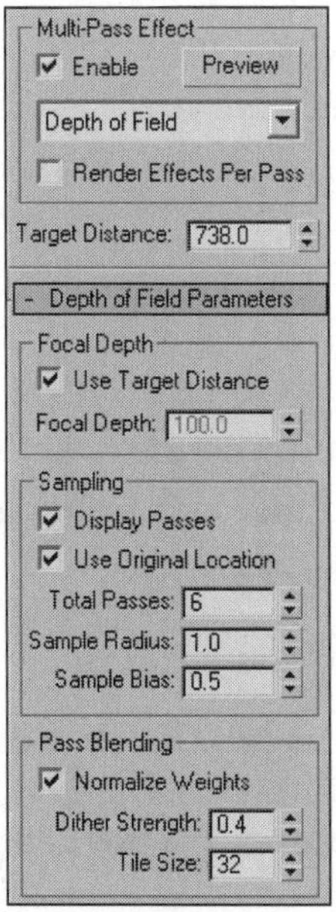

Fig. 6.8. Multi-Pass Effect for the Depth of Field

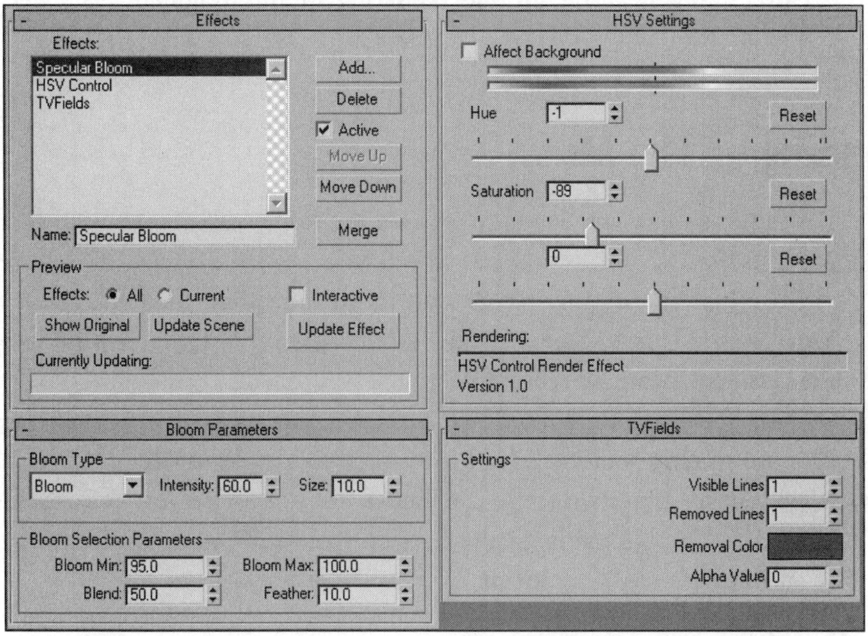

Fig. 6.9. Parameters for the effects to simulate a TV camera

There still are several effects to add that simulate shooting with a TV camera for a TV monitor. To do this, we used several effects-scripts with the parameters shown in Fig. 6.9. Try to experiment with them; it is quite possible that your result will be better than ours:

Main menu → Rendering → Effects

If you included the path to these scripts as recommended at the beginning of the lesson, you will find them in the list of effects. Otherwise, you must start the scripts. They are in the \3dsmax5\scripts\PluginScripts\ folder:

Main menu → MAXScript → Run Script

Note

In the text of the TVFields script we found and corrected an inaccuracy that led to a redundant line at the top of the image. In the line `for j = 1 to img.height do` we substituted 1 for 0. To do so, we opened the RenderEffect-TVFields.ms script (Main menu → MAXScript → Open Script), changed its value, then saved and restarted the script.

Everything is ready for the rendering of this fragment. The details of the rendering parameters are given in *Lesson 8*.

Landing on the Moon

For this fragment, you will have to build the scene with the rendering result shown in Fig. 6.10.

The building of this scene took more time than that of the previous one. You can find our scene in the lesson06(part2).max file on the CD-ROM in the Lessons\Lesson06\Scenes\ folder.

First the moonscape must be created. You can create it as a single object, but we propose another solution. There is no need to make everything "life-like." Detail is important for objects close to the viewer but not for remote objects. If you don't plan to reach mountains on the horizon, you don't have to create them life-size at such a distance — reducing them will do. Various methods (e.g., configuring the textures) can make the viewer believe that the mountains are really high and remote.

Fig. 6.10. Scene for the Moon landing

► *Tip*

To estimate the scale correctly, create an object (e.g., **Box**) at the coordinate origin with the approximate dimensions of the lunar module (e.g., 5 × 5 × 5 meters). It is convenient to do this by entering the dimensions from the keyboard. 3ds max supports automatic conversion of the units: Enter the dimensions as 5m, and 3ds max will convert them into the current units.

Length:	196.85	⬍
Width:	196.85	⬍
Height:	5m	⬍
	Create	

Create an object to simulate the mountains on the horizon; we named our object **Mountains**. We propose using a **Compound Object** of **Terrain** type, which provides surfaces by curves. The main purpose of this object is to build terrains using isolines of equal heights. We use it slightly differently.

❐ Make two concentric circles on the **Top** view — the **Donut** type will do. Make the radius of the internal ring approximately 100 m, and the external one 300 m (Fig. 6.11, *a*).

❐ Create intermediate forms for future "ridges" and "ravines" between the internal and external circumferences using **Line** curves. Make more intermediate vertices!

❐ **Attach** all lines to one.

| Attach |

❏ Select all vertices and **Smooth** them:

Context menu → Smooth

❏ Apply the **Noise** modifier (Fig. 6.11, *b*):

Main menu → Modifiers → Parametric Deformers → Noise

❏ Convert the object to an **Editable Spline** and work out the vertex level. In particular, move the extreme vertices closer to the zero level of the future terrain.

▶ *Tip*

Use **Soft Selection**.

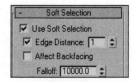

Select the **Donut01** object and split it into many segments. It is convenient to do this using the **Normalize Spline** modifier. To control the process, use the **Edit Spline** modifier on the level of vertices (Fig. 6.11, *c*):

Main menu → Modifiers → Patch/Spline Editing → Normalize Spline, Edit Spline

Now, everything is ready for the terrain creation.

❏ Select the **Donut01** object, toggle the control panel to object creation mode (**Create**), and make the **Compound Object** of **Terrain** type:

Control panel → Create → Geometry → Compound Objects → Terrain

Press the Pick Operand button and click the left mouse button on the object-lines forming the terrain.

❏ Toggle the control panel to edit mode (**Modify** tab) and specify the parameters as shown in Fig. 6.11, *d*.

▼ *Explanation*

Rename the object **Mountains**.

After you turn to **Sub-object** editing and select the operand from the list, you can edit the operand by moving down the stack. This feature is typical for most compound objects.

Select the **Graded Surface** type in the **Form** group.

In the **Simplification** group, select a value making the mesh of the object more or less uniform. This is important for further smoothing.

Leave the rest of the parameters unchanged. Try to find out yourself what they are intended for. (This is easy.)

The result is a rather crude model. Let's complicate it and smooth it a little. In general, you can use the **MeshSmooth** modifier, but this provides a regular mesh.

We propose using the Hierarchical SubDivision Surfaces (**HSDS**) modifier. This modifier lets you perform *adaptive splitting*.

❏ Apply the **HSDS Modifier**:

Main menu → Modifiers → Subdivision Surfaces → HSDS Modifier

❏ Apply adaptive splitting to the object with the parameters shown in Fig. 6.11, *e*:

Control panel → ... → Advanced Options → Adaptive Subdivision

Explanation

Three settings offered by the developers were not useful to us, so we substituted them for **Custom** settings.

We set the maximal level of splitting, or detail to 3 (**Max. LOD**), which is enough.

By setting the maximal value in the **Length** parameter, we determine the minimal length of the edges for which splitting can be done and avoid splitting the known flat planes.

We set a small value for the **Angle** parameter to determine the minimal angle between the planes for which splitting can be done.

The mountains are ready (Fig. 6.11, *f*).

We propose modeling the part of the terrain closest to the viewer using **Displacement**. To do so, use the **Plane** primitive and the texture on the **Displace** channel.

Note

We considered this process in detail in our book "3ds max 4: From Objects to Animation."

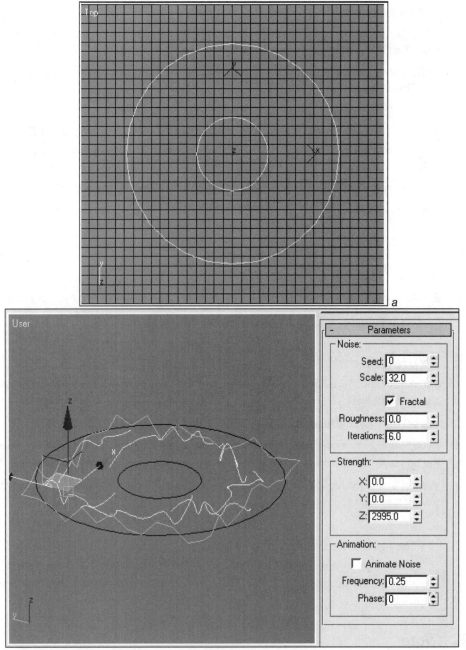

Fig. 6.11, *a* and *b*. Modeling mountains on the horizon

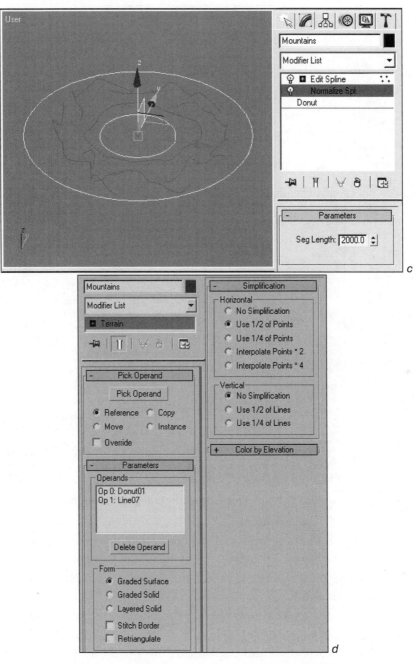

Fig. 6.11, c and d. Modeling mountains on the horizon

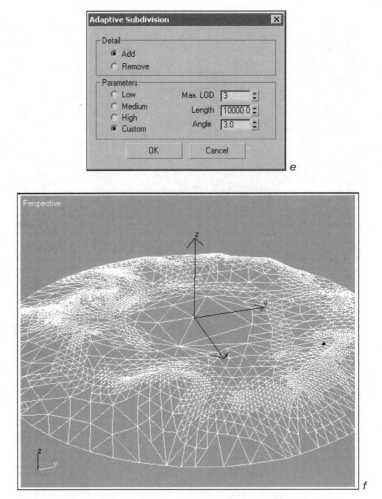

Fig. 6.11, _e_ and _f._ Modeling mountains on the horizon

❏ Create the **Plane** primitive at the coordinate origin with the approximate dimensions of 200 × 200 meters. To do this, use the keyboard (Fig. 6.12, *a*).

❏ In the object's parameters, check the **Generate Mapping Coords** flag and rename it **Ground**.

❏ Open the material editor (<M> key) and select any preview window.

❏ Specify the raster image (**Bitmap**) as the **Displacement** map in the **Maps** rollout. Select the Land-displace.tga file on the CD-ROM in the \Lessons\ Lesson06\Scenes folder.

❗ *Explanation*

Although the displacement texture may have any color depth, it is more convenient to use an image made in 256 grayscale (**Grayscale**). The brighter areas will be those with greater convexity; the darker areas will be those with deeper indention. Note that when the chart of vertices is created, the zero level is marked with a gray, not black, color. This will be helpful as you draw convex and concave figures on the surface.

☐ Assign the material to the object.

So far, you cannot see your terrain in the viewport. To do this, it is necessary to apply the **Displace Mesh** modifier. The application of the **Displacement** map is mainly intended for the object's complication during rendering. We need it to use the terrain at full resolution in the viewports.

☐ Apply the **Displace Mesh** modifier:

Control panel → Modifier List → Displace Mesh

☐ Specify the parameters so the object corresponds to the chart of vertices. Don't forget that you will place the camera in immediate proximity to the surface, so it is necessary to obtain the best quality possible (Fig. 6.12, *b*).

It will be helpful to select the parameters of the modifier and of the material on the **Perspective** view next to the pivotal object created at the beginning. For example, we reduced the height of the displacement by setting the level value (**Amount**) to 50 in the material's parameters. To follow changes in the viewport, it is necessary to press the **Update Mesh** button in the parameters of the **Displace Mesh** modifier.

After the parameters of the **Displace Mesh** modifier are specified, convert the object to the base **Editable Mesh** type. To do this, open the modifiers' stack context menu by clicking the right mouse button on the **Displace Mesh Binding** modifier in the stack and by selecting the **Collapse To** command. Remove the texture from the **Displace** channel; we don't need it anymore.

Before modeling, we looked through the photographs of the Moon's surface. We could see pebbles of various sizes densely covering the surface. Let us also "scatter" a couple of dozen of pebbles of various sizes. To do this, we propose using another compound object — **Scatter**.

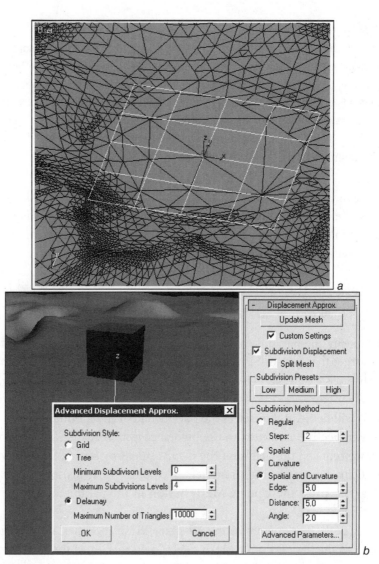

Fig. 6.12. Terrain blanks (*a*) and parameters of the **Displace Mesh** modifier (*b*)

❑ Create a pebble. This is a simple geosphere with the approximate diameter of 0.5 m rumpled with the **Noise** modifier (Fig. 6.13, *a*).

❑ Create a compound object (**Compound Objects**) of the **Scatter** type, keeping the selection on, with the parameters shown in Fig. 6.13, *b*:

Control panel → Create → Geometry → Compound Objects → Scatter

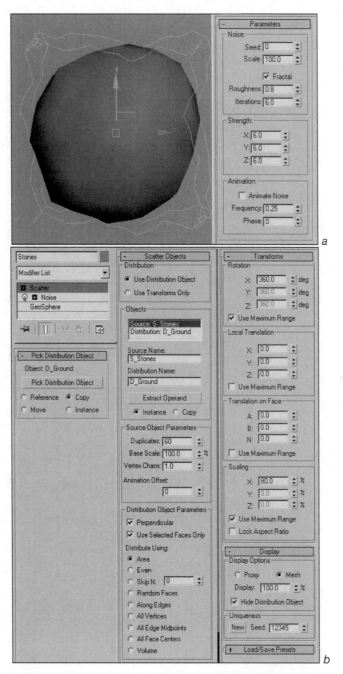

Fig. 6.13. Creation of pebbles on the Moon's surface

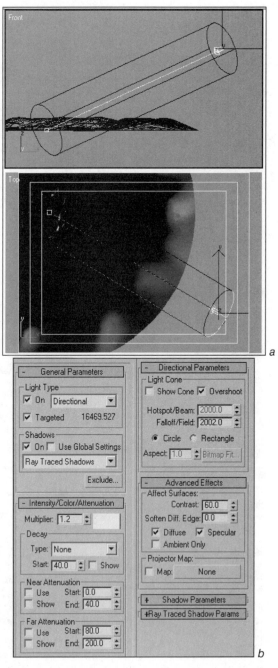

Fig. 6.14. Position (*a*) and parameters (*b*) of the light source

Explanation

In the **Pick Distribution Object** rollout, set the toggle in the **Copy** position to keep the original object independent. (It will still be of use.) Select the **Ground** object as the one the pebbles will be "scattered" on.

Set the number of copies (**Duplicates**) to about 60.

Use the **Vertex Chaos** parameter to obtain inequality of the pebbles.

Set the **Distribute Using** toggle in the **Area** position.

The **Use Selected Faces Only** flag restricts the distribution area. To use it, select the planes of the objects on the surface of which the pebbles will be distributed. You can do this before creating the **Scatter** object or directly within it. Go down the stack to the level of the sub-objects — operands and select the **D_Ground** operand. Go down the stack, select the required polygons, then go back to the **Use Selected Faces Only** level under the **Scatter** object.

In the **Transforms** rollout, specify the values for rotating and scaling the distributed object. This will diversify the appearance of the pebbles even more.

Deactivate the display of the **D_Ground** object in the **Display** rollout (**Hide Distribution Object** flag).

Now it is time to go for the materials. But first you must set a source of light (to simulate the Sun) and the camera.

☐ Set the source of light as shown in Fig. 6.14, *a*. Specify its parameters according to Fig. 6.14, *b*.

Explanation

The type of the source is **Targeted Directional**.

The type of shadows is **Ray Traced** (with value of the **Multiplier** slightly bigger than the default); the color is yellowish. Set the **Falloff/Field** parameter so that the central part of the terrain is within its view. The shadows are appropriate here.

The **Overshoot** flag will light all objects despite the **Falloff/Field** value, but there will be no shadows. The surface is quite even, so nobody should notice their absence, and you will save hours at the final rendering.

Increase the **Contrast** to 60.

❏ Create the **Target Camera** on the **Top** view and position it so that the object substituting the lunar module is within the view. The target of the camera must be in the center of the object (Fig. 6.15, *a* and *b*). Use the **Safe Frame**.

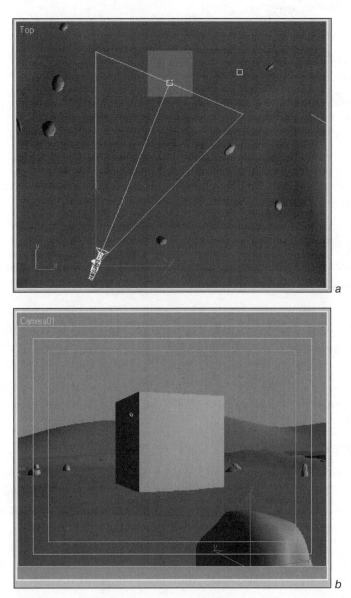

a

b

Fig. 6.15. Camera position (*a*) and the camera view (*b*)

> ### *Tip*
> Create and place a big pebble on the foreground; it will provide an additional feeling of depth.

The **Ground and Stones** material of the foreground objects should create the illusion of an uneven surface covered with a layer of dust. The material of the mountains should create the illusion that the mountains are far from the viewer. Unfortunately, there is no atmosphere on the Moon. Therefore, we cannot apply the standard method — haze.

All textures for these materials will be procedural. During the setting of the materials, you will have to perform many test renderings, but it can't be helped; the procedural textures are displayed incorrectly in the viewports.

☐ The material structure for the **Ground and Stones** object is shown in Fig. 6.16, *a*.

❗ *Explanation*

Select a shader of the **Oren-Nayar-Blinn** type. Leave the default — gray — color (Fig. 6.16, *b*). In addition, make the **Specular** color gray, but lighter. This will help you to avoid certain troubles with the **Oren-Nayar-Blinn** shader type.

Apply the texture of the **Splat** type on the **Bump** channel. Change the color of the texture to black-and-white. Select a size that shows rounded convexities in the foreground during rendering (Fig. 6.16, *c*). Apply texture of the **Noise** type on the channel for one of the colors. Select a size and type that achieves the illusion of dust during rendering (Fig. 6.16, *d*).

Reduce to 10 the level of the texture affection (**Amount**) on the **Bump** channel in the parameters of the materials. Transfer this texture to the **Roughness** channel using the **Instance** method and reduce the **Amount** parameter for this channel to 20. This will help you to obtain an uneven surface.

The material for the **Mountains** object is based on the previous material. Transfer the **Ground and Stones** material in any free preview window of the material editor and rename it **Mountains**.

The structure of the material is shown in Fig. 6.17, *a*.

❗ *Explanation*

In the main parameters of the material, make the colors on all channels lighter and yellowish to create illusion of depth (Fig. 6.17, *b*).

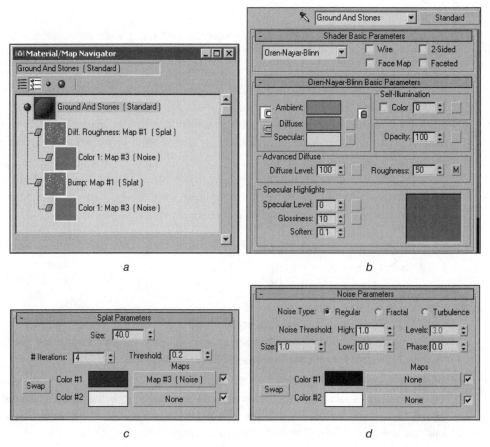

Fig. 6.16. Ground and Stones material structure (*a*), material parameters (*b*), and texture parameters (*c* and *d*)

Apply the procedural texture of the **Smoke** type on the **Bump** channel and select the size to obtain mountain ridges (Fig. 6.17, *c*).

Transfer the same texture on the **Roughness** and **Diffuse Color** channels and set the **Amount** values for these channels at 20 and 5, respectively.

Note

Do it better, if you can! Don't forget to experiment; this is the only way to master the minute details of 3D animation.

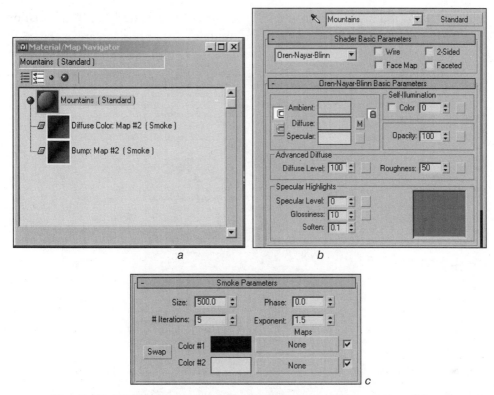

Fig. 6.17. Mountains material structure (*a*), material parameters (*b*),
and texture parameters (*c*)

Now, it is time to merge the lunar module into the scene. You can use either our Lesson06(Lunar-Ship).max file in the \Lessons\Lesson06\Scenes folder, or your own module:

Main menu → File → Merge

Select all objects in the list and press OK.

Remove the pivotal object (**Box01**). Place the lunar module by selecting the **LUNAR SHIP** object and moving it.

Move and rotate the **LUNAR SHIP** object to make it steady on its props and a little bit buried in the "lunar dust".

When the lunar module is on the surface, we should not neglect the glow from reflected light on the surface. To simulate such light, place several omnidirectional, low-powered light sources (**Omni**) under the surface — without shadows and affection on the flash channel (**Specular**) of the material. Set attenuation (**Far Attenuation** parameter) so that no mountains on the horizon are lit (Fig. 6.18).

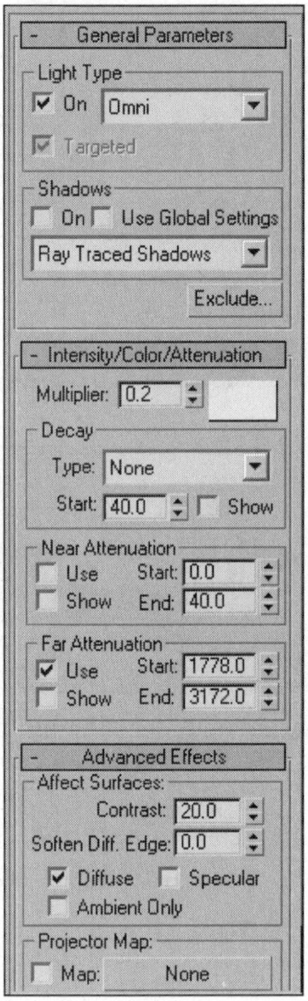

Fig. 6.18. Parameters for simulating
the light reflected by the Moon's surface

Now, the time for animation has come.

❒ Specify the parameters of the time scale. Set the picture frequency to 15 frames per second and the length to 12 seconds.

❒ **Link** the target of the camera with the **LUNAR SHIP** object to make the camera follow the lunar module.

The scene appears rather ponderous. To avoid troubles, it is better to simplify it by hiding some of the objects.

❑ Select the **Mountains**, **Stones**, and **Living Module** objects, then hide them:

Context menu → Hide Selection

❑ Select the **Ground** object on the **Top** view. (This object is of the **Editable Mesh** type.) Select the polygons inside the landing site, invert the selection (<Ctrl>+<I>), and hide them:

Control panel → Hide

Now the position of the lunar module corresponds to the final one. It would be unreasonable to set it anew.

❑ Open the **Set Key Filters** window and select the **Position** and **Custom Attributes** flags (Fig. 6.19). These parameters will be animated. There is no need to set the animation keys for the others.

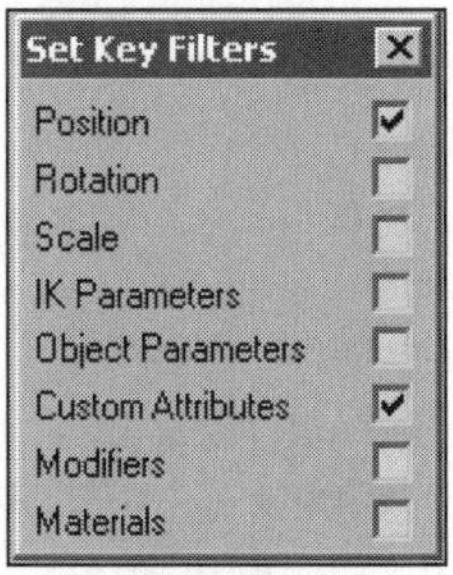

Fig. 6.19. Set Key Filters window

❑ Go to the frame **0:9:0** (9 seconds), press the **Toggle Set Key Mode** button, and set the key (**Set Key** button).
❑ Go to the start frame of the animation and raise the lunar module above the Moon surface. Extend the props slightly using the additional attribute of the **LUNAR SHIP** object, and set the key again.
❑ Edit the curves to make the module lose height as it gradually slows down and to make the landing props extend completely at the moment they touch the surface (Fig. 6.20).

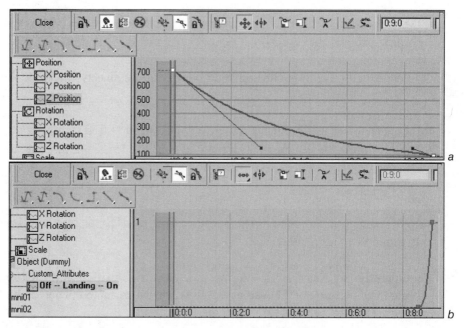

Fig. 6.20. Editing the motion curves of the object (*a*) and the extension of the landing props (*b*)

❗ *Do it yourself*

Experiment with the animation curves of other parameters. For example, you can specify the module's search path during the landing by drawing the keys on the rotation curves in the way it was done in the previous fragment.

Now, all we have to do is to add "luster" to the scene.

During the flight of an interplanetary station, the exhaust jets of the mid-flight engines would be unavailable. (The engines would start up only at the acceleration and at the moment of placement on the required orbit.) During the landing, however, the engines of the lunar module would work at full power. At the approach to the surface of the Moon, these jets would "blow" the dust off the lunar ground in the landing site. But realistically, smoke or clouds of dust cannot be created in our scene because there is no atmosphere on the Moon, only cosmic cold and vacuum.

We suggest making both of these effects — the engine reactions and the scattered dust and pebbles — using the particle system. Begin by creating the jet from the nozzle of the lunar module engine.

► *Tip*

To simplify the task of setting the particle system, make it in a separate file. We will show you how to work efficiently in one scene.

It is convenient to find all objects in the scene. You already have hidden some objects. To unhide only those required, it is worth creating a named set for these objects (**Named Selection Set**).

❑ Select all visible objects and create the set by naming it (e.g., **_MAIN OBJECT**):

> Main panel → Named Selection Set + Enter

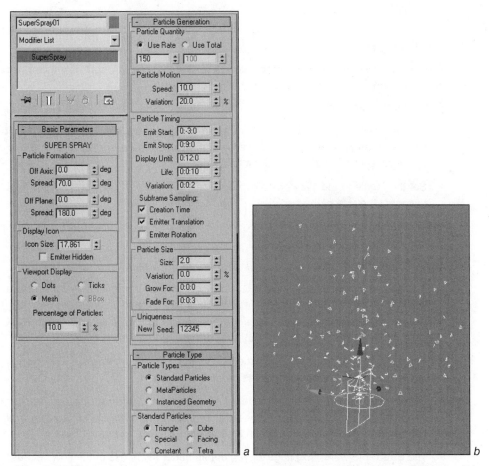

Fig. 6.21. Parameters of the **SuperSpray** particle system (*a*) and its appearance (*b*)

► *Note*

This name also appeared in the drop-down list of the animation panel.

❏   Hide all objects:

Context menu → Hide Selection

❏   Create the particle system of the **SuperSpray** type in the **Top** view:

Main menu → Create → Particles → SuperSpray

❏   Set the parameters of the system as shown in Fig. 6.21, *a*, to obtain a "fountain" (Fig. 6.21, *b*).

❗ *Explanation*

The particle system has many parameters. We will describe in detail only those necessary for this lesson.

Basic Parameters rollout:

- The parameters of the **Particle Formation** group are responsible for the direction and scatter of the particles. We specified a small value for the scatter. This creates only a vague resemblance of the jet, but it fulfills our needs.

- Set the toggle in the **Viewport Display** group to the **Mesh** position; this will enable you to control the size of the particles.

- The number of particles in the viewport (**Percentage of Particles**) displays only part of the particles.

Particle Generation rollout:

- The number of particles (**Particle Quantity** group) can be defined by an absolute value, but it is better to define the number of particles created in each frame (**Use Rate**). We will need many particles, therefore the value of this parameter is great: 2,250 particles will be created per second. But don't make the number too great!

- The value for the **Speed** of the particles also must be high. Using the **Variation** parameter, you can obtain irregularity of the particles' flow.

- Specify the values of the parameters in the **Particle Timing** group. At the start of the fragment, the engines are already on; they should be off after the landing. Therefore, the particles should be visible during the whole fragment, but their "lifespan" is short.

- The **Subframe Sampling** flags let you obtain better evenness of the flow because of the particles between the frames.

- Make the size of the particles (**Particle Size** group) small. (You can also specify their variation.) They must not grow with time, so set the **Grow For** parameter to zero. They can reduce as they become "older", so set the **Fade For** parameter to 3–5 frames.

Particle Type rollout:

- Select **Standard**, **Triangle Particles**.

- The rest of the parameters are unimportant, but there will be at least two systems of particles in the scene to simulate dust and pebbles, and many other parameters will be considered at their setting. The parameters of all four systems of particles (**SuperSpray**, **Blizzard**, **Particle Array**, and **Particle Cloud**) are similar. As for the "obsolete" systems — **Spray** and **Snow** — you should not use them in this lesson. However, their parameters are simple, and you can study them by yourself.

Now we have to put the flow of particles into the required shape. It is tempting to use a suitable parametrical modifier-deformer (e.g., **Free Form Deformer**), and such an option does exist in 3ds max! The modifier can be applied directly, but this will not provide the required result: The modifier will affect the particle emitter but not the particles. 3ds max can convert the system of particles into a geometrical object using a compound object of the **Mesher** type. This converts the original object into a mesh object that you can manipulate as you like.

❏ Create an object of the **Mesher** type (Fig. 6.22, *a*):

  Control panel → Create → ... → Compound Object → Mesher

❏ Toggle the control panel into the **Modify** mode, press the **Pick Object** button, and click the left mouse button on the system of particles. The appearance of the object will change, and it will exactly repeat the system of particles (Fig. 6.22, *b*).

❏ Rename the object **Jet** and hide the system of particles.

You could apply the **FFD Cylinder** modifier to the **Jet** object, but this will not produce the required result. The mesh of the modifier is scaled depending on its relationship with the particles. Therefore, you need to use another method.

❏ Create an **FFD (Cyl)** space warp (similar to the modifier of the same name) so that the control **Lattice** fully covers the **Jet** object (Fig. 6.22, *c*):

  Control panel → Create → Space Warps → Geometric/Deformable → FFD (Cyl)

❏ So far, the **Jet** object is "unaware" that the space warp was applied to it. Bind the **Jet** object to the **FFD01** object using the **Bind to Space Warp** command.

❏ Put the flow of particles into the required shape, working on the level of the control vertices of the **FFD01** object (Fig. 6.22, *d*).

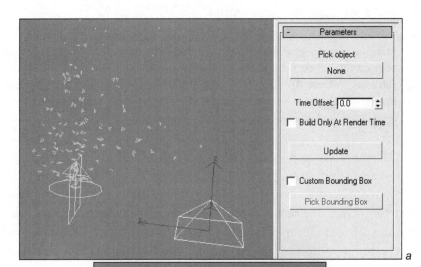

Fig. 6.22, *a* and *b*. Shaping the flow of particles

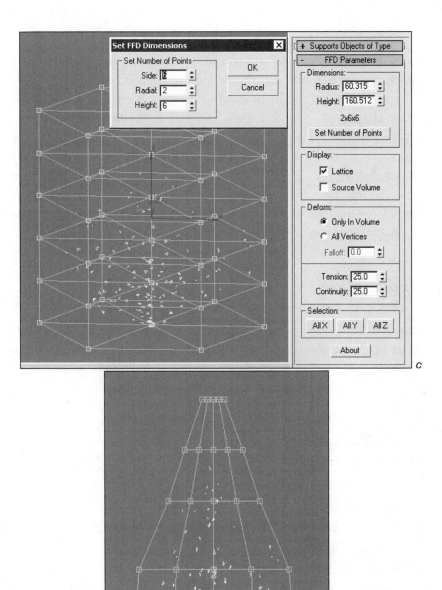

Fig. 6.22, *c* and *d*. Shaping the flow of particles

The next step is the creation and assignment of the material to the flow of particles. There is a perfect **Particle Age** texture in 3ds max for the particles that lets you assign, for example, color to the particles depending on their "age." We will use it later to simulate dilution of the dust particles; it cannot be applied now. The reason is simple: The particles, being the part of the **Mesher** type object, don't "remember" that they are particles. So, we will have to go another way.

❑ Open the material editor, select any free preview window, and rename the material **Jet**.
❑ Select **Gradient** as the texture on the **Diffuse Color** channel. Specify the parameters of the texture as shown in Fig. 6.23, *a*.

Explanation

The colors (top-down) are deep brown, vermilion, and canary.

You can obtain a shift in either direction using the **Color 2 Position** parameter.

Small **Fractal Noise** will add irregularity to the jet fire. You also can animate the noise phase.

❑ In the parameters of the object itself, specify the **Self-Illumination** value as 100% and check the **2-Sided** flag.
❑ Assign the material to the **Jet** object.

Apply the **UVW Map** modifier to the **Jet** object. Select the cylindrical type and place the gizmo of the modifier so it fully covers the **Jet** object (Fig. 6.23, *b*).

Now you can perform quick rendering. If the scene is satisfactory, leave it as it is. In our scene we had to increase the amount of particles and their size by editing the parameters of the original **SuperSpray** object. (To do this, we had to display it with the **Unhide by Name** command.) Then we had to add **Object Motion Blur** in the parameters of the **Jet** object. (**Image Motion Blur** does not work in this case.) This gave us the desired result. We also unchecked the **Cast Shadows** and **Receive Shadows** flags in the parameters of the object, which considerably accelerated the final rendering.

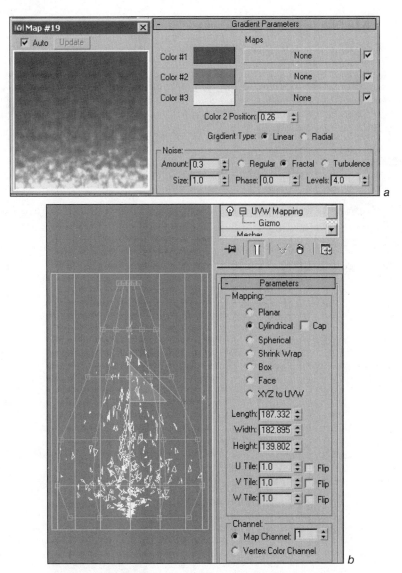

Fig. 6.23. Parameters of the material (*a*) and **UVW Mapping** (*b*)

Now we have to place the fire.

❐ Group the **Jet** and **FFD01** objects to move them together. Select the Jet and FFD01 objects:

Main menu → Group → Group → enter Jet Fire → OK

❏ Unhide the **_MAIN OBJECTS**:

> Context menu → Unhide By Name

> Choose _MAIN OBJECTS in the **Selection Sets** drop-down menu
> and press the Unhide button.

> Selection Sets
> ▼
> MAIN OBJECTS

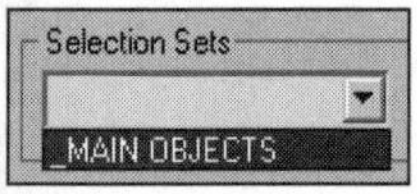

❏ Set the **Jet Fire** group into the nozzle. Scale it by all coordinates (**Uniform Scale**), if necessary.

❏ **Link** the **Jet Fire** group to the **LUNAR SHIP** object.

Now, put on the final touch. Apply the **Glow** effect (halo) to the jet fire. This procedure is described in detail in *Lessons 5* and *17*, so here we will mention only the parameters. Pay attention to the **Use Source Color** parameter. Set it to 100%, and the color of the halo will correspond to the color of particles (Fig. 6.24).

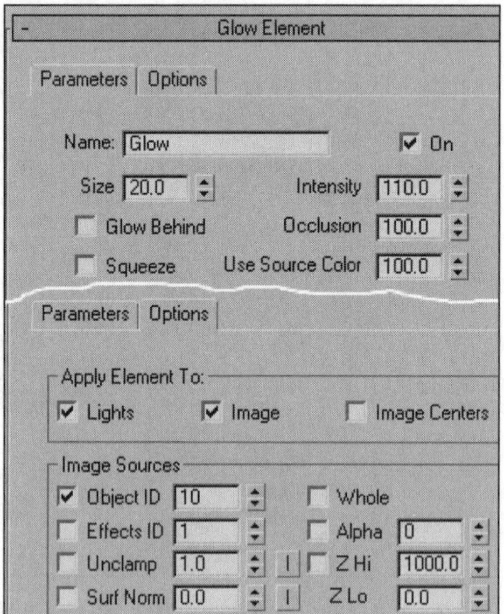

Fig. 6.24. Parameters of the halo effect for the jet fire

To create the effect of scattered dust and pebbles, you will have to make two systems of particles. Both will have the same **Particle Array** type. This type requires an object-emitter, so create one in the landing site of the lunar module.

- ❐ Build a truncated cone in the landing site (Fig. 6.25, *a*).
- ❐ Rename it **Dust Emitter**, convert it to an **Editable Mest** object, then select and remove the top and bottom polygons.
- ❐ Hide all objects except the **Dust Emitter**:

    Context menu → Hide Unselected

- ❐ Create the system of particles of the **Particle Array** type anywhere in the scene. Rename it **Dust** and set the parameters as shown in Fig. 6.25, *b*:

    Main menu → Create → Particles → PArray

Explanation

Select the **Dust Emitter** object as the particle emitter and specify the emission of particles on all surfaces of the object.

Set the amount of particles emitted in one frame (**Use Rate**) to 100. This parameter will be animated according to their distance from the lunar module.

Set the divergence angle of the particles (**Divergence**) within 20–40°.

Set the time parameters of the particles so that they are emitted and displayed during the whole fragment. Make the life-span of the particles 2–3 seconds. The type of particles should be triangle; their size should be small.

Make the particles spin quickly (**Spin Time** parameter).

- ❐ Open the curve editor and animate the **Birth Rate** parameter so that the amount of particles gradually increases within a time unit, stays at 200 for some time, then gradually decreases to zero (Fig. 6.25, *c*). To do this, use the **Add Keys** and **Move Keys** tools in the context menu of the curve editor.

There is no atmosphere on the Moon, but there is gravitation (although less than that on the Earth). Make the particles change their trajectory.

- ❐ Create the **Gravity** space warp with its vector pointed down:

    Control panel → Create → Space Warps → Forces → Gravity

- ❐ **Bind** it with the **Dust** system of particles and set it so the particles changed their trajectory (Fig. 6.25, *d*). Use the **Bind to Space Warp** command to link the **Dust** object to the **Gravity** object.

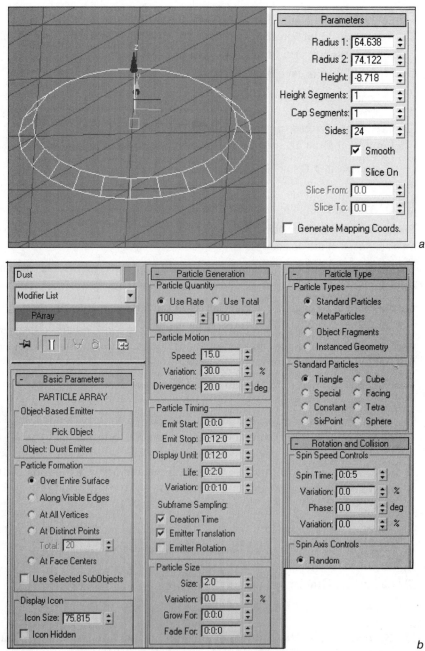

Fig. 6.25, *a* and *b*. Dust creation and animation

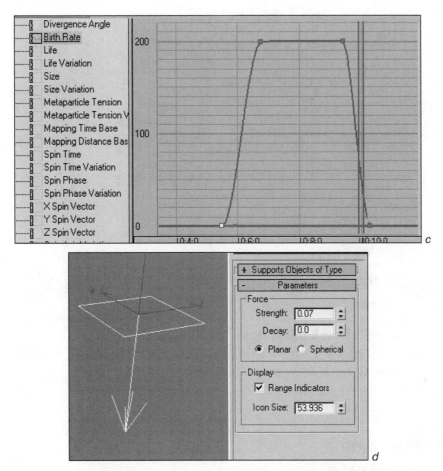

Fig. 6.25, *c* and *d*. Dust creation and animation

You can use the **Mountains** material as the original material for the dust.

☐ Open the material editor.

☐ Transfer the **Mountains** material into any preview window, rename it **Dust**, and make it double-sided (**2-sided**).

☐ Make the colors a little brighter. You can increase the value of the **Self-Illumination** parameter to 20–40%.

☐ Assign the **Particle Age** texture as **Opacity**. Make **Color #1** and **Color #2** white; this will make the dust opaque at the start of its life. Make **Color #3** black; this will make the dust gradually disappear (Fig. 6.26).

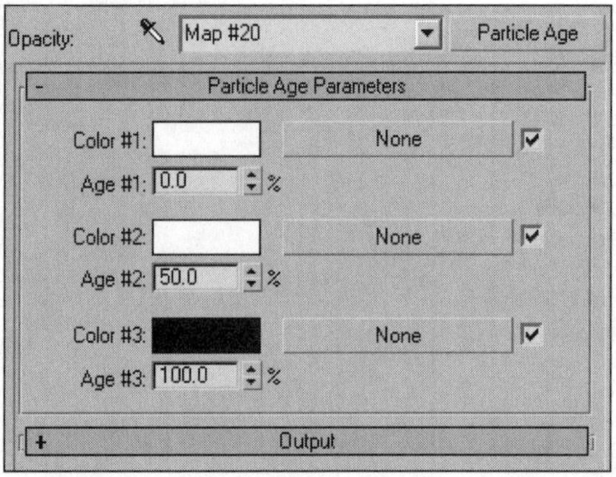

Fig. 6.26. Parameters of the **Particle Age** texture

❐   Use **Image Motion Blur** for the dust:

   Context menu → Properties

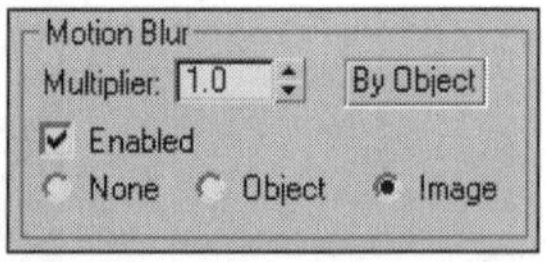

❐   Hide the **Dust Emitter** object.

❐   Duplicate the **Dust** object and rename it **Pebbles**. Move the **Dust** object by pressing and holding the <Shift> key.

❐   Change the parameters as shown in Fig. 6.27, *a*.

Explanation

Slow the **Speed** and increase its **Variation**.

Increase the size of the particles and select the **Sphere** type for them.

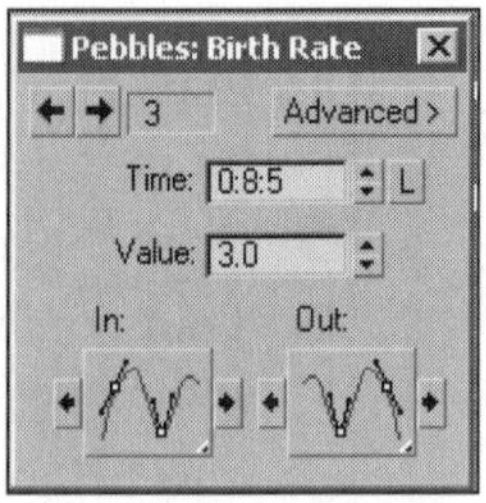

Deactivate the particle system's rotation around its axis.

To change the amount of particles, edit either the animation curves or the parameters of the keys on the time scale. To do this, click on the key with the right mouse button, select **Pebbles: Birth Rate** in the menu, and edit the key value.

Make the pebbles remain on the surface of the Moon after they fall. To do this, use a **Space Warp** of the **Deflector** type.

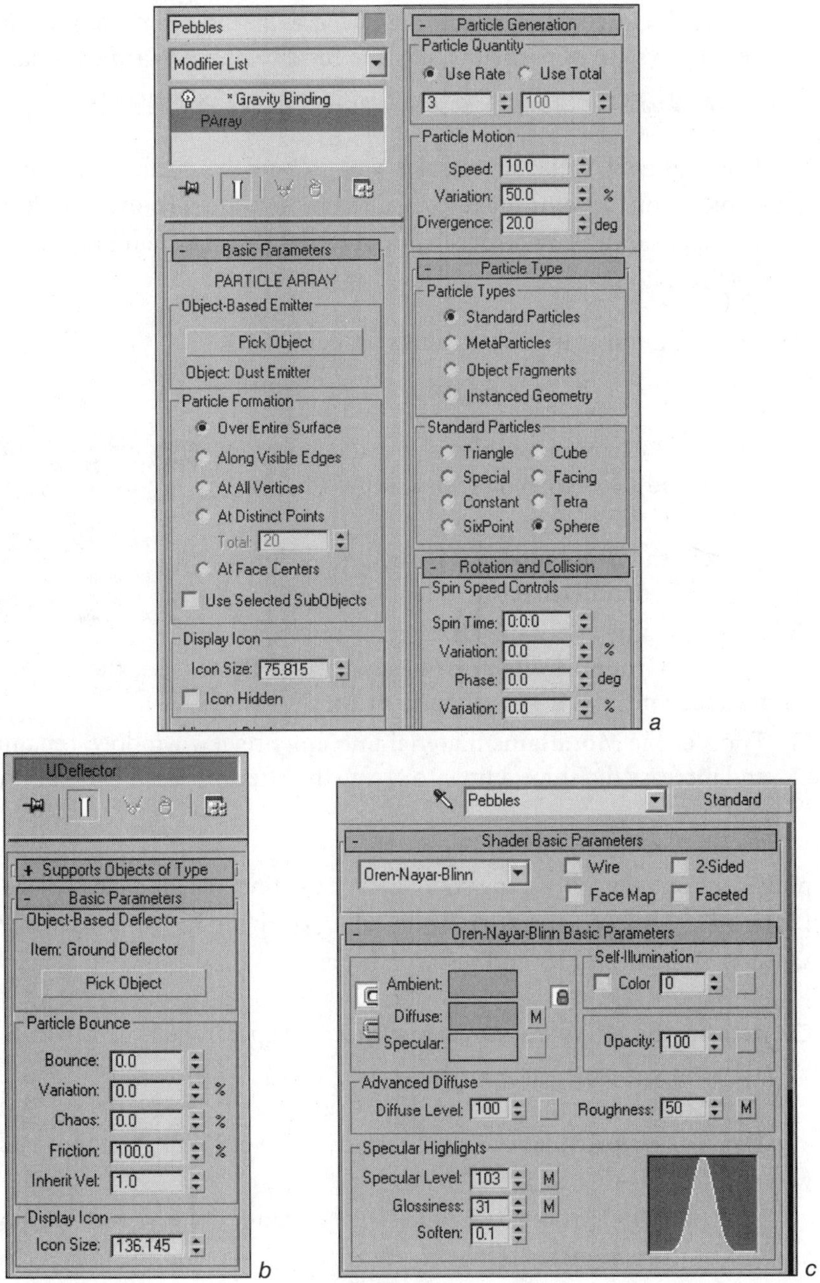

Fig. 6.27. Parameters of the particle system (*a*), deflector (*b*), and material (*c*) for the pebbles

❑ Create a **Universal Deflector** anywhere in the scene and **Bind** it with the **Pebbles** system of particles using the **Bind to Space Warp** command:

     Control panel → Create → Space Warps → Deflector → UDeflector

The universal deflector enables you to use the surface of any object as the deflector. In our case, it makes sense to employ the **Ground** object. But it is very big, and its use will lead to deceleration of the collision handling. We propose that you do the following:

❑ Unhide the **Ground** object, if it is hidden:

     Context menu → Unhide By Name

❑ Select the **Ground** object, go to the polygon mode, and select the polygons around the landing site.

❑ **Detach** them as a copy (**Detach As Clone**) named **Ground Deflector**.

❑ In the parameters of the **UDeflector** object, assign the **Ground Deflector** object as the deflector. Set the parameters so that the fallen pebbles never rebound or move (Fig. 6.27, *b*).

❑ Transfer the **Mountains** material into any preview window, rename it **Pebbles**, and increase the shine a little to create the effect of fused pebbles (Fig. 6.27, *c*).

Finally, create the stars. To do this, we propose that you use the MilkyWay plug-in from Pavel Kuznetsov. You can find it on the CD-ROM in the Plugins\Ky_MilkyWay5 folder. To install it, copy the Ky_MilkyWay.dlv file into the \3dsmax5\plugins folder and restart 3ds max.

❑ Activate the **MilkyWay** effect and specify its parameters (Fig. 6.28):

     Main menu → Rendering → Effects

This process provides excellent results, more efficient than those of the method we considered in *Lesson 5*.

Now everything is ready! Unhide the necessary objects, perform test rendering, and adjust the parameters, if necessary. You can also add the gas jets from the nozzles of the orientation engines. The **Reflection** channel of the lunar module body materials may be assigned the texture of the **Raytrace** type using a small value

(30–40) for **Amount**, since we now have something to reflect! You can perform the final rendering of the fragment, if you know how to do this. In *Lesson 8*, the settings of rendering will be considered in detail.

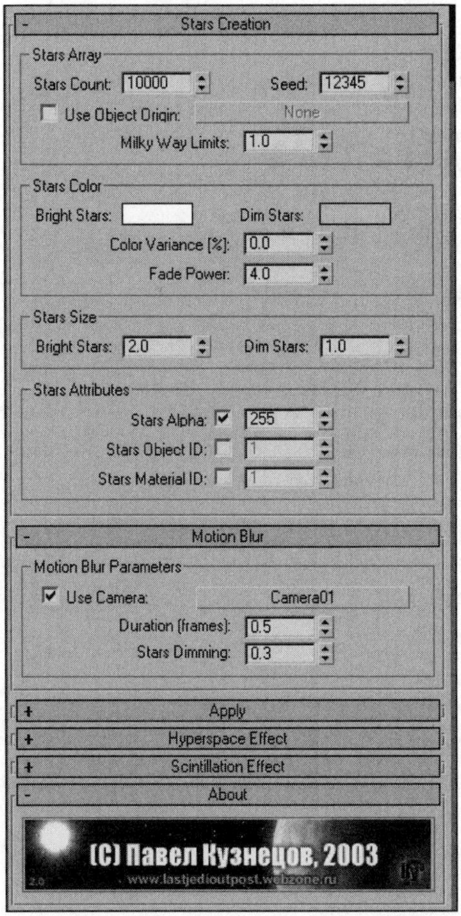

Fig. 6.28. Parameters of the **MilkyWay** effect

Lesson 7

Animating
the Astronaut
and Lunar Rover

As in the previous lesson, here you will model two fragments. The first fragment is animation of the astronaut's motion on the Moon's surface; the second is the rover's motion with the astronaut on board.

By this time, all your models should be ready, so no complicated modeling will be required. Moreover, if you did all the previous lessons, you will have no difficulty creating these two simple animations. Therefore, we will not describe the evident things in detail.

Animating of the Astronaut

The base of this fragment will be the ready scene of the second fragment in *Lesson 6*. We will touch it up a little.

- ❑ Load your scene, or load our scene from the CD-ROM (named lesson07(Start).max in the Lessons\Lesson07\Scenes folder).
- ❑ The time parameters are already specified, so don't change them.
- ❑ Unhide all objects. Go to the last frame of the animation.

What should to be changed? It is necessary to remove the animation of some objects — namely, the particle systems simulating the gases of the jet engine and the dust. The pebbles (**Pebbles** object) should remain where they fall, so start editing from them.

The **Pebbles** object will become the system of particles. Make a copy by converting it to the **Editable Mesh** type of objects using the **Snapshot** operator.

❑ Select the **Pebbles** object and apply the **Snapshot** operator (Fig. 7.1):

Main menu → Tools → Snapshot

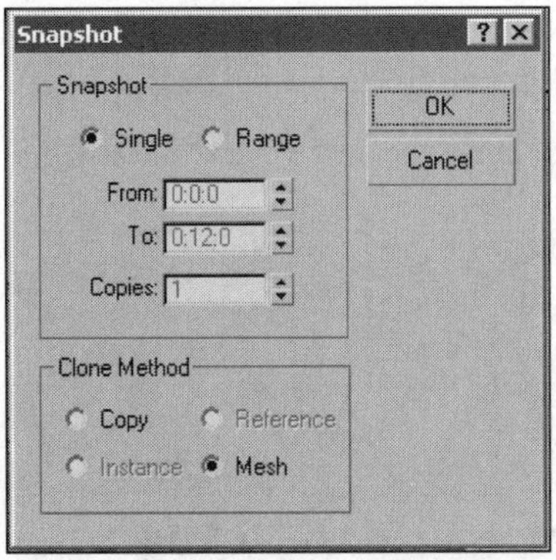

Fig. 7.1. Parameters for creating the **Snapshot** of the **Pebbles** system of particles

The result will be a geometric object named **GPebbles01** — this is the name given by 3ds max.

❑ Remove the source **Pebbles** object.
❑ Select and remove all systems of particles, deflectors (**Deflectors**), gravity (**Gravity**), auxiliary objects, and the object of the **Mesher** type.
❑ Go to the last frame and select all objects.
❑ Select and remove all animation keys on the time scale.

❗ *Attention*

If your keys are set in the last frame, first select and remove the keys in the previous frames. Only then should you remove the keys in the last frame!

Now you have to break the link between the **Camera Target** and the **LUNAR SHIP** object. This link was made to animate the camera's tracing of the lunar module.

❑ Select the **Camera01.Target** object and break the link using the **Unlink Selection** command.

You also could remove the lens effects (they are incorrect now), but we don't recommend that you do this. These effects will be used for other purposes later.

So, the scene is "clean." Now you have to hide some objects (e.g., mountains) and parts of the objects (e.g., some polygons of the Moon's surface and pebbles), leaving only those necessary (Fig. 7.2).

❐ Select the required objects. If necessary, convert them to the base type (e.g., editable poly), select the "redundant" polygons, and hide them:

Control panel → Edit Geometry → Hide Selected

Fig. 7.2. Scene preparation

❐ Merge the lunar rover:

Main menu → Merge

Position the rover at a distance from the lunar module on a sufficiently even surface. Turn it in the direction opposite to the coordinate center (Fig. 7.3). This is important for further animation; our scene will be the basis for the next fragment.

❐ Load your character:

Main menu → Character → Insert Character

Problems may occur here, but the developers of 3ds max advise you not to change the system units without utter necessity. (This recommendation was considered in the previous lessons.) The result looks approximately as shown in Fig. 7.4. The errors occur because of a lack of coincidence between the system units in the current scene and those being loaded.

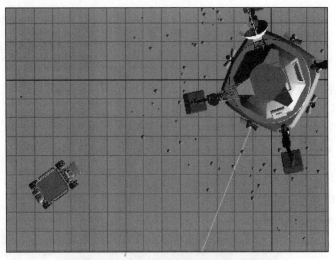

Fig. 7.3. Positioning the lunar rover

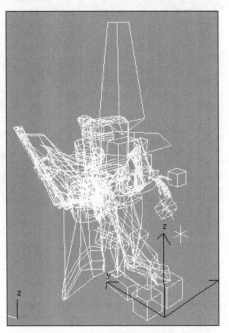

Fig. 7.4. Incorrect loading of the character

We'll help you solve this problem without going into details.

❏ Before the character is loaded, deactivate the coincidence check of the system units:

Main menu → Customize → Units Setup → System Unit Scale → uncheck Respect System Units in Files flag

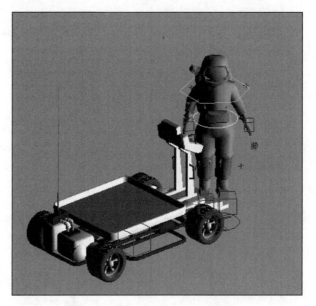

❏ After the character is loaded, check this flag again. This will ensure that all future objects are created in single units.

❏ Unlock the character, keeping the selection on:

Main menu → Character → Unlock

❏ Select the **Character01** object and adjust its size as necessary by scaling all coordinates, guided by the rover (Fig. 7.5).

Fig. 7.5. Scaling the character

► *Tip*

To simplify animation playback in the viewport, select the **SpaceSuit** object and deactivate the **MeshSmooth** and **Push**  modifiers by "switching off" the lightbulb to the left of each modifier's name in the stack.

Now, load the animation files for the character. We prepared two such files: one for step and another for jump. Let our astronaut take a step, two jumps, and then another step.

❏ Select the **Character01** object and load the step(0-60).anm file from the CD-ROM (Lessons\Lesson07\anim folder):

   Control panel → Insert Animation

❏ In the appearing dialog, select **Replace Animation** and press the **Merge Animation** button.

▶ **Note**

This animation was created for our character with the object names used here. If you completed *Lesson 4* and created your own character with other object names, then your names may not coincide. You will have to open the **Object Mapping** rollout and reassign the objects' correspondence.

Play the animation in the viewport. Your character should take a step. So far, neither his position nor orientation matter.

Load the jump(0-90).anm (twice) and step(0-60).anm files successively, not substituting but adding the animation (**Paste to Existing Animation**) to the required frame with shift (**Relative**). For example, the parameters for the first jump should be like those shown in Fig. 7.6.

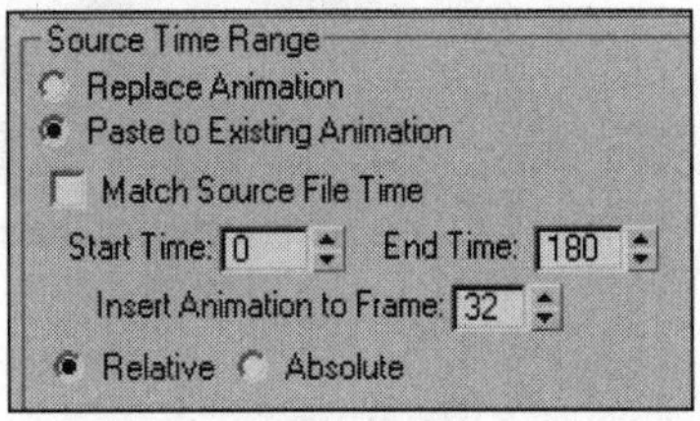

Source Time Range
- ○ Replace Animation
- ◉ Paste to Existing Animation
- ☐ Match Source File Time
- Start Time: 0   End Time: 180
- Insert Animation to Frame: 32
- ◉ Relative ○ Absolute

Fig. 7.6. Parameters for animation of the first jump

▶ **Note**

Unfortunately, when the animation files are loaded, you will have to deal with the frames. To simplify the process, switch to the frames in the time settings (**Time Configuration**).

To determine the number of the frame from which the next animation reel must be loaded, select any animated object of the character (e.g., **_BODY**). You will see the animation keys of this object on the time scale. Use these keys as guidelines.

Note that the names of our files contain the frame numbers. Actually, this is the animation time in frames. The files being loaded were made with a frequency of 30 frames per second, but the current scene uses 15 frames per second. During the loading, 3ds max takes this into account by scaling the time.

How reasonable is this process? Select any animated object and note that the keys on the time scale have different sizes. The keys of a lesser size are set between the frames, so they are called **Subframe keys**. Therefore, the smoothness of the animation remains intact, and no keys disappear.

How can the character's animation be edited if there are many animated parameters? If you want to animate the parameters' values, your only option is the animation curve editor. If the parameters of several objects need to be changed simultaneously, do this by merging the curves. Select the required tracks from the objects list (left mouse button with the <Ctrl> key pressed). After several keys are selected on these curves, you can edit them simultaneously. Fig. 7.7 shows an example of simultaneous editing of the animation curves, governing the movement on the Y axis of the **Foot_L** and **Foot_R** objects.

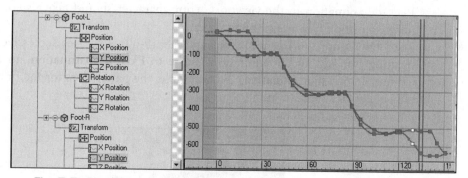

Fig. 7.7. Simultaneous editing of different tracks' keys in the curve editor

This task is rather painstaking, so we strongly recommend that you create the "correct" animation from the beginning.

The time spans, however, have to be edited frequently. Another editor — **Dope Sheet** (key chart) — is convenient for these purposes.

❑ Open the **Dope Sheet**:

Main menu → Graph Editors → Track View — Dope Sheet

▶ *Tip*

It may help to position the editor's window at the bottom of the screen by moving it to the time scale. This stops the window from "floating."

From all the features of this editor, we will consider the most necessary one in our case: the option for simultaneously working with the keys of several tracks.

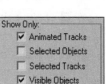

☐ Open the **Filters** dialog and set the option to display only **Animated Tracks**.

☐ Switch to the key editing mode (**Edit Keys**).

☐ Activate the **Modify Subtree** mode.

☐ Select the tracks corresponding to the upper levels of the objects. If necessary, expand the tree of the **Character01** object by pressing the "+" symbol to the left of the object's name, or reduce the tree by pressing the "–" symbol.

You should have an image similar to the one shown in Fig. 7.8.

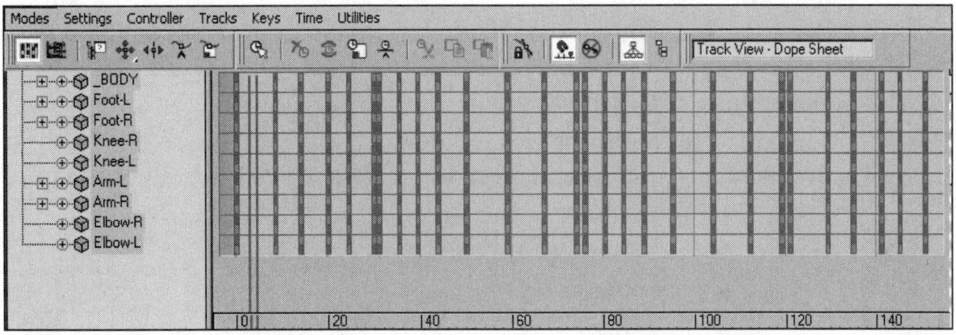

Fig. 7.8. Dope Sheet window, prepared for editing the keys of several objects

► **Note**

The figure shows the pressed **Snap Frames** button. This allows any subframe keys to move to the nearest frame when the main keys are moved. We think that in this case, this is the correct solution. Release the button if you don't like the result.

To edit keys, two groups of tools can be used: those for editing keys and those for time. When the keys are edited separately, the tools of the first group should be used. For simultaneous editing of several keys (as in our case), use the tools of the second group. Consider the main operations of these tools.

☐ You can remove the keys by eliminating their time spans. Selecting these using the **Select Time** command, then apply the **Delete Time** command.

❑ If necessary, you can copy the keys using the **Copy Time** and **Paste Time** commands.

❑ Using the **Insert Time** command, you can insert a span among the keys. Be aware that this is not a "pause" but a slowing of time!

❑ Using the **Scale Time** command, you can either accelerate or slow the animation by scaling the selected time span.

❑ Finally, using the **Reverse Time** command, you can reverse the animation playback.

▶ Note

If you opened the **Undo** window during your experiments, you likely noticed that all these operations were described in one phrase: **Move Keys**. Just so; all these operations simply move the keys on the time scale.

❑ Move the **Character01** object to the position corresponding to the start of the motion.

❑ Make the astronaut move on the surface of the Moon. You will have to animate the movement of the **Character01** object on the vertical axis. Do this using the animation record (**Auto Key**).

Now, create his footprints. It's this easy:

❑ Make one footprint — an object of the **Plane** type — slightly above the surface (Fig. 7.9, *a*).

❑ Deactivate the shadow cast by this object:

Context menu → Properties → Cast Shadows   ☐ Cast Shadows

Use the **Ground And Stones** material as the source material for the footprints by changing it as follows:

❑ Substitute the texture merged on the **Bump** channel for the image from the step.tga file.

❑ Set a big **Amount** value (100–150) for this channel.

❑ Transfer the same texture on the **Opacity** channel with copying (not inheritance!). Invert the image in the texture's properties:

Material editor → texture parameters → Output rollout → Invert flag   ☑ Invert

Here is the step we created (Fig. 7.9, *b*). On close examination it leaves much to be desired, but at a distance it looks rather good.

❑ Duplicate the footprints and place them where the astronaut's feet touch the Moon's surface.

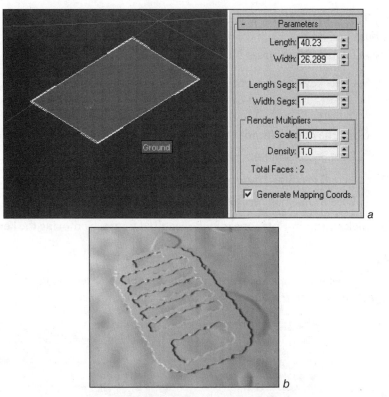

Fig. 7.9. Modeling a footprint

After you have the footprints, it is necessary to animate their appearance in accordance with the astronaut's motion. It is convenient to do this in the Dope Sheet.

☐ Select all footprints and open the **Dope Sheet.**

☐ In the **Filters** dialog, set the track display for only **Selected Objects.**

☐ Select all tracks of the objects and add the **Visibility Track:**

Dope Sheet editor menu → Tracks → Visibility Track → Add

☐ In the filters, set the display for only **Objects** and the **Visibility Tracks.**

☐ Substitute the animation controller for the visibility track of the **Step01** object with the **Boolean Controller:**

Dope Sheet editor menu → Controller → Assign

There are only two states for this controller: "1" and "0". This is what we need. A blue line on the track corresponds to the state "1". You can toggle the state of the key using the right mouse button.

☐ Set two keys on the track using the **Add Keys** tools. The first key should be set in the negative frame of the active segment, the second one in the zero frame. The first footprint should be visible at once.

☐ Copy the controller into the clipboard using the **Copy** command:

   Dope Sheet editor menu → Controller → Copy

☐ Select all visibility tracks and assign the controller from the clipboard to them:

   Dope Sheet editor menu → Controller → Paste

☐ Make the footprints appear in the required frames by moving the keys (Fig. 7.10).

▶ *Tip*

It is convenient to activate synchronization of the time slider and the cursor position (Dope Sheet editor menu → Settings → Sync Cursor Time).

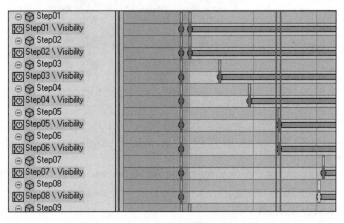

Fig. 7.10. Animating the footprints

You can obtain the camera's tracing of the astronaut by linking (**Select and Link** command) the target of the camera to the **_BODY** object. To make the camera perform only horizontal movements, deactivate inheritance (**Inherit**) of the Z-axis movement in the linkage parameters:

Control panel → Hierarchy → Link Info → Inherit → uncheck Z in the Move group

☐ Unhide all objects.

☐ Select the objects-bones and exclude them from rendering:

Context menu → Properties → uncheck Renderable flag

The last touch is to adjust a light halo around the spacesuit, which is visible in lunar photos. It would be nice if you created dust coming from under the astronaut's boots. We let you rack your brain for solutions to these tasks.

Everything is ready for rendering!

You can find our scene (lesson07(part1).max) on the CD-ROM in the Lessons\Lesson07\Scenes folder.

Animating the Motion of the Rover

Take the file of the previous scene as the base. As before, go to the last frame and remove the animation by selecting all objects in the scene and deleting the keys.

☐ Move the **Character01** object to the lunar rover and set the astronaut on the platform. Several footprints may be placed near the rover.

☐ Put the astronaut into the appropriate posture by editing the control objects (Fig. 7.11).

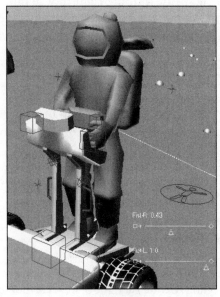

Fig. 7.11. Astronaut on the platform of the lunar rover

Tip

It is useful to switch on the **Default Lighting** (Viewport's context menu → Configure → Default Lighting).

❏ Select and **Destroy** the character assembly of **Character01**; otherwise, it will be confusing:

Main menu → Character → Destroy Character

During the motion, the astronaut must be on the platform. For this purpose, some control objects should be linked with the **ROVER** object using the **Select and Link** command. These objects are: **_BODY, Foot_R, Foot_L, Knee_R, Knee_L, Arm_R, Arm_L, Elbow_R**, and **Elbow_L**.

We propose that you animate the so-called minor movements, then animate the actual motion.

The rover should be jolting slightly during the motion. This can be simulated by assigning the controller of the **Noise** type to the rotation of the **ROVER** object:

Main menu → Animation → Rotation Controllers → Noise Rotation

You can access the parameters of this controller, for example, from the **Motion** panel, by calling the menu with the right mouse button and selecting the **Properties** item (Fig. 7.12, *a*).

The parameters of the controller are shown in Fig. 7.12, *b*. Set the extremes (**Strength**) of the rotation angles to small values on all coordinates.

Play the animation in the viewport. The rover and the astronaut are jolting, but the latter looks like a statue.

Bring the astronaut "back to life." Assign the same controller, assigning it to the **_BODY** object's motion. The parameters of this controller are shown in Fig. 7.12, *c*:

Main menu → Animation → Position Controllers → Noise

The antenna also should quiver during the motion. This can be done using the **Flex** modifier.

❏ Apply the **Flex** modifier to the antenna:

Main menu → Modifiers → Animation Modifiers → Flex

❏ Go to center editing (**Center**) and move the **Flex** modifier to the base of the antenna.

❏ Set the parameters so they create a slight quiver in the antenna (Fig. 7.12, *d*).

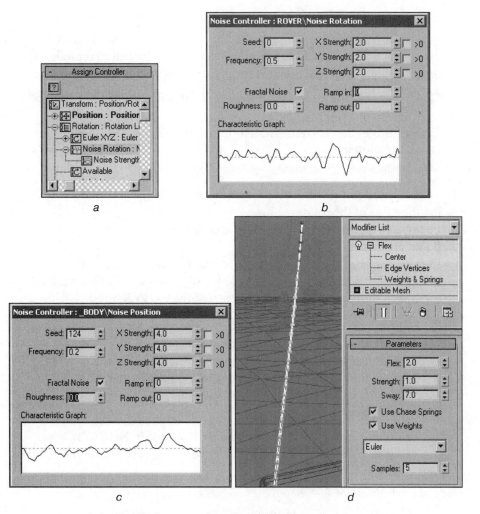

Fig. 7.12. Adjustments for minor movements

It would be more logical to animate the rover using path animation. This is not difficult — you can do it by yourself if you completed the previous lessons. The only problem is where the path should be taken from. It is necessary to cut the polygons of the surface (e.g., using the **Quick Slice** command), select the resulting edges, and convert them into a curve using the **Create Shape From Selection** command.

We recorded the animation by keys to show you another interesting method of linking the parameters using expressions. Let's animate the rotation of the wheels using this method.

Select any wheel (e.g., the right front one) and assign the controller of the **Expression** type to the rotation around the X axis. This can be done either in the **Motion** panel or in the animation editors (**Curve Editor** or **Dope Sheet**). Since the controller will have to be copied to the rest of the wheels, we propose that you use the **Dope Sheet**.

❏ Open the **Dope Sheet** and select the **X Rotation** track of the **ROVER FR Wheel** object (Fig. 7.13, *a*).

❏ Substitute the current animation controller for the **Float Expression** one:

> Animation track context menu → Assign Controller

You need to record the expression in the dialog, its result being the value of the rotation angle.

What expression do we need? The distance from the coordinates' origin to any point on a surface is calculated on the Pythagorean theorem: It is equal to the square root from the sum of the coordinates' squares. To use these values, it is necessary to introduce two scalar variables (e.g., named **PosX** and **PosY**) and link them with the corresponding parameters of the **ROVER** object.

❏ Choose the required parameter by selecting the variable and pressing the **Assign to Controller** button (Fig. 7.13, *b*).

❏ To find the value of the rotation angle (in radians), the distance should be divided by the wheel's radius. The latter is measured using the **Measure** utility:

> Control panel → Utilities

The final appearance of the expression is shown in Fig. 7.13, *c*.

The same controller should be assigned to the corresponding tracks of the rest of the wheels:

> Animation track's context menu → Copy, Paste

Now the wheels of the rover turn during the motion. This rotation may be correct only if the rover moves entirely from the coordinates' origin; that is why we proposed you position it thus.

You can obtain more interesting results using the integrated programming language MAXScript, but this feature is beyond the scope of this book.

To create tire treads in this segment, we propose that you use the system of particles.

❏ Make one object — a footprint similar to that left by a boot. The material is also similar: Use the texture with tread (wheel-step.tga file) instead of the step.tga texture.

❏ Create a system of particles of the **SuperSpray** type with the parameters shown in Fig. 7.14.

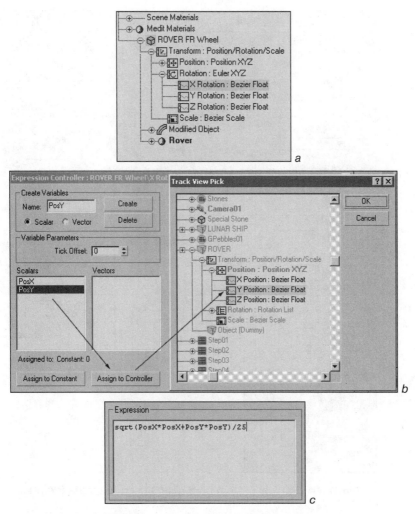

Fig. 7.13. Animation of the wheels' rotation using expressions

Explanation

The illustration shows only the necessary parameters!

Only one particle should appear in each frame; it should stay still.

The particles should be displayed on the screen during the whole animation.

The size of the particles should correspond to the original; the sizes should not be increased or reduced.

The **WheelStep** object with its material is used as particles.

The particles should stand still and be oriented in compliance with the rover's motion.

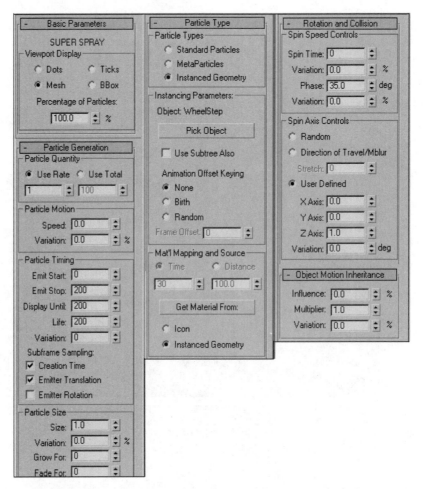

Fig. 7.14. Particle system parameters used to create footprints

❐ Move the system of particles to the wheel. Duplicate it by placing one emitter near each wheel. Link it with the **ROVER** object.

❐ Animate the camera so that it follows the rover, providing a panorama of the Moon's surface. Remember that our Moon is a rather small and flat object!

As for the Earth, we propose that you create it on your own. We used the texture merged on a disk supplied with 3ds max.

You can find our scene (lesson07(part2).max) on the CD-ROM in the Lessons\Lesson07\Scenes folder.

Lesson 8

Rendering the Scene and Assemling the Movie

This lesson explains how to create scenes using production rendering and how to compile the resulting image sequences into a video file. Before we proceed, we would like to concentrate on the main rendering parameters, so you can gain the maximal quality in the minimal amount of rendering time.

Rendering Parameters

This section summarizes the rendering parameters. They are numerous and dispersed in various windows. We will not consider each one in detail; instead, we will focus on the most important and provide some recommendations on adjustment and use.

Settings in the Render Scene Window

Main menu → Rendering → Render

Pay attention to the bottom part of the **Render Scene** window, where the **Production/Draft/ActiveShade** toggle is positioned. 3ds max allows you to assign different parameters to all three modes. As a rule, high-quality production rendering requires a large amount of time. To accelerate the process, draft rendering can be used for rough adjustments.

The **Common Parameters** rollout contains the main parameters and settings (Fig. 8.1).

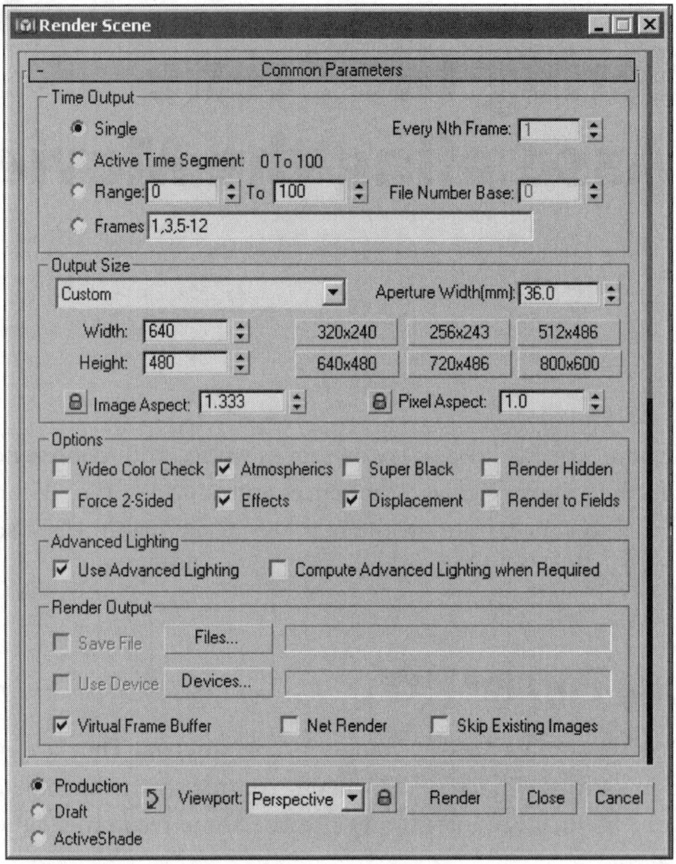

Fig. 8.1. General parameters for rendering

The **Time Output** group is used to specify the time range to be rendered. As a rule, this toggle is set to the **Active Time Segment** position for animation.

An interesting feature is the ability to render selectively, rather than in each frame. This feature allows you to set a gap using the **Every Nth Frame** parameter. For example, if this parameter is set to 5, you will have the sequence of frames rendered every five frames. If a sequence of images calculated in several frames is satisfactory, then there is no need to render them anew. This feature can be used only to render a sequence of files; it doesn't work with AVI or MOV file formats. In addition, when using this feature, the **Skip Existing Images** flag in the **Render Output** group requires special attention.

The size in *pixels* is specified in the **Output Size** group. This somehow baffles polygraphy designers; on various forums we have encountered the question: "How can a 10 × 15 cm picture of 300 dpi be rendered in 3ds max?" The answer is: "Very easily." It is sufficient to know the size in pixels. The dpi can always be adjusted.

In our case, a size of 640 × 480 pixels will do.

This group contains a drop-down list of the settings for various formats, but we are not going to consider it; these settings are beyond the scope of the book. Complete information can be obtained from the "User's Manual."

The flags in the **Options** group allow you to check on or off various features of 3ds max during rendering.

The **Force 2-Sided** flag forcibly makes 3ds max treat all the materials as double-sided during rendering. Sometimes this option is useful, sometimes not; everything depends on the situation. Activation of this option increases the rendering time.

Checking the **Render Hidden** flag allows you to render hidden objects. Two circumstances must be taken into account: Any hidden parts of the objects (polygons, patches, etc.) are rendered independently from this flag, while objects excluded in their own parameters by means of the **Renderable** flag are not rendered at all.

The **Atmospherics** and **Effects** flags allow you to include or exclude corresponding effects from the final rendering. Note that many effects can be rendered correctly only at the camera or perspective view.

The **Displacement** flag affects the display of the texture result assigned to the appropriate channel in the material editor. However, if an object is assigned the **Displace Mesh** modifier or **Displace NURBS** modifier, deactivating the **Displacement** flag does not affect the rendering result.

The rest of the flags in this group relate to the rendering of the special functions; we will describe them later. In our case, they should be deactivated.

The flags in the **Advanced Lighting** group are used jointly with the advanced lighting system. However, we are not using this system, so these flags will not affect our rendering result.

The **Render Output** group is very important. The output formats of the rendering results are specified in this group. To record the rendering results in a file, press the **Files** button. Select or create a folder, then assign the name, type, and parameters of the file (Fig. 8.2). We recommend creating a separate folder for each sequence of files.

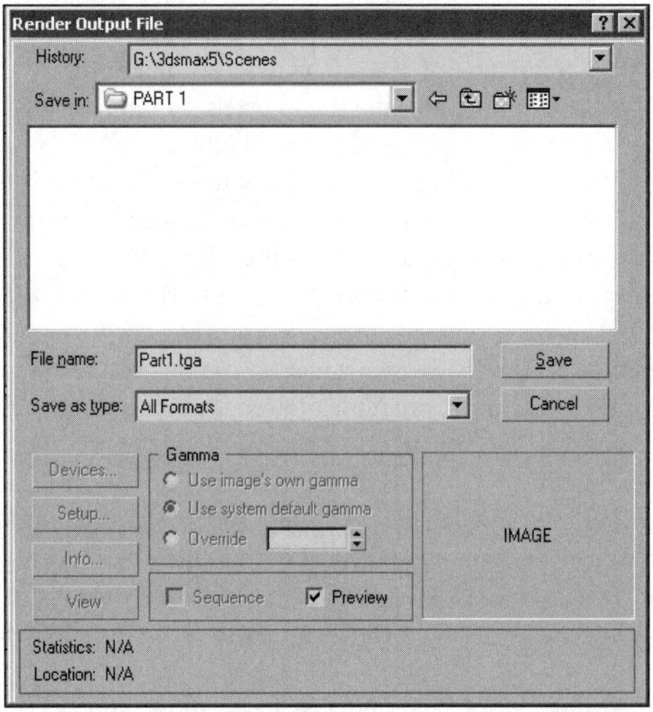

Fig. 8.2. Save window for rendering results

3ds max supports many formats, but we will dwell only on those that we recommend you use.

❏ AVI (Audio-Video Interleaved) is the main format used to record and playback video files or animation within Microsoft Windows. When recording in this format, you obtain a file that can be played at once by Windows applications. This is the only advantage of the AVI format as the rendering result. The drawbacks, however, are many. As a rule, compressing material in this format reduces the quality, making it unfit further editing. Rendering without compression, however, makes the file size enormous. It is reasonable to recommend rendering in this format if you are interested in a quick result for preview. In other cases, preference should be given to rendering in file sequence.

❏ TGA (Targa) and TIFF (Tagged Image File Format) are the best formats for rendering. Both have compression algorithms implemented without quality loss, and both support alpha-channel. The files rendered in this format look like "filename####.ext", where #### is the frame number (0001, 0002, etc.), and "ext" is the extension (tga or tif). Still, you should be aware of an annoying feature of 3ds max: When *negative* frames are rendered, the files look like "filename-####.ext". Video editing packages load such files in reverse order. Try to avoid this situation!

When rendering in the TGA format, we strongly recommend that you specify the parameters as shown in Fig. 8.3, *a*. This will help you avoid unpleasant situations as you edit and apply the effects.

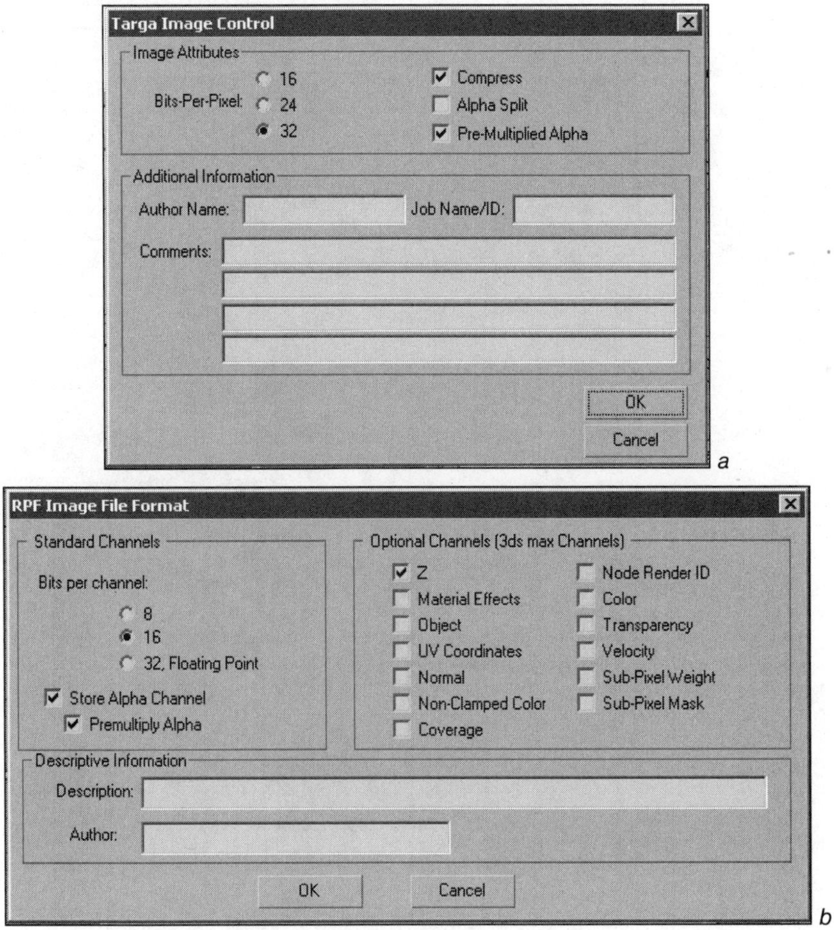

Fig. 8.3. Parameters of the TGA (*a*) and RPF (*b*) formats

❏ Apart from the alpha-channel, you can record other channels using RLA (Run-Length encoded version A) from Silicon Graphics (SGI) or RPF (Rich Pixel Format) from Discreet. These can be used for further editing in professional packages, such as Adobe After Effects or Discreet combustion (Fig. 8.3, *b*). Both RLA and RPF support color depth of 64 and 128 bits/pixel, which makes them very attractive in the film industry. However, most video editing packages of the middle class, including Adobe Premiere, do not support these formats.

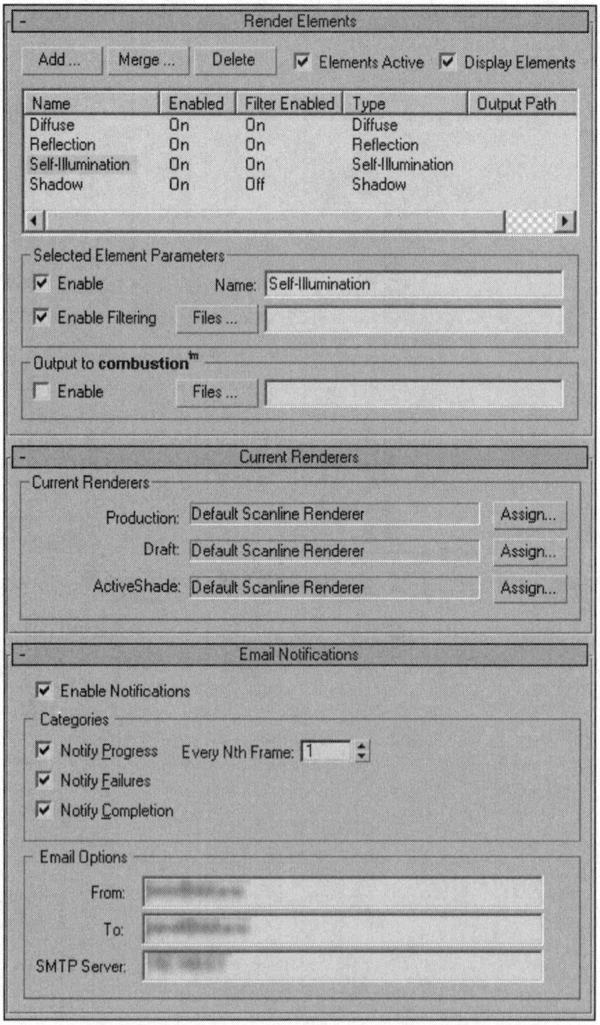

Fig. 8.4. Render Elements, Current Renderers, and Email Notifications rollouts

The rest of the formats (e.g., BMP) can be used if your editing package does not support TGA and TIFF. We strongly recommend that you *not* use JPG: It is impossible to restore the quality ruined by compression, and animation compiled from the sequence of these files tends to quiver and blink.

The **Virtual Frame Buffer** flag determines if the rendering result of the current frame should be displayed on the screen. During final rendering of the animation, it makes sense to deactivate this flag, because the screen display requires additional resources that increase the rendering time.

The **Net Render** flag activates the network rendering process. Using network rendering, you can set up *batch rendering* (**Batch Render**). This will be described below.

The next three rollouts (Fig. 8.4) allow you to use some additional features.

The parameters in the **Render Elements** rollout allow you to record each element of the image in its own file. Later, these elements can be merged to create interesting effects. For example, you can blur reflections, an option otherwise unavailable in 3ds max.

The **Current Renderers** rollout determines what rendering module is to be used.

The **Email Notifications** rollout allows you to send status messages via email.

The parameters in the **MAX Default Scanline A-Buffer** rollout are specific for this module, so they appear in the separate section (Fig. 8.5). Normally, this is a continuation of the **Common Parameters** rollout.

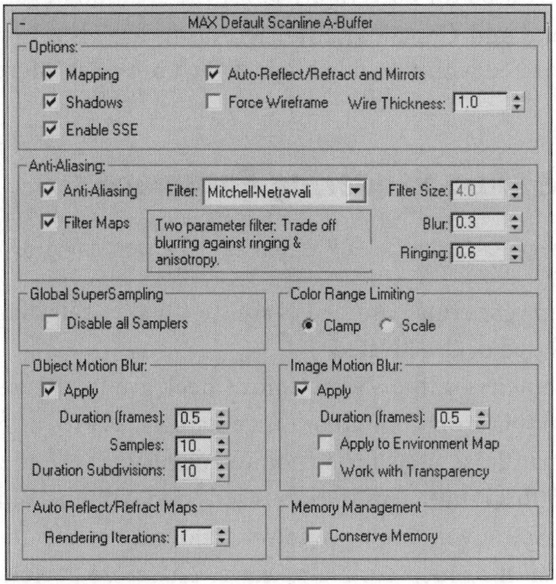

Fig. 8.5. MAX Default Scanline A-Buffer rollout

You can use the **Options** group to switch on or off some features. All of them are quite clear — except the **Auto-Reflect/Refract and Mirrors** flag. This flag lets you switch off the rendering of reflections and refractions created using textures of the **Reflect/Refract**, **Flat Mirror**, and **Thin Wall Refraction** types. This flag does not affect the rendering of reflections and refractions obtained using material and texture of the **Raytrace** type; these are controlled by their own mechanisms.

The smoothing settings (**Anti-Aliasing**) are very important, and we would like to focus on them.

There was only one algorithm in the early versions of 3ds max, which came to be called **Area**. It is rather quick, but it doesn't provide high quality; a practiced eye would easily distinguish images made in 3ds max using this algorithm from any others.

Beginning with version 3, 12 anti-aliasing algorithms were offered in 3ds max. Below are brief descriptions of some of them.

❐ In our opinion, the **Mitchell-Netravali** algorithm provides the best rendering results. The image comes out live and smooth, without excessive "soaping." This is obtained with the parameters shown in Fig. 8.5.

❐ The **Blackman** and **Catmull-Rom** algorithms provide very sharp images. They are mostly used for polygraphy or for the creation of game sprites.

❐ The **Blend** and **Cook Variable** algorithms are also captivating. Their parameters are varied within a wide range, which provides interesting results.

Dialog for the Main Rendering Parameters

Main menu → Customize → Preferences → Rendering (Fig. 8.6)

The main rendering parameters are specified in this dialog. Only some of them may be activated or deactivated.

The parameters of the **Video Color Check** group are used during rendering for television. In this group, the color range standards (PAL or NTSC) are considerably narrower than those used for a monitor display, as are the methods for reducing the image to this range. This option is activated with the **Video Color Check** flag in the **Render Scene** window. Nowadays, rendering results in draft images that have to be finished in a video-editing package. Therefore, it does not make sense to reduce quality at this stage.

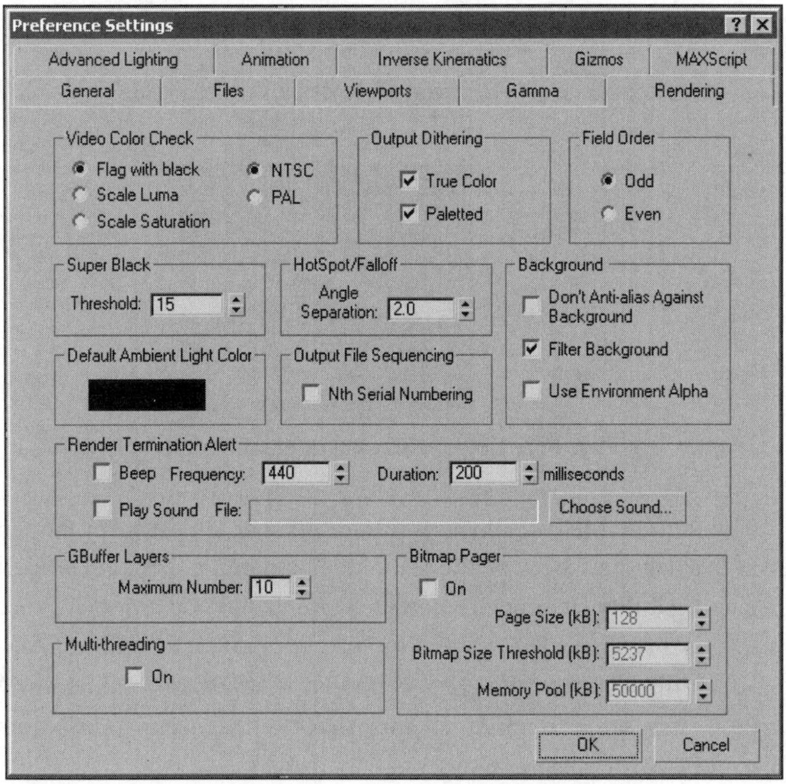

Fig. 8.6. Dialog for the main rendering parameters

The toggle in the **Field Order** group specifies the sequence of half-fields rendering for video. This parameter depends on the video output card. Half-fields rendering is activated by the **Render to Fields** flag in the **Render Scene** window.

The **Super Black** method allows you to merge black images as transparencies. When this option is checked, near-black objects will be lighter than the black background by a value specified by the **Super Black Threshold** parameter. This option was widely used to create game sprites; now it is less popular.

Activating the **Don't Anti-alias Against Background** flag helps in the creation of game sprites. Note that this option can be activated and deactivated only in this dialog.

The **Multi-threading** flag is used during rendering on multi-processor systems. The parameters of the **Bitmap Pager** group allow you to optimize the rendering process when large bitmap images are used as textures.

Object Parameters

Object's context menu → General → Rendering Control (Fig. 8.7)

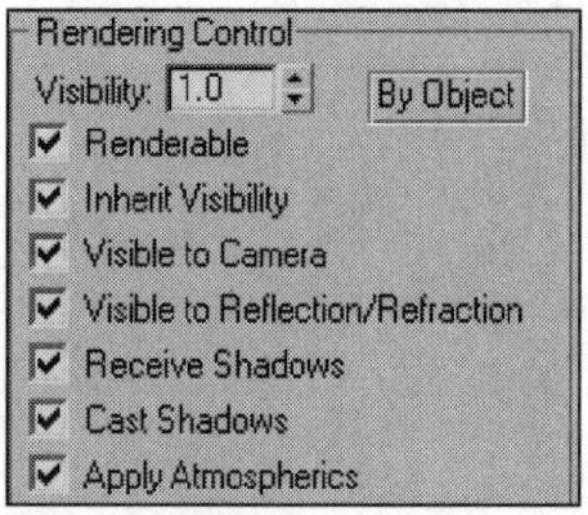

Fig. 8.7. Object parameters that affect rendering

The **Renderable** flag allows you to exclude an object from the rendering process. If this flag is unchecked, the rest of the flags don't affect the rendering process.

The **Visibility** parameter allows you to change the object's transparency, even until it is invisible. The animation of this parameter allows, for example, an object to "dissolve into thin air." Note that shadows of the **Shadow Map** type behave in the same manner if they have either semi-transparent objects or objects of semi-transparent material.

The **Inherit Visibility** flag is used to synchronize visibility on the entire hierarchical tree, from "ancestor" to "children."

The **Visible to Camera** flag lets you create an interesting effect: a shadow from a non-existent object.

The **Visible to Reflection/Refraction** flag allows you to exclude objects from reflection or refraction.

The **Receive Shadows**, **Cast Shadows**, and **Apply Atmospherics** flags allow objects to take and cast shadows and atmospherics (e.g., mist).

Material and Texture Parameters

Material editor → Texture parameters → Filtering

To improve the final image, it is possible to use some features when setting the materials and textures.

You can improve the appearance of objects by applying textures of the **Bitmap** type using **Summed Area** filtering instead of the default **Pyramidal**. However, application of this type of filtration sometimes leads to excess "soaping" of the texture (Fig. 8.8, *a*). The rendering time also is increased slightly.

Application of **SuperSampling** allows you to remove certain rendering troubles (e.g., "quivering" of a texture applied on the **Bump** channel) (Fig. 8.8, *b*):

Material editor → SuperSampling

Note that this parameter can considerably increase the rendering time.

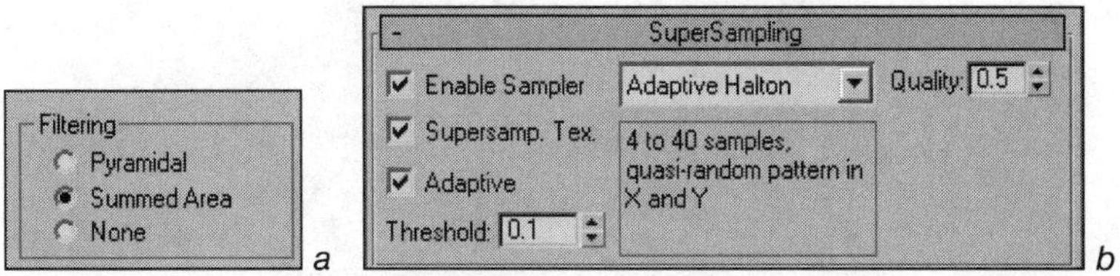

Fig. 8.8. Texture (*a*) and material (*b*) parameters that affect rendering quality

Raytracer Parameters

Main menu → Rendering → Global Raytracer Settings

You can specify global **Raytracer** parameters in the **Global Raytracer Settings** dialog (Fig. 8.9, *a*).

In addition, a material or texture of the **Raytrace** type has many similar settings that affect the rendering of only that material or texture (Fig. 8.9, *b*):

Material editor → Raytracer Controls

In general, all of these parameters are rather clear; we will dwell on the parameters of only two groups in the **Global Raytracer Settings** window.

Use the **Ray Depth Control** group to specify the maximal number of reflections and refractions of the rays (**Maximum Depth**) and the brightness cutoff (**Cutoff Threshold**). The default value (9) is sufficient in most cases. However, if there are, for example, many mirrors in your scene, then the **Maximum Depth** parameter should be increased. The **Cutoff Threshold** parameter allows you to optimize raytracing, but increasing this parameter roughens the result, and you may lose the required reflections and refractions.

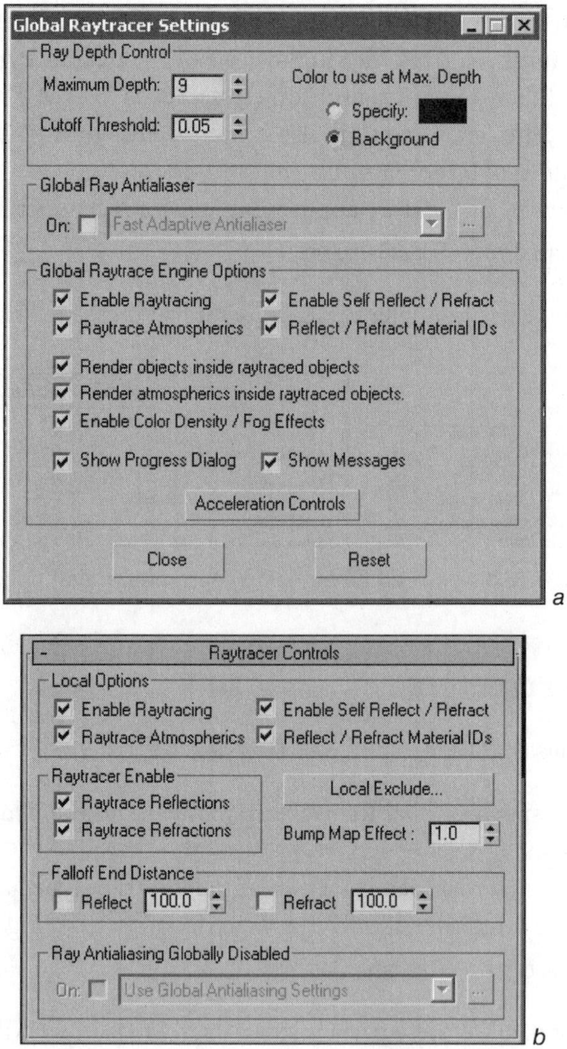

Fig. 8.9. Global (*a*) and local (*b*) settings of the **Raytracer**

You can activate and adjust smoothing of reflections and refractions in the **Global Ray Antaliaser** group. Doing so will enhance the quality of the final image, but the rendering time can increase dozens of times, so this option requires careful and competent handling.

Batch Rendering

Batch rendering in 3ds max can be set up in two ways: either with network rendering or with the Batch Render script. We recommend that you consider both options.

To use network rendering, the TCP/IP should be adjusted on your computer. If you don't have a network card or Internet connection, set the TCP/IP using Microsoft's Loopback Adapter.

▶ Note

Network rendering is available only for Windows NT/2000/XP.

The start procedure is as follows:

❏ Start **backburner Manager** and **backburner Server** sequentially:

Start → Programs → discreet → backburner 2 → Manager, Server

❏ During the first startup, the settings dialogs appear (Fig. 8.10, *a* and *b*). As a rule, the default settings are correct, so press **OK** without hesitation.

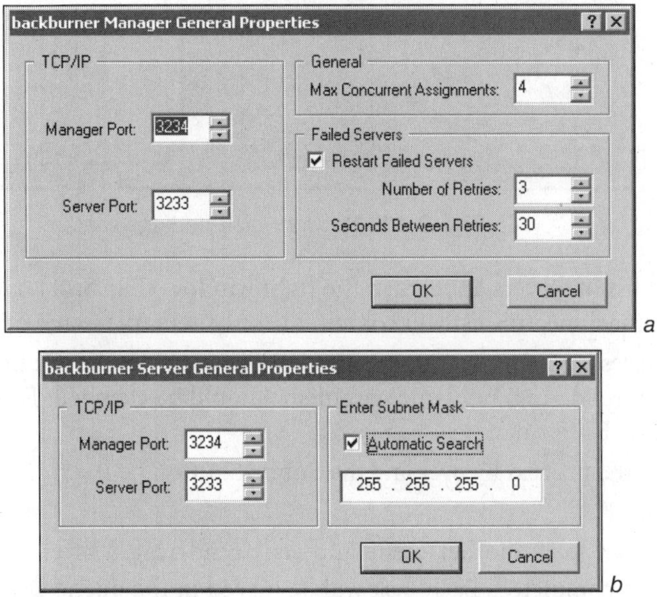

Fig. 8.10. Backburner Manager (*a*) and **Server** (*b*) setup

❑ Load your scene in 3ds max and specify the rendering parameters. Check the **Net Render** flag and start the rendering process by pressing the **Render** button.

❑ Press the **Connect** button in the opening dialog.

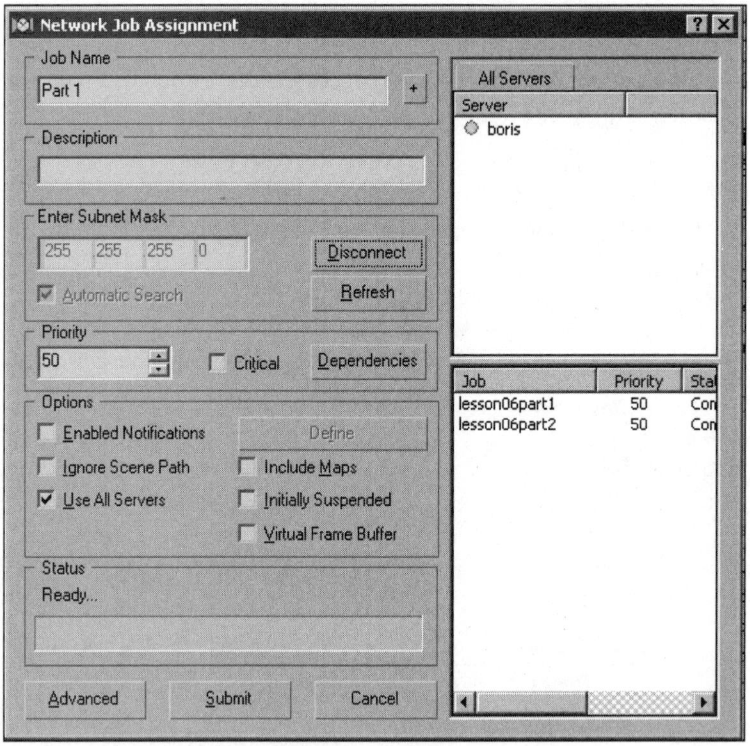

Fig. 8.11. Network task-settings window

❑ The list of servers appears in the right window (Fig. 8.11). During rendering on one machine, this list will contain the only item: the name of your computer.

❑ If necessary, specify the required parameters in the **Options** group. During batch rendering, only one parameter should be changed: Deactivate the **Virtual Frame Buffer** flag.

❑ Start the process by pressing the **Submit** button.

You can load another scene and start rendering it after the above operations have been completed. Each task will be placed in the queue and fulfilled automatically after the previous one is finished.

Use the monitor the follow and control the process (Fig. 8.12). To do so, connect to the server using the **Connect** button:

Start → Programs → discreet → backburner 2 → Monitor

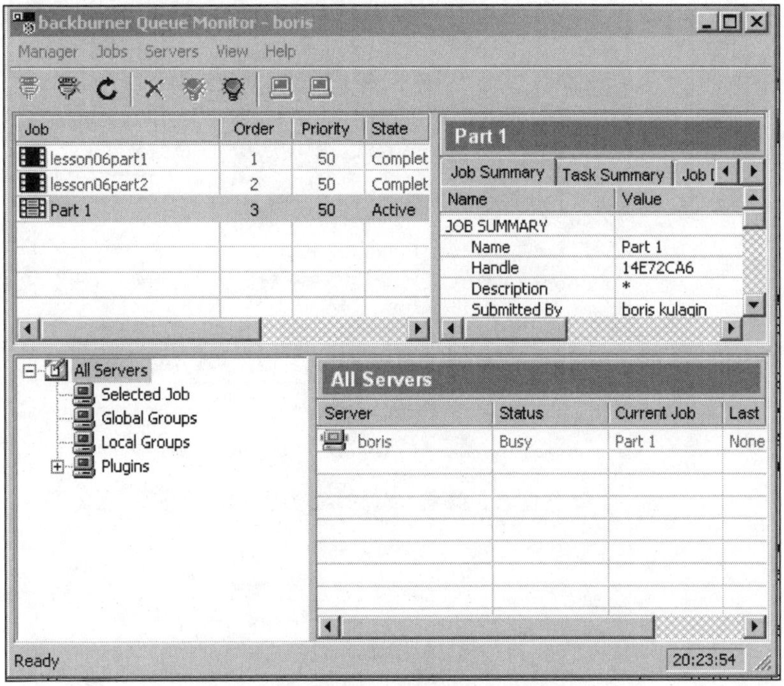

Fig. 8.12. Network monitor window

The 3ds max package includes script that allows you to set up batch rendering without using network rendering. Below is a brief summary of the script's use.

❑ Run the script:

Main menu → MAXScript → Run Script

Find and run the script's file (Macro_BatchRender.mcr); usually it is in the Scripts\MAXScriptsTools\ folder

❑ Make it available — for example, by creating a button on the main panel:

Main menu → Customize → Customize User Interface → Toolbars

Find the Batch Render command in the list and transfer it to the main panel.

❑ Press the button that appears. The settings window will open (Fig. 8.13).

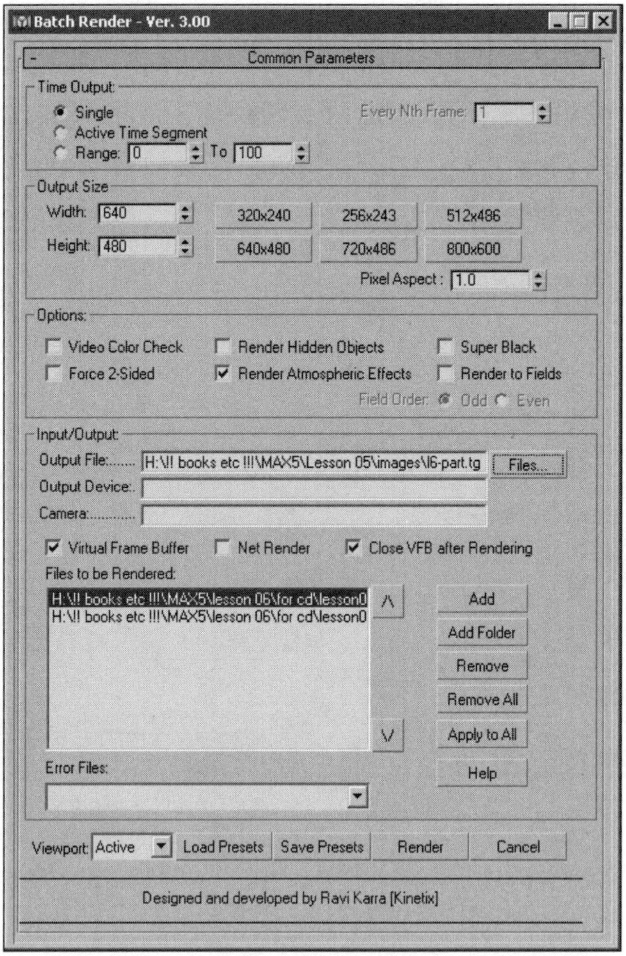

Fig. 8.13. Settings for the **Batch Render** script

❑ Use the **Add** button to choose the scenes you wish to render.
❑ Specify the parameters (e.g., determine the output folders and files).
❑ Run the process by pressing the **Render** button.

Our experience shows that this script is good but uncertain; sometimes it "hangs" the system. Network rendering is preferable.

Assembling the Movie Using the Video Post Module

After all sequences are completed, assemble the final reel in a file of the AVI format. Below we describe how to do this using the **Video Post** module. Frankly, this technique is not convenient, so we advise you to use it only as a last resort. Instead, assemble your reel in any video editor, if you have one.

❑ Adjust the frame change frequency in 3ds max; it should be 15 frames per second (this information will be used during the AVI file record):

> Time control panel → Time Configuration

❑ Open the window of the **Video Post** module:

> Main menu → Rendering → Video Post

❑ Load your sequences of files:

> Video Post Toolbar → Add Image Input Event → Files

> Select the first file of the sequence, check the Sequence flag, and press Open.

> Press OK in all dialogs.

❑ Repeat the operation for the rest of the sequences.

▶ *Note*

We will content ourselves with three tracks, but you should load all of your sequences; there should be five of them.

❑ Butt the tracks (Fig. 8.14, *a*).

❑ Add output (**Output Event**):

> Video Post Toolbar → Add Image Output Event → Files

> Enter a file name with an AVI extension.

❑ Select the appropriate **Codec** in the settings and adjust it (Fig. 8.14, *b*).

Your **Video Post** window should look like the one in Fig. 8.14, *c*.

❑ Start the rendering process:

> Video Post Toolbar → Execute Sequence

> Specify the parameters and press the Render button.

The **Video Post** module allows you to produce very interesting things. Its features are surpassed by few video-editing packages. But it is utterly inconvenient to use, so you need to have a video editor at your disposal. There are many choices, with the prices varying from thousands dollars (Combustion) to nil (VirtualDub).

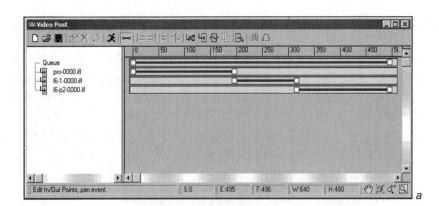

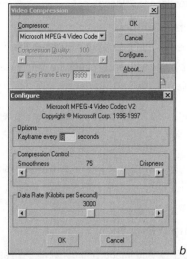

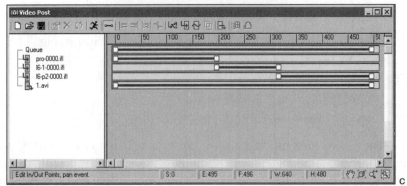

Fig. 8.14, *a–c.* Project preparation in the **Video Post** module

Project II

A Living Room

In this project, we endeavor to create a model of a small and simple living room, set up the lighting, and make a short panorama clip. We did not call it "Interior design," because of the result such an enthusiastic name implies. Nevertheless, we hope that after you read these lessons, you will be able to start more complicated and realistic projects.

Despite the number of specialized architecture programs, 3ds max and its cousin Autodesk VIZ (previously known as 3D Studio VIZ) are actively used by small designer studios to model and visualize architectural projects. There are at least two factors driving the use of comprehensive packages similar to 3ds max. First, a universal package helps solve far more tasks then special packages (e.g., creation of non-standard furniture models and design elements). Second, packages such as 3ds max possess far richer options in terms of realistic images.

There are several new options implemented in 3ds max 5 that make it more suitable for architectural design and visualization. These include indirect light rendering (**Radiosity** and **Light Tracer**), new **Photometric** and **DayLight** sources of light, realistic **Area Shadows**, and **Exposure Controls** modules. These tools enable you to obtain rather convincing images.

▶ *Note*

Currently, there are three additional rendering modules for 3ds max available from third-party manufacturers. Most of them provide higher quality results in a shorter amount of time, but it is a good idea for us to begin with those in 3ds max. Besides, the tools in 3ds max work correctly with plug-ins, materials, and procedure textures of third-party manufacturers, unlike the external rendering modules that often cannot cope with all the integrated materials and textures in 3ds max. (For example, Integra InSight has problems with double-sided materials.)

We initially planned to write a small additional lesson, where the rendering and light possibilities are considered in detail, but we gradually came to the conclusion that it is more appropriate to address that as a separate project.

So, for this project, we will do the following:

❑ **Lesson 9: Modeling the Living Room**. In this lesson, we will create a simple room and "fill" it with furniture and other objects (curtains, etc.).

❑ **Lesson 10: Daylight Adjustment**. Here, you will learn how to use the new light sources and set up global illumination (**Radiosity**) and **Exposure Control**.

❑ **Lesson 11: Global Lighting Materials**. To finish, we will create materials, assign them to objects and parts of objects, and "fight" the numerous artifacts that occur when used with global illumination. We will also execute the final rendering of the clip that loops around the room.

We must repeat that this project is not intended to cover every topic; some features were deliberately simplified, while other specific settings were not presented at all. For those, you will be able to use the 3ds max manuals.

Lesson 9

Modeling the Living Room

Room Modeling

A sketch of a room, indicating dimensions, is shown in Fig. 9.1. Let's start modeling.

First, we should specify the measurement units. Unlike the previous project, where measurements were used mainly for the sake of convenience, precise linear dimensions here will ensure correct lighting calculations.

❑ Specify the measurement units (Fig. 9.2, *a* and *b*):

    Main menu → Customize → Units Setup

▶ *Note*

Generally speaking, the developers of 3ds max recommend that you retain the system unit settings to avoid inconsistencies when other objects are loaded. In this case, you will work with the units you specify for the **Display Unit Scale**.

❑ Set the **Grid Spacing** to 10.0 cm and Snaps to **Grid Points** (Fig. 9.3, *a* and *b*):

    Main menu → Customize → Grid and Snap Settings → Home Grid and Snaps tabs

❑ Create a 750 × 450 cm rectangle in the **Top** view:

    Main menu → Create → Shapes → Rectangle

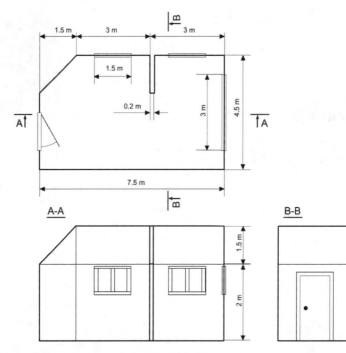

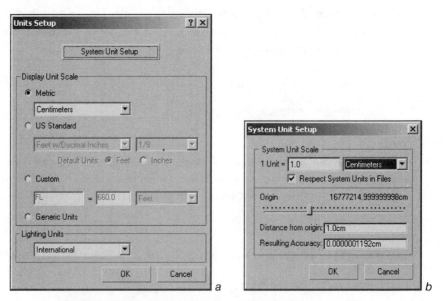

Fig. 9.1. Room sketch

Fig. 9.2. Display (*a*) and system (*b*) measurement units

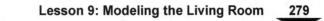

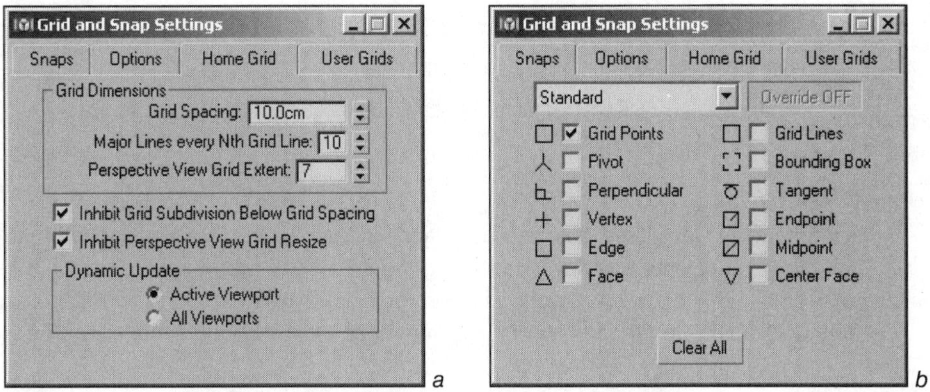

Fig. 9.3. Home Grid (*a*) and **Snaps** (*b*) parameters

▶ *Tip*

Create the rectangle by entering its parameters via the keyboard (Fig. 9.4). Position the center of the rectangle so that its bottom left corner in the **Top** view is at the coordinate origin, this will simplify further editing.

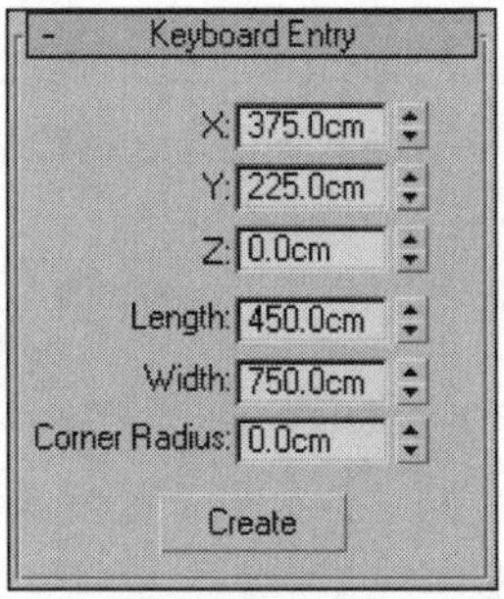

Fig. 9.4. Rectangle parameters

☐ Convert the rectangle to an **Editable Spline:**

> Context menu → Convert to → Convert to Editable Spline

☐ Activate the Snaps (<S> key).

☐ Make a bevel by selecting the top left corner and inserting vertices on the edges it joins. Delete it (Fig. 9.5, *a–c*) and convert the remaining vertices to the **Corner** type:

> Context menu → Sub-object → Vertex
>
> Context menu → Refine → insert vertices

Select the corner vertex and delete it (<Del> key)

Select all vertices (<Ctrl>+<A> key combination)

Context menu → Corner (the cursor should be on one of the selected vertices)

Note

From now on, we will not describe operations in such detail. We recommend that you use hotkeys. Sub-objects are navigated using the <1>, <2>, etc., keys. Pressing a key twice (or <Ctrl>+<B>) ends your work with sub-objects. The selection mode is changed with the <Q> key, moving mode — <W>, rotation mode — <E>, scaling mode — <R>.

There is another way to make the bevel: select the corner vertex and use the **Chamfer** command (150 cm) on the control panel.

Create a partition:

❏ Create a rectangle as shown in Fig. 9.5, *d*:

Context menu → Create Line

Build the new vertices by clicking the left mouse button

Return to the starting point, and answer "Yes" to "Close Spline?"

Exit line creation by clicking the right mouse button

❏ In spline mode (<3> key), select the main spline and subtract the rectangle out of it (Fig. 9.5, *e*):

Control panel → Geometry → activate "Boolean Subtraction"

Press the **Boolean** button and select the rectangle to be subtracted

❏ Insert two vertices on the edge opposite the partition; this will simplify further editing (Fig. 9.5, *f*).

The next step requires some explanation. It may seem that we only need to **Extrude** our plan and invert the normals for our room to be ready. Unfortunately, when external daylight is used, unpleasant "glowing" artifacts appear in the corners of the room. It comes from an error in modeling shadows from an external light source. To prevent that, add outer contours to the walls. If you don't believe us, try it yourself — maybe you'll have better luck.

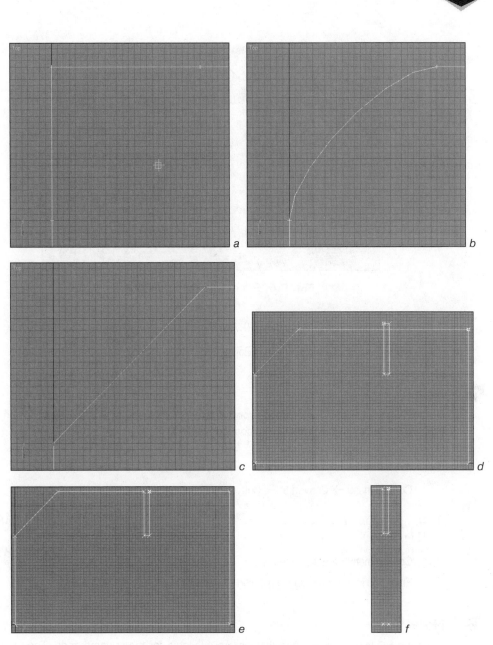

Fig. 9.5. Room editing

□   Create the outer contour around the room (Fig. 9.6):

   Context menu → Create Line

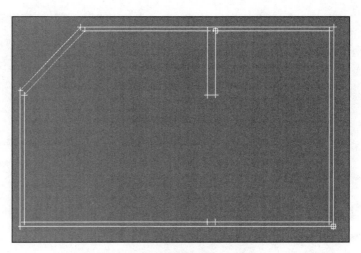

Fig. 9.6. Room with outer contour

❑ **Extrude** the walls 200 cm (Fig. 9.7, *a*):

Main menu → Modifiers → Mesh Editing → Extrude

▶ *Note*

Do not forget about the different viewport display modes and how to switch between them (<F2>,<F3>,<F4>). Use whatever is most convenient.

❑ Convert to an **Editable Poly**:

Context menu → Convert to → Convert to Editable Poly

❑ In polygon mode, select the upper polygon and **Extrude** it 150 cm (Fig. 9.7, *b*):

Context menu → Extrude rectangle

Enter 150 in the corresponding dialog and press **OK**

▶ *Note*

"Rectangles" that open settings dialogs are available for many commands. They are considered in detail in the first project.

❑ Create slants by moving vertices. **Weld** vertices where necessary (Fig. 9.7, *c*).

▶ *Tip*

This is easy to do by selecting all of the vertices and opening the **Weld** command settings dialog. Increase the **Weld Threshold** until all necessary vertices are joined, but don't go too far and weld excess vertices!

▶ *Note*

These manipulations may create strange polygons. At first, we had a triangle overlapping the ceiling diagonally. Don't panic! Just like other 3D packages, 3ds max does not "like" multi-angular polygons. One solution is to select all of the polygons and retriangulate (Control panel → Edit Polygons → Retriangulate). This functions works quite well, and the polygons that result should be more intuitive. If there is still something wrong, you probably made an error somewhere.

Now, it is time to make the windows and doorways. We suggest that you make them via **Boolean Subtraction**. In versions of 3ds max before version 5, Boolean operations were implemented poorly. If you are acquainted with our book "3ds max 4: From Objects to Animation," you might have noticed that we never mentioned them. After considerable complaint, 3ds max finally solved a lot of the problems, making Boolean operations much safer to use, even if in most cases you can do without them. We still recommend avoiding them, where possible.

There are three ways to apply logical operations to objects in 3ds max. First, you can create a **Compound Object** based on one of the operands. This method is good when you have to retain integrity in the objects and operands (e.g., for further animation). The second method applies the **Collapse** utility. The third one writes a "$object1 — $object2" command in the MAXScript Listener line, where "object1" and "object2" are the names of the objects. Since we do not have to be particularly safe in this case, we will use the second method:

❑ Create objects for the windows and doorways — we used a simple **Box** — and position them appropriately (Fig. 9.7, *d*). It is important that the boxes intersect both the inner and outer walls; otherwise, you will get cavities instead of openings.

▶ *Note*

If you do not plan to open the door, then you do not need to make the doorway.

Tip

Sometimes, it is useful to hide other objects while editing (<Alt>+<X> key combination).

❏ Select all of the boxes you created by holding the <Ctrl> key and **Collapse** them with the parameters shown in Fig. 9.7, *e*:

> Control panel → Utilities → Collapse → Collapse Selected

❏ Select the room and "openings" while holding the <Ctrl> key, change the parameters as shown in Fig. 9.7, *f*, and press the **Collapse Selected** button again.

❏ This will result in an **Editable Mesh** object. Convert it to an **Editable Poly**.

Now, we have walls with window openings and a doorway. But where is the floor and ceiling? You can create boxes for them, but this is not the best solution: It complicates the **Radiosity** calculation if the floor and ceiling are not joined perfectly. We have also forgotten the top part of the partition.

First, let's finish the partition:

❏ Select and delete the polygons shown in Fig. 9.7, *g*. (Earlier, we added two vertices to the opposing wall to simplify this operation.)

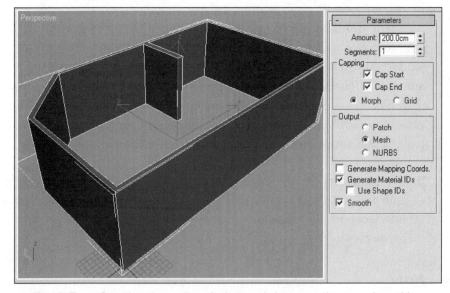

Fig. 9.7, *a*. Creating the walls, window and door openings, and partition

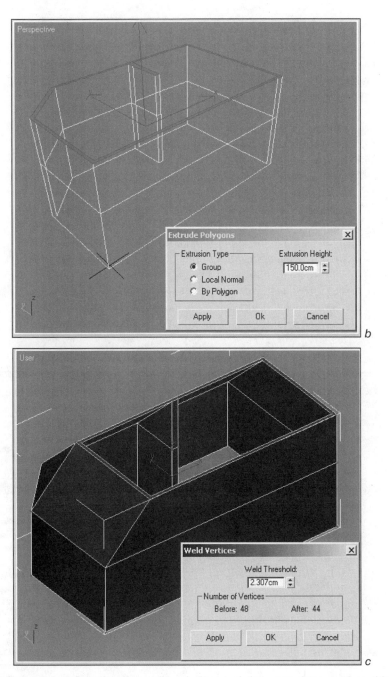

Fig. 9.7, *b* and *c*. Creating the walls, window and door openings, and partition

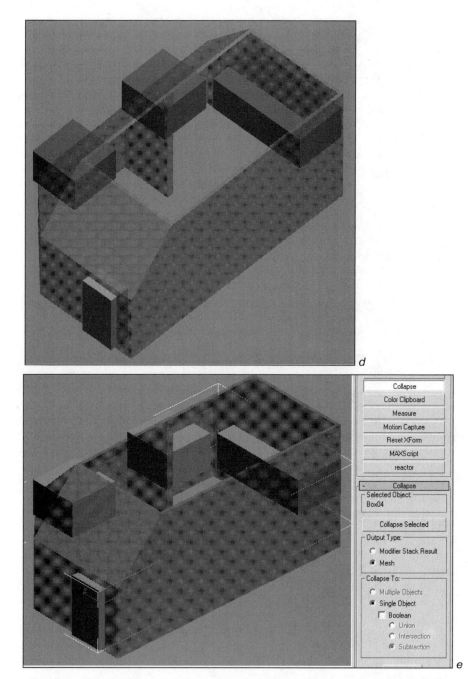

Fig. 9.7, *d* and *e*. Creating the walls, window and door openings, and partition

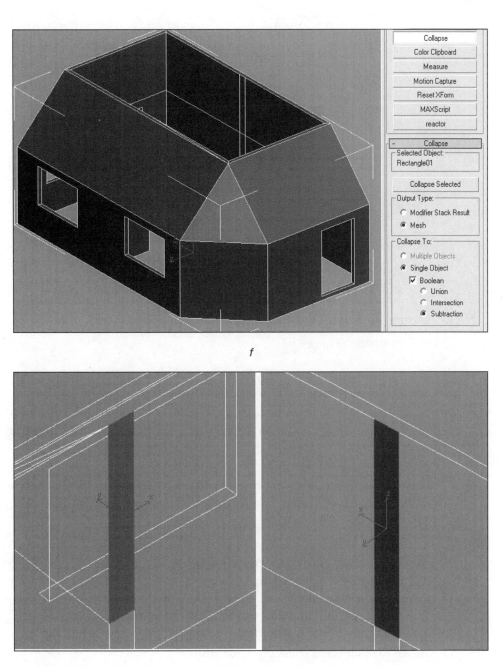

f

g

Fig. 9.7, *f* and *g*. Creating the walls, window and door openings, and partition

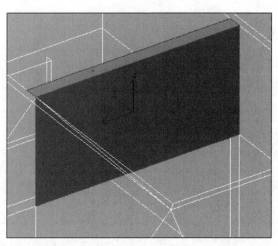

Fig. 9.7, *h*. Creating the walls, window and door openings, and partition

☐ Create polygons for the top part of the partition (Fig. 9.7, *h*):

    Context menu → Create

The following operations require some explanation. They are intended to kill two birds with one stone: first, to create polygons for the ceiling and floor defined by "open" edges (**Border**); second, to separate the outer and inner surfaces and assign them to two different objects, which will help optimize calculating global illumination.

☐ Select the polygons joining the outer and inner surfaces — those at the top and the bottom, as well as those in the window and door openings (Fig. 9.8, *a–c*).

► *Tip*

The **Ignore Backfacing** flag on the control panel may be useful here.   ☑ Ignore Backfacing

☐ Delete the selected polygons. This will divide our model into two elements. You can check this by switching to **Element** editing mode and selecting the outer and inner walls. If all surfaces are selected, you missed something.

☐ Switch to open edges selection mode (**Border**).

☐ By selecting the open edges and applying the **Cap** command, you will create both the floor and the ceiling, exactly matching | Cap |

the shape of the walls (Fig. 9.8, *d*). You will also need to make the roof above the ceiling and the surface below the floor.

☐ Position the exterior polygons to create a "shell" that will block light from outside (Fig. 9.8, *e*).

☐ Select the outer **Element, Detach** it, and rename it **Outer Walls** (Fig. 9.8, *f*). Later, you can **Hide** it to make the editing of other objects easier.

☐ Select the inside and rename it **Inner Walls**.

❗ *Do it yourself*

To make the room more realistic, you might want to bevel the corner joining the walls with the partition (by no more than 5–10 mm). It is easy to miss this when beginning, but slight adjustment considerably enlivens the image.

☐ Save your result. You can find ours on the CD-ROM in Lessons\Lesson09\ Lesson09(room).max.

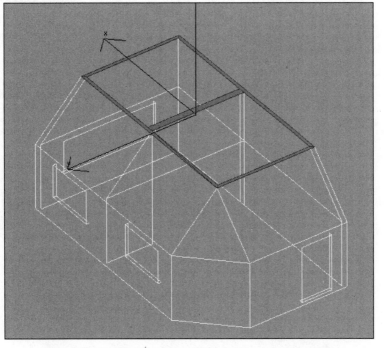

Fig. 9.8, *a*. Final development of the room geometry

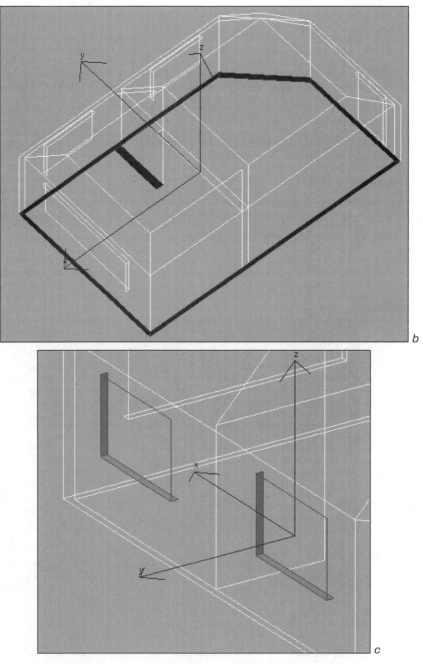

Fig. 9.8, *b* and *c*. Final development of the room geometry

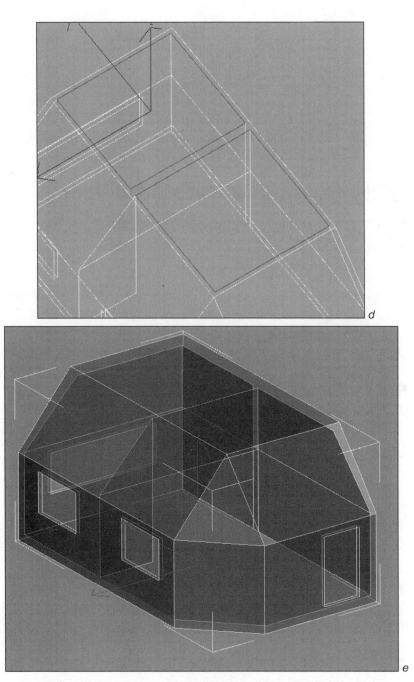

Fig. 9.8, *d* and *e*. Final development of the room geometry

Fig. 9.8, *f*. Final development of the room geometry

Modeling the Window Frames and Door

Before we start to model the window frames, select and hide the **Outer Walls** object:

Context menu → Hide Selection

We will create compound windows, but you are free to experiment with simpler constructions made of primitives.

- ❏ Create a rectangle in the shape of a window in a "direct" projection (**Front** or **Left** view).
- ❏ Create the profile of the glass panes in the same projection (Fig. 9.9, *a*) as follows: Create three triangles and convert one of them to an **Editable Spline**. Join them using the **Attach** command, use the **Boolean** command to make a single spline, and bevel all vertices by 1 cm.

- ❏ Select the rectangle, apply the **Bevel Profile** modifier to it, and select the profile (Fig. 9.9, *b*).

▶ *Note*

You will not find this modifier in the Main menu. Look for it in the modifier stack list.

▶ *Tip*

Sometimes this modifier does not work "correctly." In such a case, you may need to edit either the profile itself, or the **Gizmo** modifier (**Profile Gizmo**).

- ❏ Rename the object **Window Frame**, copy it, adjust the copies, and insert them into the openings in the walls.

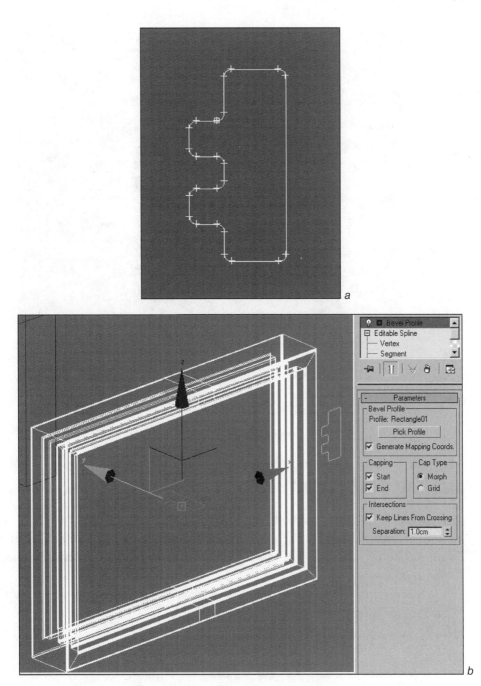

Fig. 9.9. Modeling the window frames

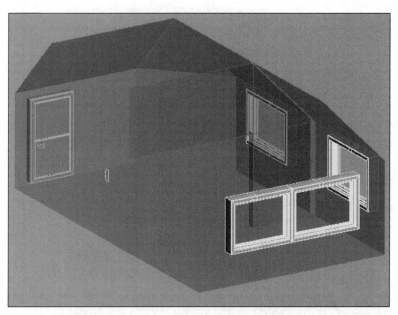

Fig. 9.10. Living room with windows and door

Now make the door, using either primitives or a "concoction" (Fig. 9.10).

❏ Save your file as Lesson09-room01.max:

Main menu → Save As → <+> key

Modeling Soft Furniture

There is no universal method for modeling soft furniture (and furniture in general). Shelves, cabinets, office tables, etc., can be made using primitives, often without getting very detailed. It is much more difficult to model soft furniture or amorphous items.

We propose that you model the armchair and sofa using splines and the **Surface** modifier.

❏ Start with a **Rectangle**:

Main menu → Create → Shapes → Rectangle
or <Ctrl>+Context menu → Rectangle

❏ Convert it to an **Editable Spline**, select the vertices at the corners, and round them off with the **Fillet** command (Fig. 9.11, *a*):

> Context menu → Convert To → Convert To Editable Spline
>
> Context menu → Sub-objects → Vertex or <1> key
>
> Control panel → Fillet

▶ *Tip*

Some commands, including **Fillet,** were deemed "unworthy" of initially being placed in the context menu (**Quad Menu**). You can put them there yourself, but be sure to put the right command in the right place. In our case, we are using the **Fillet (Spline)** command. You should place it in the **Default Viewport Quad** menu of the bottom left **tools2** quadrant in the **Context Spline Tools** branch. Actually, the branch is not so important because 3ds max will find it in any case, but we wanted to show the formal location.

❏ Copy the spline by moving it along the vertical axis while pressing the <Shift> key (Fig. 9.11, *b*).

❏ Make another copy by pressing the <Shift> key while scaling.

❏ Make a copy of the scaled spline by pressing the <Shift> key while moving it down (Fig. 9. 11, *c*).

❏ Select the lowest spline and **Attach** all the others to it in the order they were copied. The order is very important!

❏ Apply the **CrossSection** modifier (Fig. 9.11, *d*) and set the **Spline Options** to **Smooth:**

> Main menu → Modifiers → Patch/Spline Editing → CrossSection

We now have the outline of an armchair. To continue editing, use the **Edit Spline** modifier. Make any necessary adjustments to the outline, apply the **Surface** modifier to obtain the surface, and edit its **Patches**.

Finish the outline so that it consists of triangles and rectangles.

❏ Apply the **Edit Spline** modifier:

> Main menu → Modifiers → Patch/Spline Editing → Edit Spline

❏ Delete the segments that would prevent someone from sitting in the chair (Fig. 9.11, *e*).

☐ Select the vertical segments along the perimeter of the armchair (Fig. 9.11, *f*) and divide them into two halves:

> Control panel → Geometry → Divide

☐ Select the vertices that result and move them to the seat level.

☐ Copy the bottom spline by moving it to the seat level while holding the <Shift> key (Fig. 9.11, *g*).

▶ *Note*

The vertices do not need to coincide; you will be able to adjust them later. It is only important that they are close to each other.

☐ Touch up the elbow-rests (Fig. 9.11, *h*). This includes deleting unneeded segments and creating new ones with the **Create Line** command. To make the vertices of the new lines coincide exactly with the existing vertices, temporarily activate snaps to vertices (<Shift>+Context menu). You will have to do this each time you use **Create Line**; otherwise, the line will return to snaps to the grid. Alternately, you can activate snaps to vertices in the **Grid and Snap Settings** dialog window.

☐ Apply the **Surface** modifier:

> Main menu → Modifiers → Patch/Spline Editing → Surface

Most likely, the current result doesn't look so good. Increase the **Threshold** value of the **Surface** modifier. Everything should look much better! (Fig. 9.11, *i*).

If that does not help, then there is a problem somewhere — most likely there are still polygons with more than four angles. Sometimes this happens when there are no vertices where segments cross. To solve this problem, use the **CrossInsert** command when editing the splines.

Often, it is more convenient to fix holes with patches. We will do so with the hole under the cushion:

☐ Apply the **Edit Patch** modifier:

> Main menu → Modifiers → Patch/Spline Editing → Edit Patch

▶ *Tip*

You may find it useful to uncheck the **Show Interior Edges** flag in the modifier parameters.

```
Surface
  View Steps: 5       ▲▼
  Render Steps: 5     ▲▼
  ☐ Show Interior Edges
```

❐ Use the **Create Patch** command (Fig. 9.11, *j*):

Context menu → Create Patch → create patches by clicking on vertices

▶ *Note*

Two things need to be taken into account when creating patches. First, they should be created with existing vertices. The cursor will look like a "+" if that is the case. If it is cross-shaped, then a vertex will be created in addition to the patch, usually on the grid. Second, the direction of the normal should be taken into account when creating surfaces. If you want it to face toward you, traverse the vertices counter-clockwise when creating the patch.

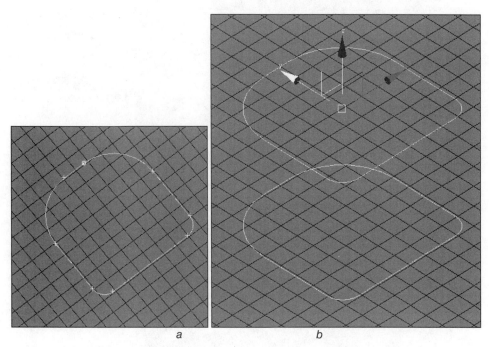

a   *b*

Fig. 9.11, *a* and *b*. Armchair modeling

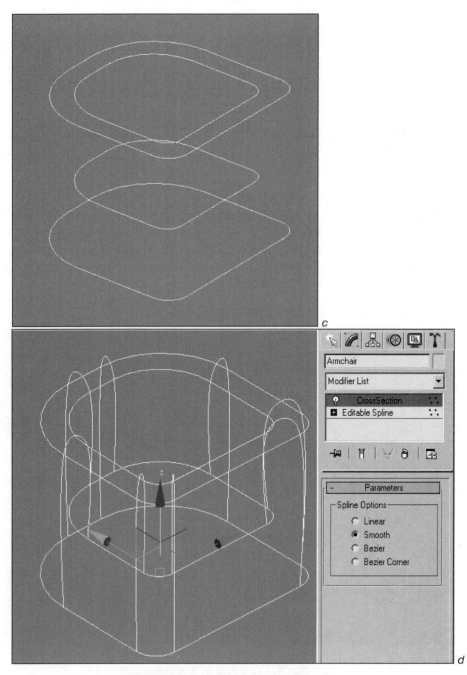

Fig. 9.11, *c* and *d*. Armchair modeling

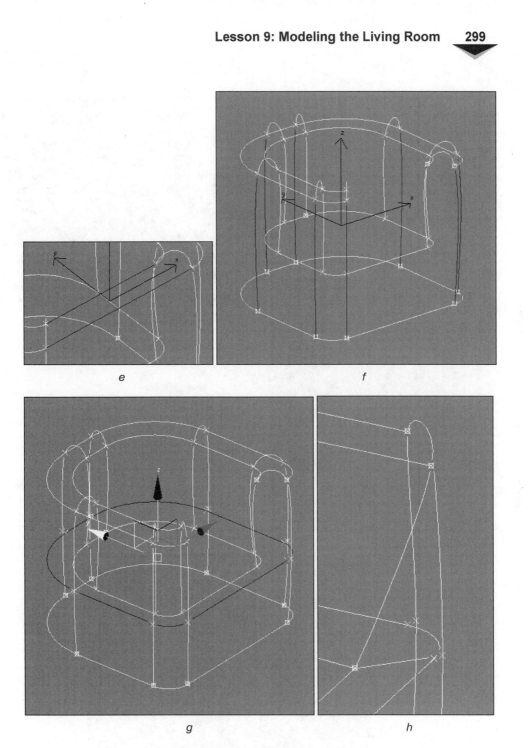

Fig. 9.11, *e–h*. Armchair modeling

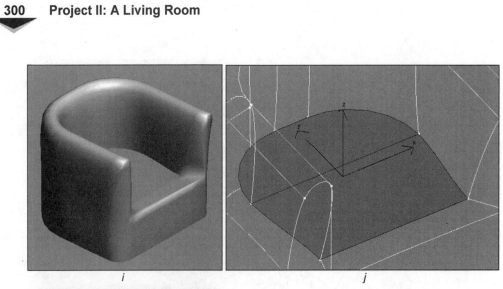

i

j

k

Fig. 9.11, *i*–*k*. Armchair modeling

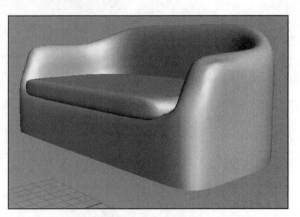

Fig. 9.12. Sofa

Practice using patches by creating a cushion. We made one by selecting the seat patches and creating a new object using the **Detach** command. We then shaped it with the **Extrude** and **Bevel** commands (Fig. 9.11, *k*). The **Relax** modifier enhances the appearance.

We made the sofa from the armchair — it was very easy. We simply moved the corresponding vertices (Fig. 9.12).

Files with the armchair and sofa are named Lesson09(armchair).max and Lesson09(sofa).max, respectively, on the CD-ROM in the Lessons\Lesson09 folder.

Curtain Modeling

To make a good curtain, you cannot do without **Cloth** imitating systems. The possibilities integrated in 3ds max 5 include the **Reactor** system and additional modules such as **SimCloth** or **Stitcher**. Beginning with version 5.0, **Reactor** is included in the package. Prior to this version, it was distributed as a plug-in.

If you do not need ultimate precision or animation of the curtains, the following method is good enough.

▶ *Tip*

If you want to create blinds in addition to the curtains, make sure they are closer to the window and have the right size.

❑ Create a broken line in the **Top** view (Fig. 9.13, *a*). Set the interpolation value to 0 (you will understand why later):

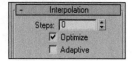

    Main menu → Create → Shapes → Line

❑ **Extrude** it by 200 cm (Fig. 9.13, *b*) and split it into five or six **Segments**. Do not forget to check the **Generate Mapping Coords.** flag!

❑ Apply the **Edit Mesh** modifier and make the folds by selecting and scaling the vertices (Fig. 9.13, *c*):

    Main menu → Modifiers → Mesh Editing → Edit Mesh

❑ Switch to vertex editing (<1> key) and non-uniform scaling (press the <R> key several times).

❑ Switch to the **Use Select Center** mode on the main panel.
❑ Move the vertices to one side.
❑ Apply the **MeshSmooth** modifier, specifying two iterations in the parameters. Apply the **Noise** modifier to "rumple" the result a little (Fig. 9. 13, *d*):

> Main menu → Modifiers → Subdivision Surfaces → MeshSmooth
> Control panel → ... → Subdivision Amount → Iterations
> Main menu → Modifiers → Parametric Deformers → Noise

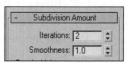

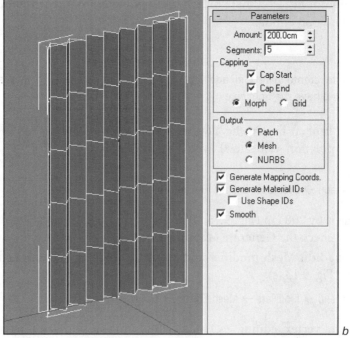

Fig. 9.13, *a* and *b*. Curtain modeling

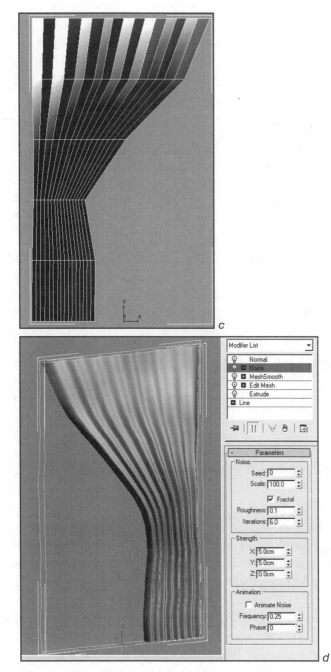

Fig. 9.13, *c* and *d*. Curtain modeling

Note

You do not need to invert the normals because we will use a two-sided material, but you should do it as a matter of practice (Main menu → Modifiers → Mesh Editing → Normal Modifier).

Do it yourself

Try to make the laces holding the curtain aside. Use a spline and the necessary rendering parameters.

So, the curtain is ready. You can convert it to an **Editable Poly**, but hold off for now. You might have to edit it on the spline level first.

❑ Rename it **Curtain** and save the file as Lesson09(curtain).max.

Assembling the Scene

The great moment has come! Everything we have done will be assembled in one scene.

❑ Load your file with the room or use our file (Lessons\Lesson09\Lesson09(room)-01.max on the CD-ROM).

Note

It is possible that you will be warned about **Units Mismatch** when opening the file (Fig. 9.14), in which case you will have to make a choice. The first option is to **Rescale the File Objects to the System Unit Scale**. The second option is to **Adopt the File's Unit Scale**. In our case, the second choice is preferable.

Before we begin adding new objects, we might want to systematize what we already have. It is not obligatory, and the objects we have are not complicated — it is up to you whether it is worth the effort. We use the empirical principle that if something is done quickly (1–2 days) and the project is doomed to be "done and forgotten," then there is no reason to waste time systematizing it. However, if it is a long-term project and we have to return to it later, then it is worthwhile to spend some time putting everything in order. This will help us recall "what is what" even if we open the project in a year. Here, we will discuss 3ds max capabilities for project systematization. It is up to you to decide whether to employ them or not.

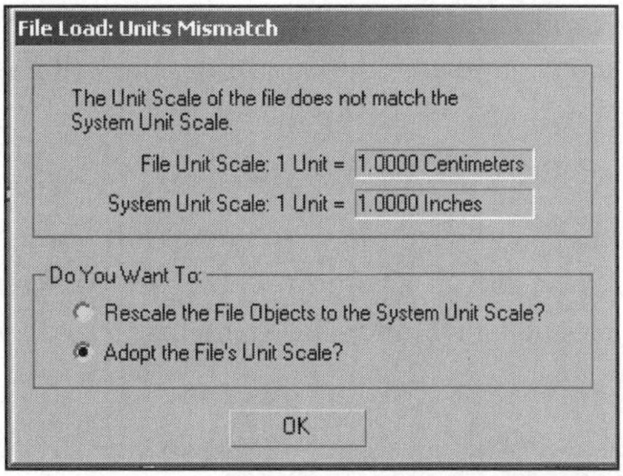

Fig. 9.14. Dialog window indicating **Units Mismatch**

The list of objects in our scene is shown in Fig. 9.15. Only **Rectangle01** is confusing. On closer examination, it turns out to be the profile for the **Bevel Profile** modifier we used to construct the window frames. If deleted, the window frames will be destroyed. Its presence by no means affects the final result, but it is irritating. There are two ways out of this situation. You can **Hide** the object and rename it (e.g., `Frame Profile`); this is recommended if you will need to edit it further on this level. Your other option is to convert the window frames to a base-level **Editable Poly** or **Editable Mesh**. In that case, you can delete the profile without affecting the final result.

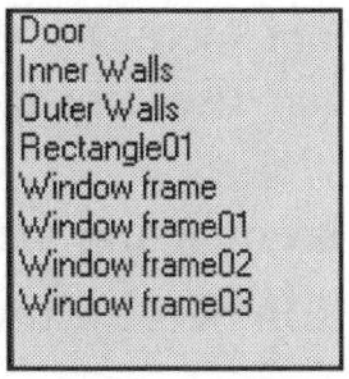

Fig. 9.15. List of objects in the scene

We chose the second way and deleted the profile after converting the window frames to **Editable Poly**.

Select the **Outer Walls** object and hide it, for we will not need it soon:

Context menu → Hide Selection

We propose that you merge the rest of the objects — the "inner" walls, window frames, and door — so that you can work with them more efficiently. There are several methods for systematizing objects in 3ds max. The most efficient (but least convenient) method is to **Attach** objects. Doing so, constituent objects lose their independence and can only be accessed as an object **Element**.

The second method is to **Group** the objects:

Main menu → Group → Group

This method is good if you have to work with objects as a whole, while leaving them independent. You can also group objects of different types (e.g., geometrical objects and sources of light). Individual elements are accessed by opening the group:

Main menu → Group → Open

That step, as well as the necessity to subsequently close it, is its main disadvantage.

The third method uses a **Named Selection** of objects. It has existed since the first versions of 3ds max, but only the fifth version made it useful. We mentioned it in the book "3ds max 4: From Objects to Animation," but only in passing, its practical use being rather limited. At that time, when you created a selection, you could neither exclude nor add objects. The new version is much more powerful and is the one we will use.

Note

There is one more way to systematize objects that we are sure users of 3D Studio VIZ, Autodesk VIZ, and AutoCAD will like — namely, layers. Fortunately for them and unfortunately for us, this tool is absolutely the same as the one integrated in AutoCAD and, in our opinion, is rather limited in 3ds max 5. For example, it does not allow you to exclude a layer from illumination by certain sources of light. Moreover, it has an unfriendly interface. You can find several scripts that make layers more user-friendly at **http://www.scriptspot.com**.

❏ Select all objects in the scene using the <Ctrl>+<A> key combination.
❏ Press the **Named Selection Sets** button on the main toolbar.
❏ In the window that opens, press **Create New Set** and give the set a name (for example, **Walls**) (Fig. 9.16).

Sooner or later, we will use all the buttons enabling you to delete objects from the selection, add new objects, etc. These are rather powerful tools, but they are not without drawbacks — the main one being the necessity of double clicking the desired object. Selecting several objects with the <Shift> and <Ctrl> keys is not supported; we hope that will be corrected in the near future.

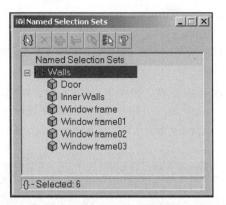

Fig. 9.16. Creating a **Named Selection Set**

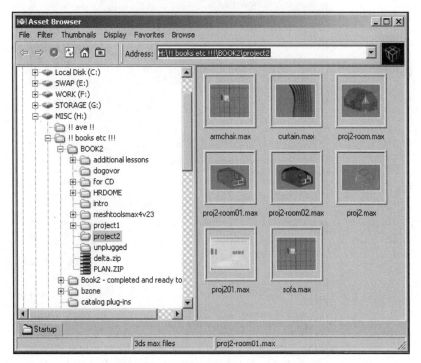

Fig. 9.17. **Asset Browser** window

Now, load the models into the scene. You can use the **Asset Browser**, which allows you to browse local disks, network drives, websites, as well as move models and textures by drag-and-drop. There are two ways to launch the **Asset Browser**: from the control panel (Control panel → Utilities), or from the viewport (Context menu → Views → Extended → Asset Browser) (Fig. 9.17).

Go to the folder with your models, or to the Lessons\Lesson09\ folder on the CD-ROM if you want to use our files. Select the Lesson09(armchair).max file and drag it to the **Top** viewport. (It is necessary to have the right model orientation.) You will have three options: **Open File**, **Merge File**, and **XRef File**. The first two items are self-explanatory, but **XRef File** requires additional attention.

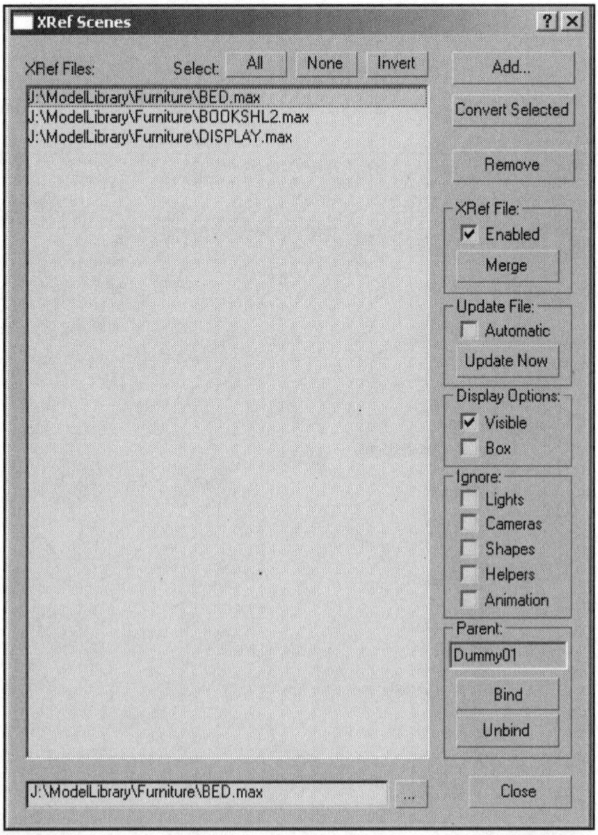

Fig. 9.18. Management window for **XRef Scenes**

You can load objects or whole scenes as references (XRef Objects or XRef Scenes, respectively) in 3ds max, which means a connection will remain with the source file. The difference between XRef Object and XRef Scene is the latter does not allow you to edit objects in the scene. To do so, you will have to **Merge** the scenes in the **XRef Scenes** window (Fig. 9.18), which will break the connection with the source file:

Main menu → File → XRef Scenes

Is working with references worthwhile? There is no doubt such an approach is beneficial for several people working on one project — it enables them to work in parallel. It is also useful if you have created a library of models and want to use them in several projects. It is much easier to edit the library models than those in every project. In other cases, the **Merge** command is preferable, which we will use here.

❑ Put the armchair in its place in the living room (Fig. 9.19, *a*).
❑ We do not know why, but the dimensions seem off, and the armchair is too small. Scale it by all coordinates (**Uniform Scale**).
❑ Make the armchair stand directly on the floor by selecting it, applying the **Align** command, and clicking on the **Inner Walls** object:

Control panel → Align

Select the alignment axis (in our case, the Z axis) and parameters so that the armchair stands on the floor (Fig. 9.19, *b*).

Load the sofa from Lesson 9-Sofa.max. It also seems small. Since we made the sofa out of the armchair, and it needs to be scaled to the same extent, we suggest that you use an interesting option of the **Align** command:

❑ Select the sofa, apply the **Align** command, and click on the armchair.
❑ Specify the alignment parameters that were used in the previous case. In addition, check all three **Match Scale** axes (Fig. 9.19, *c*). The sofa will be aligned and scaled according to the armchair.

Load your curtains and hang them on the windows by copying and rotating them (Fig. 9.19, *d*). Note that we hung the curtains on the big window slightly differently — straight, without being tied open on the sides. It was very easy to do: We selected the **Edit Mesh**

modifier, made the folds, and deactivated it again by pressing the "lamp" icon. You can also change the rumpled nature of the curtains by changing the **Noise** modifier parameters.

Note

You can use the **Merge** command of the Main menu to insert the objects. By doing so, the selected objects will be placed where they were created.

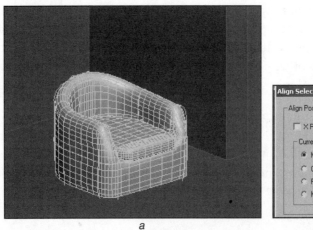

a

b

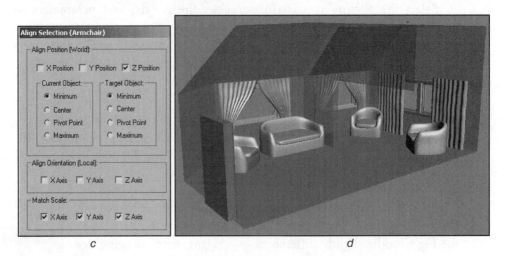

c

d

Fig. 9.19. Furniture arrangement

Do it yourself

We do not have many pieces of furniture in our room, and you may want to make more or supplement them with objects from the 3ds max library. The ModelLibrary folder on the second CD-ROM has many such models. You can use them to fill your room with furniture. Due to licensing reasons, we will not use these models, but you are free to do so.

We now propose that you join these objects and name the selection **Furniture**. You can do so quickly by the following method:

❐   Click on **Walls** in the **Named Selection Set.**

❐   Invert the selection by pressing <Ctrl>+<I>.

❐   In the selection window, type in "furniture" and press <Enter>. You have thus created a new selection named **Furniture**. You can easily select all of the constituent objects in any dialog window where the named selection is used.

❐   Save your file as Lesson09(room)-02.max.

Lesson 10

Daylight Adjustment

Adjusting Daylight without Using the Global Illumination System

Although 3ds max 5 provides two methods of global illumination rendering — **Radiosity** and **Light Tracer** — their use is hampered by a considerable drawback: The rendering time is greatly increased. Therefore, it often makes sense to simulate global illumination using additional sources of light. Fig. 10.1, *a*, shows the placement scheme for the sources of light in our room, and Figs. 10.1, *b–d* illustrate their approximate parameters. The scene file is included in \Lessons\Lesson10\ Scenes\Lesson10(GI-Imitation).max on the accompanying CD-ROM.

> ▶ *Note*
>
> This section is cognitive and may be skipped. If you are a beginner, however, don't be lazy — spend some time looking through it. We do not give a detailed description of the light sources. If you performed the first project, you should understand this process.

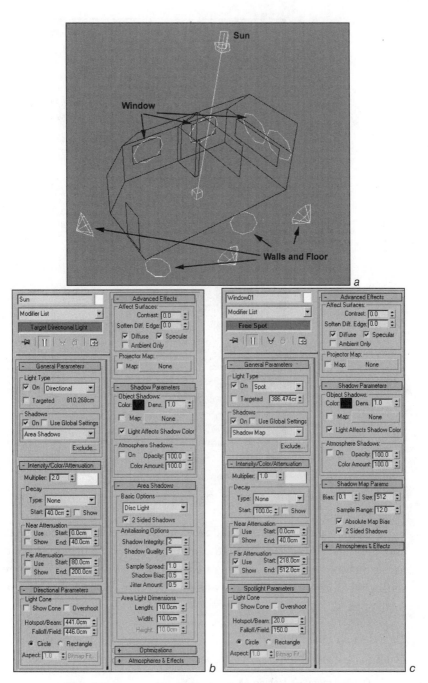

Fig. 10.1, *a–c.* Daylight simulation in the room

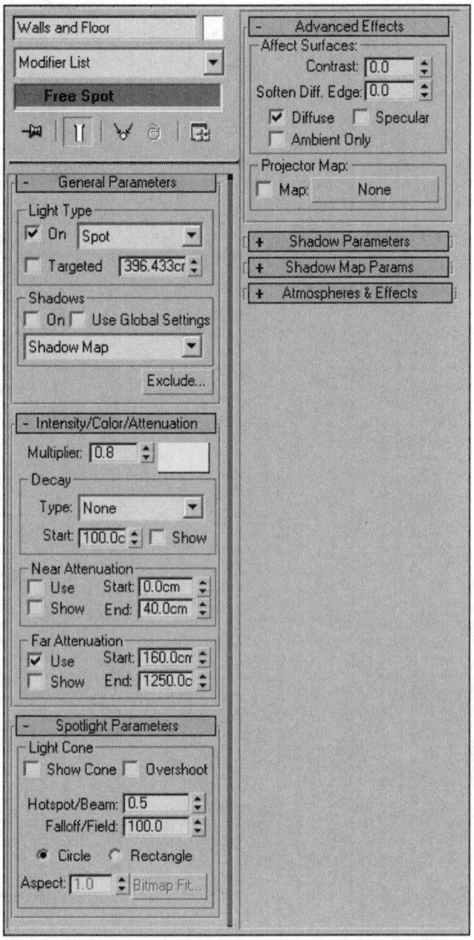

Fig. 10.1, _d_. Daylight simulation in the room

There is a good rule to be followed when you create a scene: First set the light, and then start practicing with the materials. By default, 3ds max paints objects in various colors to help you orient yourself when you model, but they are unfit for setting the illumination. The easiest way to get rid of them is to assign one material to all objects.

❐ Select all objects.

❐ If there are hidden objects in the scene, make them visible first:

Context menu → Unhide All

❏ Open the material editor by pressing the <M> key. Assign the first material named **1-Default** by dragging it from the material preview window (**Sample Slot**) on the objects and selecting the **Assign to Selection** item.

However strange it may seem, the brightest (but the least useful) source of light is the Sun. Its task is to make a bright spot on the floor and on objects within the range of its illumination. To simulate the Sun, a light source of **Direct** type is the most suitable. The color of this light source is yellowish, and it is supposed to cast shadows. However, we recommend setting the **Area Shadows** to a small size to simulate the "spotlessness" of the source (see Fig. 10.1, *b*).

In reality, the main room light goes through the windows, is scattered from the sky, and is reflected from objects (the Earth, houses, etc.). In our book "3ds max 4: From Objects to Animation," we discussed in detail how to create the so-called coelosphere. In this case, however, it does not work. Therefore, we need to create several **Spot** sources (by setting the number of windows) with the greatest attenuation angle. These sources should have a bluish color. They should produce very blurred shadows; the usual shadows of the **Shadow Map** type are good for this purpose, with a higher **Sample Range** value. In addition, it is necessary to adjust the intensiveness attenuation farther from the source. To do so, adjust the **Far Attenuation** parameter (see Fig. 10.1, *c*).

Note

The **Decay** parameter in the light source settings physically employs the most correct approach for attenuating the light. You are free to experiment with it. You can use **Decay** and **Far Attenuation** parameters together, but remember that **Decay** has priority over **Far Attenuation**.

To take into account the light from the floor, the walls, and the ceiling, set a few low-powered sources along the perimeter of your room. These sources should neither cast shadows nor affect the flash channel (**Specular**) of the material. These sources may be placed outside the room, and they may have either **Spot** or **Omni** type. It is important to accurately adjust the intensity of the attenuation (see Fig. 10.1, *d*).

Finally, you can add some ambient light, but be careful. You could lose the 3D-effect.

Main menu → Rendering → Environment → Global Lighting → Ambient

At first glance, this scheme is rather good and suitable for showing to an undemanding customer. However, as a rule, such placement of the light sources is insufficient. If there are objects in the room made of highly reflective or shiny materials (e.g., mirrors or polished wardrobes), you will need additional sources of light.

Tip

The **Light Lister** tool (Main menu → Tools → Light Lister) is useful for setting a large number of light sources. It helps to quickly change the main parameters of light sources.

Do it yourself

Sometimes it is useful to employ not only the source of light, but also the "source of shadow" — the one with the negative value of the **Multiplier** parameter. Try to use such sources to create shadows under the furniture (e.g., under the armchairs).

Adjusting Daylight Using the Global Illumination System

To adjust daylight, we propose using the system called **Daylight**. This system integrates two light sources, which simulate sunlight and scattered daylight, with a special animation controller (based on season, time, and the location of the lit object on the Earth's surface) and an auxiliary object (**Helper**) of the **Compass** type, which determines the orientation of the object.

Note

In previous versions of 3ds max there was a similar **Sunlight** system. For the sake of compatibility, it was retained in 3ds max 5. However, with the addition of the **Daylight** system, it is of no interest.

❏ Create the daylight illumination system in the viewport on the **Top** view (Fig. 10.2):

Main menu → Create → Light → Daylight

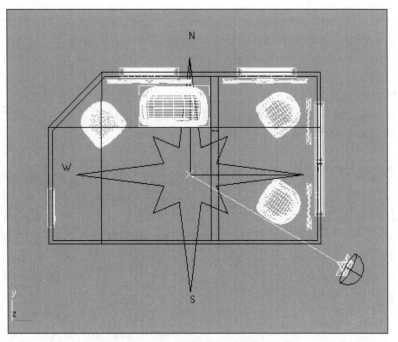

Fig. 10.2. Daylight system creation

Now, turn to the system elements. The compass is the simplest one. The entire illumination system is bound up with this auxiliary object. By default, the North direction coincides with the viewport for the top view. This is logical because it complies with principles accepted in cartography, but if it does not suit you, you can turn the compass as you like. In this case, we want North at the bottom. You can move North by turning the compass or by changing the orientation in the animation controller settings.

The next element is the special animation controller.

❐ Select the **Daylight** system and turn to the animation editing parameters (Fig. 10.3):

Control panel → Motion tab → Control Parameters

Now, let's try to find out what's it all about.

The parameters of the **Time** group determine the moment of time — such as the time of day and the day of the year — for which the lighting is to be rendered. The **Time Zone** parameter determines the time bias relative to Greenwich Mean

Time. This sometimes causes problems, but 3ds max automatically adjusts this parameter according to the system settings. The readings of the system timer at the moment of the daylight system creation are also taken automatically.

Note

You can find the value of this parameter in the Windows settings. For the English version, it is: Control panel → Date and Time → Time Zone.

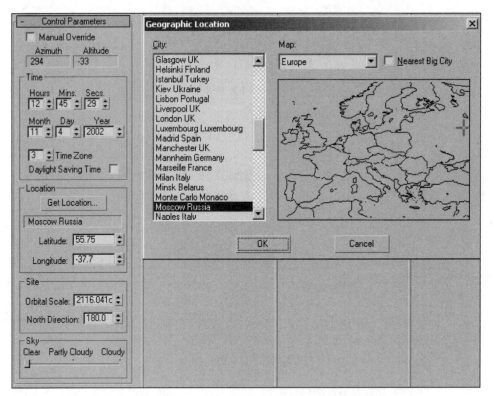

Fig. 10.3. Animation controller parameters for the **Daylight** system

The **Daylight Saving Time** flag takes into account the summer time difference.

The **Location** group enables you to enter the values of the latitude and the longitude of the object manually or using the map, where you can select the object's location.

The parameters of the **Site** group determine the distance to the Sun and sky (**Orbital Scale**), as well as the orientation (**North Direction**). The **Orbital Scale** parameter is not critical, and there is no need to enter the real distance (150 million kilometers). The important thing is that the Sun was never inside the room.

Last, but not least, the **Sky** group lets you redistribute the energy between the Sun and the sky depending on the weather conditions. Its use is justified only when **IES Sun** and **IES Sky** are used as sources of light.

Note

All parameters can be animated. You can easily animate the change of illumination (for a room or cottage) depending on the time of the day, season, or weather conditions.

Now, let us examine the parameters of the light sources. To do this, go to the **Modify** panel (Fig. 10.4).

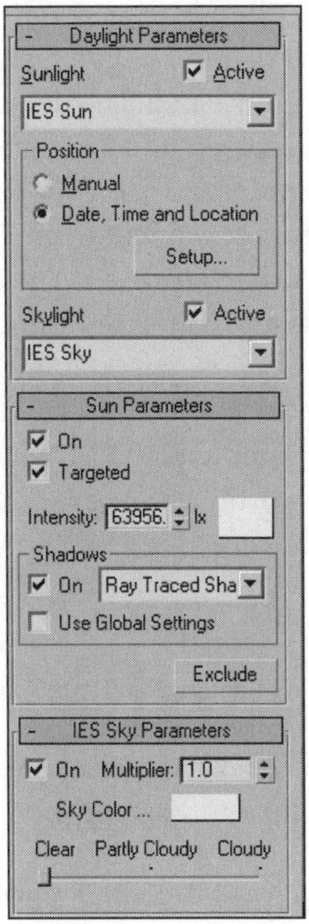

Fig. **10.4.** Adjustment parameters for **Daylight** sources

Note

We have regrouped the rollouts to discuss the most important parameters first.

The parameters in the **Daylight** rollout let you select the type of the light sources that will simulate the Sun and the sky. This selection is not big, but it is fundamental. You can use either **IES Sun** or the standard directional source of light (**Direct Light**) as the Sun. Similarly, you can use either **IES Sky** or **Skylight** as the sky. To use the system to its full advantage, we recommend that you use the **IES Sun/IES Sky** bond. Why?

The **IES** prefix stresses that these sources of light comply with the standard of the Illuminating Engineering Society of the U.S.A., which proves the sources' reliability from the physical point of view. In addition, the use of these sources makes the intensiveness of the sunlight dependent on the Sun's position above the horizon, which, in turn, depends on the season, the time of the day, and the nebulosity parameter specified in the **IES Sky Parameters** rollout. Combining all of these parameters provides realistic illumination conditions.

It is worth mentioning that in 3D-graphics, the notions of "realistic" and "beautiful" do not always go hand-in-hand. The developers of 3ds max know this and provide you with an option to correct any parameters as you like. For example, with daylight you can ignore the automatic settings by switching to the **Manual** mode.

The other rollouts are independent from the type of light source and the shadows that are used. Do not edit them at this stage. The only thing you should do is ensure that the **2 Sided Shadows** flag is checked in the **Shadows** parameters for the Sun.

We have adjusted daylight to 5:00 PM, Moscow time, June 4, 2002.

To continue, it is worth creating a camera and placing it in the room (Fig. 10.5). First, create the camera on the top view, using the **Target Camera** type.

❏ Create the camera:

Main menu → Create → Cameras → Target Camera

However, it will be more convenient to work with a camera of the **Free Camera** type. You can switch the camera type on the control panel.

❏ You can find the view from the camera by pressing the <C> key and expanding it to full screen (the <Alt>+<W> key combination). In this example, the camera turned out to be set "on the floor." Raise it a little by moving the view in the viewport using the middle mouse button. Make the camera wide-angle by pressing the **35mm** button on the control panel.

☐ Select all objects and assign one simple material to them. If there are hidden objects in your scene, make them visible beforehand:

Context menu → Unhide All

☐ Open the material editor by pressing the <M> key. Assign the first material called **1-Default** by moving it from the preview window (**Sample Slot**) on the object and selecting the **Assign to Selection** item.

☐ Make the test rendering:

Main panel → Quick Render

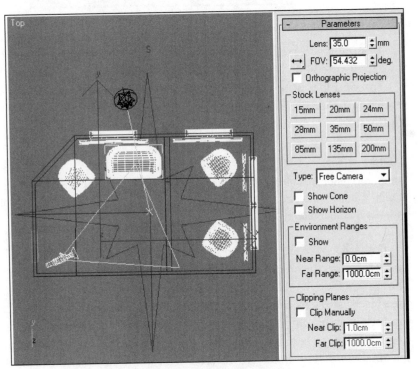

Fig. 10.5. Position and parameters of the camera

We are sure that you will have nothing but a black square and white spots from the sunlight (Fig. 10.6). So, what is the trouble?

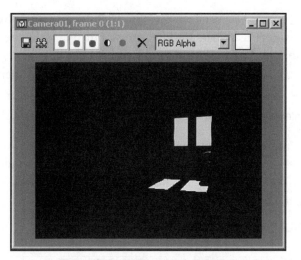

Fig. 10.6. Test rendering result

This result occurred because the daylight system is not independent. It is necessary to adjust two additional procedures: **Advanced Lighting** and **Exposure Control**.

To continue, note that there are two absolutely different global illumination rendering processes integrated in the 3ds max 5: **Light Tracer** and the so-called **Radiosity**.

▶ Note

The term "global illumination" has several synonyms: indirect lighting, reflectance lighting, etc. In the final analysis all of these terms meant the same thing, but "global illumination" was the one that took root.

Both processes are supposed to solve the same task: render the global illumination. However, they perform it differently. The **Light Tracer** employs the so-called photon method. A source of light emits particles that, when reflected from the objects' surfaces and gradually attenuated depending on the surface properties, produce a global illumination effect. This method features a considerable drawback: You must re-render the solution for each frame, which greatly increases the final rendering time. However, if you want to light the model using only the coelosphere, this method is preferable.

The **Radiosity** method is based on rendering the light energy on a surface and redistributing it on the other surfaces. Radiosity divides the surfaces into many small elements through a process called meshing. The smaller the elements, the more accurate the solution, and the more time it takes to render. The rendering time of one frame, however, is barely increased; therefore, the rendering of the camera moving within the room is rather quick. Be aware that any change to the scene geometry, parameters of the sources of light, materials, etc., makes it necessary to repeat the rendering.

In our case, we will use the **Radiosity** method.

❏ Open the **Advanced Lighting** settings window:

Main menu → Rendering → Advanced Lighting

❏ Select **Radiosity** in the drop-down menu and press the **Start** button. The global illumination rendering will start; this may take several minutes.

After the process is completed, you will see the image shown in Fig. 10.7 in the camera viewport. You will obtain almost the same image after the test rendering, and this image will leave much to be desired!

Fig. 10.7. Result of **Radiosity** rendering in the viewport

▶ *Note*

You will see this image only if you are in the shaded reflection mode in the viewport (**Smooth+Highlights**) and the **Display Radiosity in Viewport** flag is checked.

☑ Display Radiosity in Viewport

❗ *Attention*

The **Use Advanced Lighting** flag should be checked in the rendering parameters (Main menu → Rendering → Render → Common Parameters → Advanced Lighting).

Now, let's improve the appearance of the scene.

As previously mentioned, the rendering accuracy with the **Radiosity** method directly depends on the degree to which objects are divided into the triangle elements, or "meshes". In our case, the inner surfaces of the room — the **Inner Walls** object — are ideal for dividing into many triangle surfaces. 3ds max provides several options for controlling this process. You can assign the dividing degree for all objects in the scene by setting a value in the **Radiosity Meshing Parameters** rollout in the **Advanced Lighting** dialog window. This is the simplest, but not the best, solution.

| Radiosity Meshing Parameters |
| Global Subdivision Settings |
| ☐ Enabled   Meshing size: 100.0cm |
| These settings can be overriden on any object through its properties dialog. |

Indeed, the curtains and the furniture have a rather complex grid, and the outer walls need no triangulation at all. The second method is to apply the **Subdivide** modifier, which you can apply to the **Inner Walls** object. Finally, the third method is to specify the triangulation degree in the properties of the object itself. We recommend that you use this method.

☐ Select the **Inner Walls** object and open its settings:

Context menu → Properties

☐ Turn to the **Advanced Lighting** tab, uncheck the **Use Global Subdivision Settings** flag, and specify the dividing value — 10 (Fig. 10.8).

☐ Press **OK** and start the **Radiosity** rendering again. You will be warned that the properties of the **Inner Walls** object were changed. Press the **Reset and Continue** button to start the rendering from the beginning.

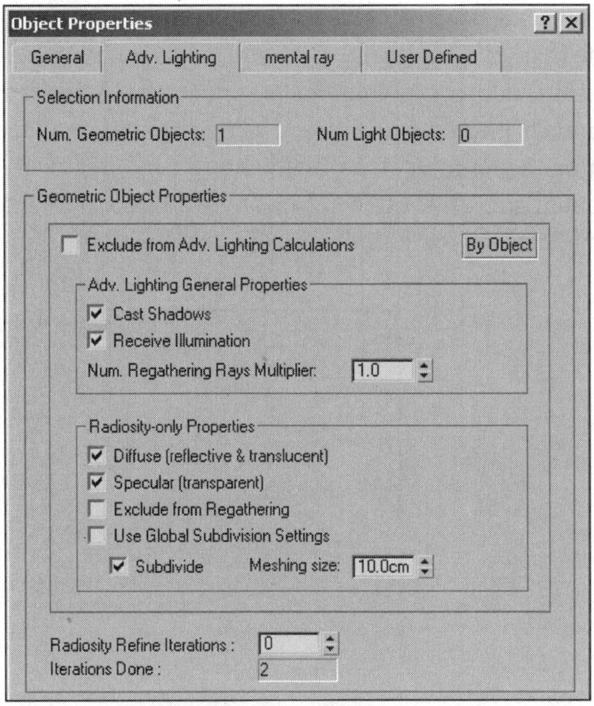

Fig. 10.8. Triangulation parameters for the object

The process will take more time, but the result will be better.

There are several ways to perform further finishing. You can increase the degree of the objects' division, although this is not the best solution from the point of view of the rendering time. You can try to improve the quality (**Initial Quality**) and refining (**Refine Iterations**). In this case, you will not have to render everything anew. Finally, you can smooth the "spots" using the **Filtering** parameter. We obtained a decent result with the parameters shown in Fig. 10.9.

Notice that the spot from the Sun is absolutely white, even too white, whereas the corners of the room are too dark. In reality, you rarely see such contrast. This point needs more detailed consideration.

Today, the most advanced optical device for a human is his eye. Neither photographic camera, nor camera-recorder, TV, or computer display can reproduce the variety of colors and tints available around us. It is not uncommon for a photo made in the most picturesque place, saturated with colors, light, and amazing effects, to become a disappointing piece of paper filled with pale spots and shadows.

This problem has become acute as "fully automatic" (and rather expensive) cameras fill the market. This is why we swore off taking pictures of the mountain landscapes; uninitiated people would fail to appreciate their beauty, and those knowing have seen such photos many times! Cinematographers and photographers have been fighting these problems by highlighting dark areas with spotlights and screening direct sunlight. They often substitute overhead spotlights for sunlight to make the dynamic range of the illumination conform with the film speed.

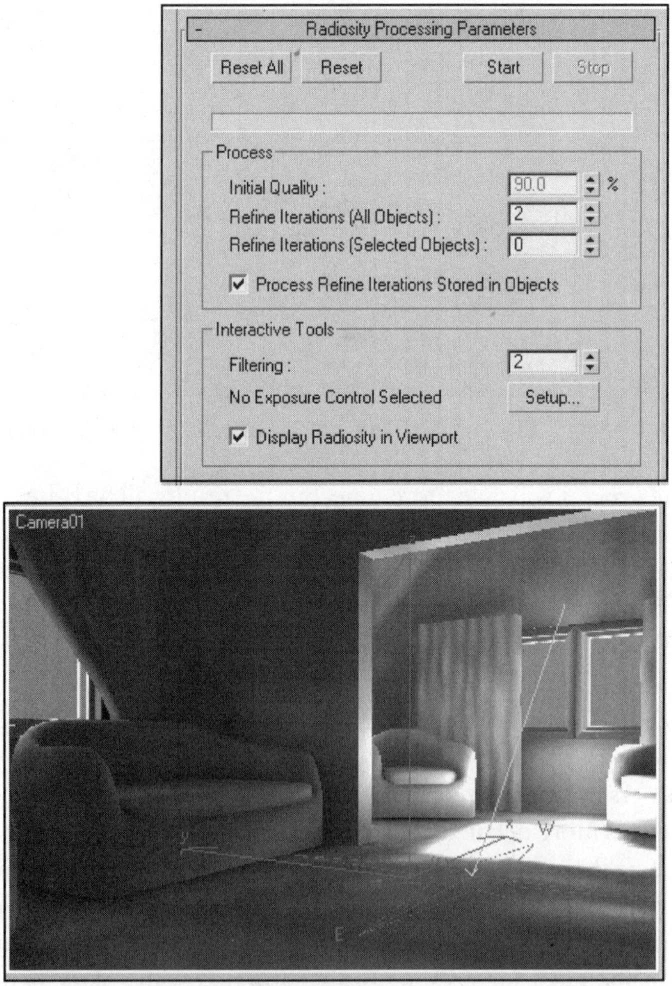

Fig. 10.9. **Radiosity** parameters and rendering result in the viewport

You can solve this problem by employing the exposure control process (**Exposure Control**). You can open the exposure control settings window from the **Advanced Lighting** settings menu or from the main menu (Rendering → Environment).

▶ *Tip*

Since you have opened this menu, make sure the background color is set to pale blue; it is daytime outside.

Open **Exposure Control** and select in the drop-down menu… What? Why are there several choices? Let us try to answer these questions.

The developers of 3ds max offer four procedures for controlling exposure (Fig. 10.10).

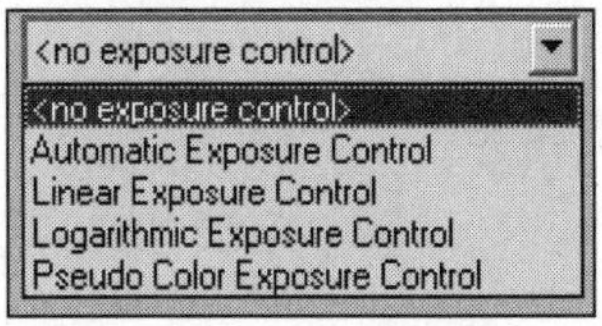

Fig. 10.10. Drop-down menu for selecting the exposure control procedure

Let us start from the end of the list by implementing the algorithm with the strangest name: **Pseudo Color Exposure Control**. The result of its application is no less strange. In our case, everything has been painted red. This happened because this process is not an exposure controller, even if it is placed in this menu. The results of this procedure let you estimate the illumination and the objects' luminance in the scene so you can correctly set the sources of light when the interior design is developed. Try to change some of the parameters in the settings (e.g., increase the **Max.** value in the **Display Range** group to 5000) and see what happens. A detailed consideration of this process is beyond the scope of this book, so refer to the "User's Manual" a physics course for more information.

The remaining three processes are variations of one algorithm used to compensate for the imperfection of the displaying devices (e.g., computer display).

❑ **Automatic Exposure Control** creates a bar chart (users of Adobe Photoshop know it well) based on the entire dynamic range and corrects the illumination by expanding the range. This provides excellent results. Unfortunately, it is not applicable to scenes with animation because a separate bar chart is created for each frame, which leads to inadmissible flickering.

❑ **Linear Exposure Control** uses the average brightness value to expand the dynamic range. This algorithm can help improve images with a very low dynamic range. Here, the problems with animation are the same as with **Automatic Exposure Control**: An average brightness is rendered for each frame.

❑ **Logarithmic Exposure Control** does not use bar charts and is perfect for animation. But you have to pay for it by using a complex setting procedure. This is comparable to a photographic camera with fully manual controls.

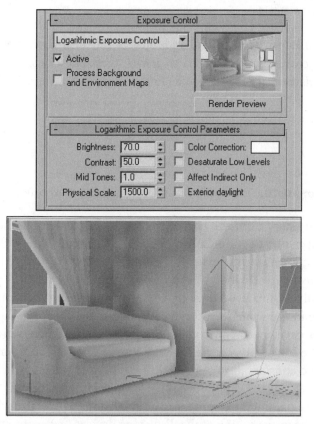

Fig. 10.11. Settings for the exposure process parameters and the result in the viewport

In general, all of these exposure controls are easy to understand and use. The only difficulty may be the **Physical Scale** parameter. Standard sources of light can appear photometrical. The **Physical Scale** parameter is provided to correctly process the light from the standard sources and convert dimensionless quantities to physical values. There are only photometrical sources of light in our scene, so this parameter does not affect the final result.

We hope that, while reading the above, you have tried all of these processes and noticed how the picture in the viewport changed. We set the parameters as shown in Fig. 10.11. You will need to return to them later.

Save your work in the file named Lesson10(room-radiosity).max.

Artificial Lighting

Although artificial lighting is beyond the scope of this book, we should mention the new features of 3ds max in this area.

To simplify the work with artificial lighting, a whole class of light sources is provided in 3ds max, called photometrical sources (**Photometric Lights**). These differ from standard sources because they use physical values to set their parameters. As an example, consider the most demonstrative type: **Area Light** (Fig. 10.12). This type simulates spatial sources of light (e.g., daylight lamps encapsulated in the plastic cases).

❑ **Light Type** is the type of light source (**Area**, in our example). The dimensions of the source of light are in the **Area Light Parameters** rollout. In this case, these are the dimensions of the luminescent surface.

❑ You can select any of the available types of **Shadows**; in this case, **Area Shadows** is appropriate. Notice that the dimensions are not controlled in **Area Shadows** because they are connected to the dimensions of the light source.

❑ **Distribution** distributes light. 3ds max supports several types of distribution, from simple (**Isotropic** and **Diffuse**) to physically correct (**Web**), based on the light distribution diagrams, or goniograms.

❑ The **Color** and **Intensity** parameters are based on the physical properties of real sources of light. Refer to the manufacturer for information on these.

Notice that the sources of artificial light have no **Decay** and **Attenuation** parameters. These properties are specified automatically.

For details on the parameters of the photometrical sources of light, see the "User's Manual."

When these types of light sources are used, the best result is obtained by jointly using the global illumination rendering system and exposure control.

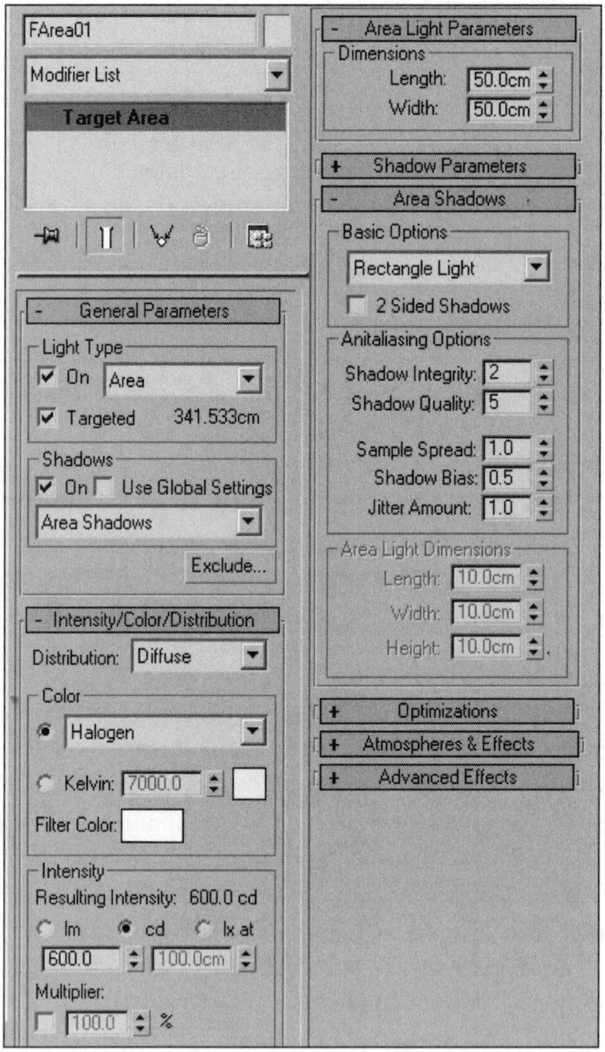

Fig. 10.12. Parameters for the **Area Light**

 Note

Despite assurances from the 3ds max developers about the physical correctness and truthfulness of the results obtained with the use of the photometrical sources of light, global illumination systems, and exposure control, you are free to experiment on your own. Don't be upset if you are not satisfied with the results. Try to change all possible parameters to get the best appearance. Combine various methods, or even tint the result in a 2D editor. And don't neglect the filters. In this case, the end justifies the means.

Lesson 11

Global Lighting Material

Now, it is time to "paint" our room and assign materials to the objects.

❏ Load the lesson11-01.max file from the \Lessons\Lesson11\Scenes folder on the CD-ROM. At present, all objects in the scene have one material assigned: **1-Default**.

▶ **Note**

If you use your own file, your scene likely contains the light distribution rendered earlier. It is worthwhile to temporarily get rid of this light; otherwise, you will have to render it many times. To do this, open the advanced lighting window and deactivate the radiosity process:

Main menu → Rendering → Advanced Lightin → Active

❏ For further work, it makes sense to activate the default sources of light:

Viewport context menu → Configure → Rendering Method → Rendering Options → Default Lighting

☑ Default Lighting
◉ 1 Light   ○ 2 Lights

The only object of our scene that requires assignment and adjustment of the **Explicit** texture coordinate is **Inner Walls**. The armchairs and the sofa will be assigned a one-color material, and a procedure texture will be used for the pattern. The sashes and the door also will be "painted" one color. The curtains were assigned texture coordinates at their creation.

❏ Select the **Inner Walls** object using selection by name (<H> key) and hide all the other objects. Thus, it will be more convenient to assign materials and texture to the object:

    Context menu → Hide Unselected

If you did the first project, then it will not be difficult for you to create materials, assign them correctly to objects, and adjust texture coordinates. We, however, would like to consider in more detail all possible methods of assigning materials and imposing texture coordinates on an object as simple as our room. You may learn something new that will be to your liking.

The first method is based on application of a **Multi/Sub-object** material, which was created automatically when materials were assigned to the various parts of the object. Then, the **Poly Select** and **UVW Map** modifiers are used to adjust the texture coordinates for each of the selected polygons. This is our favorite method, although it's not without drawbacks. The main drawback is the need for complete attention and accuracy when working with the stack, because any casual action may lead to nearly irreparable consequences.

The second method is also based on the application of a **Multi/Sub-object** material, but adjustment of the texture coordinates is carried out slightly differently. Starting from the third version of 3ds max, there is an option to assign up to 99 texture channels (**Map Channels**) to the texture using **Explicit Map Channel**. The ratio is easily defined: The **Map Channel** parameter in the material editor should correspond to the one in **UVW Map** modifiers. Then adjustment comes to successive application of **UVW Map** modifiers to the whole object, each of the modifiers determining the texture coordinates for the corresponding channel. Although this may seem complex, the process allows you to efficiently employ one simple material with a **Composite** texture. We usually try to avoid such exotics unless they are justified, but this one at times is the only solution (for example, if a logo is imposed on a surface that already has an assigned texture).

▶ *Note*

Some people may wish to make computer graphics as "showy" as possible. They often are either beginners who take every revelation as a call for action, or skilled professionals who are simply "playing to the max." However, those who treat computer graphics as a means of livelihood, not as an end in itself, are apt to find the simplest and most efficient methods for gaining their final result.

The third method that we recommend is to split the object into independent objects, assign a simple material to each object, and texture each one separately.

Before you split the object, you can assign the same **Material ID** to all polygons. This will help you avoid problems later on when you merge the objects back into one.

❑ Select all polygons and assign the same material index to all of them:

   Control panel → Polygon Properties → "1" for Material

❑ Successively select the polygons corresponding to these elements and **Detach** them to create new objects:

   Control panel → Edit Geometry → Detach

▶ *Tip*

Some polygons are convenient to select on straight projections (e.g., on the Left view). Uncheck the **Ignore Backfacing** flag.

Fig. 11.1 shows all of the resultant objects. To make the figure more demonstrative, we separated the objects. (You do not need to do this.) Note that we created a separate object (**Diagonal Wall**) for one of the walls. Later we will explain its purpose.

You have to create and assign three materials: for the floor, the walls, and the ceiling. Those for the floor and the walls will contain textures loaded from files with raster images. The corresponding objects want explicit indication of the texture coordinates. The ceiling material can be easily implemented using procedure textures; you don't have to assign texture coordinates on the ceiling.

▶ *Note*

If you've seen the final reel, you might have been horrified. We agree that a ginger polished table, tastelessly patterned blue wallpaper with no less tasteless violet curtains, and cream-colored furniture are a bit excessive. All this "grandeur" was made deliberately to demonstrate possible problems and ways of coping with them. Hopefully, you have good taste and will be able to match the textures and materials so that you would want to live in this room. If colors are matched perfectly, it is possible that no additional settings will be needed.

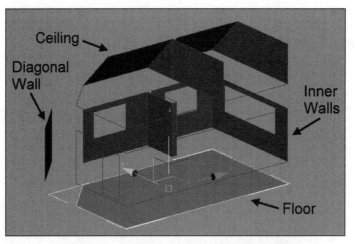

Fig. 11.1. Splitting the **Inner Walls** object

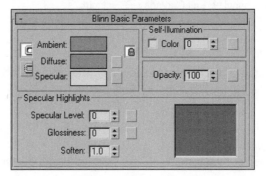

Fig. 11.2. Basic parameters of the materials for the floor, walls, and ceiling

Generally, a **Blinn** type of **Shader** may be used on all three materials. Make all materials lusterless by specifying the bas parameters shown in Fig. 11.2.

► *Tip*

Adjust one material, then duplicate it by transferring it to the neighboring preview window (**Material Slot**) of the material editor. Rename each material **Floor**, **Walls**, and **Ceiling**, respectively.

When creating materials for use with the global lighting system, remember that direct light (in our case, from the Sun (**IES Sun**)) affects the **Specular** and **Diffuse** channels, whereas reflected light and that of the "sky" (**IES Sky** or **SkyLight**) affect the **Ambient** channel. For correct rendering, the colors and the textures imposed on the **Diffuse** and **Ambient** channels must match. That is the default state of materials in 3ds max, indicated by the pressed buttons locking (**Lock**) the **Ambient** and **Diffuse** colors and textures. If you wish, you can get interesting effects by toggling off these links and "playing" with the colors and textures.

❏ Assign appropriate textures on the **Diffuse** channel of the **Floor** and **Walls** materials. We used the texture files supplied with 3ds max. You can also use any file from your own library of textures:

> Material editor → button in Diffuse line
> Material/Map Browser → Bitmap

To assign textures from raster image files, you can use the **Asset Browser** module. Select the required file and transfer it with a button.

▶ *Note*

Quite unexpectedly, we got to know another feature of 3ds max. You can transfer raster images directly on objects and selected sub-objects. The procedure creates the material, with the corresponding image merged on its **Diffuse** channel. In the case of sub-objects, a **Multi/Sub-object** material is created. Many are the mysteries of 3ds max, indeed!

❏ Assign materials to the objects: the **Floor** material to the **Floor** object, the **Walls** material to the **Inner Walls** and **Diagonal Wall** objects, the **Ceiling** material to the **Ceiling** object. It is convenient to select the objects by name and assign the materials using the **Assign Material to Selection** button.

❏ In the materials' parameters, toggle on the materials' display in the viewport. The objects will be painted the colors of the textures, but no textures will be visible.

❏ Assign texture coordinates to the objects using the **UVW Map** modifier:

> Main menu → Modifiers → UV Coordinates → UVW Map

Planar coordinates will do for the floor (Fig. 11.3, *a*). There are a few ways of setting the coordinates, but in our case it is convenient to change the size and position of the modifier's **Gizmo**. Distorting the texture looks bad, so you can bring the size of the modifier's gizmo into accordance with that of the texture file by pressing the **Bitmap Fit** button and selecting the texture file. Then scale by two coordinates, retaining the sides ratio, to change the dimensions.

For walls oriented to each other at right angles, the **Box** type will do (Fig. 11.3, *b*). If the walls are not at right angles, this type is bound to introduce inevitable distortions. Therefore, the separate **Diagonal Wall** object was created. To texture it, copy and transfer the modifier from the **Inner Walls**, then orient the modifier's gizmo using the **Normal Align** command.

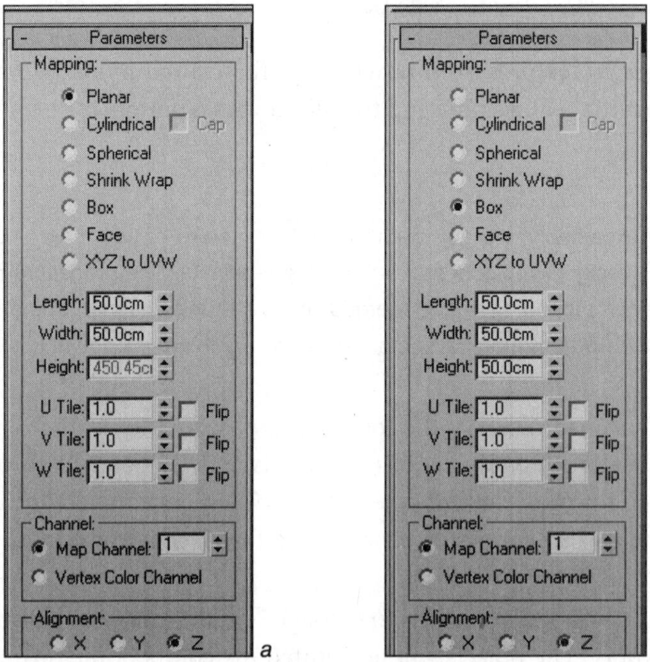

Fig. 11.3. Editing texture coordinates

Make the material of ceiling bright. Don't assign textures for existing channels. After all coordinates are adjusted, merge all of the objects into one.

❒ Select the **Inner Walls** object and **Attach** the rest of the objects to it using selection-by-name:

Context menu → Attach → select all objects in the list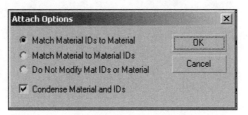

❒ In the **Attach Options** window, choose **Match Material IDs to Material** in response to the question about the materials assigned to the objects (Fig. 11.4).

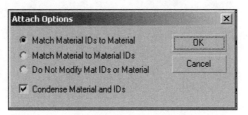

Fig. 11.4. Attach Options window

❒ Select any free preview window in the material editor and load the material into it using the "dropper" (**Pick Material from Object**). As you can see, the material consists of three sub-materials (Fig. 11.5). Rename the material **Room**.

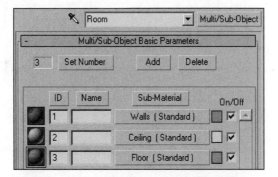

Fig. 11.5. Structure of the **Room** material

❒ Unhide the **Outer Walls** and **Window Frame##** objects:

Context menu → Unhide by Name

❒ Create a bright material, rename it **Frames**, and assign it to the sashes (**Window Frame##** objects).

❒ Assign any **Default** material to the **Outer Walls** object.

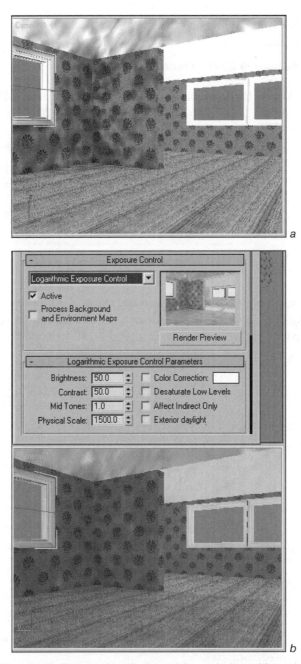

Fig. 11.6. Result of radiosity quick rendering without (*a*) and with (*b*) the exposure control process

Now you can render the global lighting. We assume that the objects' parameters responsible for global lighting are specified as described in *Lesson 10*.

❑ Open the advanced lighting window and activate radiosity:

> Main menu → Rendering → Advanced Lighting → Radiosity

❑ Specify the **Initial Quality** parameter equal to 50%. (This will do for quick rendering.) Start rendering.

The resulting scene will be overexposed (Fig. 11.6, *a*). The **Exposure Control** process can help you adjust the brightness (Fig. 11.6, *b*).

There is yet another problem: painting the walls and the ceiling with the floor-texture color. In reality, if you enter an empty room on a bright, sunny day, you will see a similar effect: The painting is too strong and needs to be reduced.

► Note

Further editing depends on the textures you applied to the objects. We already pointed out the purpose of our coloring. You will have to correct the settings yourself. You can find our file (lesson11-02.max) in the \Lessons\Lesson11\Scenes folder on the CD-ROM.

In the material editor of 3ds max 5, there is the option to redistribute the reflected and transmitted light. To use this option, activate the display of this information (Fig. 11.7, *a*):

> Main menu → Customize → Preferences → Advanced Lighting → Display Reflectance and Transmittance Information

For each material in the material editor, a line will display the average and the maximal **Reflectance** and **Transmittance** values (Fig. 11.7, *b*).

► Note

You can use this option only if your 3ds max has been updated to version 5.1 or later. It option does not work in the previous release (5.0).

The developers of 3ds max recommend adjusting materials so that the reflected energy for non-brilliant materials remains 20–50%.

Fig. 11.7. Activating the display of materials' light distribution (*a*)
and a corresponding line in the material editor (*b*)

To adjust the materials using the global lighting system, there is a special type of material provided in 3ds max: the composite **Advanced Lighting Override** material. It enables you to adjust the light without changing the original material.

❏ Use **Advanced Lighting Override**, for the **Room** material leaving the original material as a sub-material. Rename the material **Room Override**.

> Material editor → Room + Advanced Lighting Override
>
> Select "Keep old material as sub-material?" in the Replace Material window

We obtained a decent result with the parameters in Fig. 11.8. Now, let us consider in detail the meanings of these parameters.

❏ **Reflectance Scale** enables you to change the degree of reflection according to the material's surface. We slightly reduced this parameter and obtained the cherished 40% for the average value of the reflected energy.

❏ **Color Bleed** enables you to change the degree of the object's illumination by reflected light. We considerably reduced this parameter.

❏ **Transmittance Scale** enables you to change the degree of light transmission by the object. This is used for semi-transparent objects.

❏ **Luminance Scale** emits light from objects assigned a self-luminous material.

❏ **Indirect Light Bump Scale** enables you to solve problems that may occur with indirect light (e.g., "saturating" a bump).

During material adjustment, you will have to render radiosity several times. When materials' parameters are changed, new rendering is required. To do this, press the **Reset** button before rendering is started. If objects in the scene were moved, it is necessary to press the **Reset All** button.

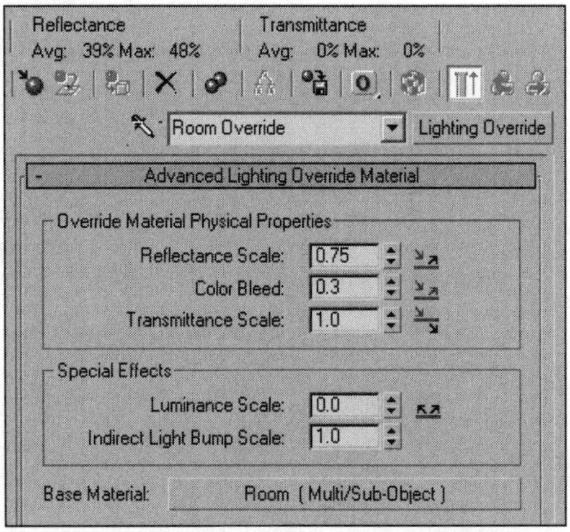

Fig. 11.8. Advanced Lighting Override parameters

After the material for the room is adjusted, all objects should be unhidden. Then creat and adjust the materials for them.

You can find our variant in the Lesson11(Final).max file on the CD-ROM in the Lessons\Lesson11\Scenes folder. Below is a brief description of what was done.

First we worked with the room materials. A texture was added to the floor material, and it was made slightly glossy by transferring the texture from the **Diffuse** channel to the **Bump**, **Glossiness**, and **Specular Level** channels. Low **Amount** values were set for these channels (Fig. 11.9, *a*).

Then we added the **Raytrace** texture to the **Reflection** channel with a small **Amount** value. Apart from the reflection itself, this gives us the option of using an interesting effect, which will be described later.

The **Oren-Nayar-Blinn** shader was used for the furniture. The colors on the **Ambient** and **Diffuse** channels were made very dark; otherwise, at final rendering, these objects would be too bright (Fig. 11.9, *b*). We applied a **Cellular** procedural texture to the bump channel (Fig. 11.9, *c*).

The **Translucency** shader was used for the curtains. This shader gives us an option to reduce overexposure. We made the color almost black on this channel; otherwise the exposure would have been too bright. This material is **2-Sided** (Fig. 11.9, *d*).

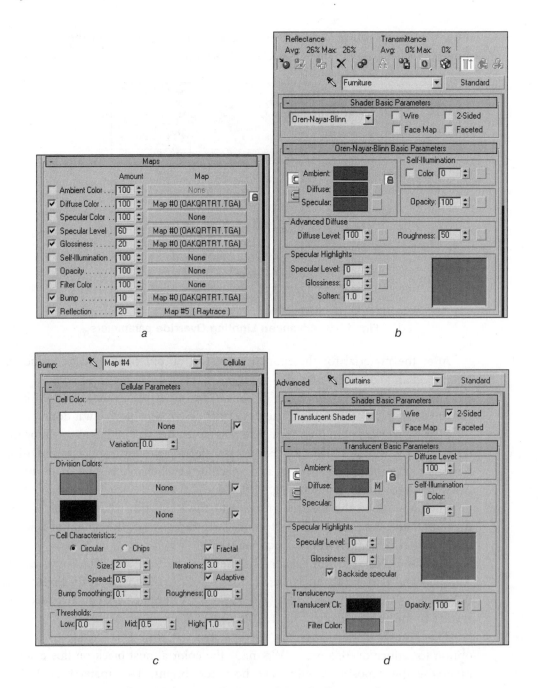

Reflectance
Avg: 0% Max: 0%

Transmittance
Avg: 98% Max: 98%

Glass ▾   Raytrace

Raytrace Basic Parameters

Shading: Blinn ▾   ☐ 2-Sided   ☐ Face Map
                    ☐ Wire   ☐ Faceted

Ambient: ☑   Luminosity: ☑

Diffuse: Transparency: ☐ 98 ⬍

Reflect: ☑ Fresnel   Index of Refr: 1.5 ⬍

Specular Highlight

Specular Color
Specular Level: 208 ⬍
Glossiness: 62 ⬍
N/A 50 ⬍
N/A 0 ⬍
Soften 0.1 ⬍

☐ Environment.................... None   🔒
☐ Bump............ 30 ⬍   None

+   Extended Parameters

−   **Raytracer Controls**

Local Options
☑ Enable Raytracing   ☑ Enable Self Reflect / Refract
☑ Raytrace Atmospherics ☐ Reflect / Refract Material IDs

Raytracer Enable
☑ Raytrace Reflections   Local Exclude...
☑ Raytrace Refractions   Bump Map Effect : 1.0 ⬍

e

Glow Element

Parameters | Options

Apply Element To:
☐ Lights   ☑ Image   ☐ Image Centers

Image Sources
☐ Object ID 1 ⬍   ☐ Whole
☑ Effects ID 15 ⬍   ☐ Alpha 0 ⬍
☐ Unclamp 1.0 ⬍ I   ☐ Z Hi 1000.0 ⬍
☐ Surf Norm 0.0 ⬍ I   Z Lo 0.0 ⬍

Glow Element

Parameters | Options

Name: Glow   ☑ On

Size 30.0 ⬍   Intensity 80.0 ⬍
☑ Glow Behind   Occlusion 100.0 ⬍
☐ Squeeze   Use Source Color 0.0 ⬍

f

Exposure Control

Logarithmic Exposure Control ▾

☑ Active
☐ Process Background
  and Environment Maps

Render Preview

−   **Logarithmic Exposure Control Parameters**

Brightness: 55.0 ⬍   ☐ Color Correction:
Contrast: 50.0 ⬍   ☐ Desaturate Low Levels
Mid Tones: 1.0 ⬍   ☐ Affect Indirect Only
Physical Scale: 15000.0 ⬍   ☐ Exterior daylight

g

Fig. 11.9, *e–g.* Final material and effects settings

We also glazed the windows. The windowpanes are typical **Plane** objects. We used an almost transparent **Raytrace** material with **Fresnel** reflection (Fig. 11.9, *e*).

To obtain a slight glow around the windows and its reflection on the floor, we added the **Glow** effect. It was adjusted so that only the windowpanes glow. To do this, we set the **Material Effect Channel** of the windowpane material to 15. Then we matched the same parameter of the effect. The intensity of the glow was slightly reduced (Fig. 11.9, *f*).

Since the material effect channel is used for this effect, a slight glow appears around the reflection of the window on the floor. To enable this effect, check the **Reflect/Refract Material ID** flag in the parameters of the **Raytrace** texture of the **Floor** material. Note that the same flag in the windowpane parameters should be deactivated; otherwise, the glow will be created only on the floor.

Finally, to make the windows are bright after rendering, we increased the **Physical Scale** value in the exposure control parameters (Fig. 11.9, *g*).

After all materials are adjusted, you can render the global lighting with high quality (Fig. 11.10).

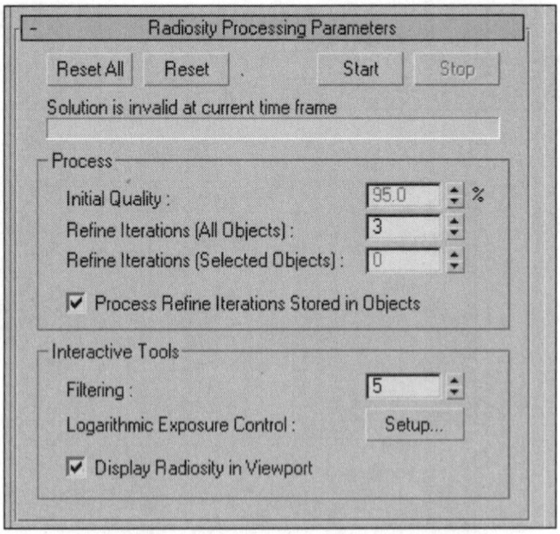

Fig. 11.10. Final radiosity parameters

► *Note*

Lately it has become all the rage to create interactive panoramas in QTVR (Quick Time Virtual Reality) format. Unfortunately, the developers of 3ds max did not deem it necessary to create such panoramas in the base supply of the package. However, Autodesk VIZ 4, the "younger brother" of 3ds max, has such a module. You can use it by loading the 3ds max supplement named Design Extensions from the **http://www.discreet.com/** website. But, to be frank, this is not the best solution. In this module, the so-called "cubic panorama" is used to create panoramas with six cameras with a 90° visual angle. Our practice proves that a panorama based on photographs works better. During the process, the file sequence is obtained by rendering from the animated camera view. Of course, the best solution is to use the RealViz Stitcher package, but it is rather expensive: about $500. You can find a panorama package at a reasonable price at **http://www.panoguide.com/**.

We propose that you make a panoramic reel for 7 seconds, with the camera rotating around its axis.

To animate the rotation of the camera:

❏ Specify the animation parameters Fig. 11.11. Set the picture frequency to 15 frames per second and the duration to 7 seconds:

   Time control panel → Time Configuration

❏ Move the camera to the center of your room and change its type to **Target Camera**.

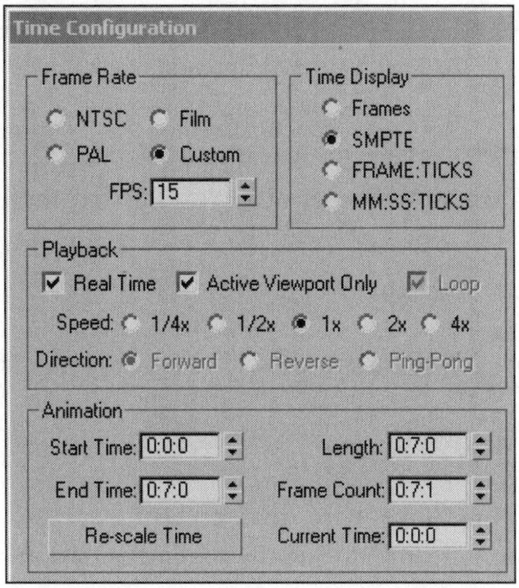

Fig. 11.11. Animation parameters

❐ Make **Circle** on the **Top** view Fig. 11.12. This will be the path for the target of the camera.

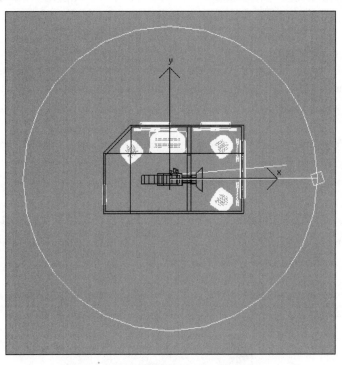

Fig. 11.12. Animation of the camera

❐ Raise it on the **Left** view to the camera level.
❐ Select the **Camera01.Target** object and assign the **Path Constraint** animation controller:

Main menu → Animation → Constraints → Path Constraint

Draw a "line" to the circle and click with the left mouse button.

Play the animation in the viewport. The camera turns around its axis following the target moving on the circle.

Now, everything is ready for final rendering!

❐ Go to the camera view and set the rendering parameters (Fig. 11.13):

Main menu → Rendering → Render

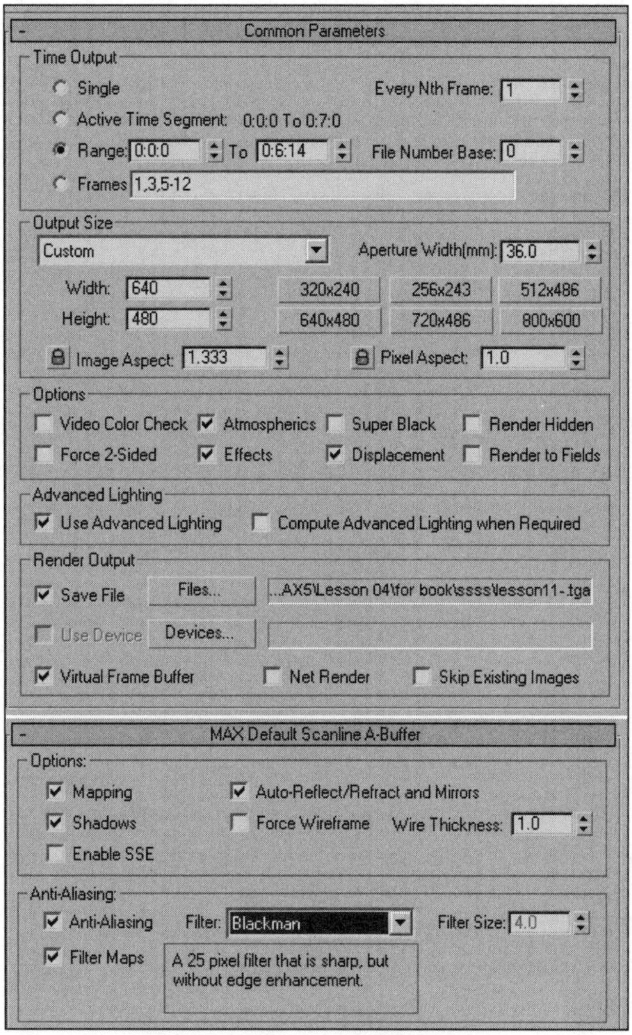

Fig. 11.13. Rendering parameters

Explanation

The rendering parameters are considered in detail in *Lesson 8*. Here we will only clarify the most pertinent points.

Set the **Range** one frame less than the duration of the animation. This will help you avoid a "break" when playing looped animation.

Set the frame size as 640 × 480 pixels.

Check the **Use Advanced Lighting** flag.

Activate the **Save File** option. You can save your animation directly as a video file (AVI or MOV). We prefer rendering to TGA files with further compilation of the reel in a video editor.

Use **Anti-Aliasing** at your own discretion. We decided that in this case, the **Blackman** type provided the best picture quality.

❐ Do the final rendering.

In the end, we recommend that you use the **IES Sun** and **IES Sky** sources of light only when you want a physically correct distribution of light. If a nice picture is your goal, it makes sense to use a **Direct** light source as the Sun, and **Skylight** as the sky. This gives you more control over the lighting.

Additional Lessons

Several separate lessons giving the solutions to various tasks are presented in this part.

- ❐ **Lesson 12: Navigation in 3ds max Viewports, Object Manipulations, and Special Features**. In this lesson, we tried to sum up these options in 3ds max to make your work more efficient. The lesson is intended for beginners, but is also useful for advanced users.

- ❐ **Lesson 13: Coordinates, Transform Centers, Alignment, and Snaps**. This lesson is also aimed at helping beginners understand their actions when working with objects.

- ❐ **Lesson 14: Texture Creation**. Every 3D package devotes a lot of space to textures created in 2D packages. Creating new textures and effectively using the existing ones considerably enhances efficiency and improves the final result.

- ❐ **Lesson 15: Modeling a car Body Using a Sketch**. In this lesson, we examine the right way to prepare a sketch for further modeling. In addition, we discuss creating a car body with minimal geometry by changing textures.

- ❐ **Lesson 16: Modeling a Human Head**. This lesson is useful for those who want to create animated characters. When we wrote this lesson, we were governed by the principle: "Less words, more action!"

- ❐ **Lesson 17: Modeling Lightning and an Electric Discharge**. Can you create special effects in 3ds max without the use of additional modules? You can and must! The simple examples in this lesson demonstrate the options for creating special effects in 3ds max.

❏ **Lesson 18: Modeling a Soccer Ball**. A soccer ball is a rather difficult object to model but because of the variety of geometrical primitives available in 3ds max, the process turns out to be very easy.

❏ **Lesson 19: Using 3ds max with Other Autodesk and Discreet Packages**. In this review lesson, we describe the joint work of 3ds max and Discreet Combustion and provide brief descriptions of the applications based on 3ds max — Autodesk VIZ, Discreet Plasma, and Discreet Gmax.

❏ **Lesson 20: 3ds max and Landscape Generators**. A wide range of landscape generators can be quite useful. In this lesson, we describe the most popular ones, as well as the options to use them with 3ds max.

❏ **Lesson 21: Useful Add-Ons**. This lesson covers a few freeware modules (plug-ins and scripts) that expand 3ds max capabilities in various areas.

Lesson 12

Navigation in 3ds max Viewports, Object Manipulations, and Special Features

We decided to cover viewport navigation in a separate lesson for two main reasons. First, we wanted to avoid cluttering other lessons, as was the case in our previous book "3ds max 4: From Objects to Animation," and to concentrate all your attention on the pertinent information. We also wanted to summarize the capabilities provided by 3ds max in this area in order to make your work more efficient. In the course of preparing this lesson, we discovered several interesting capabilities.

Customizing the Viewport Layout

When you start 3ds max for the first time, it displays a standard viewport layout — four viewports for the top view, the left view, the front view and for the perspective view. You can maximize any viewport at any time by pressing the <W> key on the keyboard. ("W" stands for the word "wide".) Furthermore, with the release of 3ds max 4, the developers introduced the capability to resize any viewport. To achieve this, place the mouse over the splitter bars (the cursor will then change to cross-hairs with bi-directional arrows), click and hold the left mouse button, and drag the mouse to change the viewport size according to your requirements. To return the viewport to its initial state, right-click any splitter bar, and select the single command — **Reset Layout** — from the right-click menu.

We would like to note that, in a decade of experience with all the versions of 3D Studio, we have only wanted to change the position of viewports a couple of times. However, sometimes this might prove to be rather useful. Let us consider how this is achieved.

❑ Open the window for configuring viewport layout (Fig. 12.1):

   Viewport right-click menu → Configure → Layout

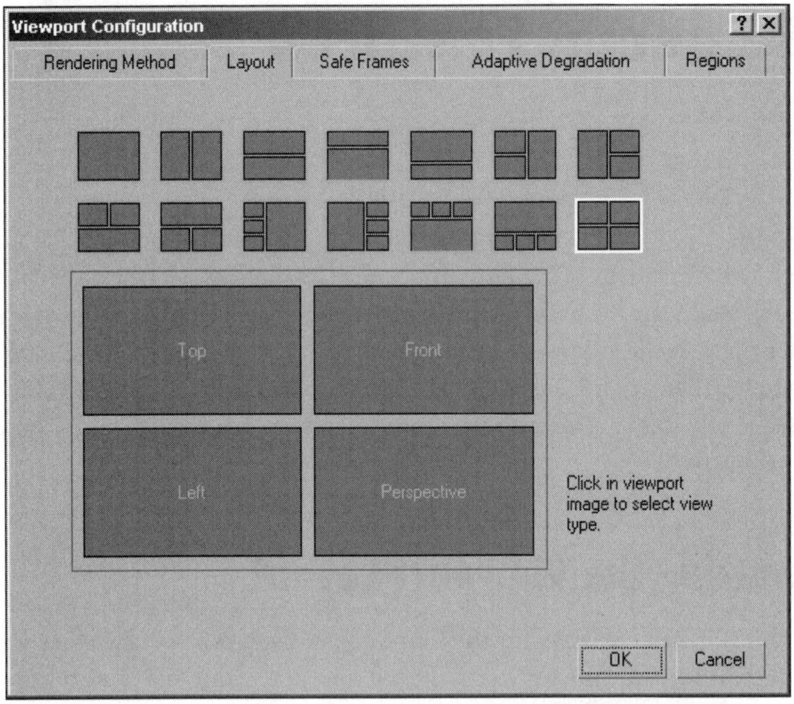

Fig. 12.1. Layout tab of the **Viewport Configuration** window

❑ Select the desired viewport-placement scheme and define their contents by clicking the windows and selecting the appropriate views.

3ds max doesn't have the built-in functionality to change viewport positions "on the fly." If you need to do this, you can use a macro script written by Fred Moreau that can be found on the companion CD-ROM in the folder named Scripts\ViewPort Layout\. Furthermore, you can always download the latest versions of this and other useful scripts from the author's website: **http://mapage.noos.fr/maxevangelists/**. To install this script, proceed as follows:

❏ Start the Vplayout.mzp script:

Main menu → MaxScript → Run Script

You'll see the message box shown in Fig. 12.2.

Fig. 12.2. ViewPort Layouts Setup message box

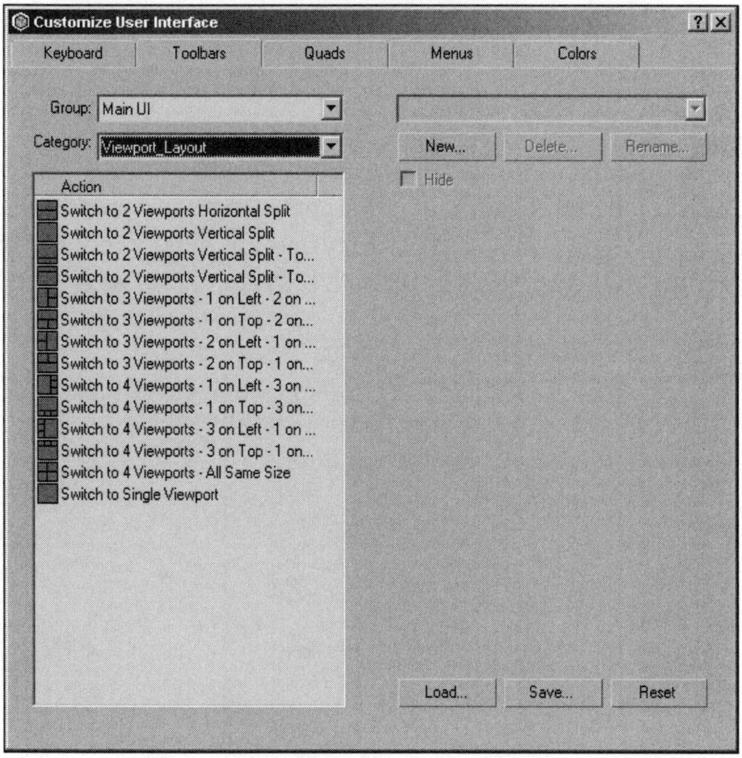

Fig. 12.3. Customize User Interface dialog box

❑ Open the dialog box for creating and editing toolbars (Fig. 12.3):

Main menu → Customize → Customize User Interface → Toolbars

❑ Create a new toolbar by clicking the **New** button and name it **Layouts**.

❑ Open the **Viewport_Layout** category and move the commands from the **Action** list to the **Layout** window.

Now try to click the buttons on the newly created toolbar. Isn't it great?

Do not forget to save your new interface settings.

► *Tip*

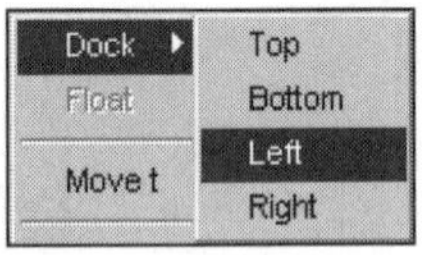

It is often convenient to position this toolbar to the left of the viewports. To do so, right-click the **Layout** toolbar and select **Dock → Left**.

Selecting the View in the Viewport

You can select the view in the viewport using the viewport right-click menu (Fig. 12.4). However, the keyboard hotkeys are much more convenient. We will provide a list of keyboard shortcuts with brief comments later.

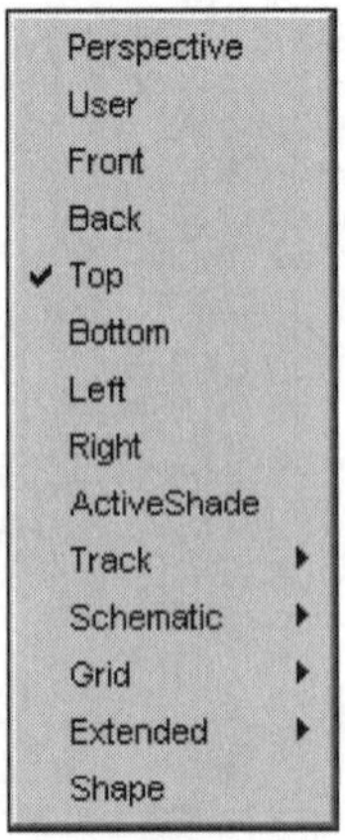

Fig. 12.4. Viewport right-click menu

The <T>,<B>,<F>,<K>,<L> keys allow you to select the following views: **Top** (T), **Bottom** (B), **Front** (F), **Back** (K), **Left** (L). These commands are self-explanatory.

Note

Users of previous versions of 3ds max may notice that there is no shortkey for the **Right** view. This will be explained below.

The <P> and <U> keys designate the **Perspective** (P) and **User** (U) views, respectively. When you switch to one of these views, the current viewing angle is saved.

The <C> and <$> keys (<Shift>+<4>) designate the **Camera** and **Light** views, respectively. If the current scene lacks objects of these types, you'll get a warning. If the scene contains several objects of this type, and none of them is currently selected, you'll be prompted to select one from a list. The view from these objects will then be available from the viewport right-click menu.

All the remaining viewport views are rather specific, and will therefore not be described further here. In addition, some of them were covered in previous lessons.

Note

Some views have no default keyboard shortcuts. If necessary, you can always assign them. (The second lesson of this book contains a detailed description of this procedure.)

Moving the Viewport Display

To switch to the moving view (or panning) mode, press the **Pan** button on the navigation toolbar, or press <Ctrl>+<P> on the keyboard. If you have a three-button mouse, you can use the middle mouse button for this purpose. By pressing and holding the <Ctrl> key, you'll increase the speed of movement of the view in the viewport. If you press and hold the <Shift> key, you'll move the viewport around one coordinate.

3ds max provides yet another interesting and useful technique with the <I> key. Move the mouse to any position within the viewport and press the key.

The viewport will move in such a way that the cursor will be centered. This technique is very convenient when the object you are working with (a curve, for example) doesn't fit within the viewport.

Note

To navigate viewports, you can also use the arrow keys. However, in reality, this capability is rarely used because the implementation is not intuitive. This is true for all types of navigation and object manipulation.

Rotating the Views in the Viewports

To switch to this mode, click the **Arc Rotate** button in the navigation toolbar. When using a three-button mouse, it is convenient to rotate the view using the middle mouse button while pressing and holding the <Alt> key. The <Shift> key can be used for rotation around one axis.

The **Arc Rotate** drop-down menu on the Navigation panel is very important. Using this menu, you can determine the rotation center for the viewport: coordinate origin, selected object (**Arc Rotate Selected**) or selected sub-object (**Arc Rotate SubObject**), for example, vertex or edge. Unfortunately, 3ds max doesn't provide a command to sequentially go through rotation centers but, generally, it isn't that important. You can simply select rotation around sub-objects. If no object is selected within a scene, the coordinate origin will be used as the rotation center.

Zooming Viewport Views

Zooming commands are quite numerous in 3ds max, being used more frequently than other commands. Let's consider these commands in more detail.

The scaling mode, which allows you to re-scale the viewport view, can be selected by clicking the **Zoom** button on the navigation toolbar or by pressing the <Z> key. When using a three-button mouse, you can also perform this task by using the middle mouse button while simultaneously pressing the <Alt> and <Ctrl> keys. If you have an IntelliMouse, the mouse wheel can also be used. You may find the <[> and <]> keys most useful, however, which when pressed produce a twofold increase or decrease, respectively, in the viewport scale.

3ds max settings provide another particularly interesting feature — namely, the use of the cursor position as the center of viewport manipulation. The usefulness of this capability is a question of personal preference:

Main menu → Customize → Preferences → Viewport → Zoom About Mouse Point

To zoom the view in all viewports, click the **Zoom All** button in the navigation panel.

To zoom a specific area, click an appropriate button on the Control panel, or press <Ctrl>+<W>.

Finally, the commands allowing you to zoom the current viewport or all viewports according to the size of all objects or the size of the selected objects/sub-objects (**Zoom Extents, Zoom Extents Selected, Zoom Extents All**) can be selected by clicking the appropriate buttons on the navigation panel or by pressing the following keyboard shortcuts, respectively: <Alt>+<Ctrl>+<Z>, <E>, <Shift>+<Ctrl>+<Z>.

Additional Navigation Commands

When working with 3ds max, we regularly use several additional capabilities. The most important one is rollback of viewport changes (**Undo View Change**). To use this feature, press the <Shift>+<Z> hotkey combination, similar to simple rollback (**Undo**, or the <Ctrl>+<Z> hotkey combination).

Another useful capability is saving and restoring parameters of the active view in any viewport.

Main menu → Views → Save/Restore Active View

And, finally, to redraw views in all viewports, press the <~> key (<Shift>+<`> keys).

Selecting Objects

You can select objects one by one or several at a time. To select a single object or sub-object, point the mouse at the object or sub-object that you need to select, and click the left button. To select several objects, click the left mouse button and encompass the required objects within a rectangle, circle or region, depending on the selection specified by the **Type Selection Region**.

Main panel → Type Selection Region

To add a new object to the selected set of objects, press the <Ctrl> key and click the desired object. To remove an object from the selected set, click that object while holding the <Alt> key.

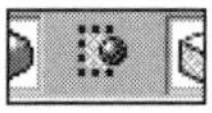

3ds max provides two methods of selecting several objects or sub- objects — using the selected area as a window or as a crossing. In the first case, the system selects all objects that completely fit within the selection, while in the second case it will select all objects, including the ones that only partially fit. You can toggle the selection mode by clicking the **Crossing/Window Selection** button. In 3ds max 4, there is away to change this mode "on the fly" by seting the following checkbox in the program settings (Fig. 12.5):

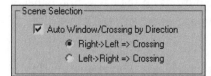

Main menu → Customize → Preferences → General → Scene Selection

Fig. 12.5. Parameters to change the selection mode "on the fly"

In this case, the selection will be performed in window mode when you drag the mouse from left to right. If you drag the mouse in the other direction, crossing mode will be used. When selecting with a region, the first segment direction determines the mode.

Finally, we have **Select All**, **Select None** and **Select Invert** possibilities in 3ds max 5. Their shortcuts are often useful: <Ctrl>+<A>, <Ctrl>+<D> and <Ctrl>+<I>, respectively.

Moving, Rotating, and Scaling Objects

The **Transform Gizmos** in 3ds max 5 are somewhat different (Fig. 12.6, *a–c*) from those in previous versions and have more settings (Fig. 12.6, *d*). Apart from everything else, you can change the appearance of the **Rotate Gizmo** in this dialog box, making it similar to that in previous versions of 3ds max, called Legacy R4:

Main menu → Customize → Preferences → Gizmos → Rotate Gizmo

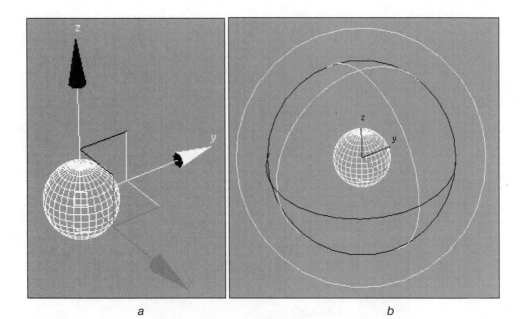

Fig. 12.6, *a–c*. Gizmo transformation (*a*), rotation (*b*), and scaling (*c*)

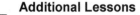

Fig. 12.6, _d._ Gizmo settings window

3ds max 5 provides the <Q>, <W>, <E>, and <R> keys to designate how to manipulate the selected objects and sub-objects. These keys correspond to: selection mode (**Smart Selection**), moving (**Move**), rotation (**Rotate**), and scaling (**Scale**), the last key indicating the scaling type (**Uniform**, **Non–Uniform**, and **Squash**).

Sometimes it is useful to switch off the gizmos. To do this, press the <X> key.

In the latest version, the main toolbar (**Main Toolbars**) no longer has the **Restrict by Axis** buttons, obviously hoping that everyone has memorized the <F5>, <F6>, <F7>, and <F8> keys corresponding to the restrictions on the X, Y, and Z axes and the XY, XZ, and YZ planes. If you want to use buttons for these commands, select the **Axis Constrains** panel (Main menu → Customize → Show UI → Show Floating Toolbars). This panel also contains buttons for the **Array**, **Snapshot** and **Spacing Tools** tools. If there is enough free space on your screen, you can move this panel onto the main line, or place it to the side.

Sub-object selection is performed with the <1>, <2>, <3>, <4> etc., keys. They can be used not only for base objects (e.g., **Editable Poly**) but modifiers, too. Pressing a key repeatedly transitions to the base level.

Working with Numeric Parameters

In 3ds max, most parameters can be entered into the appropriate fields as numeric values. All such fields for entering numeric values have spinners, which are used by clicking them with the left mouse button the required number of times, or by moving the mouse upward or downward while holding the left mouse button. To ensure that the cursor stays with the appropriate field, set the **Wrap Cursor Near Spinner** flag, as shown in Fig. 12.7:

Main menu → Customize → Preferences → General → Spinners

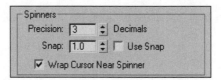

Fig. 12.7. Warp Cursor Near Spinner flag

To change this parameter quickly, press and hold the <Ctrl> key while scrolling. By pressing and holding the <Alt> key when scrolling, you will increase precision in floating-point parameters. If you right-click the parameter, you will reset the parameter to its minimum value.

When working in parameter fields, you can also perform addition and subtraction operations with the current parameter value. For example, if you want to increase the current value by 10 units, enter "r10" into the parameter field ("r" stands for *relative*) and press <Enter>. For subtraction, use the "r-" prefix, for example: r-10. You can also divide one number by another, for example: 360/5. Unfortunately, no other calculations are allowed in the parameter fields.

3ds max provides a calculator allowing you to calculate the value in a parameter field. To start the calculator, press <Ctrl>+<N> when the cursor is positioned over the parameter field (Fig. 12.8). The expression syntax used by this calculator has a lot in common with the Expression Controller. You can get more detailed information on the calculator in the "User's Manual" supplied with 3ds max.

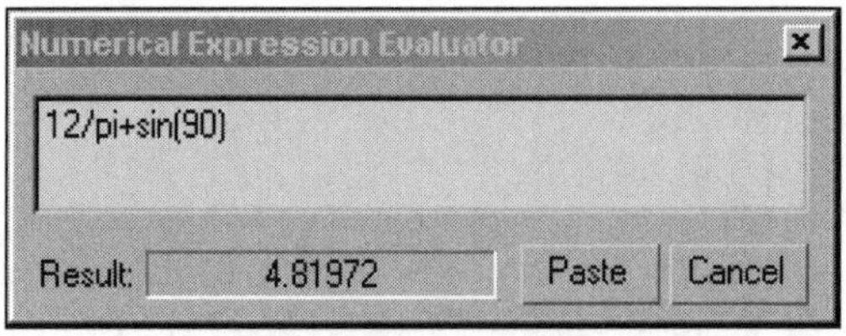

Fig. 12.8. Built-in calculator

Finally, special mention should be paid to 3ds max's gratifying capability to convert measurement units. For example, if you are working in the metric system and want to enter a value in inches, simply enter the value and specify the units explicitly (for example, 8"). 3ds max will automatically convert it to the metric scale.

Note

Unfortunately, the built-in calculator does not support automatic conversion of measurement units.

Manipulators

3ds max 4 has a new method to manage object parameters and some modifiers — manipulators, which can be switched on by clicking the **Select and Manipulate** button on the main toolbar or by selecting the **Manipulate** command from the right-click menu (sub-menu of the **Transform** command). Not many are provided with a base installation; however, you can add more manipulated objects and modifiers by installing **Bonus Scripts** and then run the SuperManipulators.mzp script (Main menu → MaxScript → Run Script), located in the 3dsmax\scripts\ MAXScriptTools\folder. After running the script, restart 3ds max. Borislav Petrov, one of the best-known 3ds max enthusiasts, developed this package of scripts.

To be honest, out of habit, we rarely used manipulators. However, in the course of preparing this lesson, we tried to use and tweak manipulators (both in a literal and figurative sense) and now advise everyone to use them, since they have proved extremely convenient and useful.

The **Bonus Scripts** package also includes the **Toggle Manipulators** script, which allows you to make specific manipulators visible or invisible (Fig. 12.9).

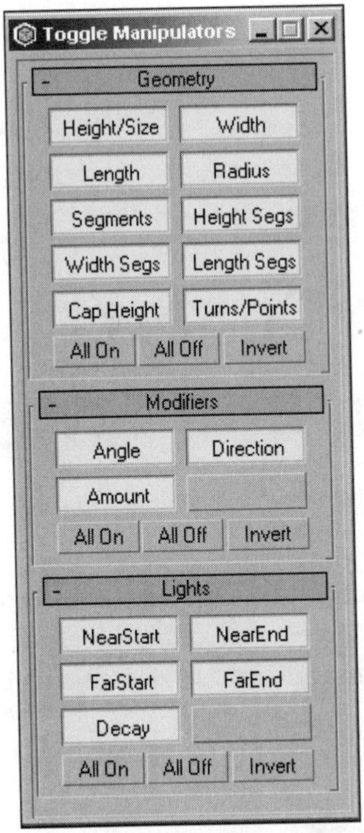

Fig. 12.9. Toggle Manipulators window

Lesson 13

Coordinates, Transform Centers, Alignment, and Snaps

Like the previous lesson, this one is mainly intended for beginners. In this lesson, we will provide detailed coverage of all the elements specified in the title. Understanding and correct usage of these elements will significantly increase your efficiency and boost your productivity.

Coordinate Systems

3ds max allows the user to apply transforms (such as moving, rotating, or rescaling) to objects and sub-objects in different coordinate systems. Usually, these coordinate systems are orthogonal (i.e., the coordinate axes are perpendicular to one another).

There are three ways to select the required coordinate system. First, you can select it from the drop-down menu on the main toolbar (Fig. 13.1, *a*). Second, you can hold the <Alt> key, right-click the mouse, and select the "coordinates" command from the right-click menu (Fig. 13.1, *b*). Lastly, you can assign a keyboard shortcut (Fig. 13.1, *c*):

Main menu → Customize → Customize User Interface

▶ *Tip*

Don't assign keyboard shortcuts to too many coordinate systems, as it is unlikely that you will need to switch between all of them. Assign key combinations only for the ones you will most frequently use.

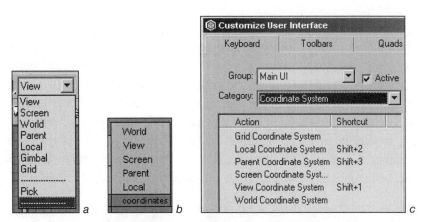

Fig. 13.1. Selecting the coordinate system

☐ **View** (Viewport coordinate system). This is the default coordinate system. It is identical in all "rectangular" views (Top, Left, etc.). The X-axis (abscissa) is always directed to the right, the Y-axis (ordinate) is always directed upward, while the Z-axis always points in a direction into the screen away from you. User and perspective viewports use the world coordinate system.

☐ **Screen** (Screen coordinate system). This coordinate system uses screen coordinates. The X-axis always points horizontally to the right, the Y-axis always points up, while Z-axis always points in a direction into the screen and away from you, independent of the view.

☐ **World** (World coordinate system). This coordinate system uses the so-called "world coordinates." In some cases, it is preferable to viewport coordinates.

☐ **Local** (Local coordinate system). This is the coordinate system of the current object. Each object, while being created, is assigned some orientation in space, with its "top" not necessarily corresponding to "up" in world coordinates. The "top" orientation depends on how the object's first element (a primitive, for example) was created. When you rotate an object, its local coordinate system rotates along with it.

▶ *Note*

If you want an object initially to be oriented along world coordinates, create it in the top viewport. However, in most cases, this is not convenient and usually unnecessary.

The confusion with local coordinates is somewhat more complex for sub-objects. Fig. 13.2, *a–c* shows local coordinates for polygons, edges and vertices of a single object. For polygons, everything is straightforward. If one polygon is selected, its Z-axis points in the direction normal to its surface. If several adjacent polygons are selected, the Z-axis points in the direction of the vector sum of the normals of the polygons. The situation is more complicated with edges and vertices — the Z-axis for these elements points in the direction of the vector sum of the normals of their adjacent polygons. Consequently, editing sets of sub-objects in local coordinates is somewhat difficult, although single sub-objects can be edited rather easily.

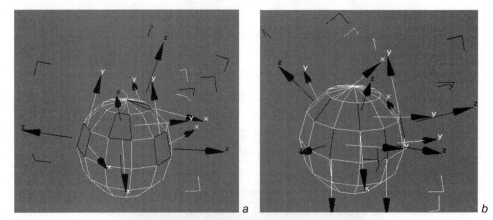

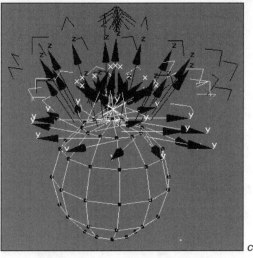

Fig. 13.2. Local coordinates for polygons (*a*), edges (*b*), and vertices (*c*)

❏ **Gimbal** (literally "joint"). This coordinate system simplifies animation curves when the object is rotated with the **Euler XYZ** rotation controller. Whereas rotation of an object in local coordinates may lead to changes in two or three curves, rotation in the **Gimbal** coordinate system affects only one curve. The axes therefore may be non-orthogonal. When moved and scaled, this coordinate system behaves in the same way as **Parent** (see below).

❏ **Parent** (Coordinate system of the parent object). When an object is not related to any other object, the "world" is considered to be its parent object and, in that case, this coordinate system coincides with the world coordinate system. When an object is linked to another object or grouped with other objects, a coordinate system of this type coincides with the local coordinate system of the parent object. In these groups, the group's gizmo is considered to be an object. The parent for sub-objects is regarded as the object itself. Therefore, for sub-objects, the parent coordinate system coincides with local coordinates of the object.

❏ **Grid** (Coordinate system of an active grid). 3ds max has a special helper object called the grid. You may use several grids at once, each with a different orientation in space, once they are activated. This coordinate system is convenient when working with a specific grid (Fig. 13.3).

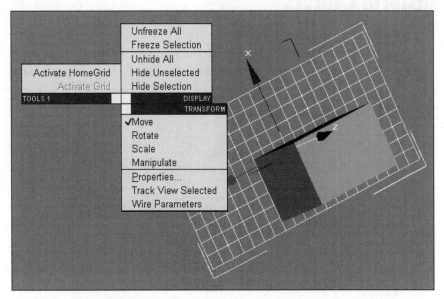

Fig. 13.3. Active grid, and an object in the grid coordinate system

□ **Pick** (Coordinate system of a designated object): Sometimes it is convenient temporarily to apply the local coordinate system of an object to another object. To do so, select **Pick** in the drop-down menu and select an object with the left mouse button. The name of the designated object will appear in the list of coordinate systems.

Note

Unfortunately, pick coordinate systems are not saved in 3ds max projects.

We would like to warn you about one aspect of 3ds max related to coordinate systems that often surprises beginners and experts alike. The problem is that if an object is scaled, its local coordinate system also changes. In other words, a centimeter in the coordinate system of such object, or coordinate system based on such an object, might not necessarily coincide with a centimeter in the world coordinate system. In addition, sometimes such systems are not orthogonal. If it is critical, the Reset XForm operation might prove helpful:

Control panel → Utilities → Reset XForm

Transform Centers

A transform center (don't confuse it with a pivot point — a center of object transformation and binding) in 3ds max defines a point around which the selected object(s) or sub-objects will be rotated or re-scaled. The transform center is selected via a fly-out on the main toolbar (Fig. 13.4, *a*). For convenience, you can also assign keyboard shortcuts (Fig. 13.4, *b*).

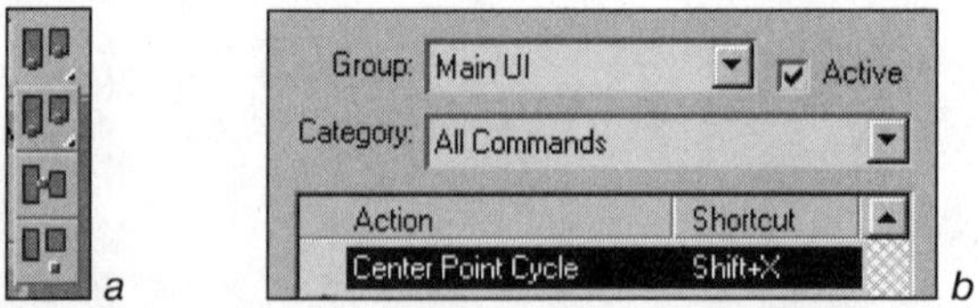

Fig. 13.4. Selection of the transform center

□ **Transform Coordinate Center**. In this case, the origin of the current coordinate system is used as the transform center. Depending on the coordinate system, this might be the center of the screen, the coordinate origin, etc. (Fig. 13.5, *a*).

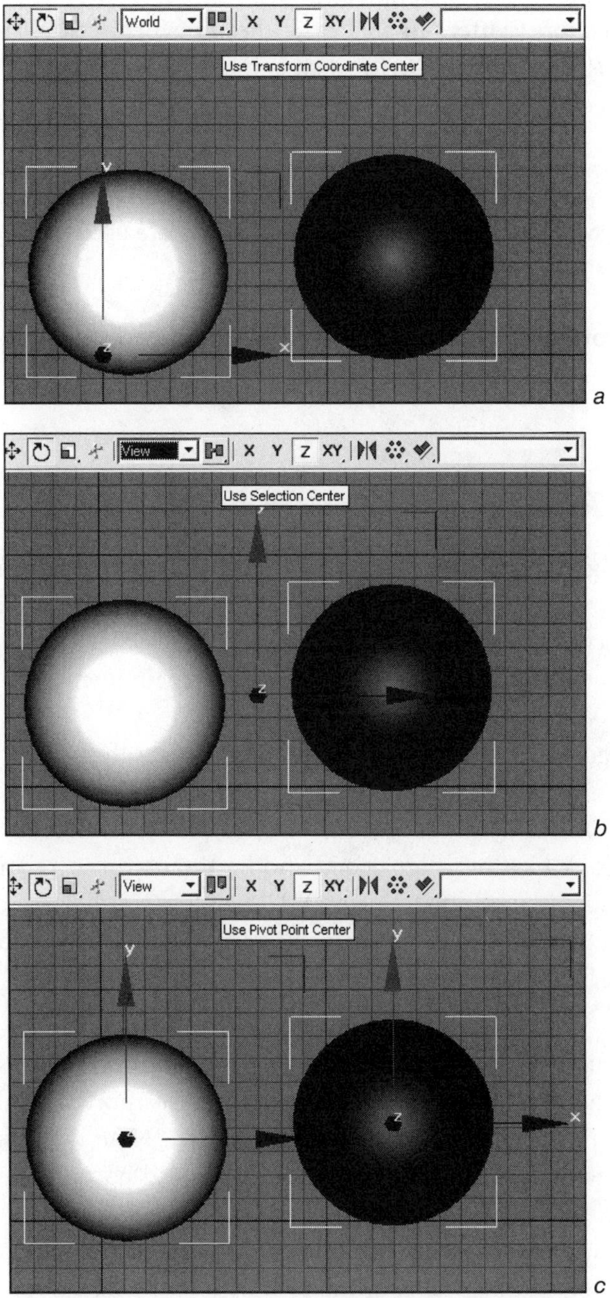

Fig. 13.5. Transform centers

❐ **Selection Center.** In this case, the transform center, in relation to which all transforms will be performed, is the geometric center of the centers of the selected objects (Fig. 13.5, *b*).

 Note

Notice that the geometric centers of the objects are used, not the pivot points — they are two different things!

❐ **Pivot Point Center.** In this case, the transform center coincides with the pivot point of the object (Fig 13.5, *c*).

Alignment

The **Align** operation is a rather powerful modeling tool. In 3ds max, there are several types of alignment intended to solve different tasks. Alignment of the selected object or sub-object is begun by selecting the required type from the fly-out on the main toolbar or from the main menu.

❐ **Align** (Aligning objects in relation to one another). This procedure is the most common. Select the required object(s) or sub-objects. Then select the **Align** command from the fly-out. The cursor will change its shape to look like the **Align** icon. Choose the object in relation to which you need to align the selected object(s). Notice that, in the case of aligning sub-objects, you may choose to align to the same object. The alignment dialog will open (Fig. 13.6).

Let us consider the parameters of this dialog in more detail.

In the **Align Position** group, select one or more axes along which to perform alignment, and select the alignment method. Note that alignment will take place in the active coordinate system. We described coordinate systems earlier in this chapter.

Besides alignment by position, the **Align** command allows you to synchronize orientation in the local coordinate system (the **Align Orientation** group) and object size (**Match Scale**), by adjusting the transform matrix of the objects.

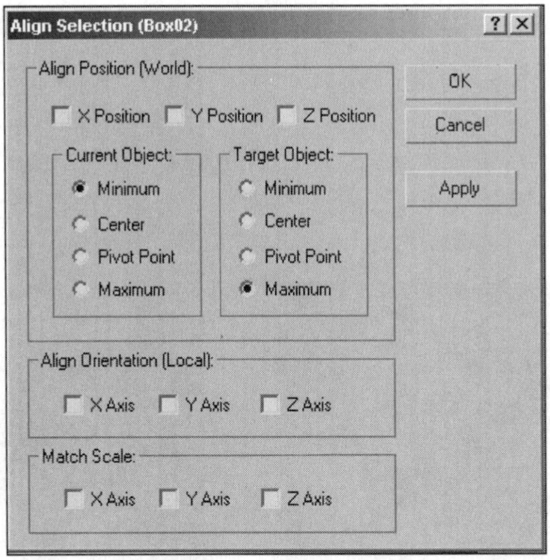

Fig. 13.6. Align dialog

❑ **Normal Align** (Alignment in relation to a normal). This command allows you to align the normals of two objects. This might be necessary, for example, if you need to place one object onto the surface of another one (Fig. 13.7). The procedure is as follows: Select an object, then select the **Normal Align** command from the **Align** fly-out on the main toolbar. Next, select the face whose normal will be aligned by clicking the left mouse button and dragging the cursor along the object's surface. Release the mouse button and select the face of another object. Release the mouse and specify the required parameters in the dialog that will appear. To finish, click **OK**.

This command, like other commands related to normals, is implemented in a specific way. If the face is smooth (i.e., belongs to one of the smoothing groups) 3ds max uses the normal interpolated with respect to this smoothing rather than the geometric normal.

❑ **Place Highlight** (Position the highlight from the light source). This command allows you to orient the light in such a way as to highlight a specific position on the model. Select the light and the **Place Highlight** command from the **Align** fly-out on the main toolbar. Then select the object face whose normal will point in the direction of the light by dragging the mouse along its surface.

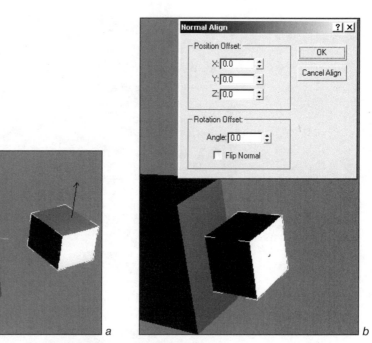

Fig. 13.7. Selecting normals (*a*)
and the result of the operation (*b*)

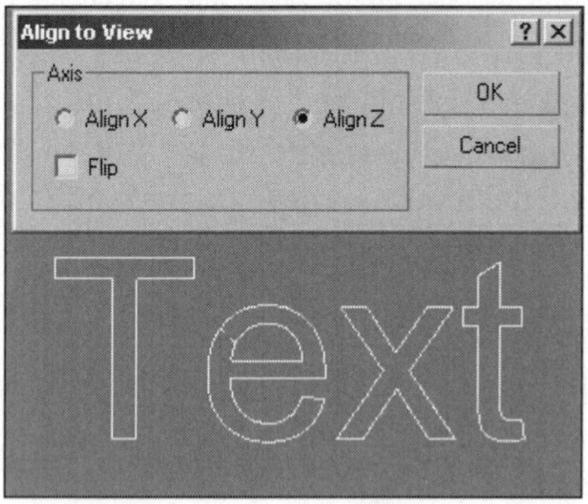

Fig. 13.8. Align to View dialog and aligned object

☐ **Align Camera** (Align the camera in relation to the object). This command allows you to align the camera in such a way as to direct it to a specific position on the object. It is similar to the **Place Highlight** command, with the only difference being that it adjusts the camera instead of a light.

▶ *Tip*

If you are working in the camera viewport, you can simply select the **Select Camera** command from the viewport right-click menu.

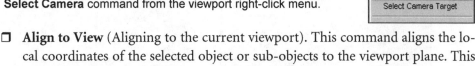

☐ **Align to View** (Aligning to the current viewport). This command aligns the local coordinates of the selected object or sub-objects to the viewport plane. This might be necessary, for example, to align explanation text in the camera viewport (Fig. 13.8).

Snaps

3ds max provides a large number of various snaps, whose usage simplifies and expedites the modeling process.

Spatial snaps are toggled on or off in the Snaps toolbar, or by pressing the <S> key. Pay special attention to the fact that there are three types of spatial snaps — 2D, 2.5D and 3D.

2D snaps, as is evident from the name, are two-dimensional. This means that the cursor only snaps to objects belonging to the active grid plane. When using 2.5D snaps, the cursor snaps to the projection of the element onto the active grid, where the projection lies in the plane of the screen. Finally, when using 3D snaps, the cursor directly snaps to all elements selected as snap objects. 3D snaps are the most frequently used.

To select a specific element as snap object, mark it in the **Grid and Snap Settings** window, which can be opened by right-clicking the Snaps toolbar (Fig. 17.9). As you can see, the possibilities are rather impressive.

3ds max also provides the capability to temporarily (for a single operation) select another snap type. Hold the <Shift> key, right-click and select the required snap from the right-click menu.

To conclude, we would like to describe several interesting ways to use snaps.

To align an object with a grid precisely, set the snaps as shown in Fig. 13.9. Switch to move mode, and drag the object by the angle vertex. In the course of this movement, the object will be positioned exactly along the grid nodes.

An object may also be rotated around a snap point when snaps are on. Switch to rotation mode and fix the selection by pressing the <Space> bar. Now point the cursor to the point around which you are going to rotate the object (for example, the grid node) and perform the rotation. Don't forget that the transform center must not coincide with the object's pivot point.

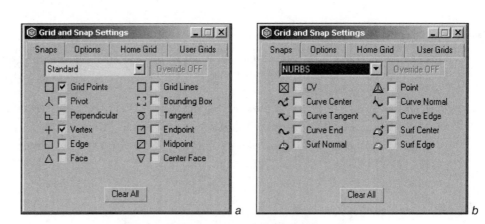

Fig. 13.9. Standard (*a*) and **NURBS** (*b*) snaps

Angle and **percentage snaps** are very useful. You can set their parameters on the **Options** tab of the **Grid and Snap Settings** window (Fig. 13.10).

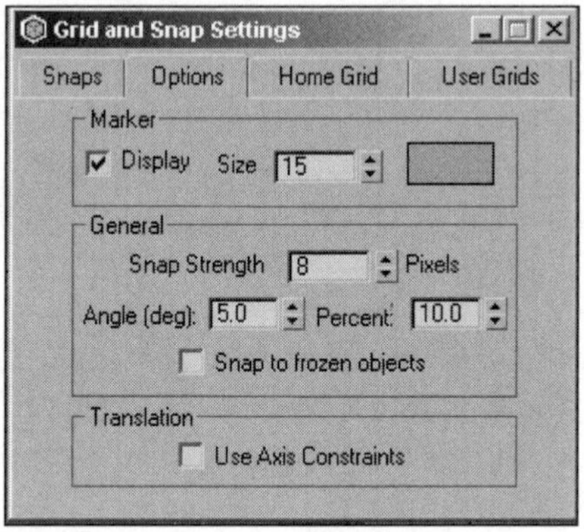

Fig. 13.10. **Options** tab of the **Grid and Snap Settings** window

Lesson 14

Texture Creation

In many lessons, we recommend you use transparent textures, also known as alpha channel textures, and seamless tiling textures. Both types of textures are useful. Transparent textures allow you to put marks and inscriptions on the surfaces of objects without affecting the material's color, while seamless tiling textures enable you to imitate such things as stucco, sand, etc., by using photos of these materials. In this lesson, we want to draw your attention to the creation of various textures.

Transparent Textures with Vector Graphics Editors

As a matter of preference, we often use vector graphics editors for creating textures similar to the one shown in Fig. 14.1. However, 3ds max doesn't recognize vector formats and, therefore, it is necessary to convert the image to a bitmap file supporting transparency. The most suitable format for this is TGA. Creating such a picture with a vector graphics editor is straightforward and will not be discussed here.

We would like to draw your attention to the following aspects.

Some editors, such as CorelDraw, crop the image when it is being exported. To avoid this, create a "blank" rectangle around your picture, without filling or lines (Fig. 14.2). Your picture should fit comfortably within the rectangle, with some extra space.

Fig. 14.1. Example of a transparent texture

Fig. 14.2. Rectangle delimiting the drawing

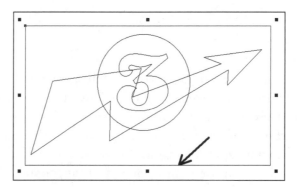

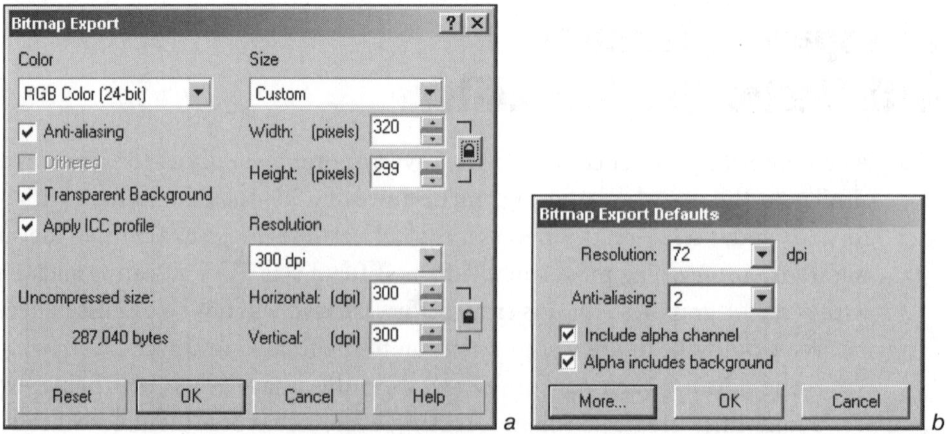

a

b

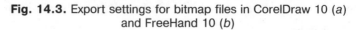

Fig. 14.3. Export settings for bitmap files in CorelDraw 10 (*a*)
and FreeHand 10 (*b*)

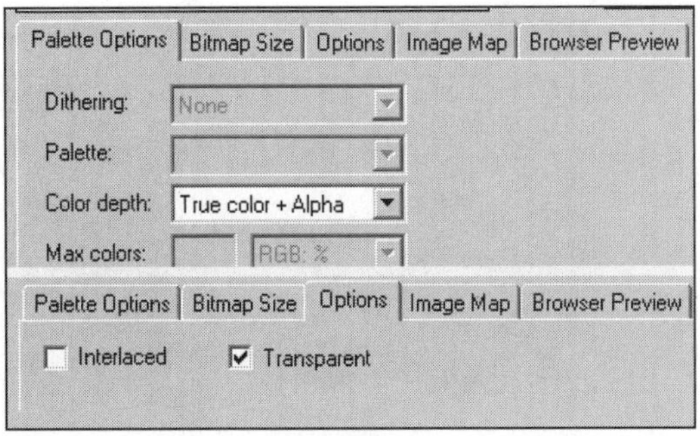

Fig. 14.4. Settings for exporting to a PNG file in Xara X 1.0

When exporting, select a reasonable size for your texture. If the frame size is 640 × 480 pixels, it isn't advisable to use a large texture with 1200 × 1200 pixels.

In the dialog allowing you to set bitmap export options, don't forget to select the checkbox for transparency, also known as the alpha channel. Fig 14.3 shows how to set the export options in CorelDraw 10 and Macromedia FreeHand 10.

Our favorite program — Xara X — deserves special attention. Unfortunately, transparency is not preserved when exporting to a TGA file. Instead, use the PNG format, which 3ds max interprets without problems. Fig. 14.4 shows the parameters to use when exporting to a PNG file in Xara X 1.0.

Transparent Textures Using Layer Support

Let's consider the process of creating a transparent texture with Adobe Photoshop 6 in more detail. This process, with small variations, is similar in most other editors that support layers, such as Jasc Paint Shop Pro 7.

❏   Create a new file with the parameters shown in Fig. 14.5.

❏   Create a new layer, where you will create your image:

   Main menu → Layer → New → Layer

❏   After you finish editing your image, load the transparency mask:

   Main menu → Select → Load selection

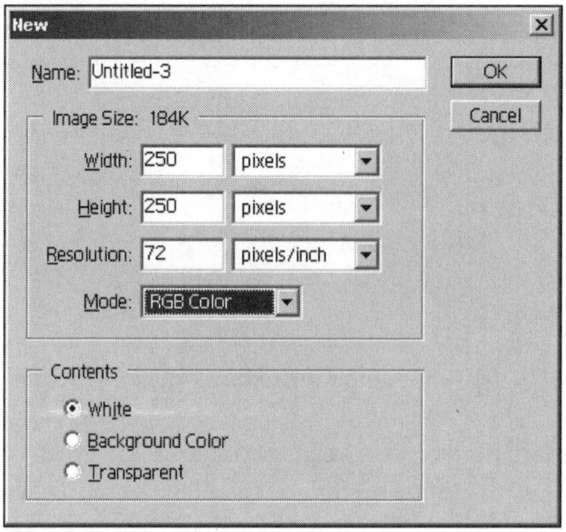

Fig. 14.5. Parameters for creating a new file in Adobe Photoshop 6

▶ *Note*

If you created additional layers in the course of editing, join these layers into a single layer (but don't join them with the background).

❑ Save the mask as a transparent (alpha) channel:

 Main menu → Select → Save selection

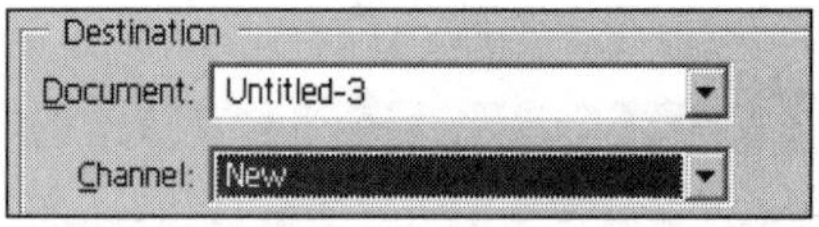

❑ Save the image as a TGA file (Fig. 14.6):

 Main menu → Save as

▶ *Note*

3ds max 5 introduced the possibility of loading Adobe Photoshop (PSD) files with layers. The transparency layer is recognized and interpreted as an alpha channel.

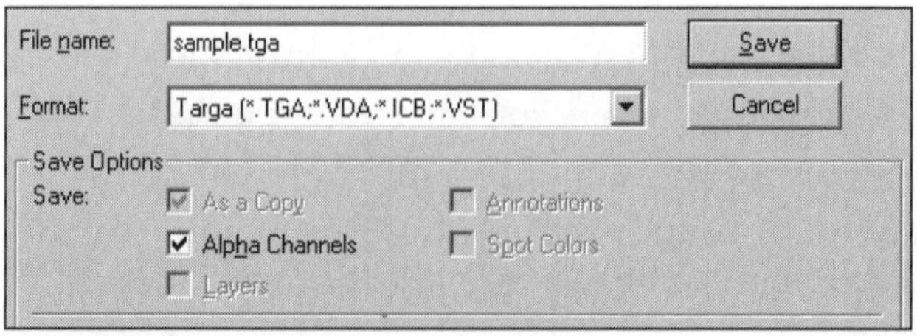

Fig. 14.6. Saving a file with the transparency (alpha) channel
in Adobe Photoshop

Seamless Tiling Textures

When creating a seamless tiling texture, we recommend you keep the process as simple as possible. This involves dividing the texture into four parts, diagonally interchanging the quadrants, and making a few adjustments to their intersections (Fig. 14.7). Here, we will consider the process in more detail with Adobe Photoshop. The procedure is applicable (with some subtle variations) to any bitmap editor supporting layers.

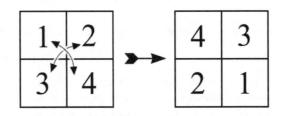

Fig. 14.7. Interchanging the quadrants in the process of creating a seamless tiling texture

❑ Open the texture.tga file, which you can find on the companion CD-ROM in the \Lessons\Lesson14 folder.

❑ Enable the rulers:

> Main menu → View → Show Rulers

❑ Create one horizontal guide and one vertical guide in such a way as to divide the image into four equal parts. Alternately, you can display the grid and adjust it in the same way.

❑ Duplicate the background twice by creating two new layers:

> Main menu → Layer → Duplicate Layer

❑ Using these layers, select the four quadrants and arrange them according to the scheme shown in Fig. 14.7. To do this, use the **Rectangular Marque Tool** and the **Move Tool**.

▶ **Note**

Don't forget to enable snaps (Main menu → View → Snap).

❏ Join the two upper layers into a single layer and disable the guides or grid:

Main menu → View → clear Show Extras checkbox

Now select the **Eraser Tool** and carefully erase parts of the upper layer to remove the seams. Be very careful with the edges of the image, and take special care not to erase more than necessary! To make the task easier, you may occasionally want to disable the background. In the end, you want the background visible with the upper layer naturally transparent. It is also recommended to rotate the background by a small angle relative to the upper layer.

► *Tip*

We advise you to create a second, larger file and periodically fill it with the texture to check how it fits.

When you have completed your work, do not forget to save it to a file.

In this way, you can get rid of the seams. However, removing the tiled "wallpaper" effect, often seen as a haunting repeating pattern, is a much more difficult task. You can slightly reduce this effect by making the texture saturation more even. The finishing touches in 3ds max are applied by mixing various types of textures.

As a final note, we would like to say a few words about software used to generate textures.

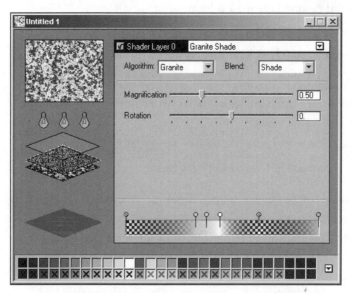

Fig. 14.8. Texture-editing window in Corel Texture

We often use the application Corel Texture, which is included in the Corel-Draw package and has a special command to create seamless textures (Fig. 14.8). The texture we used as an example was produced using this program.

The Infinity Textures package by Tobias Reichert is wonderful! You can download a free, 30-day version of this package from the author's website at **http://www.i-tex.de**. Finally, the DarkTree Textures package from DarkSim deserves special mention. It allows you to create textures of any level of complexity and of any type. It includes a plug-in module named Simbiont MAX, created especially for 3ds max, which enables you to use the textures created in DarkTree directly in 3ds max. This module is now free for any use and can be download from the owner's website at **http://www.darksim.com**. A rich library of textures created by DarkTree is supplied with it.

Spherical Textures

If you apply a flat texture to a spherical object, distortions are inevitable. These distortions are especially noticeable at the poles (Fig. 14.9). As a rule, they are undesirable and very hard to eliminate. Drawing elements in the correct shape so that they have the proper appearance after rendering is even more difficult. As a case in point, it is particularly complicated to model round illuminators on a diving bell.

Fig. 14.9. Typical distortions of flat textures on a spherical object

There are several methods to solve this problem. The simplest and recommended one uses Adobe Photoshop to transform orthogonal coordinates to polar coordinates.

❑ Create a new rectangular image with a 2:1 side length ratio, for example, 600×300 pixels.

Note

We will use geographical terms to describe the editing process, as they are the most illustrative.

❒ Draw lines representing the "equator" and "tropics" (Fig. 14.10).

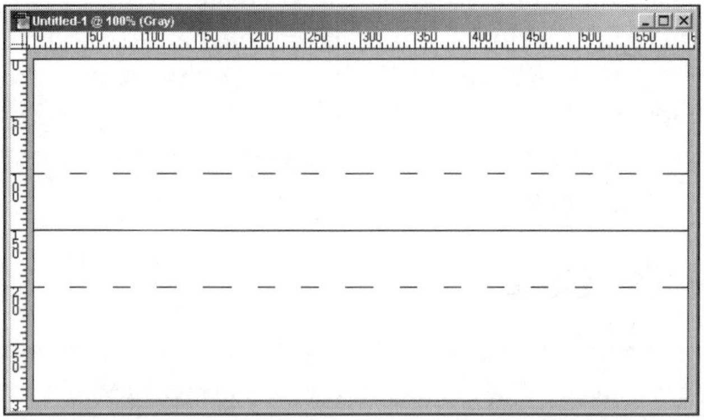

Fig. 14.10. Texture dummy

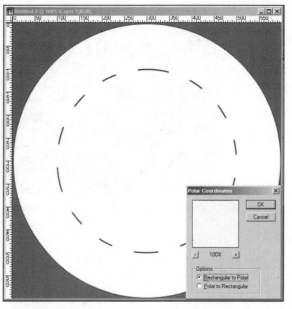

Fig. 14.11. Result of converting orthogonal coordinates to polar coordinates

- Select the "northern hemisphere" and copy it into a new file.
- Change the size of the new file in such a way as to make its side ratio 1:1. In our case, this would be a change from 600×150 pixels to 600×600 pixels.
- Apply the **Polar Coordinate** filter to convert to polar coordinates (Fig. 14.11):

    Main menu → Filter → Distort → Polar Coordinate

- Draw whatever is required within the dashed circle. When you are done, convert back to orthogonal coordinates and resize the file back to the original dimensions. In our case, this would be back to 600×150 pixels.
- Copy the area "north" of the "tropic of cancer" and insert it back into the initial texture.

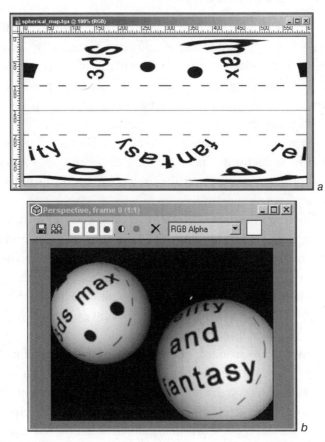

Fig. 14.12. Final texture (*a*) and an object rendered with the texture (*b*)

- ❏ Do the same for the "southern hemisphere" after rotating the image 180° so that the "south pole" is on top.
- ❏ Once you have completed the "polar" regions, draw the "equatorial zone."

The texture is now ready (Fig. 14.12, *a*). Save it in a format supported by 3ds max and try to use it (Fig. 14.12, *b*). As you can see, everything looks great. Distortions may still appear near the "poles," but supersampling in the material parameters will help solve this problem.

Animated Texture Loops

3ds max enables the use of video sequences, designated by either a video file (AVI, MOV) or a frame-file sequence, as animated textures. By "stretching" the texture onto a plane and positioning it in various places of the scene, you can create smoke trails, air bubbles rising through water, etc. You can produce such effects in the Discreet Combustion 2 or Illusion packages, among others. Unfortunately, the above packages do not create video sequences looped in time so, to avoid "skips," you have to match the sequence with the length of the final reel, which can be an unnecessarily burdensome task for long files. The recommended and simplest method to produce excellent results for smoke, fire and similar effects entails continuously replaying a short video clip.

The procedure is simple. Render the video file and load it into a video editor (e.g., Adobe Premiere). Cut it at some point (Fig. 14.13, *a*) and move that segment to another track so that it overlaps the end of the video file. Then specify a **Transition** in such a way that the main reel image gradually changes to that of the cut section (Fig. 14.13, *b*). This gives a smooth transition between the end and start of the next repeat. Of course, there is a certain amount of blur during transition, but only those aware of it usually notice.

One more problem needs to be discussed before we finish. Sometimes, you need a clip where the beginning is played once, but upon reaching some point, the remainder is repeated until the end of the scene, as in the case of burning. You can solve this problem by using two video files, where the first is played once and the second starts playing at the moment the first one ends and keeps playing for the duration of the scene. To do this, use a **Mix** texture with the two prepared video sequences. The **Mix Amount** parameter and specified **Time** parameters for each segment allow you to transition from one clip to another in an appropriate right way and at the proper time.

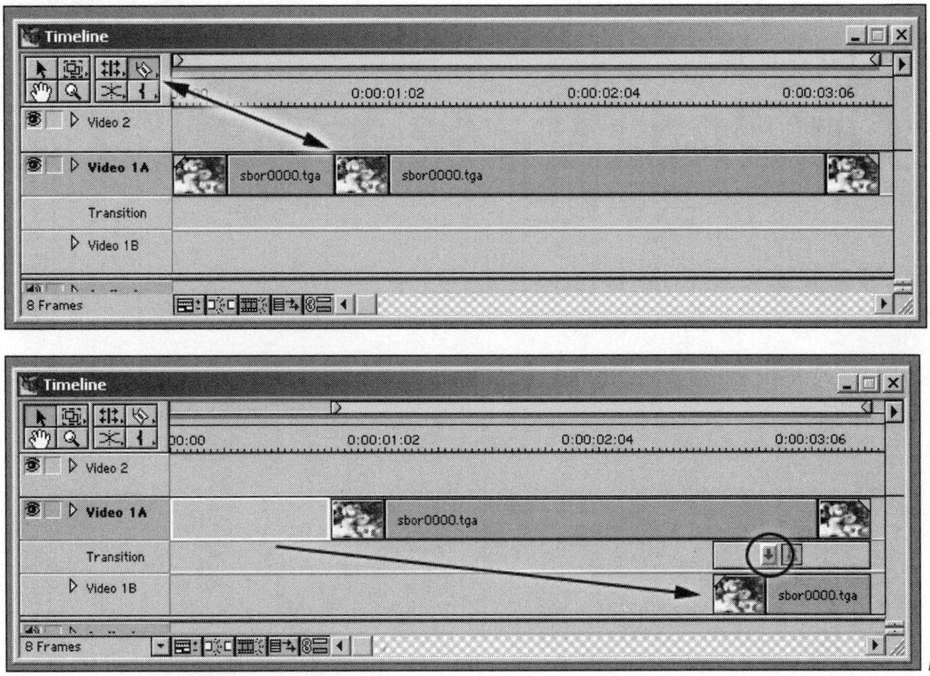

Fig. 14.13. Creating a looped video file in Adobe Premiere

Lesson 15

Modeling
a Car Body Using a Sketch

In this lesson we will describe some methods of modeling objects with sketches. As an example, we suggest modeling the body of a car. However, all materials provided here are applicable to most objects.

We propose that you use a method of creating materials that will eliminate the necessity of working on the object's geometric details. This is particularly important if you plan to develop the model for the Internet or to use it in game development.

Preparing Projections

We have selected our favorite car as a to model: the "Lancia Delta" (Fig. 15.1), whose body was designed by Giorgetto Giugiaro, the founder and head of Italdesign-Giugiaro S.p.A. from 1975 to 1979. In our opinion, this car is still modern. Furthermore, the design of this car is simple but expressive, which lets us concentrate on the basic principles without being distracted by unimportant details.

Before using this sketch, we need to prepare projections of all the main views and save them in separate files. This task can be accomplished using any bitmap editor.

Note

You can try to prepare the projection files yourself. The initial file named delta.jpg can be found on the companion CD-ROM in the Lessons\Lessons15\Delta folder.

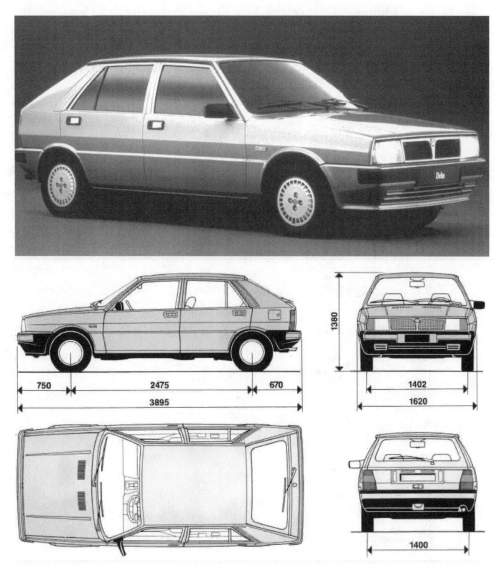

Fig. 15.1. Photo and sketch of the car (published with the permission of Italdesign-Giugiaro S.p.A.)

❏ Divide the image into four parts, each corresponding to a specific projection.

❏ When necessary, adjust image orientation according to the way that it will look in the viewports. For example, position the top view vertically.

❏ Delete the dimension lines.

❏ Draw additional lines: centerlines and clearance (extension) lines.

❏ Based on these lines, bring the linear dimensions of the files into accordance with one another. For example, the width of the projection files for the front and rear views must be equal to the width of the top view file (Fig. 15.2). Centerlines must divide the image into equal halves.

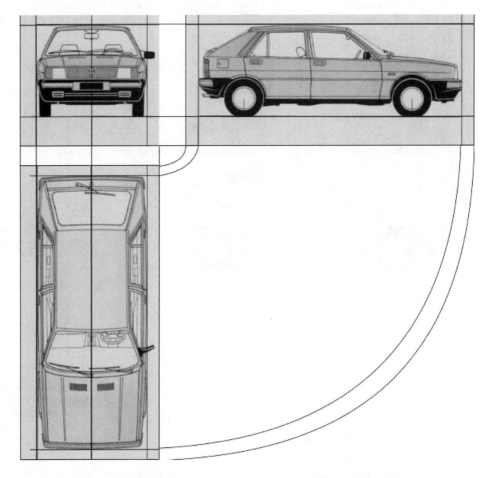

Fig. 15.2. Relation between the projection files

Note

If you have already viewed the contents of the folder containing the projection files, then you should have noticed that there are two variations of projections: normal and wide. The width of the files with the "-wide" suffix is equal to the width of the left view file. Later on we will explain why this is necessary.

❑ Fill in all projections with some color. This is not necessary, but it will be helpful because 3ds max, by default, uses white to highlight selected objects and sub-objects.

❑ Save the files using any format without compression (TGA, for example) and assign them appropriate names.

Two Methods of Using a Sketch

There are two modeling methods. We recommend that you try both and select the one that you like best.

The first method involves using projections as background. 3ds max lets you synchronize viewport zoom with the dimensions of the background images. Unfortunately, if the width of the background images doesn't match, 3ds max displays them using different scales. As a result, we had to create duplicates of the projections (the ones with the -wide suffix), adjusting their width according to that of the left view.

❑ Reset 3ds max to the default viewport display. To accomplish this, just reset 3ds max to its initial settings:

Main menu → File → Reset

❑ Replace the **Perspective** view with the **Back** view.

❑ Assign the top-wide.tga, front-wide.tga, left.tga, and back-wide.tga as background images for respective viewports. You can use one of two techniques to assign background images to the viewports: Use the viewport display settings dialog (Main menu → Views →

Viewport Background or <Alt>+<B>), or simply drag the images to the viewports using the **Asset Browser** (Control panel → Utilities → Asset Browser). In either case, the settings dialog will appear, where **A viewport background** must be selected.

Note

Instead of the **Asset Browser**, you can use a tool such as ACDSee or even Windows Explorer.

❐ Synchronize the parameters of the background images to the view dimensions in the viewports (Fig. 15.3).

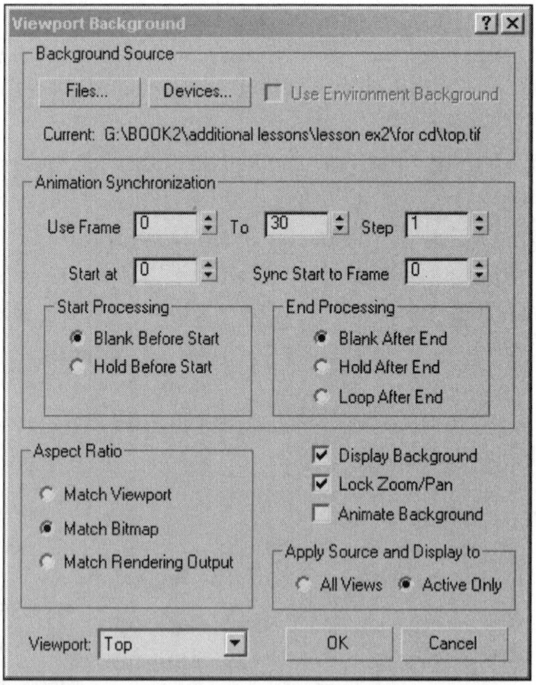

Fig. 15.3. Settings in the **Viewport Background** dialog

Try to change magnification in the viewports and move the display. As you can see, background images are linked to the viewports.

▶ *Note*

If you are using the hardware accel-
erator in OpenGL or Direct3D mode,
you may encounter problems with the
display of the background images. If
you do, switch to the Software Z Buffer
mode and restart 3ds max.

> Context menu → Customize →
> Preferences → Viewports tab →
> Choose Driver

The file named lesson15-01.max with appropriately adjusted viewport settings
can be found on the companion CD-ROM in the \Lessons\lesson15\Scenes\ folder.

Unfortunately, the drawback of this modeling method is evident: You are
limited to the side projection viewports when modeling. If you are satisfied with
this, you can start modeling.

The second modeling method requires you to create several planes and apply
the projection files to these planes as textures.

❑ Reset 3ds max to its initial state.

❑ Go to the left viewport and create a plane whose dimensions coincide with the
linear dimensions of the left.tga file (472 × 212) or represent their multiples.
Don't forget to set the **Generate Mapping Coordinates** checkbox.

▶ *Tip*

The most convenient method of creating a plane is to enter the values of its dimensions
manually from the keyboard.

❑ Create other planes (Fig. 15.4, *a*).

❑ Using the **Asset Browser**, move the projection files to the planes. Materials with
assigned **Diffuse** maps will be created (Fig. 15.4, *b*).

▶ *Tip*

You can open the **Asset Browser** in one of the viewports. (Viewport right-click menu →
Views → Extended → Asset Browser).

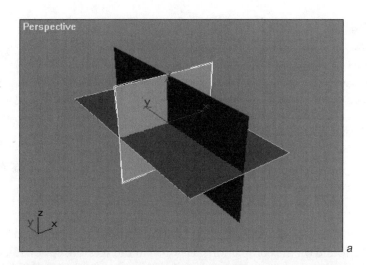

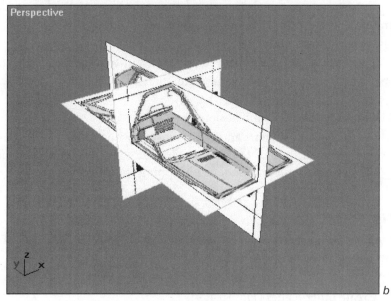

Fig. 15.4. Creating the base planes

 Note

Textures applied to objects might be displayed with distortions. If so, you can correct the situation by enabling the **Texture Correction** mode in the viewport right-click menu.

❏ If necessary, move the planes to make the center lines of the textures match the grid and one another.

The lesson15-02.max file containing correctly adjusted viewport planes can be found on the companion CD-ROM in the \Lessons\Lesson15\Scenes\ folder.

Modeling the Car Body

We propose that you model the car body using Bezier curves with a subsequent conversion to Bezier patches. We selected this method to demonstrate how this can be done. Principally, the shape is rather simple, since Giugiaro used straight lines and basic geometric shapes when designing the car body. Thus, you can model the car body by stretching polygons and moving the cube vertices. If you agree that this method is simple, create a model using this technique.

The modeling itself requires drawing the contours by curves and creating patch objects based on them. All stages of the modeling process are shown in Fig. 15.5. In these illustrations, we have intentionally made the sketches invisible. We won't concentrate on the details of creating geometry; instead, we will provide only general recommendations.

❏ It makes sense to model only half of the object. Later, you can create the second half by making a mirror copy and attaching it to the initial half.

❏ Don't try to model the whole object as a single shape. Details, such as bumpers, can be created later.

❏ If you selected the first method of modeling (using projections as background), you'll have to work in side views. If you selected the second method, it is convenient to work in the perspective or user views in the final stages. Still, most of the work is performed in side views.

❏ Switch on the snap to vertices:

Main menu → Customize → Grid and Snap Settings

❏ Draw open polygons rather than curves, since the curvature can be added later by changing vertex types.

❏ You often will have to select more than one vertex at a time, with coinciding coordinates. To simplify this task, go to the control panel and set the **Area Selection** checkbox.

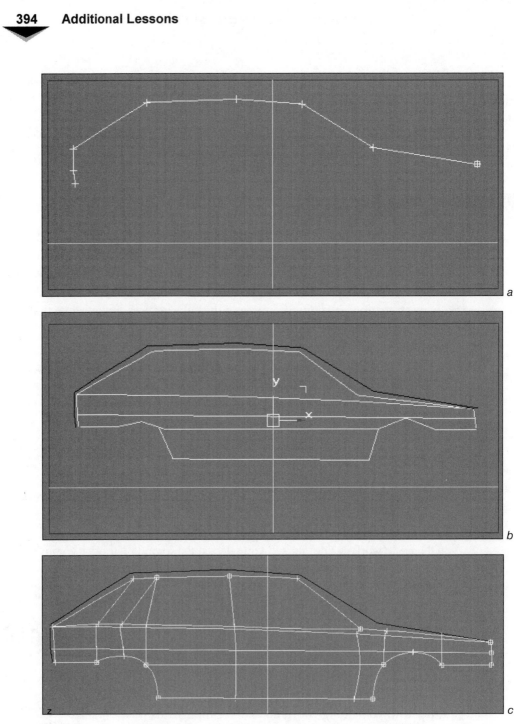

Fig. 15.5, a — c. Sequence of modeling the car body

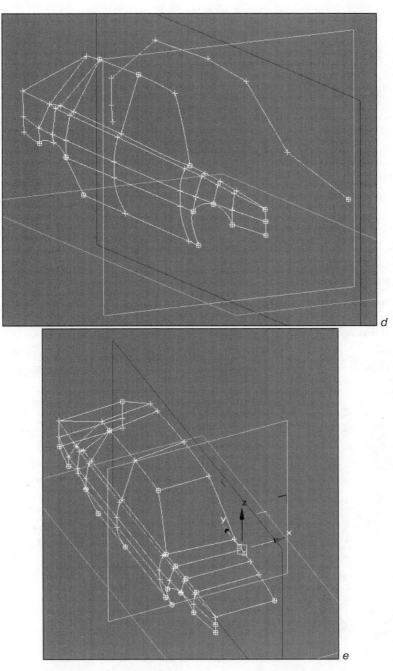

Fig. 15.5, _d_ and _e_. Sequence of modeling the car body

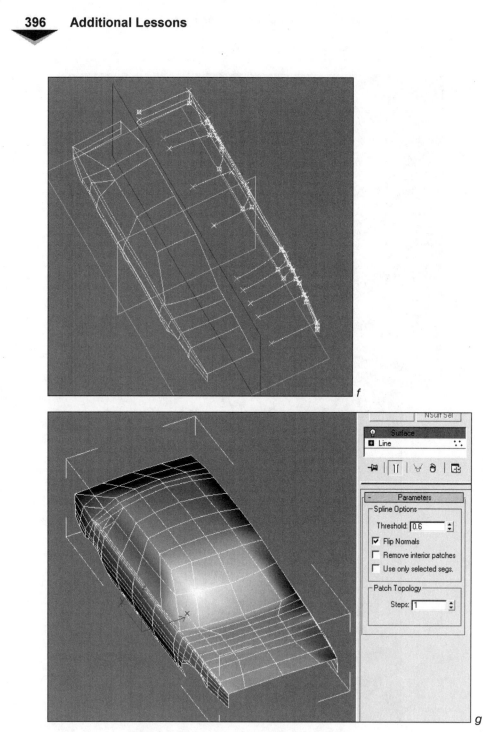

f

g

Fig. 15.5, *f* and *g*. Sequence of modeling the car body

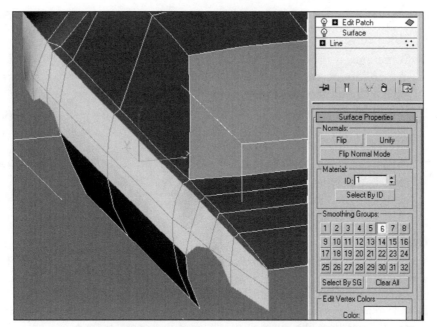

Fig. 15.5, *h*. Sequence of modeling the car body

❏ When editing vertices, 3ds max will periodically prompt you to **Weld** coinciding vertices. Don't be deceived; ignore these prompts.

❏ Since the accuracy of the sketch itself and the precision of its display in 3ds max viewports are far from perfect, try to use the same view (for example, the left view) as the basic one. Furthermore, specify the maximum possible quality for texture display in the viewports:

    Main menu → Customize → Preferences → Viewports → Configure Driver

❏ If you are using planes, you can always move them along longitudinal axes to make the modeling process more convenient.

❏ At a certain stage of your work, you'll have to join all the curves to a single object to take advantage the capabilities of curve editing. To do so, select any curve and join all other curves to it. This action is also required to apply the **Surface** modifier:

    Control panel → Geometry rollout → Attach Mult

❏ You'll get a frame consisting of quadrangular and triangular "cells." Only then will the **Surface** modifier build the patch model correctly.

❏ It is convenient to use the **Refine** command to join the obtained vertices.

❏ Sometimes it is necessary to start or finish either separating or joining in the existing vertices. In such a situation, you'll be warned that you are attempting to separate the edge in the vicinity of the existing vertex. Select the **Connect Only** option.

❏ After you convert the model to the **Editable Patch** type or apply the **Edit Patch** modifier, work on the smoothing groups to obtain the correct model.

▶ *Note*

There is another excellent feature that lets you create curves in any vector graphics editor and import them as curves into 3ds max. If you decide to do so, use Adobe Illustrator (version AI 88) or DWG/DXF formats. Note that AI 88 format can't always be loaded successfully. The import procedure could fail because of the decimal separator, which must be a period. Sometimes the success or failure of this operation depends on the operating system. (This happens occasionally under Windows 98 for unknown reasons.) Finally, note that the vector graphics software must perform the export operation correctly. We use Xara X and, usually, everything goes smoothly. Generally, we also can import successfully files saved in Adobe Illustrator. You should note that the format version supported by 3ds max is AI 88.

❏ Save your model. The results of our work are presented in the file named lesson15-05.max on the companion CD-ROM. (You can find this file in the \Lessons\Lesson15\Scenes\ folder.) The lesson15-03.max and lesson15-04.max files contain the intermediate variants.

The geometry of the model is now ready. We recommend that you accomplish all other tasks with materials that are combined using masks.

Creating Materials

To be precise, we are going to create only one material. In 3ds max, there is a general rule: One object — one material. This material can be composite and contain many sub-materials. These, in turn, can be composites, and so on.

Let us begin with sub-materials. First, we'll need the base material for the car body with the bump and color textures imitating door handles, openings, etc.; material for chromium-plated shaping strips and door handles; and material for glasses. We also will need material for the inner surface of the car body.

Thus, the list of textures and masks is as follows: the mask for mixing the main material and chromium, and the mask for mixing chromium and glasses.

- ❏ It is possible to create several sets of files for each projection. However, we recommend that you try to join every texture of each type within a single file. This will simplify the structure of the materials. (This is rather complex by itself.)
- ❏ The \Lessons\Lesson15\Scenes\ folder on the companion CD-ROM contains the textures required for the project. As you can see, nearly all of them are black-and-white images.

► *Note*

We have "merged" the models and textures. On one hand, this is awkward and inconvenient. On the other hand, when projects are moved from one computer to another, unpleasant situations will occur if 3ds max cannot find the necessary textures. In the material editor, generally the absolute path to the files is used, and 3ds max will constantly demand the paths to the texture files. You can correct this problem by adding the folders with the textures into the path settings (Main menu → Customize → Configure Paths), but note that this database is limited. Therefore, we recommend using a property of 3ds max: If a file is not found, 3ds max searches for it in the folder with the source file of the scene. By the way, the 3ds max package has the useful **Resource Collector** utility (Control panel → Utilities → More → Resource Collector) enabling the collection all the project files into one folder.

We would like to draw your attention to the texture in the diffuse_map.tga file. At first glance, it looks strange. This is because the main element of this texture is not the image itself, but rather the alpha channel that will be used to apply all required elements to the surface of the car body. It is possible to change the color of the body immediately by choosing the diffuse color of the material directly in 3ds max. Initially, the drawing was done on a white background; however, this background will probably produce an undesirable light contour when applying the texture. Therefore, we advise you either to fill in all unused space in the texture with the drawing color or to blur the image by increasing the width of the lines.

Fig. 15.6 shows the structure of the **Lancia** material. Let us consider it in more detail.

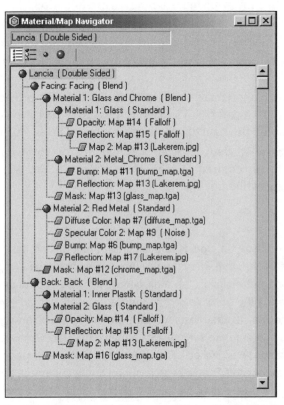

Fig 15.6. Structure of the material for the car body

The material that will be assigned to the model is composite, double-sided material. It comprises two other composite materials (**Facing** and **Back**) of the **Blend** type. These  materials are applied to the outer and inner sides, respectively. Outer sub-material consists of the standard **Red Metal** sub-material and a composite **Glass and Chrome** sub-material. These materials are mixed using the mask texture chrome_map.tga. The **Glass and Chrome** sub-material comprises two appropriate sub-materials mixed using the glass-map.tga texture. The nesting order is vitally important; the mask of the material at the deeper nesting level must be "inside" the mask of the material at the higher level.

Inner material is much simpler. It consists of the **Glass** and **Inner Plastik** sub-materials, also mixed using the glass_map.tga mask.

Now, try to study the material parameters yourself by going over the lesson15(final).max file. We hope that you're able to understand everything without additional comments. We will only emphasize some important aspects.

❏ The diffuse-map.tga texture in the **Red Metal** material is applied using the alpha channel. This enables you to alter the body color by changing the **Diffuse** color of the material. Notice that the **Premultiplied Alpha** checkbox is cleared. As for other textures, we recommended that you select the **None** option (non-transparent material).

❏ Transparency and reflection in the **Glass** material are produced using the **Falloff** map of the **Fresnel** type.

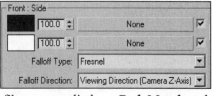

❏ The **Chrome** material is taken from the standard 3ds max library. The same bump textures from the bump_map.tga file are applied to **Red Metal** and **Chrome** materials.

❏ We advise you to enable **SuperSampling** when specifying parameters of all materials. In the parameters of all materials, we rec-ommend setting the **Summed Area** option for texture filtering to allow better smoothing of the contours.

Editing
the Texture Mapping Coordinates

Assign the **Lancia** material to the car body by dragging it from the sample slot of the material editor to the object. Make one of the textures of any material visible in the viewport (for example, bump_map.tga) and switch to the **Smooth+Highlight** mode in the viewport window by pressing the <F3> and <F4> keys.

You also need to adjust the texture coordinates. This can be done using the **Unwrap UVW** modifier.

Compared to the previous versions, this modifier in 3ds max 5 has become a powerful and excellent tool. There is no need to describe all of its novelties in this lesson because our model is very simple, but we suggest that you master these tools on your own. The options for texture application should be the first to receive your attention.

- ❑ Apply the **Unwrap UVW** modifier.
- ❑ Expand the branch of sub-objects and choose the **Select Face** option.
- ❑ Select the patches for the hood, windscreen, top, and rear glass. Notice how the coordinate plane of the modifier changes (Fig. 15.7, *a*).

▶ *Tip*

During the selection, it is convenient to use the angle specification option in which polygons are considered co-planed (**Planar Angle**).

- ❑ Align the plane on the Y-axis, click the **Planar Map** button, and switch to coordinate editing by clicking the **Edit** button (Fig. 15.7, *b*).
- ❑ In the coordinate-editing window, select the appropriate texture (pointed to by arrow 1 in Fig. 15.7, *b*).
- ❑ Adjust the texture's appearance as desired by rotating, moving, and re-scaling. For this purpose, use the **Freeform Mode** tool (arrow 2). When you use this tool, a container (gizmo) appears around the selected elements. To move it, press the left mouse button and grab at any place within the container. To rotate it, grab at the centers of the sides; to scale it, grab at the corners. The usage of the <Alt>, <Ctrl>, and <Shift> keys provides you with additional options during the editing process.
- ❑ When you open the option window (arrow 3), you can edit the texture appearance in the editing window. The texture may not be shown at all if a zero value is set for brightness (**Brightness**).

▶ *Note*

When you are editing texture mapping coordinates for patches, handles appear near the texture control vertices that are similar to the patch vertex handles. This enables you to edit the coordinate curvature in accordance with the curvature of the patches themselves.

- ❑ Select the lateral patches and correct their coordinates.

  Now, everything is ready!

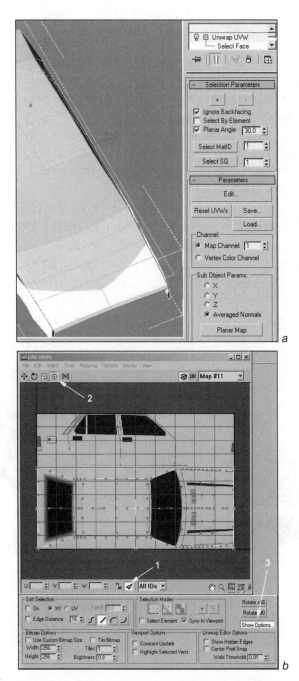

Fig. 15.7. Editing the texture mapping coordinates

Still, we would like to give you some tips and advice.

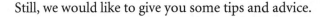

- ❑ After the texture coordinates are edited, you can apply the **Edit Patch** modifier and smooth the result slightly by using the **Relax Mesh** option. Be careful with this option: It may distort the textures.
- ❑ If you have the f-Edge plug-in extension module at your disposal, try to apply this instrument. The demo version of this module can be found on the companion CD-ROM in the Plugins folder.

As you can see, this task didn't prove to be too complicated. Therefore, the question arises: "Is it possible to create more complex shapes using this method?" Fig. 15.8 shows the set of models that we produced for one of the projects developed by Doka Media. When creating these models, we simply copied the materials from one scene to another and replaced the appropriate textures.

Fig. 15.8. Example car models (published with the permission of Doka Media)

Lesson 16

Modeling a Human Head

This lesson deals with the most complicated and interesting task of 3D graphics: human head modeling. It should be mentioned that this considerable task gives software developers no rest because of its complexity and the wish of many artists (the term is deliberate, for we ourselves are to some extent adherents of new technologies) to create convincing characters quickly. Lately, a whole range of the software has appeared that simplifies the process; Poser, FaceGen Modeller, and Head Designer are but a few of the offerings. The names convey nothing, do they? Scarcely so. We think that you probably have encountered them more than once before and could not help admiring the results obtained. Indeed, it is rather tempting to work with a true image of the human head by changing a dozen of options. (No kidding — a parametric head in the FaceGen Modeller package is described using about forty main and thirty optional parameters!)

So why, year in and year out, are virtual galleries supplemented with various characters that feature heads and bodies created in multi-purpose 3D packages, such as 3ds max or Maya? The explanation is simple. Specialized packages (those named above as well as half-dozen unlisted ones) are good and often inexpensive compared to multi-purpose packages. As a rule, they also are either direct plug-ins to multi-purpose packages or can convert models into common formats. But they do have drawbacks — sometimes substantial.

First, a model obtained with the help of a specialized generator is not optimized and contains many "redundant" polygons. This is not a disaster, for geometry optimizers are available. For example, there are two optimization modules integrated in 3ds max. One of them — MultiRes — implements one of the most progressive methods of optimization, leaving the texture coordinates intact. Unfortunately, it is painstaking to edit such a model.

Second, any model obtained by means of a generator bears the traits of the base "blank" because most generators change the proportions of an "average" model. What's more, as a rule, such blank features have a pronounced "national identity". A face of any nationality bears common signs of humanity, but few people would take into account all of the shades and variation within one source model. All of these considerations relate to a realistic head, but what if a character is fantastic? It seems that nothing prevents us from touching up the model... Yes, something does! The source topology of the model prevents us from redoing it as we like.

And the last, but not the least, argument: Did you ever think that someone produced these "blanks"? If so, why not create your own template for a further series of characters? This way, you know where and what should be amended to get the necessary result. The benefits of the approach are evident: This is your model, and you can do whatever you like with it.

Hopefully, we have persuaded you that creating your own model of a head is not only interesting, but also useful. So, let's try!

This lesson is based on a method introduced by Arild Wiro Anfinnsen, better known as simply Wiro (**http://www.secondreality.ch**). Wiro kindly permitted us to make use of some steps that will allow you to create a model of a head quickly and with high quality.

To model the head of a human being, not a monster, it is desirable to have files with projections for comparison. These can be sketches or photos of a real head, even your own. You can load them as described in *Lesson 15*. When preparing this lesson, we used our own photos, and some similarities came out.

❑ Start by creating a box (**Box**), built approximately by the sizes of the projections' images and segmented as shown in Fig. 16.1, *a*.

❑ Streamline your box by applying the **Spherify** modifier (Fig. 16.1, *b*):

Main menu → Modifiers → Parametric Deformers → Spherify

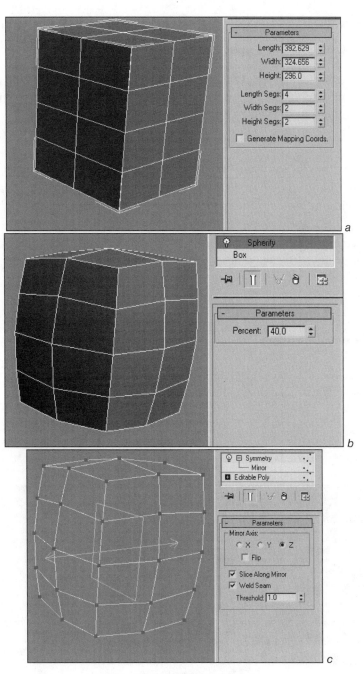

Fig. 16.1. Blank of a head

❏ Convert the object to the polygonal object type (**Editable Poly**):

Context menu → Convert to → Convert to Editable Poly

❏ On the front view, select and remove the vertices from one side, leaving the "half". Apply the **Symmetry** modifier and make the adjustment so you can see the final model while editing one side (Fig. 16.1, *c*):

Main menu → Modifiers → Mesh Editing → Symmetry

❏ Go down the stack and press the **Show End Result On/Off Toggle** button.
❏ Working on the vertices' level, put the model into the head shape (without nose or other protruding parts) (Fig. 16.2, *a*).
❏ Add the edges across the center of the eyes and lachrymal glands. Use ring selection of the edges (**Ring**) and edge connection (**Connect**), with subsequent movement of the vertices (Fig. 16.2, *b* and *c*).

▶ *Tip*

When moving the edges, it is convenient to use the constraint (**Constraints** to **Edge**). Also use the **Ignore Backfacing** mode.

❏ Make eye sockets (Fig. 16.2, *d*) and additional edges in the shape of the upper jaw (Fig. 16.2, *e*) using the same tools.

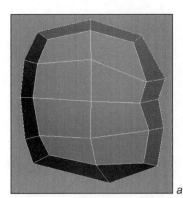
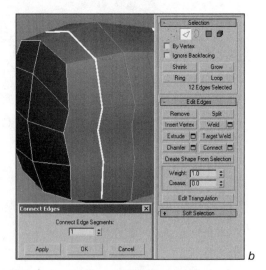

Fig. 16.2, *a* and *b*. Creating eye sockets and the upper jaw

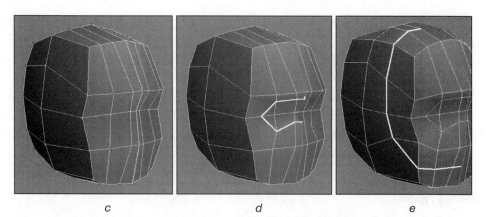

c   d   e

Fig. 16.2, *c–e.* Creating eye sockets and the upper jaw

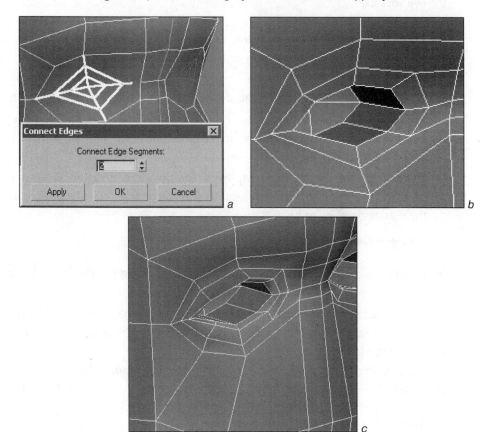

Fig. 16.3. Eye modeling

❏ Complete the eye sockets using the **Insert Vertex** and **Create** commands for the edges.

❏ To create the blanks for the eyelids, join the edges of the eye sockets twice by circles (Fig. 16.3, *a*). Then move the vertices.

❏ Make the hollows for the eyes using the **Extrude** command for the polygons (Fig. 16.3, *b*).

❏ Form the eyelids (Fig. 16.3, *c*) by dividing the edges around the eyes again and moving the vertices.

▶ *Tip*

To have eyelids of the correct shape, you can make the eye-spheres and insert them into the eye sockets.

❏ Make the nose. The **Hinge From Edge** command for polygons will be of use (Fig. 16.4, *a*). Remove the polygon formed close to the symmetry line. Move the vertex to the symmetry line.

❏ Obtain the desired shape of the nose by complicating the mesh and moving the vertices (Fig. 16.4, *b*).

❏ The **Inset** and **Bevel** commands for polygons will help you to create the nostrils (Fig. 16.4, *c* and *d*).

❏ Technology similar to that employed for the eyes' creation is used for the mouth (Fig. 16.5, *a* — *c*). The option for converting the edges' selection into the vertices is of great help:

Context menu → Convert to Vertex

❏ Finally, make the chin and the cheeks (Fig. 16.6, *a* and *b*). The face is ready!

As you can see, there was nothing difficult. We think that you will manage to finish the model by yourself. By the way, the Wiro's website contains a perfect lesson on ear modeling.

By creating our model in this way, it does not require further complication of the mesh — if the smoothing groups are set up correctly. But applying the **MeshSmooth** modifier once may help smooth the sharp angles where necessary.

And the final tip: Look in the mirror often when you model a human head. You may discover interesting features there!

Fig. 16.4. Nose modeling

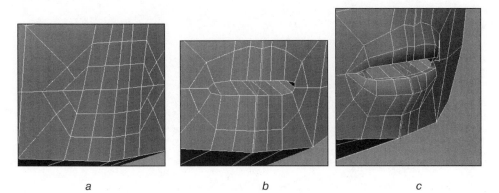

Fig. 16.5. Creating the mouth and lips

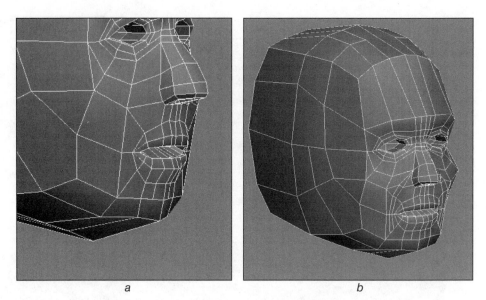

a *b*

Fig. 16.6. Creating the chin and cheeks

Lesson 17

Modeling Lightning and an Electric Discharge

In this lesson we will create simple electrical effects. There are several plug-ins that enable the creation of rather realistic and beautiful effects of this type. In this lesson, however, we suggest that you create these effects using only 3ds max's built-in tools.

Modeling Lightning

☐ Go to the **Front** viewport and create a tree-like broken line (open polygon) that resembles chained lightning (Fig. 17.1, *a*):

Main menu → Create → Shapes → Line

▶ *Tip*

To avoid subsequent joining of your lines, clear the **Start New Shape** checkbox in control panel.

AutoGrid ☐
Start New Shape ☐

☐ Set the parameters as shown in Fig. 17.1, *b*.

▶ *Tip*

Make the curve renderable. Set the parameters in such a way as to make the line thin. Then select the **Display Render Mesh** checkbox. This is necessary because later we are going to apply the modifiers for editing mesh objects.

☐ Apply the **Slice** modifier.

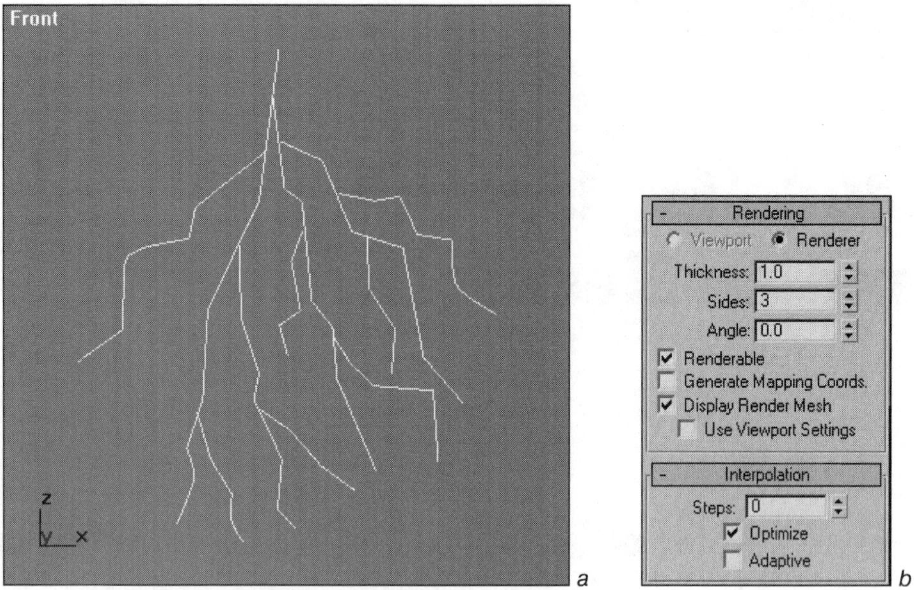

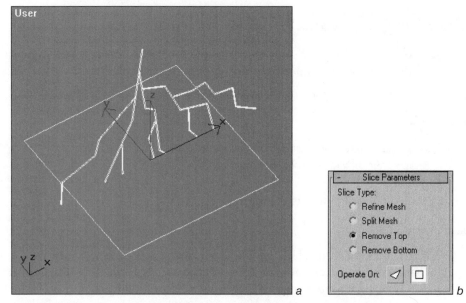

Fig. 17.1. Geometry of the lightning (a) and its parameters (b)

Fig. 17.2. Positioning the **Slice** modifier's gizmo (a)
and its parameters (b)

❏ Position the modifier's gizmo at an angle normal for a thunderbolt (Fig. 17.2, *a*):

    Right-click menu → Sub-object → Slice Plane

    Right-click menu → Rotate

❏ Configure the modifier parameters to "cut off" the lower part of the bolt (Fig. 17.2, *b*).

Try to move the modifier's gizmo up and down. As you can see, the lightning "grows." That's the effect we need.

Now, before we proceed with animation, let's create some materials and adjust the settings.

❏ Open the material editor by pressing the <M> key.

❏ Create a bright-blue, self-illuminating material (Fig. 17.3).

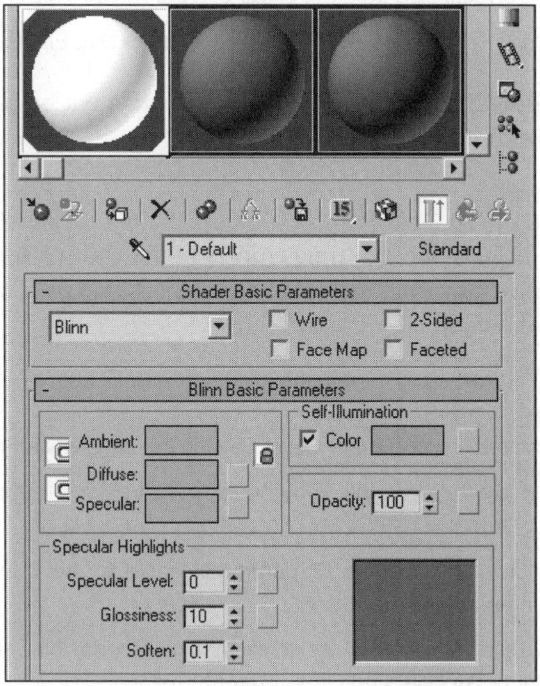

Fig. 17.3. Material parameters for the lightning

Tip

Set the bright-blue color for the **Ambient**, **Diffuse**, **Specular**, and **Self-Illumination** channels. You could merely set the **Self-Illumination** parameter to 100%, but doing this would make to the discharge non-uniform.

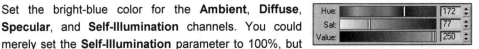

Specify any number but zero for the effects channel (for example, 15). You'll use this setting to specify the illumination area (Material editor → Material Effect Channel).

Now adjust the **Glow** parameter. We recommend that you do this in the **Perspective** viewport of the camera. (You need to create a camera, if you haven't done so already.)

Glow effects in 3ds max can be created by two methods: through rendering effects or through the Video Post module effect. We recommend that you use both methods.

❐ Open the effects and add the **Lens Effects** to the scene:

Main menu → Rendering → Effects → ... → Add → Lens Effects

❐ Select **Glow** from the list of effects and activate it by clicking the ">" button.

In *Lesson 5*, you created an effect for imitating the glow of the solar corona. The process of adjusting the lightning glow is similar, with a single exception — now we need to create a glow that will follow the object's shape. To do this, set the glow parameters as shown in Fig. 17.4.

Note

We have renamed the effect **Inner Glow**. Later in this chapter we will explain why we did so.

To make the glow follow the lightning shape, set the **Image** checkbox in the **Apply Element To** group.

Make the value of the **Effects ID** parameter equal to the value of the similar parameter for the lightning material.

Set the glow size so it produces a slight blur. To do this, set the **Size** parameters in the **Lens Effects Globals** and **Glow Element** rollouts.

The first color in the **Radial Color** group must be bright blue.

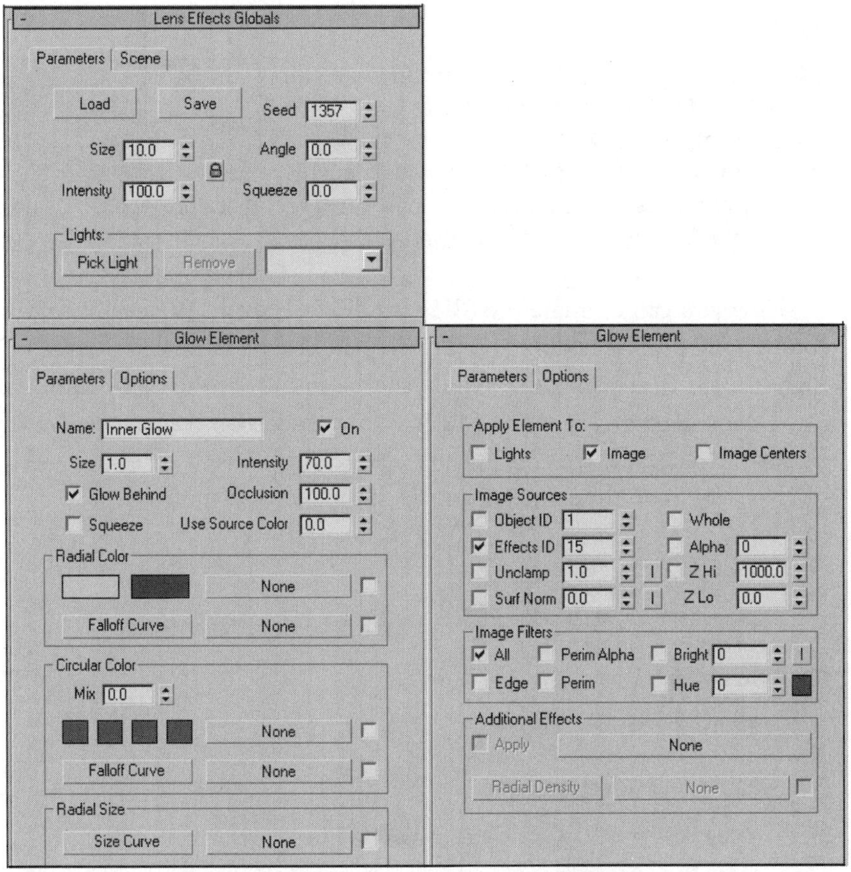

Fig. 17.4. Parameters of the **Inner Glow**

Thus, you have set the parameters. However, a single **Glow** element isn't sufficient. If the object has glowing contours, the parameters from the **Radial Color**, **Circular Color**, and **Radial Size** don't work (with the exception of the first color in the **Radial Color** group). Consequently, you'll have to create **Glow** elements of various sizes and intensities. You can create them yourself or use our settings that we have created. You can find our settings in the electric bolt.lzv file on the companion CD-ROM in the Lessons\Lesson17\plugcfg\ folder if you press the **Load** button in the **Lens Effects Globals** rollout. If you have created your own settings, don't forget to save them for the future use.

▶ *Note*

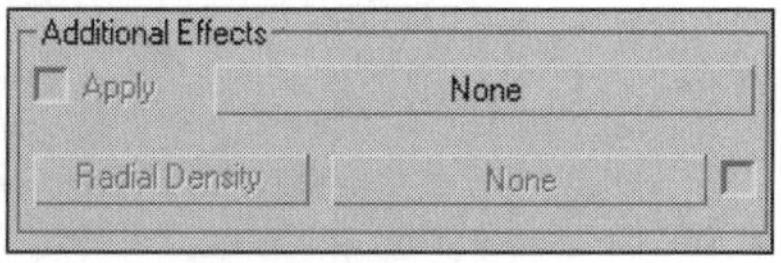

You can create additional effects by applying a texture to the transparency channel of one of the effects from the **Additional Effects** group an the **Options** tab. Try to do this and understand its working principles. We can add only one comment: A texture applied using this method works as a transparency mask. Its colors are ignored.

Now you can animate the **Slice** modifier's gizmo. We doubt that you will encounter any problems doing so. To view the results of our work, open the lesson17 (lightning - effects).max file, which can be found on the companion CD-ROM in the Lessons\Lesson17\scenes folder. The rendering results are in the Lessons\Lesson17\Images\lesson17 (lightning - effects).avi file.

Now try to do the same task using the Video Post module.

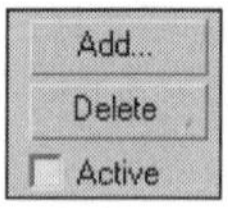

❑ Turn off all effects:

   Main menu → Rendering →Effects → clear the Active checkbox

❑ Open **Video Post**:

   Main menu → Rendering → Video Post

❑ Create the rendering sequence (Fig. 17.5):

   Video Post → Add Scene Event → viewport (Camera01 or Perspective)
   Video Post → Add Image Effect Event → Lens Effect Glow
   Video Post → Add Image Output Event → select a file

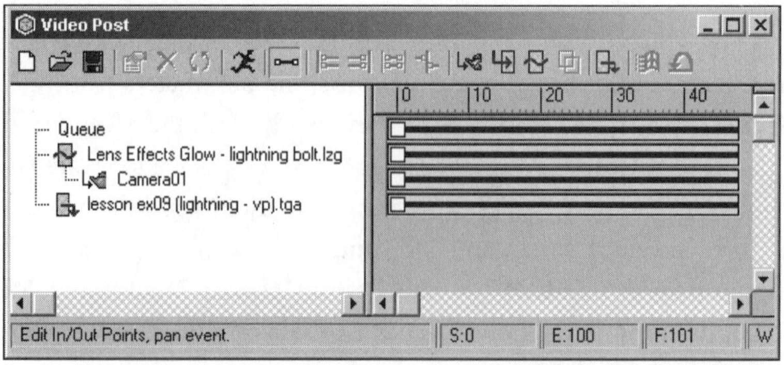

Fig. 17.5. Rendering sequence in the **Video Post** window

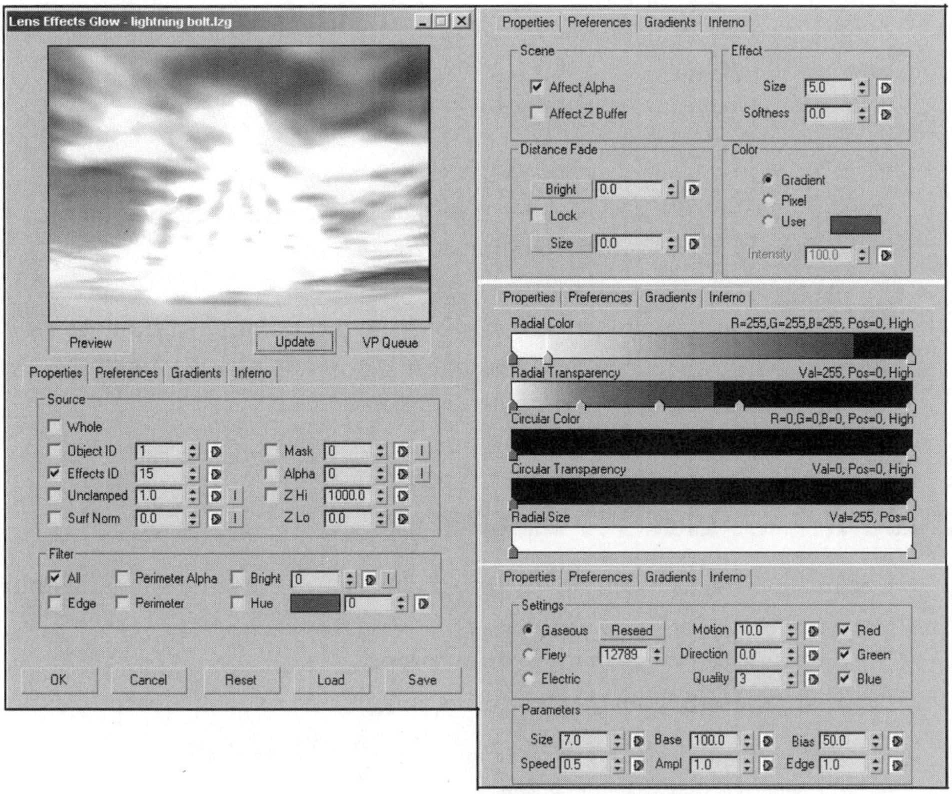

Fig. 17.6. Lens Effects Glow parameters

❐ Adjust the **Glow** parameters for a stunning effect (Fig. 17.6).

▶ *Tip*

Make the value of the **Effects ID** parameter equal that of the similar parameter for the lightning material.

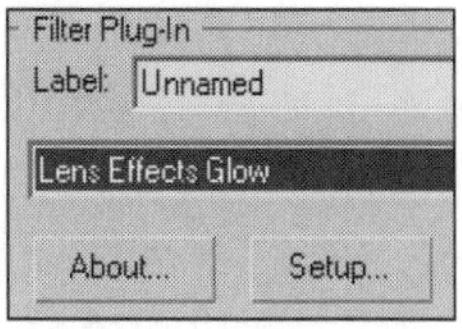

At color settings, select **Gradient** (Preferences → Color) and adjust the color and transparency gradients.

Set the **Inferno** effect on all color channels to make it partially influence all other **Glow** elements.

▶ *Tip*

You can see a preview of the effect by clicking the **VP Queue** and **Preview** buttons.

We have saved our settings, which you can download from the Lessons\ Lesson17\plugcfg\lightning bolt.lzg file on the companion CD-ROM. If you like your settings better, save them for the future use.

❏ Now, render the sequence by clicking the **Execute Sequence** button and specifying a segment duration of 20–25 frames.

To view the results of our work, open the lesson17 (lightning — video-post).max file by pressing the **Load** button. Rendering results are in the Lessons\ Lesson17\images\lesson17 (lightning - vpost).avi file.

Modeling an Electric Discharge

Electric discharge between two objects can be done in the same way as lightning.

❏ Create a straight line in the **Front** viewport.
❏ Adjust the settings in the **Rendering** rollout just as you did for the lightning.
❏ Select the single line segment and divide it into 10-12 parts:

Control panel → Selection → Segment
Control panel → Geometry rollout → Divide
Apply the Edit Mesh modifier

❏ Select all vertices except the ones at the margins.
❏ Apply the **Noise** modifier and set it to make the resulting "discharge" randomly change its shape (Fig. 17.7).

Now, both the geometry and animation of the electric discharge are ready. Materials and effects are adjusted in the same way as they were for lightning.

▶ *Note*

Project files and clips are in the Scenes and Images subfolders, respectively, in the Lessons\Lesson17 folder on the companion CD-ROM. Try to work on them, or on your own projects, to make them more interesting and better-looking than ours. Experiment with effect animation, visibility, and so on. Now, everything is up to you.

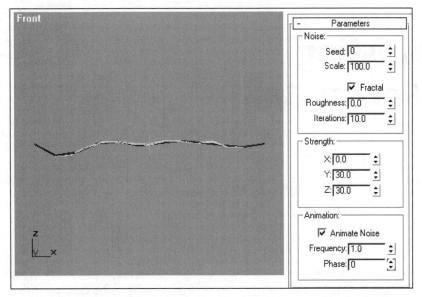

Fig. 17.7. Noise modifier parameters for animating an electric discharge

Lesson 18

Modeling a Soccer Ball

Creating this object, at first glance, might seem like an elementary task. But this is deceptive. The ball's geometry is not trivial and can be created with various techniques. The method described in this lesson represents our own way of approaching the task. You can think of this lesson as an interesting 'mental training' exercise and try to invent your own solutions.

The set of geometric primitives provided by 3ds max contains numerous parametric objects, including the Hedra, a parametric polyhedron. Using this primitive, you can create a large number of polyhedrons of various types, including the basis for the soccer ball.

❑ Create a polyhedron with parameters shown in Fig. 18.1:

Main menu → Create → Extended Primitives → Hedra

▶ *Tip*

Select the Dodec/Icos type (dodecahedron).

Select the **P** value experimentally so as to obtain evenly distributed equilateral pentagons and hexagons.

❑ Convert it to an editable polygon:

Right-click menu → Convert to → Convert to Editable Poly

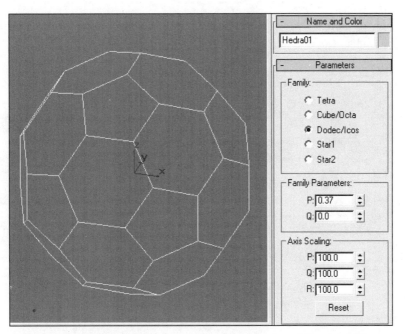

Fig. 18.1. Polyhedron basis for the soccer ball and its parameters

❐ Create the seams.

- Select all polygons, slightly extrude them independently, and decrease their size:

  Control panel →...→ Edit Geometry → By Polygon

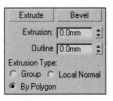

- Enter a small positive value into the **Extrusion** field and a small negative value in the **Outline** field.

❐ Without deselecting the polygons, apply the **Tessellate** modifier with parameters shown in Fig. 18.2, *a*:

  Control panel → Modifier List → Tessellate

❐ Apply the **Spherify** modifier (Fig. 18.2, *b*), then the **Smooth** modifier (Fig 18.2, *c*), with the required parameters.

The ball's geometry is now ready.

Next, let us create the necessary materials. We do not think it will be difficult for you to paint the ball as you wish. To carry this out, convert the object back to an editable polygon. Note that polygon selection corresponds to the initial selection. Select the polygons by name and apply materials on them.

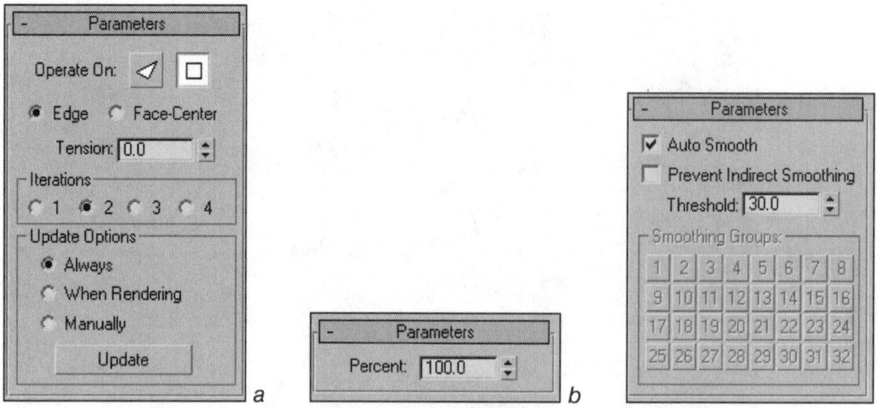

Fig. 18.2. Parameters of the modifiers: Tessellate (*a*), Spherify (*b*), and Smooth (*c*)

Fig. 18.3. Final view of the ball

Fig. 18.3 shows what the ball will look like. The lesson18-01.max file contains the ball with the modifier stack, while the lesson18(final).max file contains the final result — the ball with the applied materials.

Lesson 19

Using 3ds max with Other Autodesk and Discreet Packages

This lesson and the two following are brief reviews. Their goal is to show ways of increasing your efficiency when working with 3ds max and software from the Autodesk group, third-party companies, or independent developers.

Discreet Combustion

After the Autodesk group acquired Discreet Logic and transformed the Kinetix division into Discreet, the Combustion package was created. It was based on the Paint and Effect packages, combining the features of these two and adding new ones. The subsequent version of the package expanded the options for creating video effects and for follow–up editing. Here we want to consider one feature — texture drawing and editing directly on model surfaces in 3ds max.

There is no similar tool integrated in 3ds max. Third-party companies provide several packages that solve these problems to varying degrees. You may be aware of DeepPaint 3D, GhostPainter, or BodyPaint. Discreet offers its own solution: joint use of 3ds max and Combustion. Let us consider the preparations for drawing and the actual drawing in more detail.

❑ The Combustion package features the original interface. First, note that you cannot resize a window as in other Windows applications. You can specify the size of the working window (Fig. 19.1) in the package settings. Do this and re-start the package.

Note

If your system has two monitors, you don't need to use this feature. Simply position Combustion on one monitor and 3ds max on the other.

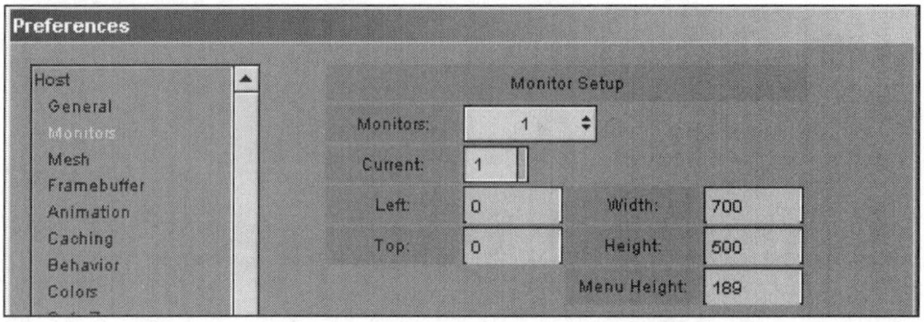

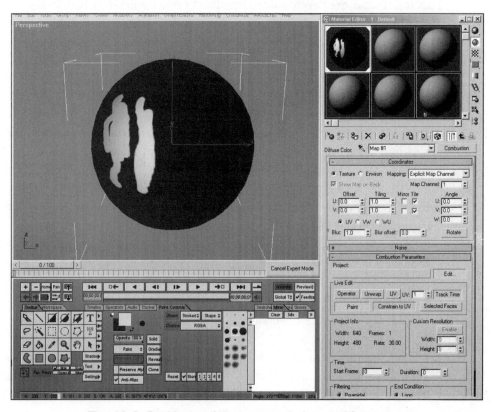

Fig. 19.1. Combustion window-size adjustment

Fig. 19.2. Positioning the program windows on the screen

☐ Start 3ds max, open the material editor, and select **Combustion** as the texture.

☐ Assign this material to an object and ensure the texture is displayed in a viewport.

☐ Start Combustion by pressing the **Edit** button.

☐ Position the applications as you wish (Fig. 19.2). Use **Expert Mode** (<Ctrl>+<X>) in 3ds max.

☐ Press the **Paint** button in the material editor and draw using the **Combustion** tools.

Apart from this feature, you can use Combustion to create rather impressive effects similar to those that you can create in 3ds max (glowing, mist, motion-blur, etc.). In Combustion, use the special Rich Pixel Format (RPF) for rendering and writing various channels (Fig. 19.3). This often is much quicker, and the final results turn out to be of higher quality.

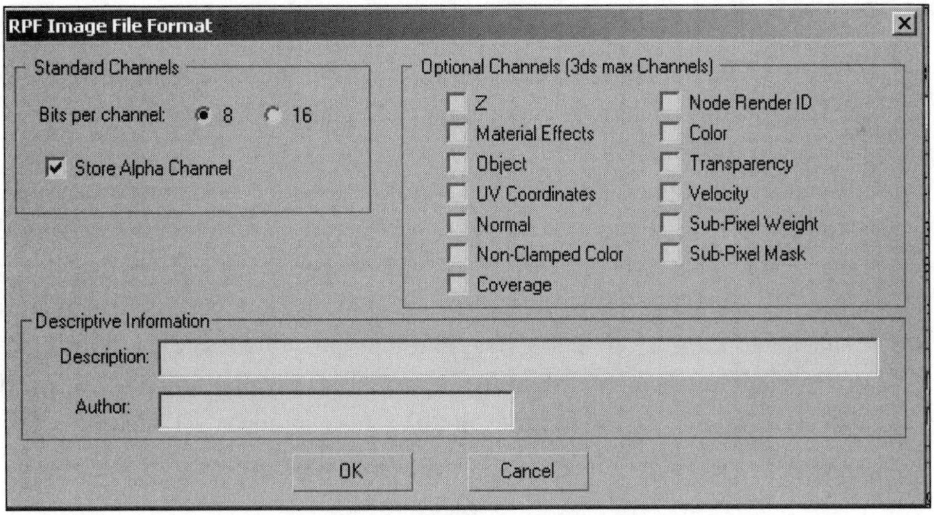

Fig. 19.3. Rendering adjustment in the RPF window

Finally, there is an option for rendering by layers (elements) and compiling them in a Combustion file for further compositing (Fig. 19.4).

You can find more details in the manuals of 3ds max and Combustion.

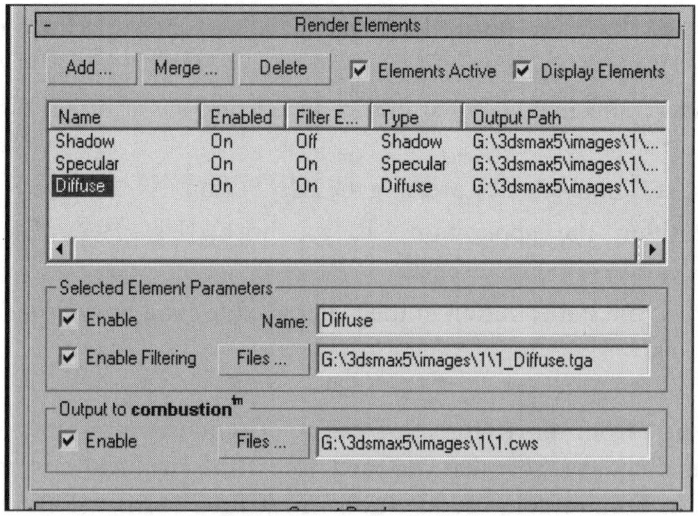

Fig. 19.4. Rendering-by-elements window

Autodesk VIZ

A team of developers from the Autodesk group, incorporating Discreet, used the 3D Studio MAX package as a basis for creating the 3D Studio VIZ package, which is now called Autodesk VIZ.

Initially this package was intended as a visualizer for projects created in the AutoCAD series, including Autodesk Architectural Desktop and Mechanical Desktop. In time, however, VIZ turned into an independent package possessing its own means for modeling, animation, and visualization. These means are similar to those available in 3ds max. In fact, global illumination, soft shades, photometric sources of light, and the daylight system first appeared in VIZ, not in 3ds max. In addition, VIZ features a range of unique modules (e.g., rendering QuickTime VR panoramas) that allow you to create parametric walls, windows, doors, stairways, etc. (Fig. 19.5).

Although Autodesk VIZ has no formal relationship with 3ds max, the packages have much in common. They use the same File format to allow you to easily move projects from one package to another. In order not to "offend" the users of 3ds max, the developers also offer a set of modules known as 3ds max Design Extensions (see details at **http://www.discreet.com/subscription/extensions.html**).

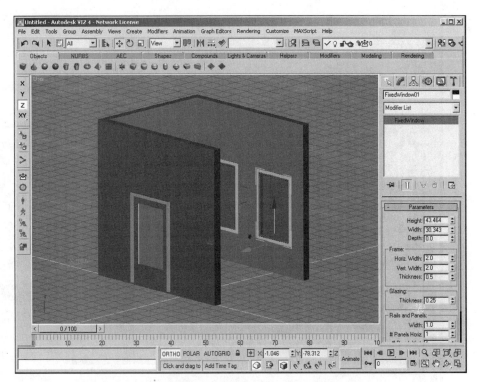

Fig. 19.5. Autodesk VIZ 4 interface

Taking into account the fact that VIZ is considerably less expensive than 3ds max, this package is popular among small companies involved in interior design and visualization.

Discreet Plasma

Discreet has released a product called Plasma, a relatively inexpensive package of 3D modeling and animation based on 3ds max 4 and intended for creating Web content in Flash, ShockWave 3D, and VRML formats (Fig. 19.6). There is also the option to render in Adobe Illustrator vector format and raster formats.

Plasma includes advanced tools for polygon modeling, texturing, animation with the use of ribs, inverse kinematics, and solids' dynamics. The package enables loading objects in 3ds max formats (with some limitations), 3D Studio, and VRML. The package also supplies a plug-in for 3ds max that lets you render in Flash format in 3ds max.

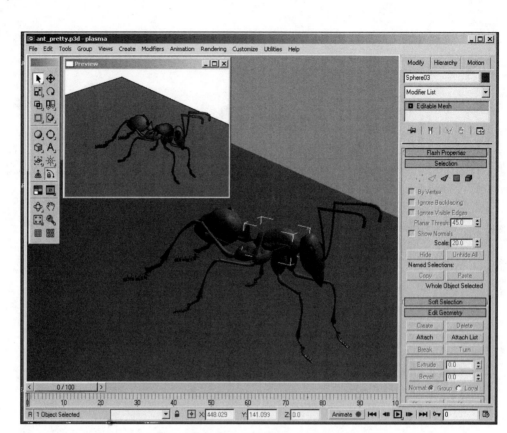

Fig. 19.6. Discreet Plasma interface

Discreet Gmax

During active promotion of 3ds max as the main package for creating computer games, the developers of Discreet released the Gmax package. Gmax integrates all of the tools necessary for creating models and animations for 3D games (Fig. 19.7). This is a full-value 3D-graphics package, but without rendering. The package loads objects in 3ds and DXF formats, but it saves only in its own format. This format is incompatible with 3ds max. (Beginning with version 1.2, Gmax supports export in the Plasma format, p3d.) So, why the new package? By releasing this package, Discreet meant to integrate with game developers. Apart from games, some developers produce so-called "game packs" that use Gmax as the level editor, creating models for a given game through "modifications" (mod). This seems to enjoy some success;

a couple of dozen games already support "mod" (e.g., Flight Simulator 2002 Pro from Microsoft and C&C:Renegade from Westwood) and contain sets of plug-ins for Gmax as expansion software. This trend seems to be developing quickly, especially because Gmax is free for this category of users.

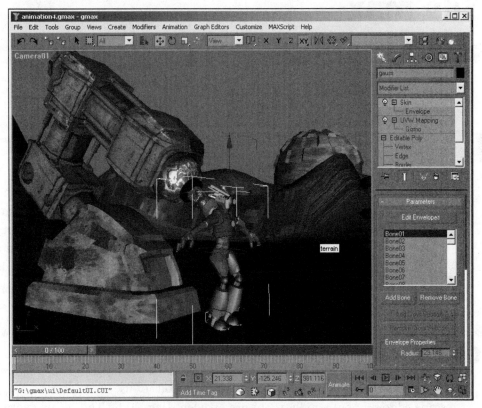

Fig. 19.7. Discreet Gmax interface

Gmax also may be of interest to game developers using the MAXScript language that is part of Gmax. Skilled programmers can easily write their own software to convert Gmax models into their own format.

Finally, Gmax is excellent educational software. (Don't forget that it is free!)

You can find details on all of these packages in the corresponding sections of the **http://www.discreet.com** website. You can also download demo-versions, updates, and the latest full–scale version of Gmax from this site.

Lesson 20

3ds max and Landscape Generators

3ds max is often used for architecture modeling and visualization. When an exterior form is developed, it is impossible not to take into account the peculiarities of the landscape. Of course, you can create a landscape using only 3ds max; here and in the book "3ds max 4: From Objects to Animation" we already described some methods. However, there is a range of applications specially intended for landscape creation and visualization, and it would be wrong to leave them out. In this lesson we will briefly discuss using them as plug-ins to 3ds max.

Corel Bryce 5 and E-on Vue D'Esprit 4

These packages are similar in features and methods of use with 3ds max. The landscape editors in both applications are excellent (Fig. 20.1). They enable you to interactively create landscapes by simply squeezing or dragging areas on the surfaces. In addition, many effects allow you to imitate wind erosion, changes of season, and so on. The material editors in both packages are powerful, although not traditional (especially in Bryce). Fortunately, both packages include good material libraries.

The only way to use landscapes created in these packages in 3ds max is to export them in the 3DS format. For this reason, Bryce enables the creation of an adaptive grid, while Vue D'Esprit can export only an object with a regular structure. Both packages export not only landscape geometry, but also textures (Fig. 20.2).

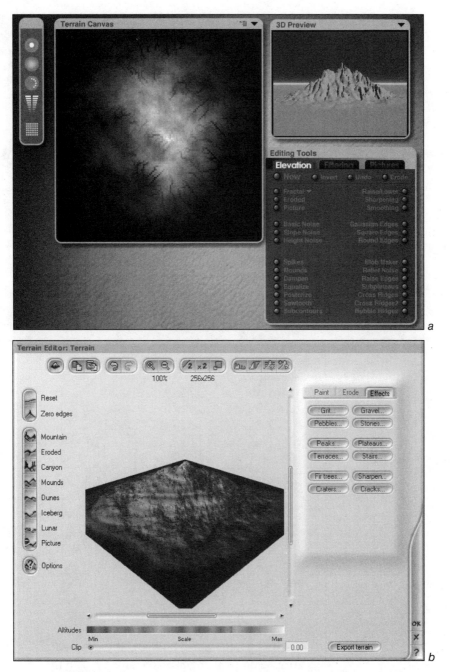

Fig. 20.1. Landscape editor in Bryce 5 (*a*) and Vue D'Esprit 4 (*b*)

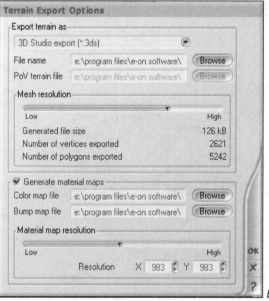

Fig. 20.2. Export into the 3DS format in Bryce 5 (*a*)
and the corresponding dialog in Vue D'Esprit 4 (*b*)

It is worth mentioning that to render landscapes, Bryce uses voxel technology, creating an image from colored "columns," or voxels. This provides surface smoothness that is impossible when common algorithms are used. Therefore, conversion to the polygonal format leads to an inevitable loss of detail.

Both packages (especially Vue D'Esprit) allow the generation of beautiful skies (Fig. 20.3). Since each packages provides an option for creating panoramas, they can be used as environment textures.

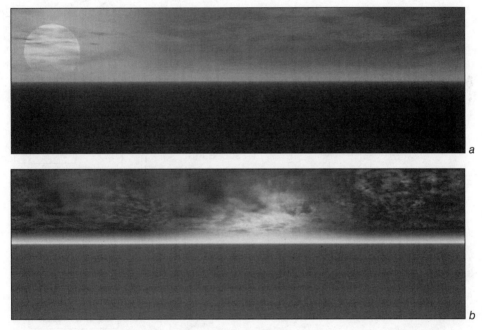

Fig. 20.3. Cylindrical panoramas created in Bryce (*a*) and Vue D'Esprit (*b*)

Neither of these packages can convert images into files supporting the Z-Buffer (for example, RLA). Nevertheless, each package features an option for making a black-and-white (256 gradations of gray) image containing depth information, which makes it possible to use them as masks. For animation, however, such an option is practically useless. You cannot synchronize the camera position — neither package allows 3DS camera import, nor do they allow the export of their own cameras in a common format.

You can download demo-versions of the packages for free from these websites: **http://www.corel.com** and **http://www.e-onsoftware.com**.

3D Nature World Construction Set 5

A recognized authority among landscape generators, World Construction Set (WCS) provides unlimited options for obtaining realistic images and animation — not only from the appearance point of view, but also with respect to a range of specific parameters, such as geographical location and season.

WCS allows you to work with the LightWave 3D and 3ds max packages by merging the images obtained in these packages with the image from WCS using the Z-Buffer. Let us consider the queue of operations for a static image (Fig. 20.4).

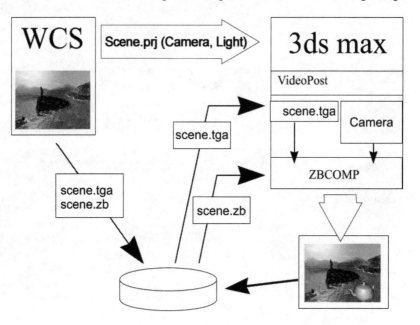

Fig. 20.4. Operations for a static image

- ❏ After you make a scene in WCS, export it in the PRJ format. You can export only the camera and sources of light, or you can export them with the landscape for more accurate model adjustment.
- ❏ Render the image in WCS by saving it in two formats: in a plain image format compatible with 3ds max (for example, TGA), and in the ZB format (Z-Buffer) for further use as a mask overlap in Video Post.
- ❏ Load the PRJ file in 3ds max and create the necessary objects, materials, etc.
- ❏ Open the Video Post module and create the structure shown in Fig. 20.5.

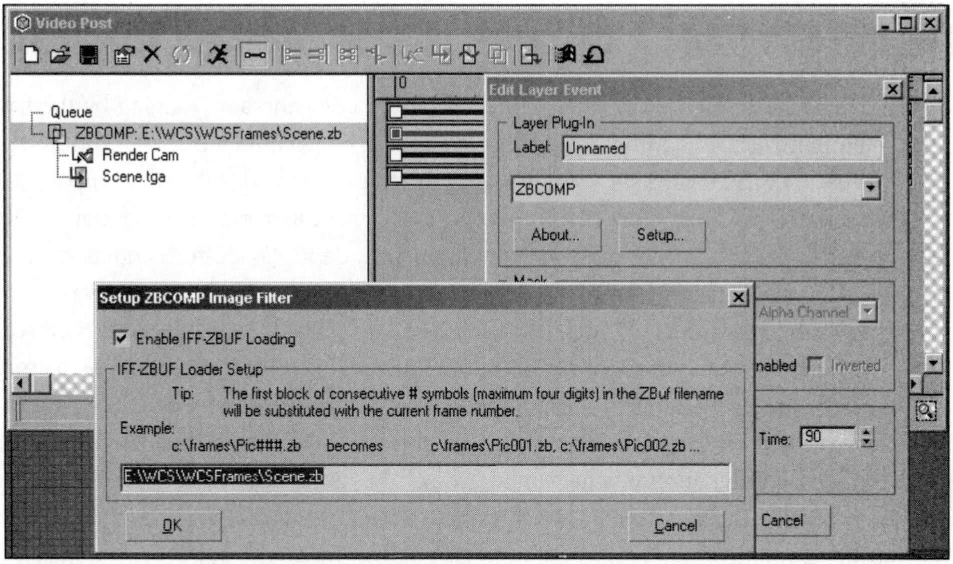

Fig. 20.5. Queue in **Video Post**

❑ Indicate the Z-Buffer file (with the ZB extension) in the settings of the ZBCOMP module.

▶ Note

The Zbcompr4.flt plug-in should be located in the \3dsmax\plugins folder.

With animation everything is a little more complicated, but the principle remains the same.

Unfortunately, this method does not allow you to have shadows of 3ds max objects on the landscape. However, if you use a file with the landscape, you can include shadows by assigning the **Matte/Shadow** landscape material.

It is worth mentioning that WCS is an uncommon application from the interface point of view. But if you are seriously involved in landscape modeling, you should pay attention to it.

You can find more detailed information and download the demo-version of the package at **http://www.3dnature.com**.

Digital Element Animatek World Builder 3

This package, can be considered the best landscape generator judging by the flashy resulting images. In addition to this, from the realism point of view, World Builder far exceeds WCS. The clips show an amazing development of details. Its trump card is flora generation without geometrical objects. Trees and other plants are drawn on the prepared landscape image with respect to its surface, depth (Z-Buffer), and illumination.

The developers of Animatek World Builder (AWB) offer their own way of interacting with 3ds max. Although this package contains the option to export scenes in 3DS format and to compose with the Z-Buffer in the Video Post module, its main feature lies in the availability of the so-called "communicator" between 3ds max and AWB. The principle is easy: 3ds max renders its objects, while AWB renders its own in parallel. An ideal combination is achieved because of the use of shared sources of light and camera. Movement and position of 3ds max objects in the AWB scene are determined by using simplified images of these objects. You can move the objects either in AWB or in 3ds max; all changes will followed automatically in both packages. The rendering also can be performed in AWB or in 3ds max using the Video Post module. An example image obtained via joint rendering in AWB and 3ds max is shown in Fig. 20.6.

Fig. 20.6. Example of using Animatek World Builder in conjunction with 3ds max

You can find more detailed information on AWB and download the demo-version from **http://www.digi-element.com/**. This version contains the commutators for 3ds max version 3 to version 5.

Lesson 21

Useful Add-Ons

In this lesson, we will draw your attention to some useful and interesting scripts and plug-in modules for 3ds max. Before we proceed, we would like to give you a historical overview.

Even the early versions of 3D Studio for DOS implemented additional modules, known as IPAS-processes, to enhance system functionality. The built-in scripting language was also developed and available at that time. For some reason, however, it was not included in the first two versions of 3ds max (to be more precise, 3D Studio MAX 1.x). Instead, these included a complete version of Software Developers Kit (SDK), libraries used to develop custom plug-in modules. That situation, combined with the limitations of the first 3D Studio MAX version, led to an abundance of plug-in modules (most of which are free). Some of those modules later became part of 3ds max. At present, there are more than 700 plug-in modules available for different 3ds max versions, some freeware and some commercial.

Starting with version 2.0, 3ds max began to include the scripting language MAXScript, which was greeted by a storm of enthusiasm from 3ds max users with programming skills.

Currently, there are more than 600 scripts of various kinds. This process was aided by an excellent user manual on MAXScript that contains a large number of examples.

MeshTools

This package of scripts, developed by Laszlo Sebo, enhances 3ds max built-in capabilities to edit polygonal objects. The MeshTools package that was initially developed for 3D Studio MAX 3.1 and later improved for 3ds max 4 has somehow lost its importance in 3ds max 5, where the majority of its functions are integrated into the main interface. Laszlo understood that and re-wrote the script, leaving only the original tools.

You can find this package on the second 3ds max 5 CD-ROM in the \Scripts\ Samples folder.

To install these scripts, proceed as follows:

1. Unpack the Laszlo_Scripts.zip file into a temporary folder.
2. Copy the Meshtools3-Functions.ms file from the Meshtools_v3_max5 folder into the 3dsmax5\stdplugs\stdscripts folder.
3. Copy the Meshtools3-Macroscripts.mcr file from the Meshtools_v3_max5 folder into the 3dsmax5\ui\macroscripts folder.
4. Copy the .bmp icon files into the 3dsmax5\ui\icons and 3dsmax5\ui\discreet folders.
5. Pray! (Laszlo assuresus us that it works better if you do so.)
6. Start or restart 3ds max.
7. Create the **MeshTools** toolbar:

    Main menu → Customize → Customize User Interface → Toolbars → New

8. Sequentially move the commands from the **MeshTools** category of the **Main UI** group to the toolbar (Fig. 21.1).

These commands work with Editable Poly objects and are partially applicable to Editable Mesh. Their names succinctly describe the functions they perform, so feel free to experiment with them by yourself.

Laszlo's home page is **http://www.s21net.com/meshtools/**.

We should mention an extension to the Meshtools package, csPolyTools, developed by Christopher Subagio (**http://www.3dluvr.com/subagio**). Several scripts written by Borislav Petrov (**http://www.gfxcentral.com/bobo/**) also simplify the modeling process. They were written, however, for 3ds max 4, and we are not sure if they will work correctly in 3ds max 5.

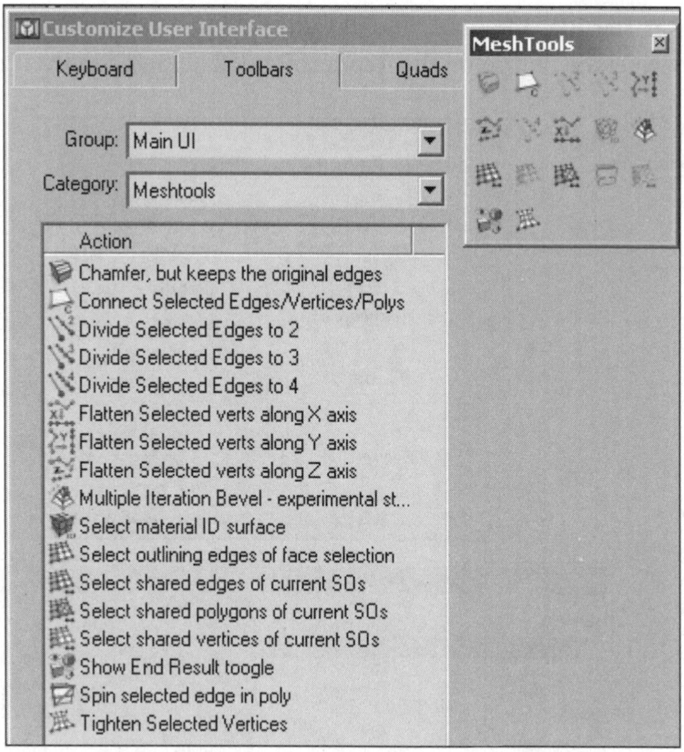

Fig. 21.1. Putting **MeshTools** on the toolbar

Domelight

This script, written by Steve Johnson, solves the problem of simulating uniform light coming from the sky. In "3ds max 4: From Objects to Animation," we gave detailed instructions on how to create such a dome yourself, using a large number of directed lights. The task is rather complicated, however, since it requires numerous lights and fine adjustments. The Domelight script described here eases the process.

The required files are on the companion CD-ROM in the \Scripts\DomeLight 1.2\ folder. To install this script, create a folder named \3dsmax4\UI\callbacks\ and copy the builddomelights.ms file into it. The chugg_domelight.mcr file must be placed in the \3dsmax4\UI\macroscripts\ folder, and the chugg_global_setup.ms file should go in the \3dsmax4\stdplugs\stdscripts\ folder.

After starting 3ds max, find the **domelight** command in the **Chugg's Tools** category, set the button on the **Rendering** toolbar, and run the script (Fig. 21.2).

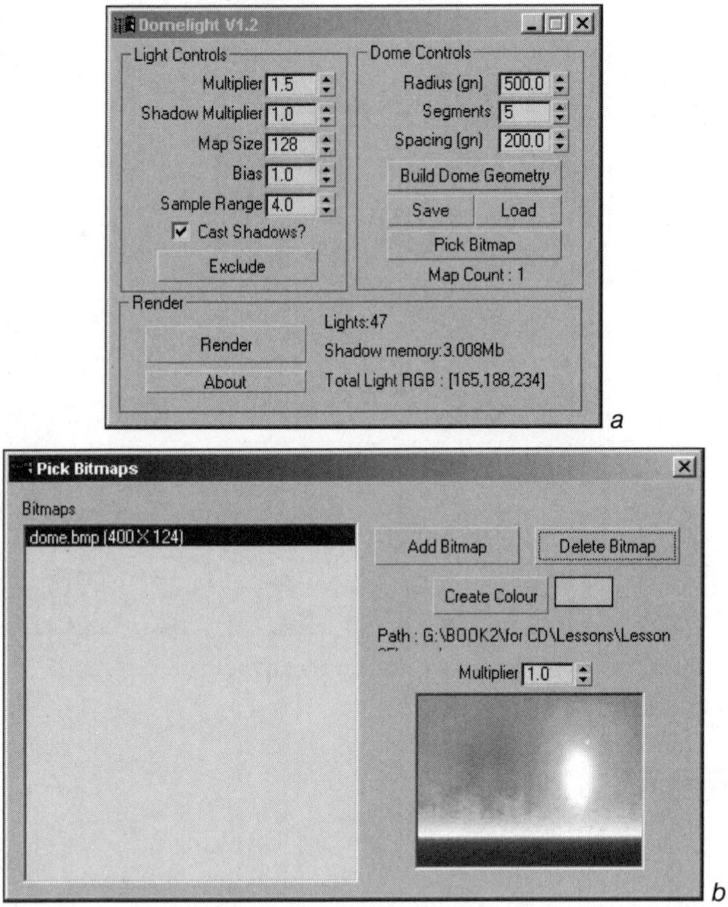

Fig. 21.2. Parameters of the **Domelight** script (*a*) and dialog for selecting the image (*b*)

The process is rather simple. First, you need to create the "sky" by clicking the **Build Dome Geometry** button. A hemisphere will be created. Then select one or more textures for the sky and click the **Render** button in the **Domelight** dialog, followed by the **Render** button in the 3ds max **Render Scene** dialog. Domelight will create the required number of lights with predefined parameters. The color of these lights is determined by the "sky" texture color.

There are several things to keep in mind when using this script:

❑ Select and hide the sky-dome geometry (the **Dome Sample** object).

❑ Save the settings immediately with the **Save** button. If you close the script dialog without doing so, your settings will be lost.

❑ Since the lights are created before rendering and deleted afterward, click the **Render** button in the **Domelight** dialog before beginning the 3ds max render process.

❑ You can use the animated file with "flowing clouds" as one of the sky textures — the result is rather impressive.

More detailed information and newer versions of the script can be downloaded from Steve's home page at **http://www.chuggnut.com**.

The HDRdomeLight script developed by Christopher Subagio is also worth mentioning. This script is very similar to the Domelight script, but it has a larger number of settings and wider functional capabilities. For example, it allows you to space the lights in accordance with a texture's brightness, which enables you to enhance shadows from the texture of the Sun. The main advantage of this script, however, is that it imitates so-called High Dynamic Range lighting. More detailed information can be found at **http://www.3dluvr.com/subagio/**.

And, of course, we should point out the SkyDome script written by Borislav Petrov (**http://www.gfkcentral.com/bobo/**).

Combustion Stuff

This freeware package of plug-ins, written by Peter Watje, is based on algorithms developed by Rolf Berteig, the creator of the Combustion/Fire Effect module. With Peter's permission, we have included these modules on the companion CD-ROM in the \Plugins\Combusion Stuff\ folder. To use these plug-ins, simply copy them to the \3dsmax4\plugins\ folder and restart 3ds max.

▶ *Tip*

Put plug-in modules in separate sub-folders under the one quoted above and include their paths in the plugin.ini file. For example:

```
[Directories]

...

watje=E:\3dsmax4\plugins\watje

...
```

This allows us to easily disable the plug-ins we do not intend to use by simply inserting the comment symbol (";") at the beginning of the lines containing the unnecessary paths.

If you only want to use a module from time to time, you can also load it with the Plug-in Manager (Main menu → Customize → Plug-in Manager → Load).

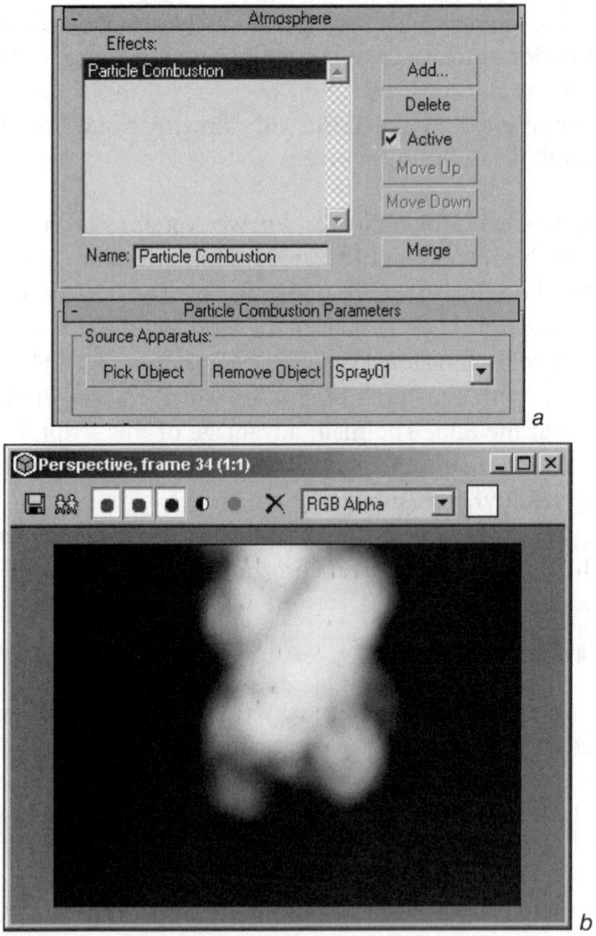

Fig. 21.3. Applying the **Particle Combustion** effect (*a*), and how it looks after rendering (*b*)

Now, let's consider one of these plug-ins, namely, Particle Combustion, in more detail. As is evident from its name, this plug-in uses a particle system as a gizmo. Thus, to use this module, proceed as follows:

❐ Create a particle system of any type.

❏ Add the **Particle Combustion** atmospheric effect to the scene and select the particle system as a gizmo (Fig. 21.3, *a*):

   Main menu → Rendering → Environment → Atmosphere → Add

   Particle Combustion Parameters → Pick Object → select the particle system

❏ Go to frame zero and render the **Perspective** viewport (Fig. 21.3, *b*).

Its parameters are a lot like the built-in Fire Effects module, but we will only mention one of its uses — backlighting. Simply include the appropriate light sources in the list of objects.

It runs rather slow and, in contrast to AfterBurn and PyroCluster plug-ins, looks a bit rough. However, the results are decent (Fig. 21.4) and it is absolutely free.

Fig. 21.4. Example illustrating the Particle Combustion plug-in

The Vertex Combustion and Object Combustion plug-ins, respectively, use object vertices and internal volume as the gizmo. They are set in a way similar to Particle Combustion, with only a few insignificant differences.

Painter Modifier

This module was also written by Peter Watje. It is mainly intended to model embossings but has a range of other interesting uses.

❑ Copy the files in the \Plugins\Paint Modifier\ folder on the companion CD-ROM to the \3dsmax4\Plugins\ folder and restart 3ds max.
❑ Create a sufficiently large plane (20×20, for example).
❑ Apply the Paint Modifier by selecting it from the modifier list and clicking the **Paint** button. Proceed with your drawing (Fig. 21.5)!

Besides embossing and engraving, you can also create surface curves, draw with objects, smoothen them out, etc. The module supports graphical plotters. Try it out!

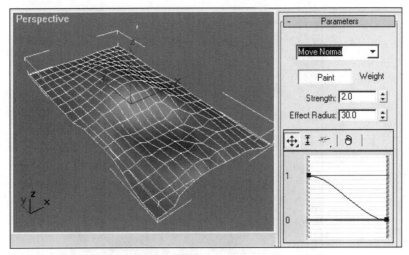

Fig. 21.5. Paint Modifier

Both packages described above are included on the companion CD-ROM with Peter Watje's permission. Peter's home page is **http://www.max3dstuff.com**.

SimCloth

This module, developed by the Chaos Group, was initially intended to simulate various types of cloth. Later, however, it also integrated the ability to imitate the dynamics of soft and hard physical bodies. It should be noted that, from a physical accuracy point of view, commercial products such as Stitch do much better. How-ever, like the Combustion Stuff module, it is advantageous in terms of its wide-spread use and because it is free. The developers have kindly provided us with version 2.52 (version 2.51 is available on their website at http:www.chaosgroup.com/). You must install it with a program on the companion CD-ROM (in the \Plugins\SimCloth\ folder). Follow the instructions on the screen.

You might encounter some difficulties when starting to work with this module. We will therefore discuss it in more detail.

- Create a scene similar to the one shown in Fig. 21.6 — a single **Box** object and two spheres of the **Geosphere** type. The second condition is important, since the module requires **Cloth** objects to have a regular mesh to work correctly.
- Position the spheres above the box's surface.
- Select all objects and apply the **SimClothMod** modifier. Disassociate the objects by clicking the **Make Unique** button in the modifier stack.
- For one of the spheres, select the **Cloth** type; for the second, select **Rigid body**; for the box, select the **Deflector** type.
- Click the **Start Calculation** button. Note that it doesn't matter which object is selected. One of the spheres will fall to the surface of the box, while the second will fall and crumple.

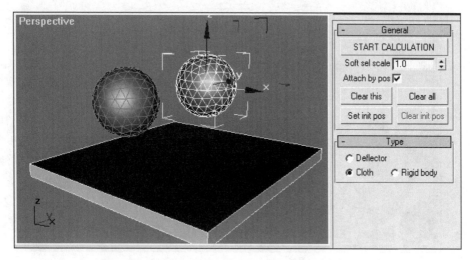

Fig. 21.6. Example using the SimCloth module

The module comes with comprehensive documentation illustrated by a large number of examples. We therefore won't discuss its parameters here but, rather, will draw your attention to two aspects. First, you need to make sure that there are no intersections between objects or between an object and itself (unless this is desirable). If there are, and the module is unable to handle the situation, increase **Min. Subdivs** and **Max. Subdivs** in the **Simulation** group. This increases the calculation time but also improves accuracy.

The second aspect is the fact that the object's pivot point retains its position during calculation. Thus, you can animate the object however you'd like afterward. On the other hand, the animation recorded before the calculation is lost (to be more precise, it is distorted), except when the object is of a deflector type.

And, finally, it should be mentioned that this module has one rather unpleasant drawback: You cannot record its settings for future use. Therefore, you have to adjust it from scratch each time you use it.

Unwrap Object Texture

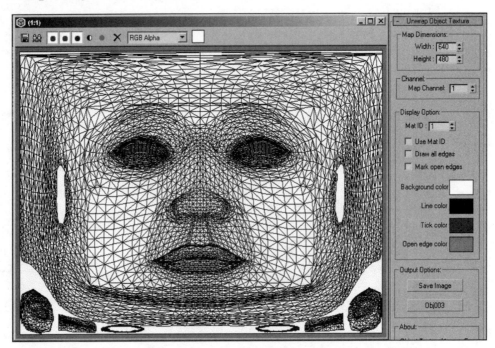

Fig. 21.7. Bitmap file produced by the **Unwrap Object Texture** plug-in

This module, developed by Peter Watje, allows you to save a texture unwrapped from an object to a bitmap file (Fig. 21.7). This file can then be used as a template to create a texture in any bitmap editor. Spherical and cylindrical coordinates are most commonly used. After you install the module in 3ds max, you can access it in **Utilities** on the control panel by clicking the **More** button.

There is another module called Texporter, developed by Cuneyt Ozdas, that is similar but has somewhat broader capabilities. For example, it produces a colored map, where each color corresponds to the Material ID, etc. For more detailed information on this module and to download the latest version, visit Cuneyt's site at **http://www.cuneytozdas.com**.

f-Edge

This add-on, written by Ivan Kolev, solves a single but important problem of 3D graphics — smoothing sharp angles. In reality, nearly every angle has a bend radius, however small. Light reflects off this bending surface in all directions, instead of strictly off the adjoining surfaces. In 3ds max, you can produce this effect by creating additional faces, chamfering sharp angles, and assigning smoothing groups. All of this makes the model more complicated, increases hardware requirements (RAM), extends the time required for rendering, etc. Furthermore, such models are much harder to texture. The f-Edge module solves this problem. Look at Fig. 21.8. It shows a pyramid with a simple material (*a*) and the same pyramid using a material with the F-Edge texture (*b*). The second pyramid looks much more realistic, doesn't it?

The \Plugins\F-Edge 1.0 Trial\ folder on the companion CD-ROM contains a time-limited demo version of the module, included with the author's permission. More information, including prices and purchase conditions, can be found at **http://www.chaoticdimension.com**.

To install the module, copy the f-Edge.dlt file to the 3dsmax4\plugins\ folder or load it directly from the CD-ROM using the Plug-in Manager. The 3ds max material and texture browser will then contain two new textures — the **f-Edge** texture itself and a texture named **Stack**.

Here, we'll discuss how to apply these textures and set some parameters.

❏ Go to the material editor, and assign the f-Edge texture to the bump channel of any material.

❏ Set the **Amount** value of the bump channel to 100.

❏ Editing the f-Edge texture parameters (Fig. 21.9).

Tip

To keep things simple, use a box object in material editor.

Material editor → Sample Type

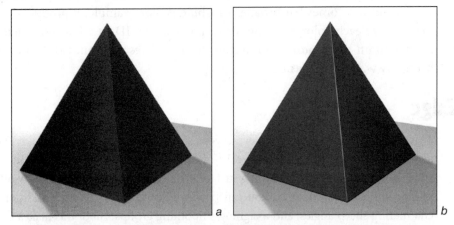

Fig. 21.8. Pyramid before (*a*) and after (*b*) applying the **f-Edge** texture

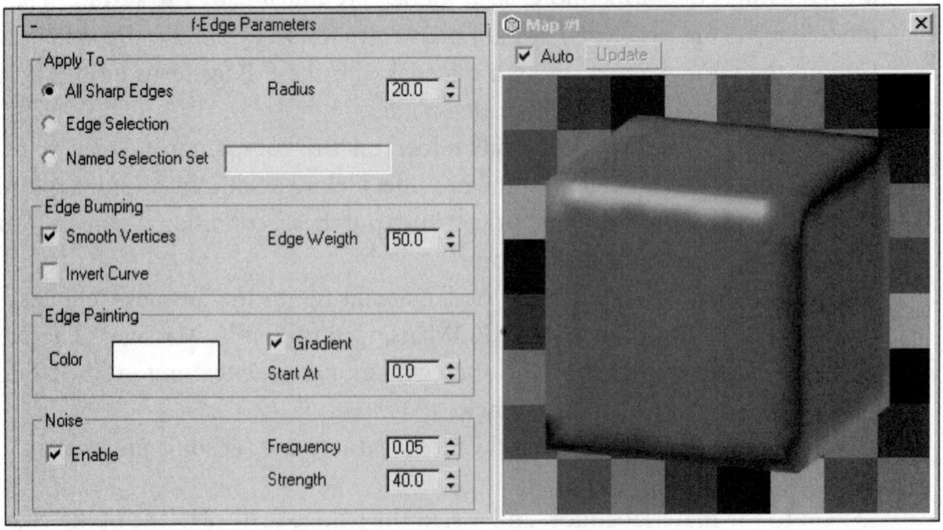

Fig. 21.9. f-Edge texture parameters

The **Radius** parameter determines the "curvature" extent. However, don't get into the habit of uncontrollably increasing this value — it only approximates the effect; the object's geometry doesn't actually change!

This texture can be applied to both unsmoothed edges and selected edges. You can also use the f-Edge texture as a part of composite texture and assign textures with different parameters to different edges.

The **Noise** group allows you to make uneven angles in the course of rendering.

To use several bump channel textures together, you need to assign the **Stack** texture, one of which is the f-Edge texture.

The f-Edge texture is not limited to the bump channel — try to apply it to other channels and see the result.

Surface Blur

This small module was developed by Pavel Kuznetsov, a Russian 3ds max enthusiast. It makes surfaces less glossy in the process of blurring images obtained by reflection or radiographing objects. Setting its parameters is easy (Fig. 21.10, *a*), and the results are self-evident (Fig. 21.10, *b* and *c*). It works correctly on the edges of objects, unlike the **Blur** process integrated in 3ds max (Fig. 21.10, *d*), and is the best way we found to achieve this effect.

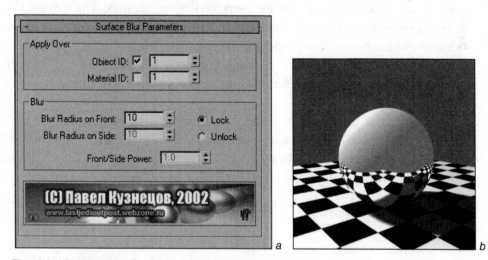

Fig. 21.10, *a* and *b*. **Surface Blur** parameters (*a*), the image before it is applied (*b*), after it was applied (*c*), and the result of the **Blur** process (*d*)

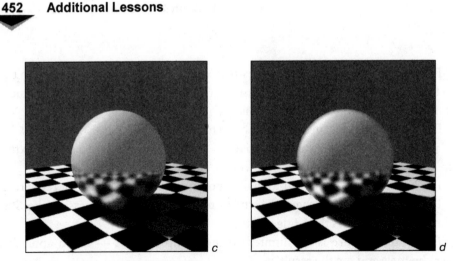

Fig. 21.10, *c* and *d*. Surface Blur parameters (*a*), the image before it is applied (*b*),
after it was applied (*c*), and the result of the **Blur** process (*d*)

The Ky_SurfaceBlur.dlv file is on the CD-ROM in the \Plugins\Ky_SurfaceBlur5
folder.

Internet Resources for Scripts and Plug-Ins

http://www.maxplugins.de/ is the most complete 3ds max plug-in database. It has
every current plug-in available for every version of 3ds max. The website also has
descriptions of most commercial plug-ins and addresses where to get more detailed
information. The database is updated daily.

http://www.tdp.nu/ — Tech Design Production (Sthlm) — is a great resource,
entirely dedicated to scripts for 3ds max, Autodesk VIZ, and Gmax. It is updated
daily.

Finally, it is impossible to forget the virtual "Boboland Republic" — 3ds max
fans' favorite portal, created and supported by Borislav Petrov. You can find it at:
http://www.gfxcentral.com/bobo/. If you have never visited this site before, take a
look. You won't be disappointed!

Appendixes

Appendixes

Appendix A

Brief 3D Graphics Glossary

This glossary is organized as follows: Terms encountered in 3ds max and this book, followed by their definitions and brief descriptions.

Note that the terms and concepts provided only relate to 3ds max.

More detailed information is provided in the 3ds max "User Manual's", online help system, and reference.

General Concepts

Gizmo. A virtual object or sub-object, represented by a wireframe that initially surrounds the selected object and to which a modifier or specific effect is applied.

Material. A set of surface parameters defining how the object will look after rendering. Note that the concept of material relates only to surfaces and doesn't address volume. (The reason is simple — there is no concept of volume in 3ds max). The only exceptions are the Dynamics module and RayTrace material.

Modifier. A procedure applied to a selected object, set of objects, or selected sub-objects.

Modifier Stack. A list of modifiers applied to an object. 3ds max applies modifiers sequentially, going from the bottom to the top. You can return to any modifier in the stack at any time and change its parameters, move it to another level, or copy or delete it. You can also move modifiers from stack to stack. Be very careful, however! Some modifiers (Edit Mesh, for example) are destructive, which means that the effect of editing object parameters below it on the stack might be unpredictable. As a rule, 3ds max warns the user when such consequences are possible.

Normal. In 3ds max, each surface is oriented in a particular direction and has front and rear sides. In general, the back side is not rendered, except when a two-sided material is used and rendering parameters are set in such a way as to render both sides. The normal is the direction pointing perpendicularly away from the face side. The term "flip normals" means pointing the normals in the opposite direction. The term "unify normals" means changing the orientation in such a way as to make multiple normals point the same way (usually outward).

Object. Any element of the scene. Objects can be renderable (e.g., geometric primitives) or invisible (e.g., light sources, deformations, or virtual objects).

Scene. The entire set of objects, materials, animations, and program settings, containing everything written in the project file.

Sub-object. One of the most fundamental concepts of 3ds max. Each object is composed of a set of sub-objects (e.g., vertices or faces) that you can edit independently. However, sub-objects always belong to a parent object. For each object type, there is a predefined set of sub-objects.

Transformation Matrix. When you create an object, 3ds max creates a transformation matrix in which it records all transformations of that object (such as changes in position, scale, or rotation) in relation to its initial state.

Viewport. Program windows used to edit objects, which are displayed as wireframes or shaded solids.

Visualization or Rendering. The process of turning a scene into an image, based on the objects that make up the scene, their material parameters, lighting, and camera. The term "rendering" is becoming common, since the process involves more than simple "visualization." Interestingly, it is being used not only in 3D graphics, but also in non-linear mastering (software such as Digital Fusion, for example) and even in sound-processing software.

Modeling

Polygon Modeling

When working with 3ds max 4 and 5, it is important to distinguish mesh objects (Mesh) from "true" polygons (PolyMesh). Although every object is converted to mesh in the course of rendering, sometimes the process of editing these types beforehand can be different.

Border. A group of open edges (i.e., edges that have only one adjacent polygon). Only applicable to polygonal objects.

Edge. A line connecting two vertices. A mesh object may contain both visible and invisible edges. Note that, even if an edge is invisible, it still exists. In contrast, polygonal objects do not have the concept of visible or invisible edges — edges either exist or don't exist.

Editable Mesh. A basic mesh object. It is common to simply call it a "mesh" among 3D artists.

Editable Poly. A basic polygonal object.

Element. Several faces or polygons that form a single whole and have no vertices or edges in common with other elements. Elements are created, for example, by attaching objects to one another.

Face. A minimal surface created by three vertices. For mesh objects, faces are analogous to "molecules." For polygonal objects, this concept does not explicitly exist.

Polygon. For mesh objects, a polygon consists of several faces joined by "invisible" edges. For polygonal objects, it is a real surface delimited by edges.

Smooth/Smoothing Group. Each model has a discrete number of faces. Smoothing is intended to produce the impression that some models (e.g., spheres) are smooth, rather than composed of a multitude of flat faces, by rendering smooth transitions between them. If this is not necessary (e.g., the walls of a rectangular shaft), faces and polygons can be grouped according to the required characteristics.

Vertex. A point in a 3D environment. All object geometry is based on vertices. Generally speaking, a vertex is an "atom" of any object in 3ds max.

Bezier Curves

Editable Spline. One of the basic objects in 3ds max. Editing these curves has a lot in common with similar processes in vector graphics software. The only difference is that, in 3ds max 4, you edit in a 3D environment.

Handle. For each Bezier vertex, there are two nodes (known as handles) for editing the curve's shape.

Segment. The portion of a curve that connects two vertices. A segment can be linear (Line) or curvilinear (Curve).

Spline. A set of several segments connected by common vertices.

Vertex. A point in 3D space on which curves are based. In contrast to polygonal object vertices, curve vertices are classified by the following types: smooth, Bezier, and corner. The type influences the shape of the curve.

Patch Modeling

Edge. An edge in patch modeling is similar to an edge in polygon modeling. The only difference is that, in this case, the edge is a segment of a curve.

Editable Patch. One of the basic objects. In general, patches are surfaces with the same principles as Bezier curves.

Patch. The minimal editable surface.

Vertex. In contrast to a curve vertex, a patch vertex has three or four control nodes (handles) that define the surface's shape. Surfaces can have both inner vertices and outer vertices belonging to edges — each defines the shape of the patch.

Materials

Ambient Color. Determines the color of objects' faces when they are in shadow (i.e., not illuminated by any direct light source). The color of these faces depends only on the ambient light of the scene.

Diffuse Color. The primary parameter determining the color of faces illuminated by direct light. The color depends on the angle of incidence of the light rays.

Filtering. A way to improve the appearance of textures in the course of rendering.

Highlight Graph. A curve that defines color mixing with respect to the angle of incidence of the light rays at the surface.

Map. An image assigned to any number of different parameters. Depending on the parameter type, the map may determine an object's color or roughness (Bump), for example. In the latter case, only the brightness channel (Level) is used. There are many kinds of maps, the simplest being an image from a bitmap file. To the other extreme, you can also use a procedural map defined by a mathematical algorithm and calculated in the course of the rendering.

Mapping Coordinates. A set of parameters required to determine how the map will be applied to the surface of the object.

Shader. The procedure used to calculate how faces and materials are combined to create a colored surface, depending on the parameters of the light sources.

Specular Color. Determines the color of faces directly illuminated by light at an angle close to 90°.

SuperSampling. A way to improve an object's appearance when rendering through the use of sophisticated algorithms. Useful, for example, for surfaces that have a small bump channel map.

Animation

Controller. The set of parameters that control how a specific aspect of animation proceeds. There are controllers that determine intermediate positions between keyframes, as well as controllers based on mathematical algorithms (such as noise) or external effects (sound).

Keyframe. Positions in animation where all object parameters are recorded. There must be at least two for any given animation — one at the start and one at the end.

Pivot Point. The point of an object, around which all transformations take place in the course of animation. It can be located anywhere in the scene, even outside the object.

Rendering

Antialiasing. Removing jagged distortions as a result of limited resolution (aliasing) in the course of rendering.

Global Illumination. The amount of light reflected by objects in the scene back onto themselves.

Motion Blur. Blurring objects that are moving relative to the camera. In real life, this happens as a result of non-zero camera exposure times. In graphics, it is used to make the images look more realistic.

Appendix B

Main Keyboard Shortcuts

The table below lists the main interface commands that have shortcuts defined after installing 3ds max 5. The list of all main interface commands and additional modules can be found in the **Default Keyboard Shortcuts** section of interactive help in 3ds max.

Command	Description	Shortcut
Object commands		
Align	Begins the alignment operation	\<Alt>+\<A>
Cycle Selection Method	Changes the selection method	\<Ctrl>+\<F>
Delete Objects	Removes objects from the scene	\<Del>
Isolate Selection	Works with the selection, hiding all other objects	\<Alt>+\<Q>
Normal Align	Aligns objects by their normals	\<Alt>+\<N>
Place Highlight	Positions a light source relative to a surface normal	\<Ctrl>+\<H>
Polygon Counter	Counts the number of polygons in the selection	\<7>
Redo Scene Operation	Reapplies a cancelled operation	\<Ctrl>+\<Y>
Restrict Plane Cycle	Changes the restricted plane for moving/rotating/scaling	\<F8>

continues

Continued

Command	Description	Shortcut
Restrict to X	Restricts moving/rotating/scaling along the X axis	\<F5\>
Restrict to Y	Restricts moving/rotating/scaling along the Y axis	\<F6\>
Restrict to Z	Restricts moving/rotating/scaling along the Z axis	\<F7\>
Rotate Mode	Switches to Rotate Mode	\<E\>
Scale Cycle	Switches to Scale Mode and cycles the method	\<Ctrl\>+\<E\>
See-Through Display Toggle	Displays objects in a semi-transparent state	\<Alt\>+\<X\>
Select All	Selects all objects/sub-objects	\<Ctrl\>+\<A\>
Select Ancestor	Selects an object's "ancestor" in the hierarchical chain	\<Page Up\>
Select Child	Selects an object's "child" in the hierarchical chain	\<Page Down\>
Select Invert	Inverts which objects/sub-objects are selected	\<Ctrl\>+\<I\>
Select None	Deselects all objects/sub-objects	\<Ctrl\>+\<D\>
Select-by-Name Dialog	Allows objects to be selected by name	\<H\>
Selection Lock Toggle	Activates/deactivates the ability to change the selection	\<Space\>
Smart Scale	Switches to Smart Scale mode	\<R\>
Smart Select	Switches to Smart Select mode	\<Q\>
Snap Percent Toggle	Snaps when scaling	\<Shift\>+\<Ctrl\>+\<P\>
Snap Toggle	Snaps when moving	\<S\>
Snaps Cycle	Switches the snaps type	\<Alt\>+\<S\>
Spacing Tool	Distributes objects along a path	\<Shift\>+\<I\>

continues

Continued

Command	Description	Shortcut
Sub-object Level 1	Switches to the 1st sub-object level	<1>
Sub-object Level 2	Switches to the 2nd sub-object level	<2>
Sub-object Level 3	Switches to the 3rd sub-object level	<3>
Sub-object Level 4	Switches to the 4th sub-object level	<4>
Sub-object Level 5	Switches to the 5th sub-object level	<5>
Sub-object Level Cycle	Changes the active sub-object level	<Insert>
Sub-object Selection Toggle	Switches between object and sub-object work	<Ctrl>+<B>
Transform Gizmo Size Down	Decreases the extent of the transform gizmo	<->
Transform Gizmo Size Up	Increases the extent of the transform gizmo	<=>
Transform Gizmo Toggle	Displays the transform gizmo	<X>
Transform Type-In Dialog	Takes keyboard input for transformation values	<F12>
Undo Scene Operation	Undoes an operation	<Ctrl>+<Z>
Viewport commands		
Adaptive Degradation Toggle	Dynamically drops the rendering level in shaded viewports, based on display performance	<O>
Angle Snap Toggle	Snaps when rotating	<A>
Background Lock Toggle	Locks the background	<Alt>+<Ctrl>+<B>
Bottom View	Switches to the Bottom view	<B>
Camera View	Switches to the Camera view	<C>
Default Lighting Toggle	Switches to the default lighting	<Ctrl>+<L>

continues

Continued

Command	Description	Shortcut
Disable Viewport	Freezes a viewport with respect to changes in other views	<D>
Expert Mode	Closes all screen controls except viewports and menus	<Ctrl>+<X>
Front View	Switches to the Front view	<F>
Hide Cameras Toggle	Hides cameras from view	<Shift>+<C>
Hide Geometry Toggle	Hides geometric objects from view	<Shift>+<G>
Hide Grids Toggle	Hides grids from view	<G>
Hide Helpers Toggle	Hides helper objects from view	<Shift>+<H>
Hide Lights Toggle	Hides light sources from view	<Shift>+<L>
Hide Particle Systems Toggle	Hides particle systems from view	<Shift>+<P>
Hide Space Warps Toggle	Hides space warps from view	<Shift>+<W>
Isometric User View	Switches to an isometric view	<U>
Left View	Switches to the Left view	<L>
Match Camera to View	Synchronizes the camera view with the perspective viewport	<Ctrl>+<C>
Maximize Viewport Toggle	Expands one viewport to occupy the space allotted to all	<Alt>+<W>
Pan View	Shifts the view visible in a viewport	<Ctrl>+<P> or middle mouse button
Pan Viewport	Shifts a viewport so that the mouse position is centered	<I>
Perspective User View	Switches to a perspective view	<P>
Redo Viewport Operation	Reapplies an operation cancelled in a viewport	<Shift>+<Y>
Redraw All Views	Redraws the view in all viewports	<'>

continues

Continued

Command	Description	Shortcut
Shade Selected Faces Toggle	Displays selected faces as shaded	\<F2\>
Show Main Toolbar Toggle	Shows the main toolbar	\<Alt\>+\<6\>
Show Safeframes Toggle	Shows the proportions of rendered output, which is useful when the output has a different aspect ratio (e.g., TV screen)	\<Shift\>+\<F\>
Show Selection Bracket Toggle	Shows the container surrounding the selected objects	\<J\>
Show Tab Panel Toggle	Shows the tab panel	\<Y\>
Spot/Directional Light View	Shows the view from a light source	\<Shift\>+\<4\>
Top View	Switches to the Top view	\<T\>
Undo Viewport Operation	Undoes an operation in a viewport	\<Shift\>+\<Z\>
Update Background Image	Redraws the background image	\<Alt\>+\<Shift\>+\<Ctrl\>+\<B\>
View Edged Faces Toggle	Shows individual object faces	\<F4\>
Viewport Background	Opens the background dialog	\<Alt\>+\<B\>
Wireframe/ Smooth+Highlights Toggle	Switches between displaying wireframes and shaded objects in a viewport	\<F3\>
Zoom Extents	Adjusts the view in a viewport so that all objects are visible	\<Alt\>+\<Ctrl\>+\<Z\>
Zoom Extents All	Adjusts the view in all viewports so that all objects are visible	\<Shift\>+\<\<Ctrl\>+\<Z\>
Zoom Extents Selected All	Adjusts the view in all viewports so that all selected objects or sub-objects are visible	\<Z\>

continues

Continued

Command	Description	Shortcut
Zoom Mode	Switches the zoom mode in a viewport	\<Alt>+\<Z> or \<Ctrl>+\<Alt>+middle mouse button
Zoom Region Mode	Zooms in on a selected area in a viewport	\<Ctrl>+\<W>
Zoom Viewport In	Zooms in on the mouse position in a viewport	\<[>
Zoom Viewport Out	Zooms out on the mouse position in a viewport	\<]>
File commands		
Fetch	Restores the state recorded by the Hold command	\<Alt>+\<Ctrl>+\<F>
Hold	Records the current state	\<Alt>+\<Ctrl>+\<H>
New Scene	Creates a new scene	\<Ctrl>+\<N>
Open File	Opens a scene from a file	\<Ctrl>+\<O>
Save File	Saves the scene into a file	\<Ctrl>+\<S>
Rendering commands		
Environment Dialog	Opens the environment dialog	\<8>
Material Editor	Opens the material editor	\<M>
Quick Render	Quickly renders the current viewport	\<Shift>+\<Q>
Render Last	Quickly renders the viewport again, incorporating changes	\<F9>
Render Scene	Opens the rendering settings	\<F10>
Render To Texture	Opens the "Render To Texture" settings	\<0>
Animation commands		
Auto Key Toggle	Turns on keyframing of movement/rotation/scaling; otherwise, all changes are applied to frame 0	\<N>
Backup Time One Unit	Moves one frame back	\<,>

continues

Continued

Command	Description	Shortcut
Forward Time One Unit	Advances one frame forward	<.>
Go to End Frame	Goes to the last frame	<End>
Go to Start Frame	Goes to the first frame	<Home>
Play Animation	Plays/stops the animation in the current viewport	</>
Set Key	Sets the animation key	<K>
Set Key Mode	Sets the animation key mode	<'>
Sound Toggle	Activates/deactivates sound	<\>

Appendix C

Internet Resources

Naturally, the table provided below cannot be considered an exhaustive reference of all available Internet resources dedicated to 3ds max. However, if you are an experienced Internet user, you will have no problem following the links provided by the sites below.

http://www.discreet.com **http://www.autodesk.com**	The sites of the developers and publishers of 3ds max. You can find the latest news and updates for 3ds max on the first site and information on other products from the Autodesk group on the second.
http://www.digimation.com **http://www.cebas.com** **http://www.maxplugins.com** **http://www.afterworks.com** **http://www.trinity3d.com**	The sites of the leading developers and publishers of commercial plug-ins for 3ds max, where you can get the latest information on new plug-in modules. Registered users can download updates for free.
http://max3d.3dluvr.com **http://www.3dcafe.com** **http://www.raph.com** **http://www.3dartist.com** **http://www.scriptspot.com** **http://www.maxplugins.de**	Interesting sites with additional information on the development of 3D graphics software, including works from independent artists, both professional and amateur. A large number of freeware plug-ins for 3ds max are also available.

Appendix D

About
the Companion CD-ROM

The CD-ROM that comes with this book contains the following folders: Projects, Lessons, Plugins, and Scripts.

❏ There are two reels in the Projects folder: project1.avi and project2.avi.
❏ The Lessons folder comprises the Lesson02–Lesson07, Lesson09–Lesson11 and Lesson14–Lesson18 folders. These hold all files necessary to start the work, intermediate and final variants of the scenes, and reels and images for some scenes.
❏ The Plugins and Scripts folders include useful plug-ins. Most of them are described in Lesson 21. All of the plug-ins are included with the author's permission and are free for noncommercial use. Before you use them for commercial purposes, study their license agreements in the attached text files.

System Requirements

❏ Intel-compatible processor with a clock rate of 300 MHz (Pentium III 500 MHz or greater is preferable)
❏ 256 MB RAM and at least 300 MB of free disk space for the swap file (512 MB or more is preferable)
❏ Video system with 1024 × 768 pixels, 32 bits resolution (1280 × 1024 pixels is preferable); GForce 3; Ati Radeon 8500 or better video display board; 64 MB video buffer; OpenGL 1.2 or Direct3D 8.1 (or better) hardware support
❏ Three-button mouse
❏ CD-ROM drive
❏ Microsoft Windows NT4 SP 6, 2000 SP 2, XP SP 1 (officially, the operating system Windows 98/ME is not supported, but it also is not excluded)

Index